The Dramatized
Old Testament

The Dramatized Old Testament

Volume 2: Job to Malachi

New International Version

Edited by Michael Perry

Baker Books

A Division of Baker Book House Co
Grand Rapids, Michigan 49516

Copyright 1996 by Michael Perry and Jubilate Hymns

Based on *The Dramatized Bible*, first published in 1989 by Marshall Pickering and Bible Society. Marshall Pickering is an imprint of the Collins Religious Division, part of the Collins Publishing Group, London. Copyright © 1989 by Michael Perry.

Library of Congress Cataloging-in-Publication Data

Bible. O.T. English. New International. 1994.
    The dramatized Old Testament: New International Version/Edited by Michael Perry.
        p. cm.
    Includes indexes.
    ISBN 0-8010-5396-X (v. 2)
    1. Bible. O.T.—Liturgical use. I. Perry, Michael, 1942– II. Title.
BS895.N37   1993
221.5'208—dc 20   94-5701

Printed in the United States of America

To Helen and Simon
for whom may the Book live
as it has for me.

Contents

Editor's Preface

The Dramatized Bible—here, the Old Testament—creates the opportunity for a vivid presentation of Bible narrative and teaching. Generations of ministers, teachers, and youth and children's leaders have done it before—turned the Bible text into drama so that worshipers or students can become actively involved in its teaching. But publication has always been piecemeal. Episodes have been available previously in dramatized form (the events leading up to Easter in various books, and the Christmas story in Hope Publishing Company's *Carols for Today*), but never, so far as we are aware, all the Bible narrative.

It is remarkable how much of the Bible uses the device of "reported speech" and so lends itself to dramatic presentation. For instance, we would not immediately think of the Book of Jeremiah in this way. And yet Jeremiah has a narrative form quite as amenable to dramatic presentation as, say, Genesis. It is the Hebrew tradition of storytelling that makes the task so inviting and the outcome so effective.

Old Testament Precedent

We like to think that further encouragement is given to the exercise of dramatizing the Bible for worship by one special discovery. It does appear that the Hebrew people in temple worship used drama to rehearse the acts of God in their history—notably the crossing of the Red Sea and their deliverance from the slavery of Egypt. Such dramatic presentations were not entertainment—though they would have been marvelously entertaining. And they were far more than visual aids—though Hebrew faith did require each generation to recall before the next, God's saving interventions, so that his mercy and his demands would not be forgotten. The Hebrew dramas had a teaching role, and they were acts of worship too—precedents of our own "anamnesis," that is, the calling to mind of the saving work of Christ in the drama we term, according to our Christian tradition, the Lord's Supper, the Holy Communion/the Eucharist, the Mass.

Evidence for a more extended use of drama in Hebrew worship comes from the Psalms. We have only to look at Psalm 118 to see that it is neither a hymn nor merely a meditation. There are obvious character parts and choral parts. And there are even "stage" instructions embedded in the text. For example, verse 27—"With boughs in hand, join in the festal procession / up to the horns of the altar"—which, in some traditions, we blindly *sing* as though the psalm were homogeneous. It does not take much imagination to see that what we are dealing with is the script of a drama or the libretto of an opera, set in the context of a magnificent act of worship. Here the intending (and noble?) worshiper approaches the door of the temple and asks to enter to give thanks for God's deliverance. The ministers/priests tell him righteousness is a prerequisite of an approach to God. And the drama progressed from there. Permeating the drama are the resonant choruses of the Hebrew liturgy:

Leader	Let Israel say:
All	His love endures forever.
Leader	Let the house of Aaron say:
All	His love endures forever.
Leader	Let those who fear the LORD say:
All	His love endures forever!

Finally, the worshiper is admitted ("Blessed is he who comes in the name of the LORD"), and the celebration begins ("With boughs in hand . . ."). As long as we consider the Old Testament dour and prosaic, its exciting suggestions for our own worship practice will be missed.

Barriers Broken

Much of my life's work has been in the interests of a clearer presentation of the facts of the faith in worship. Centrally within this context, *The Dramatized Old Testament* brings the text of Scripture to life. Using *The Dramatized Old Testament* means involving people in recalling and recounting their salvation history. The experience is memorable and challenging.

Those who listen to *The Dramatized Old Testament* are drawn into the presentation. As the story moves from voice to voice it is very difficult for attention to wander. Useful in all forms of church worship, *The Dramatized Old Testament* is especially an ideal focus for the "word" aspect of all-age (so-called family) worship. Even young children, who naturally grow restive during a long and uneventful reading, find their interest and imagination caught up in the narrative as the Scriptures are presented in dramatized form.

We confidently commend this book to churches, youth groups, schools, study groups, and all who work in the area of education. It may be that producers and presenters of religious programs for radio and television will also find inspiration here. We happily anticipate that *The Dramatized Old Testament* will enrich our worship by granting us a clearer vision of God and a surer knowledge of the revelation of the eternal purpose for our world in Jesus Christ.

Michael Perry

Preface to NIV

The New International Version is a completely new translation of the Holy Bible made by over a hundred scholars working directly from the best available Hebrew, Aramaic and Greek texts. It had its beginning in 1965 when, after several years of exploratory study by committees from the Christian Reformed Church and the National Association of Evangelicals, a group of scholars met at Palos Heights, Illinois, and concurred in the need for a new translation of the Bible in contemporary English. This group, though not made up of official church representatives, was transdenominational. Its conclusion was endorsed by a large number of leaders from many denominations who met in Chicago in 1966.

Responsibility for the new version was delegated by the Palos Heights group to a self-governing body of fifteen, the Committee on Bible Translation, composed for the most part of biblical scholars from colleges, universities and seminaries. In 1967 the New York Bible Society (now the International Bible Society) generously undertook the financial sponsorship of the project—a sponsorship that made it possible to enlist the help of many distinguished scholars. The fact that participants from the United States, Great Britain, Canada, Australia and New Zealand worked together gave the project its international scope. That they were from many denominations—including Anglican, Assemblies of God, Baptist, Brethren, Christian Reformed, Church of Christ, Evangelical Free, Lutheran, Mennonite, Methodist, Nazarene, Presbyterian, Wesleyan and other churches—helped to safeguard the translation from sectarian bias.

How it was made helps to give the New International Version its distinctiveness. The translation of each book was assigned to a team of scholars. Next, one of the Intermediate Editorial Committees revised the initial translation, with constant reference to the Hebrew, Aramaic or Greek. Their work then went to one of the General Editorial Committees, which checked it in detail and made another thorough revision. This revision in turn was carefully reviewed by the Committee on Bible Translation, which made further changes and then released the final version for publication. In this way the entire Bible underwent three revisions, during each of which the translation was examined for its faithfulness to the original languages and for its English style.

All this involved many thousands of hours of research and discussion regarding the meaning of the texts and the precise way of putting them into English. It may well be that no other translation has been made by a more thorough process of review and revision from committee to committee than this one.

From the beginning of the project, the Committee on Bible Translation held to certain goals for the New International Version: that it would be an accurate translation and one that would have clarity and literary quality and so prove suitable for public and private reading, teaching, preaching, memorizing and liturgical use. The Committee also sought to preserve some measure of continuity with the long tradition of translating the Scriptures into English.

In working toward these goals, the translators were united in their commitment to the authority and infallibility of the Bible as God's Word in written form. They believe that it contains the divine answer to the deepest needs of humanity, that it sheds unique light on our path in a dark work, and that it sets forth the way to our eternal well-being.

The first concern of the translators has been the accuracy of the translation and its fidelity to the thought of the biblical writers. They have weighed the significance of the lexical and grammatical details of the Hebrew, Aramaic and Greek texts. At the same time, they have striven for more than a word-for-word translation. Because thought patterns and syntax differ from language to language, faithful communication of the meaning of the writers of the Bible demands frequent modifications in sentence structure and constant regard for the contextual meanings of words.

A sensitive feeling for style does not always accompany scholarship. Accordingly the Committee on Bible Translation submitted the developing version to a number of stylistic consultants. Two of them read every book of both the Old and New Testaments twice—once before and once after the last major revision—and made invaluable suggestions. Samples of the translation were tested for clarity and ease of reading by various kinds of people—young and old, highly educated and less well educated, ministers and laymen.

Concern for clear and natural English—that the New International Version should be idiomatic but not idiosyncratic, contemporary but not dated—motivated the translators and consultants. At the same time, they tried to reflect the differing styles of the biblical writers. In view of the international use of English, the translators sought to avoid obvious Americanisms on the one hand and obvious Anglicisms on the other. A British edition reflects the comparatively few differences of significant idiom and of spelling.

As for the traditional pronouns "thou," "thee" and "thine" in reference to the Deity, the translators judged that to use these archaisms (along with the verb forms such as "doest," "wouldest" and "hadst") would violate accuracy in translation. Neither Hebrew, Aramaic nor Greek uses special pronouns for the persons of the Godhead. A present-day translation is not enhanced by forms that in the time of the King James Version were used in everyday speech, whether referring to God or man.

For the Old Testament the standard Hebrew text, the Masoretic Text as published in the latest editions of *Biblia Hebraica,* was used throughout. The Dead Sea Scrolls contain material bearing on an earlier stage of the Hebrew text. They were consulted, as were the Samaritan Pentateuch and the ancient scribal traditions relating to textual changes. Sometimes a variant Hebrew reading in the margin of the Masoretic Text was followed instead of the text itself. Such instances, being variants within the Masoretic tradition, are not specified by footnotes. In rare cases, words in the consonantal text were divided differently from the way they appear in the Masoretic Text. Footnotes indicate this. The translators also consulted the more important early versions—the Septuagint; Aquila, Symmachus and Theodotion; the Vulgate; the Syriac Peshitta; the Targums; and for the Psalms the *Juxta Hebraica* of Jerome. Readings from these versions were occasionally followed where the Masoretic Text seemed doubtful and where accepted principles of textual criticism showed that one or more of these textual witnesses appeared to provide the correct reading. Such instances are footnoted. Sometimes vowel letters and vowel signs did not, in the judgment of the translators, represent the correct vowels for the original consonantal text. Accordingly some words were read with a different set of vowels. These instances are usually not indicated by footnotes.

The Greek text used in translating the New Testament was an eclectic one. No other piece of ancient literature has such an abundance of manuscript witnesses as does the New Testament. Where existing manuscripts differ, the translators made their choice of readings according to accepted principles of New Testament textual criticism. Footnotes call attention to places where there was uncertainty about what the original text was. The best current printed texts of the Greek New Testament were used.

There is a sense in which the work of translation is never wholly finished. This applies to all great literature and uniquely so to the Bible. In 1973 the New Testament in the New International Version was published. Since then, suggestions for corrections and revisions have been received from various sources. The Committee on Bible Translation carefully considered the suggestions and adopted a number of them. These were incorporated in the first printing of the entire Bible in 1978. Additional revisions were made by the Committee on Bible Translation in 1983 and appear in printings after that date.

As in other ancient documents, the precise meaning of the biblical texts is sometimes uncertain. This is more often the case with the Hebrew and Aramaic texts than with the Greek text. Although archaeological and linguistic discoveries in this century aid in understanding difficult passages, some uncertainties remain. The more significant of these have been called to the reader's attention in the footnotes.

In regard to the divine name *YHWH*, commonly referred to as the *Tetragrammaton*, the translators adopted the device used in most English versions of rendering that name as "LORD" in capital letters to distinguish it from Adonai, another Hebrew word rendered "Lord," for which small letters are used. Wherever the two names stand together in the Old Testament as a compound name of God, they are rendered "Sovereign LORD."

Because for most readers today the phrases "the LORD of hosts" and "God of hosts" have little meaning, this version renders them "the LORD Almighty" and "God Almighty." These renderings convey the sense of the Hebrew, namely, "he who is sovereign over all the 'hosts' (powers) in heaven and on earth, especially over the 'hosts' (armies) of Israel." For readers unacquainted with Hebrew this does not make clear the distinction between *Sabaoth* ("hosts" or Almighty") and *Shaddai* (which can also be translated "Almighty"), but the latter occurs infrequently and is always footnoted. When *Adonai* and *YHWH Sabaoth* occur together, they are rendered "the Lord, the LORD Almighty."

As for other proper nouns, the familiar spellings of the King James Version are generally retained. Names traditionally spelled with "ch," except where it is final, are usually spelled in this translation with "k" or "c," since the biblical languages do not have the sound that "ch" frequently indicates in English—for example, in *chant*. For well-known names such as Zechariah, however, the traditional spelling has been retained. Variation in the spelling of names in the original languages has usually not been indicated. Where a person or place has two or more different names in the Hebrew, Aramaic or Greek texts, the more familiar one has generally been used, with footnotes where needed.

To achieve clarity the translators sometimes supplied words not in the original texts but required by the context. If there was uncertainty about such materiel, it is enclosed in brackets. Also for the sake of clarity or style, nouns, including some proper nouns, are sometimes substituted for pronouns, and vice versa. And though the Hebrew writers often shifted back and forth between first, second and third personal pronouns without change of antecedent, this translation often makes them uniform, in accordance with English style and without the use of footnotes.

Poetical passages are printed as poetry, that is, with indentation of lines and with separate stanzas. These are generally designed to reflect the structure of Hebrew poetry. This poetry is normally characterized by parallelism in balanced lines. Most of the poetry in the Bible is in the Old Testament, and scholars differ regarding the scansion of Hebrew lines. The translators determined the stanza divisions for the most part by analysis of the subject matter. The stanzas therefore serve as poetic paragraphs.

As an aid to the reader, italicized sectional headings are inserted in most of the books. They are not to be regarded as part of the NIV text, are not for oral reading, and are not intended to dictate the interpretation of the sections they head.

The footnotes in this version are of several kinds, most of which need no explanation. Those giving alternative translations begin with "Or" and generally introduce the alternative with the last word preceding it in the text, except when it is a single-word alternative; in poetry quoted in a footnote a slant mark indicates a line division. Footnotes introduced by "Or" do not have uniform significance. In some cases two possible translations were considered to have about equal validity. In other cases, though the translators were convinced that the translation in the text was correct, they judged that another interpretation was possible and of sufficient importance to be represented in a footnote.

In the New Testament, footnotes that refer to uncertainty regarding the original text are introduced by "Some manuscripts" or similar expressions. In the Old Testament, evidence for the reading chosen is given first and evidence for the alternative is added after a semicolon (for example: Septuagint; Hebrew *father*). In such notes the term "Hebrew" refers to the Masoretic Text.

It should be noted that minerals, flora and fauna, architectural details, articles of clothing and jewelry, musical instruments and other articles cannot always be identified with precision. Also measures of capacity in the biblical period are particularly uncertain (see the table of weights and measures following the text).

Like all translations of the Bible, made as they are by imperfect man, this one undoubtedly falls short of its goals. Yet we are grateful to God for the extent to which he has enabled us to realize these goals and for the strength he has given us and our colleagues to complete our task. We offer this version of the Bible to him in whose name and for whose glory it has been made. We pray that it will lead many into a better understanding of the Holy Scriptures and a fuller knowledge of Jesus Christ the incarnate Word, of whom the Scriptures so faithfully testify.

The Committee on Bible Translation

June 1978
(Revised August 1983)

Names of the translators and editors may be secured
from the International Bible Society,
translation sponsors of the New International Version,
1820 Jet Stream Drive, Colorado Springs, Colorado 80921-3896 U.S.A.

Acknowledgments

As editor of *The Dramatized Old Testament* I gladly acknowledge the skills of the teams of experts who prepared the outstanding and now celebrated New International Version of the Bible. I have appreciated the advice of the Reverend Kathleen Bowe upon the translation of my Liturgical Psalms, of the Reverend Robert Backhouse on all aspects of dramatization and typesetting and of Miss Janet Henderson on matters of copyright. My thanks go to my typist, Ann, my secretary, Bunty, and my daughter, Helen, for their conscientious work on copy, proofs, and indexes. I am grateful to church leaders and other authorities for their kind commendations and encouragement. I am indebted to the friendly staff at Baker Book House. I know that all who have cooperated in its production will find great satisfaction in the enthusiasm with which I am confident *The Dramatized Old Testament* will be received.

M.A.P.

Using *The Dramatized Old Testament*

Welcome to a new and powerful resource! If you are a minister, teacher, or leader, you will want to know how you can use this book to the greatest effect.

Realism

In designing *The Dramatized Old Testament* we have tried to be realistic about the pressure upon ministers, teachers, and leaders: on the whole they require a book that can be used spontaneously and without great forethought, preparation, or rehearsal. We suggest that each organization using *The Dramatized Old Testament* eventually needs five copies because, on average, there are five characters to a script. Then, at a moment's notice, willing readers can be given a copy each and invited to fill a character part. All characters are listed at the foot of each reading.

Superfluous "he said"s and the like are already excised from the text (with the permission of the copyright holders). While appropriate in prose, they are intrusive—sometimes even humorous—in drama. Usually in *The Dramatized Old Testament* they are left in at the beginning of the piece, in order to establish the character, and then omitted thereafter. Further phrases that for similar reasons might be thought to make performance stilted are enclosed in bold square brackets: [and]. But such phrases or sentences should not be omitted without considering the particular implications. To omit them may well enliven the drama, but it will require the cast to compensate for the omission. This can be done either visually, by turning to one of the other characters, or aurally, by a change of voice. The best solution will depend on the local circumstances, the initiative of the leader, and the availability of the participants. Therefore, a rule of thumb might be—only when consultation or rehearsal is possible, omit phrases in bold square brackets.

The proprietors of the NIV text have required the insertion of additional square brackets (not bold) to show where explanatory text has been added. Please distinguish between this and the phrases suitable for omission. Also, to aid in effective dramatic reading, words have been italicized for emphasis occasionally that do not appear in italics in the NIV. Please note that, unless they designate foreign words, all italics in the text have been added by us.

This book does not contain the entire NIV text, and many passages have been shortened or otherwise altered in punctuation or format. Please refer to an NIV Bible for actual Scripture needs and NIV copyright information.

Shortening an Episode

Bold square brackets have a different function when they enclose one or more paragraphs: they indicate where the reading may sensibly be shortened. Unless a sermon, service, talk, or discussion requires use of these longer sections, they are best left out in the interests of lively presentation and greater impact upon an audience.

Liturgical (LIT) Psalms

This volume of the *Dramatized Old Testament* contains forty psalms prepared for congregational or worship-group use. They are marked "LIT" (Liturgical Version), to indicate that they are the translation work of the Jubilate group, and they complement the other readings from the NIV text. The Liturgical Psalms, but no other material, may be photocopied freely in sufficient quantities for use by the whole congregation or local organization, on condition that any item so used is marked "© the Dramatized Bible, Jubilate Liturgical Psalms."

Local Reproduction

Applications for reproduction of material from *The Dramatized Old Testament* in the world outside North America may be addressed to Hope Publishing Company, Carol Stream, Illinois 60188 (phone 708-665-3200, FAX 708-665-2552, WATS 800-323-1049). For further information see the copyright page.

Audibility

Use of *The Dramatized Old Testament* has a positive effect on the attention that a reading is given by a congregation, class, youth group, or study group. It also makes the content of the reading more memorable—not least to those who have participated. Much depends on audibility; so care needs to be taken in larger buildings. In church, or in a school assembly hall, a stage holding a minimum of five people can be used to advantage. Where appropriate, a microphone with a wide field that will pick up all the speakers should be used; or separate microphones might be considered. This sort of preparation will enable the minister/leader to involve people whose voices are less clear and not so strong.

Casting

It is obviously important that a strong voice should be cast for any key character, such as the **Narrator.** In a church service, this part can most usefully be given to the person who would have taken the Scripture reading if it had not been dramatized, thus ensuring that no one feels usurped by what should be a welcome development in worship. It is worth noting that more male than female characters speak in the Bible. However, when using *The Dramatized Old Testament*, a good balance can still be obtained by employing female voices for narration, for the frequent anonymous **Persons**, and in the teaching passages that divide into **Voice 1**, **Voice 2.** Here it is good to have a contrast between the speakers.

Where **Voices 1–3** or **Persons 1–3** are used, participants should stand together in a group. Where **the Lord** or **God** speaks as a prophetic utterance and not in direct conversation, it is best for the reader to stand apart from the rest—even to be unseen.

Actions

There will be occasions—both formal and informal—when participants can add actions to a presentation from *The Dramatized Old Testament*. Then, prior agreement over what is to be done is a safeguard against unintended humorous accidents! A rehearsal will be necessary unless the actors are very confident and experienced. At the rehearsal it is sensible to have someone watching who is able to assess the drama's impact on the proposed audience, and for the cast to listen and respond to that person's objective criticism. When actions are used in the context of large gatherings, visibility and audibility (especially when the speaker turns away from the audience) are of utmost importance. In seminar and class work, or in small groups, carefully prepared actions will add a startlingly fresh dynamic.

Job

Job's First Test

Job 1:1–12

Narrator	In the land of Uz there lived a man whose name was Job. This man was blameless and upright; he feared God and shunned evil. He had seven sons and three daughters, and he owned seven thousand sheep, three thousand camels, five hundred yoke of oxen and five hundred donkeys, and had a large number of servants. He was the *greatest* man among all the people of the East.
	His sons used to take turns holding feasts in their homes, and they would invite their three sisters to eat and drink with them. When a period of feasting had run its course, Job would send and have them purified. Early in the morning he would sacrifice a burnt offering for each of them:
Job (thinking)	Perhaps my children have sinned and cursed God in their hearts.
Narrator	This was Job's regular custom.
	One day the angels came to present themselves before the LORD, and Satan also came with them. The LORD said to Satan:
The Lord (voice only)	Where have you come from?
Satan (casually)	From roaming through the earth and going back and forth in it.
The Lord (voice)	Have you considered my servant Job? There is no one on earth like him; he is blameless and upright, a man who fears God and shuns evil.
Satan	Does Job fear God for nothing? Have you not put a hedge around him and his household and everything he has? You have blessed the work of his hands, so that his flocks and herds are spread throughout the land. But stretch out your hand and strike everything he has, and he will surely curse you to your face.
The Lord (voice)	Very well, then, everything he has is in your hands, but on the man himself do not lay a finger.
Narrator	Then Satan went out from the presence of the LORD.

Cast: **Narrator, Job, the Lord** (voice only), **Satan**

Job's Children and Wealth Are Destroyed

Job 1:13–22

Narrator	One day when Job's sons and daughters were feasting and drinking wine at the oldest brother's house, a messenger came to Job:
Messenger 1	The oxen were plowing and the donkeys were grazing nearby, and the Sabeans attacked and carried them off. They put the servants to the sword, and I am the only one who has escaped to tell you!
Narrator	While he was still speaking, another messenger came:
Messenger 2	The fire of God fell from the sky and burned up the sheep and the servants, and I am the only one who has escaped to tell you!
Narrator	While he was still speaking, another messenger came:
Messenger 3	The Chaldeans formed three raiding parties and swept down on your camels and carried them off. They put the servants to the sword, and I am the only one who has escaped to tell you!
Narrator	While he was still speaking, yet another messenger came:
Messenger 4	Your sons and daughters were feasting and drinking wine at the oldest brother's house, when suddenly a mighty wind swept in from the desert and struck the four corners of the house. It collapsed on them and they are dead, and I am the only one who has escaped to tell you!
Narrator	At this, Job got up and tore his robe and shaved his head. Then he fell to the ground in worship:

Job	Naked I came from my mother's womb,
	    and naked I will depart.
	The LORD gave and the LORD has taken away;
	    may the name of the LORD be praised.

Narrator	In all this, Job did not sin by charging God with wrongdoing.

Cast: **Narrator, Messenger 1, Messenger 2, Messenger 3, Messenger 4, Job**

Job's Second Test

Job 2:1–10

Narrator	The angels came to present themselves before the LORD, and Satan also came with them to present himself before him. And the LORD said to Satan:
The Lord (voice only)	Where have you come from?
[Narrator	Satan answered the LORD:]

Satan (casually)	From roaming through the earth and going back and forth in it.
The Lord (voice)	Have you considered my servant Job? There is no one on earth like him; he is blameless and upright, a man who fears God and shuns evil. And he still maintains his integrity, though you incited me against him to ruin him without any reason.
Satan	Skin for skin! A man will give all he has for his own life. But stretch out your hand and strike his flesh and bones, and he will surely curse you to your face.
The Lord (voice)	Very well, then, he is in your hands; but you must spare his life.
Narrator	So Satan went out from the presence of the LORD and afflicted Job with painful sores from the soles of his feet to the top of his head. Then Job took a piece of broken pottery and scraped himself with it as he sat among the ashes. His wife said to him:
Wife	Are you still holding on to your integrity? Curse God and die!
Job (replying)	You are talking like a foolish woman. Shall we accept good from God, and not trouble?
Narrator	In all this, Job did not sin in what he said.

Cast: **Narrator, the Lord** (voice only), **Satan, Wife, Job**

Job and His Friends—the Dialogue

From Job 2:11–42:6

Narrator	When Job's three friends, Eliphaz the Temanite, Bildad the Shuhite and Zophar the Naamathite, heard about all the troubles that had come upon him, they set out from their homes and met together by agreement to go and sympathize with him and comfort him. When they saw him from a distance, they could hardly recognize him; they began to weep aloud, and they tore their robes and sprinkled dust on their heads. Then they sat on the ground with him for seven days and seven nights. No one said a word to him, because they saw how great his suffering was.
	After this, Job opened his mouth and cursed the day of his birth.

Job
(crying out
to God)
	May the day of my birth perish,
	     and the night it was said, "A boy is born!"
	That day—may it turn to darkness;
	     may God above not care about it;
	     may no light shine upon it. . . .

21

(musing)   Why did I not perish at birth,
     and die as I came from the womb? . . .
For now I would be lying down in peace;
     I would be asleep and at rest
with kings and counselors of the earth. . . .
There the wicked cease from turmoil,
     and there the weary are at rest.
Captives also enjoy their ease;
     they no longer hear the slave driver's shout.
The small and the great are there,
     and the slave is freed from his master.

Why is light given to those in misery,
     and life to the bitter of soul,
to those who long for death that does not come,
     who search for it more than for hidden treasure,
who are filled with gladness
     and rejoice when they reach the grave?
Why is life given to a man
     whose way is hidden,
     whom God has hedged in?
For sighing comes to me instead of food;
     my groans pour out like water.
What I feared has come upon me;
     what I dreaded has happened to me.
I have no peace, no quietness;
     I have no rest, but only turmoil.

Eliphaz
(to Job)   If someone ventures a word with you, will you be impatient?
     But who can keep from speaking?
Think how you have instructed many,
     how you have strengthened feeble hands.
Your words have supported those who stumbled;
     you have strengthened faltering knees. . . .
Should not your piety be your confidence
     and your blameless ways your hope?

(naïvely)   Consider now: Who, being innocent, has ever perished?
     Where were the upright ever destroyed?
As I have observed, those who plow evil
     and those who sow trouble reap it.
At the breath of God they are destroyed;
     at the blast of his anger they perish. . . .
Yet man is born to trouble
     as surely as sparks fly upward.

But if it were I, I would appeal to God;
     I would lay my cause before him.
He performs wonders that cannot be fathomed,

Miracles that cannot be counted. . . .

Blessed is the man whom God corrects;
    so do not despise the discipline of the Almighty.
For he wounds, but he also binds up;
    he injures, but his hands also heal.
From six calamities he will rescue you;
    in seven no harm will befall you.
In famine he will ransom you from death,
    and in battle from the stroke of the sword.
You will be protected from the lash of the tongue,
    and need not fear when destruction comes. . . .

(pleading)   We have examined this, and it is true.
    So hear it and apply it to yourself.

Job
(to
Eliphaz)   If only my anguish could be weighed
    and all my misery be placed on the scales!
It would surely outweigh the sand of the seas—
    no wonder my words have been impetuous.
The arrows of the Almighty are in me,
    my spirit drinks in their poison;
    God's terrors are marshaled against me. . . .

Oh, that I might have my request,
    that God would grant what I hope for,
that God would be willing to crush me,
    to let loose his hand and cut me off! . . .

A despairing man should have the devotion of his friends,
    even though he forsakes the fear of the Almighty.
But my brothers are as undependable as intermittent streams . . .
that cease to flow in the dry season,
    and in the heat vanish from their channels. (PAUSE)

(resigned)   Teach me, and I will be quiet;
    show me where I have been wrong.
How painful are honest words!
    But what do your arguments prove?
Do you mean to correct what I say,
    and treat the words of a despairing man as wind? . . .

But now be so kind as to look at me.

(looking up
at Eliphaz)   Would I lie to your face?
Relent, do not be unjust;
    reconsider, for my integrity is at stake.
Is there any wickedness on my lips?
    Can my mouth not discern malice? . . .

23

(to God,
in prayer)   Remember, O God, that my life is but a breath;
        my eyes will never see happiness again. . . .

(to God,
angrily)   Therefore I will not keep silent;
        I will speak out in the anguish of my spirit,
        I will complain in the bitterness of my soul.
    Am I the sea, or the monster of the deep,
        that you put me under guard? . . .
    Why do you not pardon my offenses
        and forgive my sins?
    For I will soon lie down in the dust;
        you will search for me, but I will be no more.

Bildad
(to Job)   How long will you say such things?
        Your words are a blustering wind.
    Does God pervert justice?
        Does the Almighty pervert what is right?
    When your children sinned against him,
        he gave them over to the penalty of their sin.
    But if you will look to God
        and plead with the Almighty,
    if you are pure and upright,
        even now he will rouse himself on your behalf
        and restore you to your rightful place. . . .
    Can reeds thrive without water?
    While still growing and uncut,
        they wither more quickly than grass.
    Such is the destiny of all who forget God;
        so perishes the hope of the godless. . . .
    He is like a well-watered plant in the sunshine,
        spreading its shoots over the garden;
    it entwines its roots around a pile of rocks
        and looks for a place among the stones.
    But when it is torn from its spot,
        that place disowns it and says, "I never saw you." . . .

    Surely God does not reject a blameless man
        or strengthen the hands of evildoers. . . .

Job
(to Bildad)   Indeed, I know that this is true.
        But how can a mortal be righteous before God?
    Though one wished to dispute with him,
        he could not answer him one time out of a thousand.
    His wisdom is profound, his power is vast.
        Who has resisted him and come out unscathed? . . .
    When he passes me, I cannot see him;
        when he goes by, I cannot perceive him.

If he snatches away, who can stop him?
Who can say to him, "What are you doing?"
God does not restrain his anger;
even the cohorts of Rahab cowered at his feet.

How then can I dispute with him?
How can I find words to argue with him?
Though I were innocent, I could not answer him;
I could only plead with my Judge for mercy.
Even if I summoned him and he responded,
I do not believe he would give me a hearing.
He would crush me with a storm
and multiply my wounds for no reason.
He would not let me regain my breath
but would overwhelm me with misery.
If it is a matter of strength, he is mighty!
And if it is a matter of justice, who will summon him?
Even if I were innocent, my mouth would condemn me;
if I were blameless, it would pronounce me guilty.

(musing)   Although I am blameless,
I have no concern for myself;
I despise my own life.
It is all the same; that is why I say,
"He destroys both the blameless and the wicked."

(bitterly)   When a scourge brings sudden death,
he mocks the despair of the innocent.
When a land falls into the hands of the wicked,
he blindfolds its judges.
If it is not he, then who is it? . . .

(despairing)   He is not a man like me that I might answer him,
that we might confront each other in court.
If only there were someone to arbitrate between us,
to lay his hand upon us both,
someone to remove God's rod from me,
so that his terror would frighten me no more.

(angrily)   Then I would speak up without fear of him,
but as it now stands with me, I cannot.

I loathe my very life;
therefore I will give free rein to my complaint
and speak out in the bitterness of my soul.

(to God,
quietly
pleading)   [I will say to God:] Do not condemn me,
but tell me what charges you have against me.
Does it please you to oppress me,
to spurn the work of your hands,

while you smile on the schemes of the wicked?
Do you have eyes of flesh?
　　Do you see as a mortal sees?
Are your days like those of a mortal
　　or your years like those of a man . . . ?

Your hands shaped me and made me.
　　Will you now turn and destroy me?
Remember that you molded me like clay.
　　Will you now turn me to dust again?
Did you not pour me out like milk
　　and curdle me like cheese,
clothe me with skin and flesh
　　and knit me together with bones and sinews?
You gave me life and showed me kindness,
　　and in your providence watched over my spirit.

(to God,
petulantly)　But this is what you concealed in your heart,
　　and I know that this was in your mind:
If I sinned, you would be watching me
　　and would not let my offense go unpunished.
If I am guilty—woe to me!
　　Even if I am innocent, I cannot lift my head,
for I am full of shame
　　and drowned in my affliction.
If I hold my head high, you stalk me like a lion
　　and again display your awesome power against me.

(to God,
exas-
perated)　Why then did you bring me out of the womb?
　　I wish I had died before any eye saw me.
If only I had never come into being,
　　or had been carried straight from the womb to the grave!
Are not my few days almost over?
　　Turn away from me so I can have a moment's joy
before I go to the place of no return,
　　to the land of gloom and deep shadow,
to the land of deepest night,
　　of deep shadow and disorder,
　　where even the light is like darkness.

Zophar
(to Bildad
and
Eliphaz)　Are all these words to go unanswered?
　　Is this talker to be vindicated?

(to Job)　Will your idle talk reduce men to silence?
　　Will no one rebuke you when you mock?

You say to God, "My beliefs are flawless
    and I am pure in your sight."
Oh, how I wish that God would speak,
    that he would open his lips against you
and disclose to you the secrets of wisdom,
    for true wisdom has two sides.
    Know this: God has even forgotten some of your sin. . . .

(patroniz-
ingly)   Yet if you devote your heart to him
    and stretch out your hands to him,
if you put away the sin that is in your hand
    and allow no evil to dwell in your tent,
then you will lift up your face without shame;
    you will stand firm and without fear.
You will surely forget your trouble,
    recalling it only as waters gone by.
Life will be brighter than noonday,
    and darkness will become like morning. . . .

Job
(sarcas-
tically)   Doubtless you are the people,
    and wisdom will die with you!
But I have a mind as well as you;
    I am not inferior to you.
    Who does not know all these things?

(to
audience)   I have become a laughingstock to my friends,
    though I called upon God and he answered—
    a mere laughingstock, though righteous and blameless!
Men at ease have contempt for misfortune
    as the fate of those whose feet are slipping.
The tents of marauders are undisturbed,
    and those who provoke God are secure—
    those who carry their god in their hands. . . .

(to friends)   My eyes have seen all this,
    my ears have heard and understood it.
What you know, I also know;
    I am not inferior to you.
But I desire to speak to the Almighty
    and to argue my case with God.
You, however, smear me with lies;
    you are worthless physicians, all of you!
If only you would be altogether silent!
    For you, that would be wisdom. . . .

(to
audience)   Though [God] slay me, yet will I hope in him;

          I will surely defend my ways to his face.
          Indeed, this will turn out for my deliverance,
             for no godless man would dare come before him!

(to friends) Listen carefully to my words;
             let your ears take in what I say.
          Now that I have prepared my case,
             I know I will be vindicated.
          Can anyone bring charges against me?
             If so, I will be silent and die.

(to God)   Only grant me these two things, O God,
             and then I will not hide from you:
          Withdraw your hand far from me,
             and stop frightening me with your terrors.
          Then summon me and I will answer,
             or let me speak, and you reply.
          How many wrongs and sins have I committed?
             Show me my offense and my sin.
          Why do you hide your face
             and consider me your enemy?
          Will you torment a windblown leaf?
             Will you chase after dry chaff? . . .

(to
audience,
musing)   Man born of woman
             is of few days and full of trouble.
          He springs up like a flower and withers away;
             like a fleeting shadow, he does not endure. . . .

          At least there is hope for a tree:
             If it is cut down, it will sprout again,
             and its new shoots will not fail.
          Its roots may grow old in the ground
             and its stump die in the soil,
          yet at the scent of water it will bud
             and put forth shoots like a plant.
          But man dies and is laid low;
             he breathes his last and is no more.
          As water disappears from the sea
             or a riverbed becomes parched and dry,
          so man lies down and does not rise;
             till the heavens are no more, men will not awake
             or be roused from their sleep. . . .

(to God)   As water wears away stones
             and torrents wash away the soil,
             so you destroy man's hope.
          You overpower him once for all, and he is gone;
             you change his countenance and send him away.
          If his sons are honored, he does not know it;

if they are brought low, he does not see it.
He feels but the pain of his own body
and mourns only for himself.

Eliphaz
(patroniz-
ingly)   Would a wise man answer with empty notions
      or fill his belly with the hot east wind?
    Would he argue with useless words,
      with speeches that have no value?
    But you even undermine piety
      and hinder devotion to God.
    Your sin prompts your mouth;
      you adopt the tongue of the crafty.
    Your own mouth condemns you, not mine;
      your own lips testify against you. (PAUSE)

(calmly)   Are you the first man ever born?
      Were you brought forth before the hills?
    Do you listen in on God's council?
      Do you limit wisdom to yourself?
    What do you know that we do not know?
      What insights do you have that we do not have?
    The gray-haired and the aged are on our side,
      men even older than your father.
    Are God's consolations not enough for you,
      words spoken gently to you?
    Why has your heart carried you away,
      and why do your eyes flash,
    so that you vent your rage against God
      and pour out such words from your mouth?

    What is man, that he could be pure,
      or one born of woman, that he could be righteous? . . .
    All his days the wicked man suffers torment,
      the ruthless through all the years stored up for him. . . .
    Distress and anguish fill him with terror;
      they overwhelm him, like a king poised to attack,
    because he shakes his fist at God
      and vaunts himself against the Almighty,
    defiantly charging against him
      with a thick, strong shield. . . .

Job
(to
Eliphaz)   I have heard many things like these;
      miserable comforters are you all!
    Will your long-winded speeches never end?
      What ails you that you keep on arguing?
    I also could speak like you,

            if you were in my place;
        I could make fine speeches against you
            and shake my head at you.
        But my mouth would encourage you;
            comfort from my lips would bring you relief. . . .

(to God)   Surely, O God, you have worn me out;
            you have devastated my entire household.
        You have bound me—and it has become a witness;
            my gauntness rises up and testifies against me. . . .

(musing)   Men open their mouths to jeer at me;
            they strike my cheek in scorn
            and unite together against me.
        God has turned me over to evil men
            and thrown me into the clutches of the wicked.
        All was well with me, but he shattered me;
            he seized me by the neck and crushed me.
        He has made me his target;
            his archers surround me. . . .
        Again and again he bursts upon me;
            he rushes at me like a warrior. . . .
        My face is red with weeping,
            deep shadows ring my eyes;
        yet my hands have been free of violence
            and my prayer is pure.

(to the
ground)   O earth, do not cover my blood;
            may my cry never be laid to rest!
        Even now my witness is in heaven;
            my advocate is on high.
        My intercessor is my friend
            as my eyes pour out tears to God;
        on behalf of a man he pleads with God
            as a man pleads for his friend. . . .

(to God)   Give me, O God, the pledge you demand.
            Who else will put up security for me?
         You have closed their minds to understanding;
            therefore you will not let them triumph. . . .

(musing)   Upright men are appalled at this;
            the innocent are aroused against the ungodly.
        Nevertheless, the righteous will hold to their ways,
            and those with clean hands will grow stronger. . . .

(to
audience)   My days have passed, my plans are shattered,
            and so are the desires of my heart.
        These men turn night into day;

in the face of darkness they say, "Light is near."
If the only home I hope for is the grave,
    if I spread out my bed in darkness . . .
where then *is* my hope? . . .

Bildad

(frustrated)   When will you end these speeches?
    Be sensible, and then we can talk. . . .

(delibe-
rately)   The lamp of the wicked is snuffed out;
    the flame of his fire stops burning. . . .
The vigor of his step is weakened;
    his own schemes throw him down.
His feet thrust him into a net
    and he wanders into its mesh.
A trap seizes him by the heel;
    a snare holds him fast. . . .
He has no offspring or descendants among his people,
    no survivor where once he lived.
Men of the west are appalled at his fate;
    men of the east are seized with horror.
Surely such is the dwelling of an evil man;
    such is the place of one who knows not God.

Job

(to Bildad) How long will you torment me
    and crush me with words?
Ten times now you have reproached me;
    shamelessly you attack me.
If it is true that I have gone astray,
    my error remains my concern alone.
If indeed you would exalt yourselves above me
    and use my humiliation against me,
then know that God has wronged me
    and drawn his net around me.

Though I cry, "I've been wronged!" I get no response;
    though I call for help, there is no justice.
He has blocked my way so I cannot pass;
    he has shrouded my paths in darkness. . . .

(to friends) Have pity on me, my friends, have pity,
    for the hand of God has struck me.
Why do you pursue me as God does?
    Will you never get enough of my flesh? . . .

If you say, "How we will hound him,
    since the root of the trouble lies in him,"
you should fear the sword yourselves;
    for wrath will bring punishment by the sword,
    and then you will know that there is judgment.

Zophar

(crossly)   My troubled thoughts prompt me to answer
        because I am greatly disturbed. . . .

    Surely you know how it has been from of old,
        ever since man was placed on the earth,
    that the mirth of the wicked is brief,
        the joy of the godless lasts but a moment.
    Though his pride reaches to the heavens
        and his head touches the clouds,
    he will perish forever, like his own dung;
        those who have seen him will say, "Where is he?" . . .
    The youthful vigor that fills his bones
        will lie with him in the dust. . . .
    What he toiled for he must give back uneaten;
        he will not enjoy the profit from his trading.
    For he has oppressed the poor and left them destitute;
        he has seized houses he did not build. . . .
    In the midst of his plenty, distress will overtake him;
        the full force of misery will come upon him.
    When he has filled his belly,
        God will vent his burning anger against him
        and rain down his blows upon him. . . .
    The heavens will expose his guilt;
        the earth will rise up against him.
    A flood will carry off his house,
        rushing waters on the day of God's wrath.
    Such is the fate God allots the wicked,
        the heritage appointed for them by God.

Job

(patiently,
to friends)   Listen carefully to my words;
        let this be the consolation you give me.
    Bear with me while I speak,
        and after I have spoken, mock on.

    Is my complaint directed to man?
        Why should I not be impatient? . . .
    Why do the wicked live on,
        growing old and increasing in power?
    They see their children established around them,
        their offspring before their eyes.
    Their homes are safe and free from fear;
        the rod of God is not upon them.
    Their bulls never fail to breed;
        their cows calve and do not miscarry.
    They send forth their children as a flock;
        their little ones dance about.
    They sing to the music of tambourine and harp;

             they make merry to the sound of the flute.
They spend their years in prosperity
    and go down to the grave in peace.
Yet they say to God, "Leave us alone!
    We have no desire to know your ways.
Who is the Almighty, that we should serve him?
    What would we gain by praying to him?"
But their prosperity is not in their own hands,
    so I stand aloof from the counsel of the wicked.

Yet how often is the lamp of the wicked snuffed out?
    How often does calamity come upon them,
    the fate God allots in his anger?
How often are they like straw before the wind,
    like chaff swept away by a gale?

(to Bildad)   ⌊It is said,⌋ "God stores up a man's punishment for his sons."
    Let him repay the man himself, so that he will know it!
Let his own eyes see his destruction;
    let him drink of the wrath of the Almighty. . . .

(to Zophar) Have you never questioned those who travel?
    Have you paid no regard to their accounts—
that the evil man is spared from the day of calamity,
    that he is delivered from the day of wrath?
Who denounces his conduct to his face?
    Who repays him for what he has done?
He is carried to the grave,
    and watch is kept over his tomb.
The soil in the valley is sweet to him;
    all men follow after him,
    and a countless throng goes before him.

So how can you console me with your nonsense?
    Nothing is left of your answers but falsehood!

Eliphaz
(to Job)   Can a man be of benefit to God?
    Can even a wise man benefit him?
What pleasure would it give the Almighty if you were righteous?
    What would he gain if your ways were blameless?

Is it for your piety that he rebukes you
    and brings charges against you?
Is not your wickedness great?
    Are not your sins endless? . . .

Is not God in the heights of heaven?
    And see how lofty are the highest stars!
Yet you say, "What does God know?
    Does he judge through such darkness?
Thick clouds veil him, so he does not see us

as he goes about in the vaulted heavens."
Will you keep to the old path
   that evil men have trod? . . .

(persua-
sively)   Submit to God and be at peace with him;
   in this way prosperity will come to you.
Accept instruction from his mouth
   and lay up his words in your heart.
If you return to the Almighty, you will be restored:
   If you remove wickedness far from your tent . . .
Surely then you will find delight in the Almighty
   and will lift up your face to God.
You will pray to him, and he will hear you,
   and you will fulfill your vows.
What you decide on will be done,
   and light will shine on your ways. . . .
He will deliver even one who is not innocent,
   who will be delivered through the cleanness of your hands.

Job
(musing
wearily)   Even today my complaint is bitter;
   his hand is heavy in spite of my groaning.
If only I knew where to find him;
   if only I could go to his dwelling!
I would state my case before him
   and fill my mouth with arguments.
I would find out what he would answer me,
   and consider what he would say. (PAUSE)

(to
Eliphaz)   Would he oppose me with great power?
   No, he would not press charges against me.
There an upright man could present his case before him,
   and I would be delivered forever from my judge.

(indicating) But if I go to the east, he is not there;
   if I go to the west, I do not find him.
When he is at work in the north, I do not see him;
   when he turns to the south, I catch no glimpse of him.
But he knows the way that I take;
   when he has tested me, I will come forth as gold.
My feet have closely followed his steps;
   I have kept to his way without turning aside.
I have not departed from the commands of his lips;
   I have treasured the words of his mouth more than my
      daily bread. . . .

(to
audience)   There are those who rebel against the light,

who do not know its ways
　or stay in its paths.
When daylight is gone, the murderer rises up
　and kills the poor and needy;
　in the night he steals forth like a thief.
The eye of the adulterer watches for dusk;
　he thinks, "No eye will see me,"
　and he keeps his face concealed.
In the dark, men break into houses,
　but by day they shut themselves in;
　they want nothing to do with the light.
For all of them, deep darkness is their morning;
　they make friends with the terrors of darkness.

(precisely)　Yet they are foam on the surface of the water;
　their portion of the land is cursed,
　so that no one goes to the vineyards.
As heat and drought snatch away the melted snow,
　so the grave snatches away those who have sinned. . . .
He may let them rest in a feeling of security,
　but his eyes are on their ways.
For a little while they are exalted, and then they are gone;
　they are brought low and gathered up like all others;
　they are cut off like heads of grain. . . .

Bildad
(airily)　Dominion and awe belong to God;
　he establishes order in the heights of heaven.
Can his forces be numbered?
　Upon whom does his light not rise?
How then can a man be righteous before God?
　How can one born of woman be pure?
If even the moon is not bright
　and the stars are not pure in his eyes,
how much less man, who is but a maggot—
　a son of man, who is only a worm!

Job
(to friends,
with irony)　How you have helped the powerless!
　How you have saved the arm that is feeble!
What advice you have offered to one without wisdom!
　And what great insight you have displayed!
Who has helped you utter these words?
　And whose spirit spoke from your mouth? (PAUSE)

(musing)　The dead are in deep anguish,
　those beneath the waters and all that live in them.
Death is naked before God;
　Destruction lies uncovered.

He spreads out the northern ⌞skies⌟ over empty space;
    he suspends the earth over nothing.
He wraps up the waters in his clouds,
    yet the clouds do not burst under their weight. . . .
And these are but the outer fringe of his works;
    how faint the whisper we hear of him!
Who then can understand the thunder of his power?

(to
audience)   As surely as God lives, who has denied me justice,
    the Almighty, who has made me taste bitterness of soul,
as long as I have life within me,
    the breath of God in my nostrils,
my lips will not speak wickedness,
    and my tongue will utter no deceit.

(to friends) I will never admit you are in the right;
    till I die, I will not deny my integrity.
I will maintain my righteousness and never let go of it;
    my conscience will not reproach me as long as I live. . . .

(musing)   Here is the fate God allots to the wicked,
    the heritage a ruthless man receives from the Almighty:
However many his children, their fate is the sword;
    his offspring will never have enough to eat. . . .
He lies down wealthy, but will do so no more;
    when he opens his eyes, all is gone.
Terrors overtake him like a flood;
    a tempest snatches him away in the night.
The east wind carries him off, and he is gone;
    it sweeps him out of his place. . . .

Where then does wisdom come from?
    Where does understanding dwell? . . . (PAUSE)
God understands the way to it
    and he alone knows where it dwells. . . .
And he said to man,
    "The fear of the Lord—that is wisdom,
    and to shun evil is understanding."

(to
audience)   How I long for the months gone by,
    for the days when God watched over me,
when his lamp shone upon my head
    and by his light I walked through darkness!
Oh, for the days when I was in my prime,
    when God's intimate friendship blessed my house. . . .
Whoever heard me spoke well of me,
    and those who saw me commended me. . . .

I thought, "I will die in my own house,
    my days as numerous as the grains of sand. . . ."

(brighten-
ing)

Men listened to me expectantly,
    waiting in silence for my counsel.
After I had spoken, they spoke no more;
    my words fell gently on their ears.
They waited for me as for showers
    and drank in my words as the spring rain.
When I smiled at them, they scarcely believed it;
    the light of my face was precious to them.
I chose the way for them and sat as their chief;
    I dwelt as a king among his troops;
    I was like one who comforts mourners.

(sadly)

But now they mock me,
    men younger than I. . . .

And now their sons mock me in song;
    I have become a byword among them.
They detest me and keep their distance;
    they do not hesitate to spit in my face.
Now that God has unstrung my bow and afflicted me,
    they throw off restraint in my presence. . . .
Terrors overwhelm me;
    my dignity is driven away as by the wind,
    my safety vanishes like a cloud.

(deliber-
ately)

And now my life ebbs away;
    days of suffering grip me.
Night pierces my bones;
    my gnawing pains never rest.
In his great power ⌊God⌋ becomes like clothing to me;
    he binds me like the neck of my garment.
He throws me into the mud,
    and I am reduced to dust and ashes.

(to God)

I cry out to you, O God, but you do not answer;
    I stand up, but you merely look at me.
You turn on me ruthlessly;
    with the might of your hand you attack me. . . .

(musing)

Yet when I hoped for good, evil came;
    when I looked for light, then came darkness. . . .
Does he not see my ways
    and count my every step?

(to friends) If I have walked in falsehood
    or my foot has hurried after deceit—
let God weigh me in honest scales
    and he will know that I am blameless. . . .

If I have denied the desires of the poor

or let the eyes of the widow grow weary,
if I have kept my bread to myself,
    not sharing it with the fatherless, . . .
if I have seen anyone perishing for lack of clothing,
    or a needy man without a garment, . . .
then let my arm fall from the shoulder,
    let it be broken off at the joint. . . .

If I have put my trust in gold
    or said to pure gold, "You are my security,"
if I have rejoiced over my great wealth,
    the fortune my hands had gained, . . .
then these also would be sins to be judged,
    for I would have been unfaithful to God on high. . . .

Oh, that I had someone to hear me!
    I sign now my defense—let the Almighty answer me;
    let my accuser put his indictment in writing. . . .

Narrator   So these three men stopped answering Job, because he was righteous in
his own eyes. But Elihu son of Barakel the Buzite, of the family of Ram,
became very angry with Job for justifying himself rather than God. He
was also angry with the three friends, because they had found no way to
refute Job, and yet had condemned him. Now Elihu had waited before
speaking to Job because they were older than he. But when he saw that
the three men had nothing more to say, his anger was aroused. So Elihu
son of Barakel the Buzite said:

Elihu
(to Job's
friends)   I am young in years,
    and you are old;
that is why I was fearful,
    not daring to tell you what I know.
I thought, "Age should speak;
    advanced years should teach wisdom."
But it is the *spirit* in a man,
    the breath of the Almighty, that gives
        him understanding.
It is not only the *old* who are wise,
    not only the aged who understand what is right.

Therefore I say: Listen to me;
    I too will tell you what I know.
I waited while you spoke,
    I listened to your reasoning;
while you were searching for words,
    I gave you my full attention.
But not one of you has proved Job wrong;
    none of you has answered his arguments.
Do not say, "We have found wisdom;

let God refute him, not man."
But Job has not marshaled his words against me,
    and I will not answer him with your arguments.

(to Job)   They are dismayed and have no more to say;
    words have failed them. . . .

But you have said in my hearing—
    I heard the very words—
"I am pure and without sin;
    I am clean and free from guilt.
Yet God has found fault with me;
    he considers me his enemy.
He fastens my feet in shackles;
    he keeps close watch on all my paths."

But I tell you, in this you are not right,
    for God is greater than man.
Why do you complain to him
    that he answers none of man's words?
For God does speak—now one way, now another—
    though man may not perceive it. . . .

(to friends) Job says, "I am innocent,
    but God denies me justice.
Although I am right,
    I am considered a liar;
although I am guiltless,
    his arrow inflicts an incurable wound."
What man is like Job,
    who drinks scorn like water?
He keeps company with evildoers;
    he associates with wicked men.
For he says, "It profits a man nothing
    when he tries to please God." . . .

Do you think this is just?

(to Job)   You say, "I will be cleared by God."
Yet you ask him, "What profit is it to me,
    and what do I gain by not sinning?" . . .
He does not answer when men cry out
    because of the arrogance of the wicked.
Indeed, God does not listen to their empty plea;
    the Almighty pays no attention to it.
How much less, then, will he listen
    when you say that you do not see him,
that your case is before him
    and you must wait for him,
and further, that his anger never punishes
    and he does not take the least notice of wickedness.

So Job opens his mouth with empty talk;
without knowledge he multiplies words.

Narrator Elihu continued:

Elihu

(declaiming) The godless in heart harbor resentment;
even when he fetters them, they do not cry for help.
They die in their youth. . . .
But those who suffer he delivers in their suffering;
he speaks to them in their affliction. . . .

God is exalted in his power.
Who is a teacher like him?
Who has prescribed his ways for him,
or said to him, "You have done wrong"?

(to
audience) Remember to extol his work,
which men have praised in song.
All mankind has seen it;
men gaze on it from afar.

(resuming
soliloquy) How great is God—beyond our understanding!
The number of his years is past finding out. . . .

His thunder announces the coming storm;
even the cattle make known its approach.

At this my heart pounds
and leaps from its place.
Listen! Listen to the roar of his voice,
to the rumbling that comes from his mouth.
He unleashes his lightning beneath the
whole heaven
and sends it to the ends of the earth.
After that comes the sound of his roar;
he thunders with his majestic voice.
When his voice resounds,
he holds nothing back.
God's voice thunders in marvelous ways;
he does great things beyond our understanding. . . .

Listen to this, Job;
stop and consider God's wonders. . . .

Narrator
(slowly and
deliber-
ately) Then the LORD answered Job out of the storm.

40

The Lord
  (voice only,
  to Job)   Who is this that darkens my counsel
                      with words without knowledge?
                  Brace yourself like a man;
                      I will question you,
                      and you shall answer me.

                  Where were you when I laid the earth's foundation?
                      Tell me, if you understand.
                  Who marked off its dimensions? Surely you know!
                      Who stretched a measuring line across it?
                  On what were its footings set,
                      or who laid its cornerstone—
                  while the morning stars sang together
                      and all the angels shouted for joy?

                  Who shut up the sea behind doors
                      when it burst forth from the womb,
                  when I made the clouds its garment
                      and wrapped it in thick darkness,
                  when I fixed limits for it
                      and set its doors and bars in place,
                  when I said, "This far you may come and no farther;
                      here is where your proud waves halt"?

                  Have you ever given orders to the morning,
                      or shown the dawn its place,
                  that it might take the earth by the edges
                      and shake the wicked out of it? . . .

                  Have you journeyed to the springs of the sea
                      or walked in the recesses of the deep?
                  Have the gates of death been shown to you?
                      Have you seen the gates of the shadow of death?
                  Have you comprehended the vast expanses of the earth?
                      Tell me, if you know all this.

                  What is the way to the abode of light?
                      And where does darkness reside?
                  Can you take them to their places?
                      Do you know the paths to their dwellings? . . .

                  Do you hunt the prey for the lioness
                      and satisfy the hunger of the lions
                  when they crouch in their dens
                      or lie in wait in a thicket?
                  Who provides food for the raven
                      when its young cry out to God
                      and wander about for lack of food?

                  Do you know when the mountain goats give birth?
                      Do you watch when the doe bears her fawn? . . .

41

Who let the wild donkey go free?
Who untied his ropes? . . .

Do you give the horse his strength
or clothe his neck with a flowing mane? . . .

Does the hawk take flight by your wisdom
and spread his wings toward the south?
Does the eagle soar at your command
and build his nest on high? . . .

Will the one who contends with the Almighty correct him?
Let him who accuses God answer him!

Job   I am unworthy—how can I reply to you?
I put my hand over my mouth.
I spoke once, but I have no answer—
twice, but I will say no more.

Narrator
(slowly and
deliberately) Then the Lord spoke to Job out of the storm:

The Lord
(voice)   Brace yourself like a man;
I will question you,
and you shall answer me.

Would you discredit my justice?
Would you condemn *me* to justify your*self?*
Do you have an arm like God's,
and can your voice thunder like his?
Then adorn yourself with glory and splendor,
and clothe yourself in honor and majesty. . . .

Narrator   Then Job replied to the LORD:

Job
(humbly)   I know that you can do all things;
no plan of yours can be thwarted.
˻You asked,˼ "Who is this that obscures my counsel without
knowledge?"
Surely I spoke of things I did not understand,
things too wonderful for me to know.

˻You said,˼ "Listen now, and I will speak;
I will question you,
and you shall answer me."
My ears had heard of you
but now my eyes have seen you.
Therefore I despise myself
and repent in dust and ashes.

Cast: **Narrator, Job, Eliphaz, Bildad, Zophar, Elihu** (a younger person), **the Lord** (voice only)

Conclusion

Job 42:7–13

Narrator	After the LORD had said these things to Job, he said to Eliphaz the Temanite:
The Lord (voice only)	I am angry with you and your two friends, because you have not spoken of me what is right, as my servant Job has. So now take seven bulls and seven rams and go to my servant Job and sacrifice a burnt offering for yourselves. My servant Job will pray for you, and I will accept his prayer and not deal with you according to your folly. You have not spoken of me what is right, as my servant Job has.
Narrator	So Eliphaz the Temanite, Bildad the Shuhite and Zophar the Naamathite did what the LORD told them; and the LORD accepted Job's prayer.
	After Job had prayed for his friends, the LORD made him prosperous again and gave him twice as much as he had before. All his brothers and sisters and everyone who had known him before came and ate with him in his house. They comforted and consoled him over all the trouble the LORD had brought upon him, and each one gave him a piece of silver and a gold ring.
	The LORD blessed the latter part of Job's life more than the first. He had fourteen thousand sheep, six thousand camels, a thousand yoke of oxen and a thousand donkeys. And he also had seven sons and three daughters.

Cast: **Narrator, the Lord** (voice only)

Psalms

True Happiness

Psalm 1:1–6

Voice 1 Blessed is the man
      who does not walk in the counsel of the wicked
or stand in the way of sinners
      or sit in the seat of mockers.
But his delight is in the law of the LORD,
      and on his law he meditates day and night.
He is like a tree planted by streams of water,
      which yields its fruit in season
and whose leaf does not wither.
      Whatever he does prospers.

Voice 2 Not so the wicked!
      They are like chaff
      that the wind blows away.
Therefore the wicked will not stand in the judgment,
      nor sinners in the assembly of the righteous.

Voice 1 For the LORD watches over the way of the righteous—

Voice 2 But the way of the wicked will perish.

Cast: **Voice 1** (happy voice), **Voice 2** (serious voice)

God's Chosen King

Psalm 2:1–12

Psalmist Why do the nations conspire
      and the peoples plot in vain?
The kings of the earth take their stand
      and the rulers gather together
against the LORD
      and against his Anointed One. [They say:]

Ruler 1 Let us break their chains—

Ruler 2 And throw off their fetters.

Psalmist The One enthroned in heaven laughs;
      the Lord scoffs at them.
Then he rebukes them in his anger
      and terrifies them in his wrath, saying:

The Lord
  (voice only) I have installed my King
         on Zion, my holy hill.
         [The King says:]

The King   I will proclaim the decree of the Lᴏʀᴅ.

         He said to me:

The Lord
  (voice)   You are my Son;
         today I have become your Father.
     Ask of me,
         and I will make the nations your inheritance,
         the ends of the earth your possession.
     You will rule them with an iron scepter;
         you will dash them to pieces like pottery.

Psalmist   Therefore, you kings, be wise;
         be warned, you rulers of the earth
     Serve the Lᴏʀᴅ with fear
         and rejoice with trembling.
     Kiss the Son, lest he be angry
         and you be destroyed in your way,
     for his wrath can flare up in a moment.
         Blessed are all who take refuge in him.

Cast: **Psalmist, Ruler 1, Ruler 2** (can be same as Ruler 1), **the Lord** (voice only), **the King**

A Morning Prayer for Help

Psalm 3:1–8

Worshiper 1 O Lᴏʀᴅ, how many are my foes!
         How many rise up against me!
     Many are saying of me:

Enemy   God will not deliver him.

Worshiper 1 But you are a shield around me, O Lᴏʀᴅ;
         you bestow glory on me and lift up my head.

Worshiper 2 To the Lᴏʀᴅ I cry aloud,
         and he answers me from his holy hill.

     I lie down and sleep;
         I wake again, because the Lᴏʀᴅ sustains me.
     I will not fear the tens of thousands
         drawn up against me on every side.

Worshiper 1 Arise, O Lᴏʀᴅ!

Worshiper 2	Deliver me, O my God!
Worshiper 1	Strike all my enemies on the jaw.
Worshiper 2	break the teeth of the wicked.
Worshipers 1 and 2	From the LORD comes deliverance.
Worshiper 1	May your blessing be on your people.

Cast: **Worshiper 1, Enemy, Worshiper 2**

An Evening Prayer for Help

Psalm 4:1–8

Worshiper
(praying)
Answer me when I call to you,
    O my righteous God.
Give me relief from my distress;
    be merciful to me and hear my prayer.

The Lord
(voice only)
How long, O men, will you turn my glory into shame?
    How long will you love delusions and seek false gods?

Worshiper
Know that the LORD has set apart the godly for himself;
    the LORD will hear when I call to him.

Teacher
In your anger do not sin;
    when you are on your beds,
    search your hearts and be silent.

Offer right sacrifices
    and trust in the LORD.

Worshiper
Many are asking:

Person
(praying)
Who can show us any good?
    Let the light of your face shine upon us, O LORD.

Worshiper
You have filled my heart with greater joy
    than when their grain and new wine abound.

(praying)
I will lie down and sleep in peace,
    for you alone, O LORD,
    make me dwell in safety.

Cast: **Worshiper, the Lord** (voice only), **Teacher, Person**

God's Glory and Our Dignity

Psalm 8:1–9

Voices 1–3	O LORD, our Lord, how majestic is your name in all the earth!
Voice 1	You have set your glory above the heavens.
Voice 2	From the lips of children and infants—
Voice 3	You have ordained praise because of your enemies, to silence the foe and the avenger.
Voice 1	When I consider your heavens, the work of your fingers, the moon and the stars, which you have set in place, what is man that you are mindful of him,
Voice 3	The son of man that you care for him?
Voice 1	You made him a little lower than the heavenly beings and crowned him with glory and honor.
Voice 2	You made him ruler over the works of your hands.
Voice 3	You put everything under his feet—
Voice 1	All flocks and herds, and the beasts of the field.
Voice 2	The birds of the air, and the fish of the sea.
Voice 3	All that swim the paths of the seas.
Voices 1–3	O LORD, our Lord, how majestic is your name in all the earth!

Cast: **Voice 1**, **Voice 2** (soprano voice), **Voice 3**

God and Humanity

Psalm 8:1–9 (LIT)

Leader	O Lord, our Lord:
All	**how great is your name in all the world!**

A (group 1)	**Your glory fills the skies.**
B (group 2)	**Your praise is sung by children.**
C (group 3)	**You silence your enemies.**

Leader	I look at the sky your hands have made,
	the moon and stars you put in place:
All	**Who are we that you care for us?**

Leader	You made us less than gods:
All	**to crown us with glory and honor.**

Leader	You put us in charge of creation:
A (group 1)	**the beasts of the field.**
B (group 2)	**the birds of the air.**
C (group 3)	**the fish of the sea.**

Leader	O Lord, our Lord:
All	**how great is your name in all the world!**

All	**Glory to the Father, and to the Son,**
	and to the Holy Spirit:
	as it was in the beginning, is now,
	and shall be forever. Amen.

Cast: **Leader**, **All** (all cast members or the entire congregation), **A** (group 1—two or more persons/part of the congregation), **B** (group 2—two or more persons/part of the congregation), **C** (group 3—two or more persons/part of the congregation)

Thanksgiving to God for His Justice

Psalm 9:1–20

Worshiper 1	I will praise you, O LORD, with all my heart;
	I will tell of all your wonders.
	I will be glad and rejoice in you;
	I will sing praise to your name, O Most High.

Worshiper 2	My enemies turn back;
	they stumble and perish before you.
	For you have upheld my right and my cause;
	you have sat on your throne, judging righteously.

Worshiper 1	You have rebuked the nations and destroyed the wicked;
	you have blotted out their name for ever and ever.

Worshiper 2	Endless ruin has overtaken the enemy,
	you have uprooted their cities;
	even the memory of them has perished.

Teacher 1	The LORD reigns forever;
	he has established his throne for judgment.
	He will judge the world in righteousness;
	he will govern the peoples with justice.

Teacher 2	The Lord is a refuge for the oppressed, a stronghold in times of trouble.
Worshiper 1	Those who know your name will trust in you, for you, Lord, have never forsaken those who seek you.
Worshipers 1 and 2	Sing praises to the Lord, enthroned in Zion—
Teachers 1 and 2	Proclaim among the nations what he has done.
Teacher 2	For he who avenges blood remembers; he does not ignore the cry of the afflicted.

Worshiper 1	O Lord, see how my enemies persecute me!
	    Have mercy and lift me up from the gates of death,
	that I may declare your praises
	    in the gates of the Daughter of Zion
	    and there rejoice in your salvation.

Teacher 1	The nations have fallen into the pit they have dug;
	    their feet are caught in the net they have hidden.
	The Lord is known by his justice;
	    the wicked are ensnared by the work of their hands.

Teacher 2	The wicked return to the grave,
	    all the nations that forget God.
	But the needy will not always be forgotten,
	    nor the hope of the afflicted ever perish.

Worshiper 2	Arise, O Lord, let not man triumph; let the nations be judged in your presence.
Worshiper 1	Strike them with terror, O Lord; let the nations know they are but men.

Cast: **Worshiper 1, Worshiper 2, Teacher 1, Teacher 2**

A Prayer for Justice

Psalm 10:1–18

Worshiper	Why, O Lord, do you stand far off? Why do you hide yourself in times of trouble?
Voice 1	In his arrogance the wicked man hunts down the weak, who are caught in the schemes he devises.
Voice 2	He boasts of the cravings of his heart; he blesses the greedy and reviles the Lord.

Voice 1	In his pride the wicked does not seek him; in all his thoughts there is no room for God.
Voice 2	His ways are always prosperous—
Voice 1	He is haughty and your laws are far from him; he sneers at all his enemies.
Voice 2	He says to himself:
Wicked man	Nothing will shake me; I'll always be happy and never have trouble.
Voice 1	His mouth is full of curses and lies and threats; trouble and evil are under his tongue.

Voice 2	He lies in wait near the villages;
	    from ambush he murders the innocent,
	    watching in secret for his victims.

Voice 1	He lies in wait like a lion in cover;
	    he lies in wait to catch the helpless;
	    he catches the helpless and drags them off in his net.

Voice 2	His victims are crushed, they collapse; they fall under his strength.
Voice 1	He says to himself:
Wicked man	God has forgotten; he covers his face and never sees.

Worshiper	Arise, LORD! Lift up your hand, O God.
	    Do not forget the helpless.
	Why does the wicked man revile God?
	    Why does he say to himself:

Wicked man	He won't call me to account.

Worshiper	But you, O God, do see trouble and grief;
	    you consider it to take it in hand.
	The victim commits himself to you;
	    you are the helper of the fatherless.
	Break the arm of the wicked and evil man;
	    call him to account for his wickedness
	    that would not be found out.

Voice 1	The LORD is King for ever and ever—
Voice 2	The nations will perish from his land.

Worshiper	You hear, O LORD, the desire of the afflicted;
	    you encourage them, and you listen to their cry,
	defending the fatherless and the oppressed,
	    in order that man, who is of the earth, may terrify no more.

Cast: **Worshiper**, **Voice 1**, **Voice 2** (can be the same as Voice 1), **Wicked man**

Confidence in the Lord

Psalm 11:1–7

Worshiper 1 In the LORD I take refuge.
How then can you say to me:

Adviser Flee like a bird to your mountain.
For look, the wicked bend their bows;
they set their arrows against the strings
to shoot from the shadows
at the upright in heart.
When the foundations are being destroyed,
what can the righteous do?

Worshiper 1 The LORD is in his holy temple;

Worshiper 2 the LORD is on his heavenly throne.

Worshiper 1 He observes the sons of men;

Worshiper 2 his eyes examine them.

Worshiper 1 The LORD examines the righteous,
but the wicked and those who love violence
his soul hates.

Worshiper 2 On the wicked he will rain
fiery coals and burning sulfur;
a scorching wind will be their lot.

Worshiper 1 For the LORD is righteous,
he loves justice;

Worshiper 2 Upright men will see his face.

Cast: **Worshiper 1, Adviser, Worshiper 2**

A Prayer for Help

Psalm 12:1–8

**Worshipers
1 and 2** Help, LORD—

Worshiper 1 For the godly are no more;
the faithful have vanished from among men.

Worshiper 2 Everyone lies to his neighbor;
their flattering lips speak with deception.

Worshiper 1 May the LORD cut off all flattering lips
and every boastful tongue
that says:

Person 1
(boasting)   We will triumph with our tongues.

Person 2
(proudly)   We own our lips—who is our master?

Worshiper 1   [The LORD says:]

The Lord
(voice only) Because of the oppression of the weak
      and the groaning of the needy,
  I will now arise. . . .
      I will protect them from those who malign them.

Worshiper 1   And the words of the LORD are flawless,
      like silver refined in a furnace of clay,
      purified seven times. . . .

Worshiper 2   The wicked freely strut about
      when what is vile is honored among men.

Worshipers
1 and 2   [O LORD, you will keep us safe
      and protect us from such people forever.]

Cast: **Worshiper 1**, **Worshiper 2** (can be the same as Worshiper 1), **Person 1**, **Person 2**, **the Lord** (voice only)

A Prayer for Help

Psalm 13:1–6

Worshiper 1   How long, O LORD? Will you forget me forever?

Worshiper 2   How long will you hide your face from me?

Worshiper 1   How long must I wrestle with my thoughts
      and every day have sorrow in my heart?

Worshiper 2   How long will my enemy triumph over me?

Worshiper 1   Look on me and answer, O LORD my God.

Worshiper 2   Give light to my eyes, or I will sleep in death—

Worshiper 1   My enemy will say:

Enemies
1 and 2   I have overcome him.

Worshiper 1   And my foes will rejoice when I fall.

Worshiper 2   But I trust in your unfailing love—

Worshiper 1   My heart rejoices in your salvation.

Worshiper 2   I will sing to the LORD,
for he has been good to me.

Cast: **Worshiper 1**, **Worshiper 2**, **Enemy 1**, **Enemy 2** (can be the same as Enemy 1)

Wickedness and Ignorance

Psalm 14:1–7

Voice 1   The fool says in his heart:

Fool(s)   There is no God.

Voice 1   They are corrupt, their deeds are vile;
there is no one who does good.

Voice 2   The LORD looks down from heaven
on the sons of men
to see if there are any who understand,
any who seek God.

Voice 1   All have turned aside,
they have together become corrupt;
there is no one who does good,
not even one.

Voice 2   [The Lord asks:]

The Lord
(voice only)   Will evildoers never learn—
those who devour my people as men eat bread
and who do not call on the LORD?

Voice 2   There they are, overwhelmed with dread,
for God is present in the company of the righteous.

Voice 1   You evildoers frustrate the plans of the poor,
but the LORD is their refuge.

Voice 2   Oh, that salvation for Israel would come out of Zion!

Voice 1   When the LORD restores the fortunes of his people,
let Jacob rejoice and Israel be glad!

Cast: **Voice 1**, **Fool(s)**, **Voice 2** (can be the same as Voice 1), **the Lord** (voice only)

What God Requires

Psalm 15:1–5

Enquirer 1   LORD, who may dwell in your sanctuary?

Enquirer 2	Who may live on your holy hill?

Voice 1	He whose walk is blameless
	    and who does what is righteous,
	who speaks the truth from his heart
	    and has no slander on his tongue—

Voice 2	Who does his neighbor no wrong and casts no slur on his fellow man.
Voice 1	Who despises a vile man but honors those who fear the LORD—
Voice 2	Who keeps his oath even when it hurts—
Voice 1	Who lends his money without usury and does not accept a bribe against the innocent.

**Voices
  1 and 2**
	He who does these things
	    will never be shaken.

Cast: **Enquirer 1**, **Enquirer 2** (can be the same as Enquirer 1), **Voice 1**, **Voice 2**

A Prayer of Confidence

Psalm 16:1–11

Voice 1	Keep me safe, O God, for in you I take refuge. I said to the LORD:
Voice 2	You are my Lord; apart from you I have no good thing.
Voice 3	As for the saints who are in the land, they are the glorious ones in whom is all my delight.
Voice 1	The sorrows of those will increase who run after other gods.
Voice 3	I will not pour out their libations of blood or take up their names on my lips.

Voice 2	LORD, you have assigned me my portion and my cup;
	    you have made my lot secure.
	The boundary lines have fallen for me in pleasant places;
	    surely I have a delightful inheritance.

Voice 3	I will praise the LORD, who counsels me; even at night my heart instructs me.

Voice 2	I have set the Lord always before me.
	Because he is at my right hand,
	I will not be shaken.
	Therefore my heart is glad and my tongue rejoices;
	my body also will rest secure—
Voice 1	Because you will not abandon me to the grave,
	nor will you let your Holy One see decay.
Voice 2	You have made known to me the path of life—
Voices 1–3	You will fill me with joy in your presence—
Voice 3	With eternal pleasures at your right hand.

Cast: **Voice 1, Voice 2, Voice 3**

God's Glory and Law

Psalm 19:1–14

Voice 1	The heavens declare the glory of God—
Voice 2	The skies proclaim the work of his hands.
Voice 1	Day after day they pour forth speech—
Voice 2	Night after night they display knowledge.
Voice 1	There is no speech or language
	where their voice is not heard.
	Their voice goes out into all the earth,
	their words to the ends of the world.
Voice 3	In the heavens he has pitched a tent for the sun,
	which is like a bridegroom coming forth from his pavilion,
	like a champion rejoicing to run his course.
	It rises at one end of the heavens
	and makes its circuit to the other;
	nothing is hidden from its heat.
Voice 1	The law of the Lord is perfect,
	reviving the soul.
Voice 2	The statutes of the Lord are trustworthy,
	making wise the simple.
Voice 1	The precepts of the Lord are right,
	giving joy to the heart.
Voice 2	The commands of the Lord are radiant,
	giving light to the eyes.

Voice 1	The fear of the LORD is pure, enduring forever.
Voice 2	The ordinances of the LORD are sure and altogether righteous.
Voice 1	They are more precious than gold than much pure gold—
Voice 2	They are sweeter than honey, than honey from the comb.
Voice 1	By them is your servant warned; in keeping them there is great reward.

Voice 3	Who can discern his errors?
	    Forgive my hidden faults.
	Keep your servant also from willful sins;
	    may they not rule over me.
	Then will I be blameless,
	    innocent of great transgression.

Voices
  1 and 2
	May the words of my mouth and the meditation of my heart
	    be pleasing in your sight,
	    O LORD, my Rock and my Redeemer.

Cast: **Voice 1**, **Voice 2**, **Voice 3** (can be the same as Voice 2)

A Prayer for Victory

Psalm 20:1–9

Voice 1	May the LORD answer you when you are in distress—
Voice 2	May the name of the God of Jacob protect you.
Voice 1	May he send you help from the sanctuary and grant you support from Zion.
Voice 2	May he remember all your sacrifices and accept your burnt offerings.
Voice 1	May he give you the desire of your heart and make all your plans succeed.
Voice 2	We will shout for joy when you are victorious and will lift up our banners in the name of our God.
Voices **1 and 2**	May the LORD grant all your requests.

Worshiper	Now I know that the LORD saves his anointed;

Worshiper Now I know that the LORD saves his anointed;
  he answers him from his holy heaven
  with the saving power of his right hand.
Some trust in chariots—and some in horses,
  but we trust in the name of the LORD our God.
They are brought to their knees and fall,
  but we rise up and stand firm.

Voice 1 O LORD, save the king!

Voice 2 Answer us when we call!

Cast: **Voice 1, Voice 2, Worshiper**

A Cry of Anguish and a Song of Praise

Psalm 22:1–31

Lonely person My God, my God, why have you forsaken me?
  Why are you so far from saving me,
  so far from the words of my groaning?
O my God, I cry out by day, but you do not answer,
  by night, and am not silent.

Singer You are enthroned as the Holy One;
  you are the praise of Israel.
In you our fathers put their trust;
  they trusted and you delivered them.
They cried to you and were saved;
  in you they trusted and were not disappointed.

Despised person But I am a worm and not a man,
  scorned by men and despised by the people.
All who see me mock me;
  they hurl insults, shaking their heads:

Accuser 1 He trusts in the LORD;
  let the LORD rescue him.

Accuser 2 Let him deliver him,
  since he delights in him.

Lonely person You brought me out of the womb;
  you made me trust in you
  even at my mother's breast.
From birth I was cast upon you;
  from my mother's womb you have been my God.
Do not be far from me,

for trouble is near
and there is no one to help.

**Despised
person**

Many bulls surround me;
strong bulls of Bashan encircle me.
Roaring lions tearing their prey
open their mouths wide against me.

**Lonely
person**

I am poured out like water,
and all my bones are out of joint.
My heart has turned to wax;
it has melted away within me.
My strength is dried up like a potsherd,
and my tongue sticks to the roof of my mouth;
you lay me in the dust of death.

**Despised
person**

Dogs have surrounded me;
a band of evil men has encircled me,
they have pierced my hands and my feet.
I can count all my bones;
people stare and gloat over me.
They divide my garments among them
and cast lots for my clothing.

But you, O Lord, be not far off;
O my Strength, come quickly to help me.
Deliver my life from the sword,
my precious life from the power of the dogs.
Rescue me from the mouth of the lions;
save me from the horns of the wild oxen.

**Lonely
person**

I will declare your name to my brothers;
in the congregation I will praise you.

Singer

You who fear the Lord, praise him!
All you descendants of Jacob, honor him!
Revere him, all you descendants of Israel!
For he has not despised or disdained
the suffering of the afflicted one;
he has not hidden his face from him
but has listened to his cry for help.

**Lonely
person**

From you comes the theme of my praise in the great assembly;
before those who fear you will I fulfill my vows.

**Despised
person**

The poor will eat and be satisfied;

they who seek the LORD will praise him—
may your hearts live forever!

Lonely
person   All the ends of the earth
   will remember and turn to the LORD,
and all the families of the nations
   will bow down before him,
for dominion belongs to the LORD
   and he rules over the nations.

Despised
person   All the rich of the earth will feast and worship;
   all who go down to the dust will kneel before him—
   those who cannot keep themselves alive.

Lonely
person   Posterity will serve him;
   future generations will be told about the Lord.
They will proclaim his righteousness
   to a people yet unborn—
   for he has done it.

Cast: **Lonely person, Singer, Despised person, Accuser 1, Accuser 2** (can be the same as Accuser 1)

The Lord Our Shepherd

Psalm 23:1–6

Voices 1–3   The LORD is my shepherd, I shall not be in want.

Voice 1   He makes me lie down in green pastures,
he leads me beside quiet waters,
   he restores my soul.
He guides me in paths of righteousness
   for his name's sake.

Voice 2
(prayer-
fully)   Even though I walk
   through the valley of the shadow of death,
I will fear no evil,
   for you are with me;
your rod and your staff,
   they comfort me.

Voice 3   You prepare a table before me
   in the presence of my enemies.
You anoint my head with oil;
   my cup overflows.

Voices

1 and 2	Surely goodness and love will follow me all the days of my life—
Voice 3	And I will dwell in the house of the LORD forever.

Cast: **Voice 1, Voice 2, Voice 3**

The Great King

Psalm 24:1–10 (LIT)

Leader **All**	The earth is the Lord's, and everything in it: **the world, and all who live here.**
Leader **All**	He founded it upon the seas: **and established it upon the waters.**
Enquirer **All**	Who has the right to go up the Lord's hill; who may enter his holy temple? **Those who have clean hands and a pure heart,** **who do not worship idols or swear by what is false.**
Leader **All**	They receive blessing continually from the Lord: **and righteousness from the God of their salvation.**
Leader **All**	Such are the people who seek for God: **who enter the presence of the God of Jacob.**
Director **All**	Fling wide the gates, open the ancient doors: **that the king of glory may come in.**
Enquirer **All**	Who is the king of glory? **The Lord, strong and mighty,** **the Lord mighty in battle.**
Director **All**	Fling wide the gates, open the ancient doors: **that the king of glory may come in.**
Enquirer **All**	Who is he, this king of glory? **The Lord Almighty,** **he is the king of glory.**
All	**Glory to the Father, and to the Son,** **and to the Holy Spirit:** **as it was in the beginning, is now,** **and shall be forever. Amen.**

Cast: **Leader, All** (two or more persons/part of congregation), **Enquirer** (positioned in the back or within the congregation), **Director**

A Prayer of Praise

Psalm 27:1–14

Worshiper 1 The Lord is my light and my salvation—
    whom shall I fear?
The Lord is the stronghold of my life—
    of whom shall I be afraid?
When evil men advance against me
    to devour my flesh,
when my enemies and my foes attack me,
    they will stumble and fall.
Though an army besiege me,
    my heart will not fear;
though war break out against me,
    even then will I be confident.

Worshiper 2 One thing I ask of the Lord,
    this is what I seek:
that I may dwell in the house of the Lord
    all the days of my life,
to gaze upon the beauty of the Lord
    and to seek him in his temple.

Worshiper 1 For in the day of trouble
    he will keep me safe in his dwelling;
he will hide me in the shelter of his tabernacle
    and set me high upon a rock.
Then my head will be exalted
    above the enemies who surround me;
at his tabernacle will I sacrifice with shouts of joy;
    I will sing and make music to the Lord.

Worshiper 2 Hear my voice when I call, O Lord;
    be merciful to me and answer me.

Worshiper 1 My heart says of you, "Seek his face!"

Worshiper 2 Your face, Lord, I will seek.

Worshiper 1 Do not hide your face from me,
    do not turn your servant away in anger;
    you have been my helper.
Do not reject me or forsake me,
    O God my Savior.

(to
audience) Though my father and mother forsake me,
    the Lord will receive me.

Worshiper 2 Teach me your way, O Lord;
    lead me in a straight path
    because of my oppressors.

Do not turn me over to the desire of my foes,
    for false witnesses rise up against me,
    breathing out violence.

Worshiper 1   I am still confident of this:
    I will see the goodness of the LORD
    in the land of the living.

Worshipers
1 and 2   Wait for the Lord—

Worshiper 2   Be strong and take heart—

Worshipers
1 and 2   And wait for the LORD.

Cast: **Worshiper 1, Worshiper 2**

A Prayer of Thanksgiving

Psalm 30:1–12

Worshiper 1   I will exalt you, O LORD,
    for you lifted me out of the depths
    and did not let my enemies gloat over me.
    O LORD my God, I called to you for help
    and you healed me.
    O LORD, you brought me up from the grave;
    you spared me from going down into the pit.

Worshiper 2   Sing to the LORD, you saints of his;
    praise his holy name.

Worshiper 1   For his anger lasts only a moment,
    but his favor lasts a lifetime—

Worshiper 2   Weeping may remain for a night,
    but rejoicing comes in the morning.

    When I felt secure, I said:

Worshiper 3   I will never be shaken.

Worshiper 2   O LORD, when you favored me,
    you made my mountain stand firm;
    but when you hid your face,
    I was dismayed.

    To you, O LORD, I called;
    to the Lord I cried for mercy.

Worshiper 3   What gain is there in my destruction,
    in my going down into the pit?

Will the dust praise you?
Will it proclaim your faithfulness?
Hear, O LORD, and be merciful to me;
O LORD, be my help.

Worshiper 2 You turned my wailing into dancing;
you removed my sackcloth and clothed me with joy,
that my heart may sing to you and not be silent.

Worshiper 1 O LORD my God, I will give you thanks forever.

Cast: **Worshiper 1, Worshiper 2, Worshiper 3**

Confession and Forgiveness

Psalm 32:1–11

Worshiper 1 Blessed is he
whose transgressions are forgiven,
whose sins are covered.
Blessed is the man
whose sin the LORD does not count against him
and in whose spirit is no deceit.

Worshiper 2 When I kept silent,
my bones wasted away
through my groaning all day long.
For day and night
your hand was heavy upon me;
my strength was sapped
as in the heat of summer.
Then I acknowledged my sin to you
and did not cover up my iniquity.
I said, "I will confess
my transgressions to the LORD"—
and you forgave
the guilt of my sin.

Worshiper 1 Therefore let everyone who is godly pray to you
while you may be found;
surely when the mighty waters rise,
they will not reach him.

Worshiper 2 You are my hiding place;
you will protect me from trouble
and surround me with songs of deliverance.

The Lord
(voice only) I will instruct you and teach you in the way you should go;
I will counsel you and watch over you.

> Do not be like the horse or the mule,
>   which have no understanding
> but must be controlled by bit and bridle
>   or they will not come to you.

Worshiper 2   Many are the woes of the wicked,
        but the LORD's unfailing love
        surrounds the man who trusts in him.

**Worshipers
    1 and 2**   Rejoice in the LORD and be glad, you righteous;
        sing, all you who are upright in heart!

Cast: **Worshiper 1** (bright voice), **Worshiper 2** (serious voice), **the Lord** (voice only)

A Song of Praise

From Psalm 33:1–22 (LIT)

Leader   Sing joyfully to the Lord, you righteous:
All   **it is right that his people should praise him.**

Leader   Praise the Lord with the harp:
 A (group 1) **make music to him on the strings.**

Leader   Sing to the Lord a new song:
 B (group 2) **play skillfully, and shout for joy.**

Leader   For the word of the Lord is right and true:
All   **and all his work is faithfulness.**

Leader   The Lord loves righteousness and justice:
 A (group 1) **his endless love fills the earth.**

Leader   By the word of the Lord the skies were formed:
 B (group 2) **his breath created moon and stars.**

Leader   Let all the earth fear the Lord:
All   **the people of the world revere him.**

Leader   For he spoke, and it came to be:
 A (group 1) **he commanded, and all was made.**

Leader   The Lord holds back the nations:
 B (group 2) **he thwarts their evil intent.**

Leader   God's purposes are sure:
All   **his plans endure for ever.**

Leader   Happy is the nation whose God is the Lord:
 A (group 1) **happy the people he makes his own.**

Leader	The eyes of the Lord are on those who fear him:
B (group 2)	**who trust in his unfailing love.**
Leader	We wait in hope for the Lord:
A (group 1)	**he is our help and shield.**
Leader	In him our hearts rejoice:
B (group 2)	**we trust his holy name.**
Leader	May your constant love be with us, Lord:
All	**as we put our hope in you. Amen.**

Cast: **Leader, All** (two or more persons/the entire congregation), **A** (group 1—two or more persons/part of congregation), **B** (group 2—two or more persons/part of congregation)

A Prayer for Help

From Psalm 35:9–28

Worshiper   My soul will rejoice in the LORD
  and delight in his salvation.

New person   My whole being will exclaim,
  "Who is like you, O LORD?
You rescue the poor from those too strong for them,
  the poor and needy from those who rob them."

Worshiper   Ruthless witnesses come forward;
  they question me on things I know nothing about.
They repay me evil for good
  and leave my soul forlorn. . . .
O Lord, how long will you look on?
  Rescue my life from their ravages,
  my precious life from these lions.
I will give you thanks in the great assembly;
  among throngs of people I will praise you.

Let not those gloat over me
  who are my enemies without cause;
let not those who hate me without reason
  maliciously wink the eye.
They do not speak peaceably,
  but devise false accusations
  against those who live quietly in the land.
They gape at me and say:

Enemies
  1 and 2   Aha! Aha!
  With our own eyes we have seen it.

Worshiper	O LORD, you have seen this; be not silent.
	Do not be far from me, O Lord.
	Awake, and rise to my defense!
	Contend for me, my God and Lord.
	Vindicate me in your righteousness, O LORD my God;
	do not let them gloat over me.
	Do not let them think:
Enemy 1	Aha, just what we wanted!
Enemy 2	We have swallowed him up.
Worshiper	May all who gloat over my distress
	be put to shame and confusion;
	may all who exalt themselves over me
	be clothed with shame and disgrace.
	May those who delight in my vindication
	shout for joy and gladness;
	may they always say:
Friend	The LORD be exalted,
	who delights in the well-being of his servant.
Worshiper	My tongue will speak of your righteousness
	and of your praises all day long.

Cast: **Worshiper**, **New person**, **Enemy 1**, **Enemy 2** (can be the same as Enemy 1), **Friend**

Our Wickedness and God's Goodness

Psalm 36:1–12

Psalmist	An oracle is within my heart
	concerning the sinfulness of the wicked:
	There is no fear of God
	before his eyes.
	For in his own eyes he flatters himself
	too much to detect or hate his sin.
	The words of his mouth are wicked and deceitful;
	he has ceased to be wise and to do good.
	Even on his bed he plots evil;
	he commits himself to a sinful course
	and does not reject what is wrong.
Worshiper 1	Your love, O LORD, reaches to the heavens,
	your faithfulness to the skies.
Worshiper 2	Your righteousness is like the mighty mountains,
	your justice like the great deep.
	O LORD, you preserve both man and beast.

Worshiper 1	How priceless is your unfailing love! Both high and low among men find refuge in the shadow of your wings.

Worshiper 2	They feast on the abundance of your house;
	    you give them drink from your river of delights.
	For with you is the fountain of life;
	    in your light we see light.

Worshiper 1	Continue your love to those who know you, your righteousness to the upright in heart.
Worshiper 2	May the foot of the proud not come against me, nor the hand of the wicked drive me away.
Psalmist	See how the evildoers lie fallen— thrown down, not able to rise!

Cast: **Psalmist, Worshiper 1, Worshiper 2**

The Goodness of God

Psalm 36:5–9 (LIT)

Leader 1 **A** (group 1)	Your love, O Lord, reaches the heavens; **your faithfulness extends to the skies.**
Leader 2 **B** (group 2)	Your righteousness is towering like the mountains: **your justice is like the great deep.**
Leader 1 **A** (group 1)	How precious is your love, O God: **we find shelter beneath your wings!**
Leader 2 **B** (group 2)	We feast on the food you provide: **we drink from the river of your goodness:**
Leader 1 **All**	For with you is the fountain of life: **in your light we see light. Amen.**

Cast: **Leader 1**, **A** (group 1—two or more persons/part of congregation), **Leader 2**, **B** (group 2—two or more persons/part of congregation), **All** (all cast/congregation)

Confessions

Psalm 39:1–13

Psalmist	I said:

**Young
  psalmist**
	I will watch my ways
	    and keep my tongue from sin;

I will put a muzzle on my mouth
as long as the wicked are in my presence.

Psalmist But when I was silent and still,
not even saying anything good,
my anguish increased.
My heart grew hot within me,
and as I meditated, the fire burned;
then I spoke with my tongue:

Young
psalmist Show me, O LORD, my life's end
and the number of my days;
let me know how fleeting is my life.
You have made my days a mere handbreadth;
the span of my years is as nothing before you.
Each man's life is but a breath.

Man is a mere phantom as he goes to and fro:
He bustles about, but only in vain;
he heaps up wealth, not knowing who
will get it. (PAUSE)

Psalmist But now, Lord, what do I look for?
My hope is in you.
Save me from all my transgressions;
do not make me the scorn of fools.
I was silent; I would not open my mouth,
for you are the one who has done this.
Remove your scourge from me;
I am overcome by the blow of your hand.
You rebuke and discipline men for their sin;
you consume their wealth like a moth—
each man is but a breath.

Hear my prayer, O LORD,
listen to my cry for help;
be not deaf to my weeping.
For I dwell with you as an alien,
a stranger, as all my fathers were.
Look away from me, that I may rejoice again
before I depart and am no more.

Cast: **Psalmist, Young psalmist**

A Song of Praise (i)

From Psalm 40:1–3 (LIT)

Leader I waited patiently for the Lord:
All **he turned and heard my cry.**

Leader	He pulled me out of the slimy pit:
All	**out of the mud and mire.**
Leader	He set my feet upon a rock:
All	**and made my step secure.**
Leader	He put a new song in my mouth:
All	**a hymn of praise to God.**
Leader	Many will see it and fear;
All	**and put their trust in the Lord. Amen.**

Cast: **Leader, All** (two or more persons/part of congregation)

A Song of Praise (ii)

From Psalm 40:4–16 (LIT)

Leader 1	Happy are those who trust in God:
All	**who do not worship idols.**
Leader 1	Sacrifice and offering you do not desire:
A (group 1)	**but you want my ears to be open.**
Leader 2	So I said, "Lord, I come:
B (group 2)	**obedient to your word."**
Leader 2	I delight to do your will, O God:
A (group 1)	**and keep your teaching in my heart.**
Leader 2	I'll tell the world your saving news:
B (group 2)	**you know my lips will not be sealed.**
Leader 2	I have not hid your righteousness:
A (group 1)	**but speak of your salvation, Lord.**
Leader 2	I do not hide your faithful love:
B (group 2)	**but share your mercy with them all.**
Leader 1	May all who come to you be glad; may all who know your saving power forever say:
All	**How great is the Lord! Amen.**

Cast: **Leader 1, All** (two or more persons/entire congregation), **A** (group 1—two or more persons/part of congregation), **Leader 2, B** (group 2—two or more persons/part of congregation)

The Prayer for Health

Psalm 41:1–13

Worshiper 1	Blessed is he who has regard for the weak;
	the Lord delivers him in times of trouble.

Worshiper 2	The LORD will protect him and preserve his life; he will bless him in the land—
Worshiper 1	And not surrender him to the desire of his foes.
Worshiper 2	The LORD will sustain him on his sickbed and restore him from his bed of illness.
Worshiper 1	I said:
Worshiper 2	O LORD, have mercy on me; heal me, for I have sinned against you.
Worshiper 1	My enemies say of me in malice,
Enemy	When will he die and his name perish?

Worshiper 2	Whenever one comes to see me,
	    he speaks falsely, while his heart gathers slander;
	    then he goes out and spreads it abroad.

Worshiper 1	All my enemies whisper together against me; they imagine the worst for me, saying:
Enemy	A vile disease has beset him; he will never get up from the place where he lies.

Worshiper 1	Even my close friend, whom I trusted,
	    he who shared my bread,
	    has lifted up his heel against me.

Worshiper 2	But you, O LORD, have mercy on me;
	    raise me up, that I may repay them.
	I know that you are pleased with me,
	    for my enemy does not triumph over me.
	In my integrity you uphold me
	    and set me in your presence forever.

Worshiper 1	Praise be to the LORD, the God of Israel—
Worshiper 2	From everlasting to everlasting.
Cast/All	Amen and Amen.

Cast: **Worshiper 1, Worshiper 2, Enemy**

Prayers in Exile

Psalm 42:1–11

Worshiper 1	As the deer pants for streams of water,
	    so my soul pants for you, O God.
	My soul thirsts for God, for the living God.
	    When can I go and meet with God?

	My tears have been my food day and night, while men say to me all day long:
Enemies	Where is your God?

Worshiper 2	These things I remember
	    as I pour out my soul:
	how I used to go with the multitude,
	    leading the procession to the house of God,
	with shouts of joy and thanksgiving
	    among the festive throng. (PAUSE)

Worshiper 1	Why are you downcast, O my soul?
Worshiper 2	Why so disturbed within me?
Worshipers 1 and 2	Put your hope in God.
Worshiper 1	For I will yet praise him, my Savior and my God.

Worshiper 2	My soul is downcast within me;
	    therefore I will remember you
	from the land of the Jordan,
	    the heights of Hermon—from Mount Mizar.

Worshiper 1	Deep calls to deep
	    in the roar of your waterfalls;
	all your waves and breakers
	    have swept over me.
	
	By day the LORD directs his love,
	    at night his song is with me—
	a prayer to the God of my life.

Worshiper 2	I say to God my Rock:
Worshiper 1	Why have you forgotten me? Why must I go about mourning, oppressed by the enemy?
Worshiper 2	My bones suffer mortal agony as my foes taunt me, saying to me all day long:
Enemies	Where is your God?
Worshiper 1	Why are you downcast, O my soul?
Worshiper 2	Why so disturbed within me?
Worshipers 1 and 2	Put your hope in God.

Worshiper 1	For I will yet praise him, my Savior and my God.

Cast: **Worshiper 1**, **Enemies** (two or more), **Worshiper 2**

God Is with Us

Psalm 46:1–11

Psalmist	God is our refuge and strength, an ever-present help in trouble.
Worshiper 1	Therefore we will not fear—
Worshiper 2	Though the earth give way and the mountains fall into the heart of the sea—
Worshiper 3	Though its waters roar and foam and the mountains quake with their surging.
Psalmist	There is a river whose streams make glad the city of God, the holy place where the Most High dwells. God is within her, she will not fall; God will help her at break of day. Nations are in uproar, kingdoms fall; he lifts his voice, the earth melts.
Worshiper 1	The LORD Almighty is with us—
Worshipers 2 and 3	The God of Jacob is our fortress.
Psalmist	Come and see the works of the LORD, the desolations he has brought on the earth. He makes wars cease to the ends of the earth; he breaks the bow and shatters the spear, he burns the shields with fire.
The Lord (voice only)	Be still, and know that I am God; I will be exalted among the nations, I will be exalted in the earth.
Psalmist	The LORD Almighty is with us;
Worshipers 1–3	The God of Jacob is our fortress.

Cast: **Psalmist**, **Worshiper 1** (can be the same as Psalmist), **Worshiper 2**, **Worshiper 3**, **the Lord** (voice only)

God Is with Us

From Psalm 46:1–11 (LIT)

Leader	God is our refuge and strength:
All	**an ever-present help in trouble.**

Leader	Therefore we will not fear:
A (group 1)	**though the earth should shake,**
B (group 2)	**though the mountains fall into the sea,**
A (group 1)	**though the waters surge and foam,**
B (group 2)	**though the mountains shake and roar.**

Leader	The Lord Almighty is with us:
All	**the God of Jacob is our fortress.**

Leader	There is a river whose streams make glad the city of God: the holy place where the Most High dwells.
A (group 1)	**God is within her, she will not fall:**
B (group 2)	**God will help her at break of day.**

Leader	Nations are in uproar, kingdoms fall:
A (group 1)	**God lifts his voice—**
B (group 2)	**the earth melts away.**

Leader	The Lord Almighty is with us:
All	**the God of Jacob is our fortress.**

Leader	Come and see what God has done:
All	**his devastation on the earth!**

Leader	He stops the wars throughout the world:
A (group 1)	**he breaks the bow and shatters the spear—**
B (group 2)	**he sets the shield on fire.**

Voice of God	Be still, and know that I am God: I will be exalted over the nations, I will be exalted over the earth.

Leader	The Lord Almighty is with us:
All	**the God of Jacob is our fortress. Amen.**

Cast: **Leader, All** (two or more persons/entire congregation), **A** (group 1—two or more persons/part of congregation), **B** (group 2—two or more persons/part of congregation), **Voice of God** (can be a distant voice, or said by the minister)

The Supreme Ruler

From Psalm 47:1–9 (LIT)

Leader	Clap your hands, all you nations:
All	**shout to God with cries of joy.**

Leader	How awesome is the Lord most high:
A (group 1)	**the King who rules the whole wide earth!**
Leader	God has ascended to his throne:
B (group 2)	**with shouts of joy and sound of trumpets.**
Leader	Sing praises to our God, sing praises:
A (group 1)	**sing praises to our King, sing praises.**
Leader	For God is King of all the earth:
B (group 2)	**sing to him a psalm of praise.**
Leader	God is seated on his throne:
A (group 1)	**he rules the nations of the world.**
Leader	The leaders of the nations come:
B (group 2)	**as subjects of our holy God.**
Leader	The lords of earth belong to God:
All	**he reigns supreme. Amen.**

Cast: **Leader, All** (the entire congregation; the congregation may divide at **A** and **B**)

The City of God

Psalm 48:1–14

Worshiper   Great is the LORD, and most worthy of praise,
          in the city of our God, his holy mountain.

Psalmist   It is beautiful in its loftiness,
          the joy of the whole earth.
     Like the utmost heights of Zaphon is Mount Zion,
          the city of the Great King.
     God is in her citadels;
          he has shown himself to be her fortress.

     When the kings joined forces,
          when they advanced together,
     they saw ⌐her⌐ and were astounded;
          they fled in terror.
     Trembling seized them there,
          pain like that of a woman in labor.

Worshiper   You destroyed them like ships of Tarshish
          shattered by an east wind.

Psalmist   As we have heard,
          so have we seen
     in the city of the LORD Almighty,
          in the city of our God:
          God makes her secure forever.

74

Worshiper	Within your temple, O God,
	    we meditate on your unfailing love.
	Like your name, O God,
	    your praise reaches to the ends of the earth;
	    your right hand is filled with righteousness.
	Mount Zion rejoices,
	    the villages of Judah are glad
	    because of your judgments.

Psalmist	Walk about Zion, go around her,
	    count her towers,
	consider well her ramparts,
	    view her citadels,
	    that you may tell of them to the next generation.

Worshiper	For this God is our God for ever and ever; he will be our guide even to the end.

Cast: **Worshiper, Psalmist**

True Worship

Psalm 50:1–23

Worshiper 1	The Mighty One, God, the Lord,
	    speaks and summons the earth
	    from the rising of the sun to the place where it sets.

Worshiper 2	From Zion, perfect in beauty, God shines forth.
Worshipers 1 and 2	Our God comes and will not be silent—
Worshiper 1	A fire devours before him, and around him a tempest rages.
Worshiper 2	He summons the heavens above, and the earth, that he may judge his people:
God (voice only)	Gather to me my consecrated ones, who made a covenant with me by sacrifice.
Worshiper 1	And the heavens proclaim his righteousness, for God himself is judge.

God (voice)	Hear, O my people, and I will speak,
	    O Israel, and I will testify against you:
	    I am God, your God.
	I do not rebuke you for your sacrifices
	    or your burnt offerings, which are ever before me.

I have no need of a bull from your stall
  or of goats from your pens,
for every animal of the forest is mine,
  and the cattle on a thousand hills.
I know every bird in the mountains,
  and the creatures of the field are mine.
If I were hungry I would not tell you,
  for the world is mine, and all that is in it.
Do I eat the flesh of bulls
  or drink the blood of goats?
Sacrifice thank offerings to God,
  fulfill your vows to the Most High,
and call upon me in the day of trouble;
  I will deliver you, and you will honor me.

Worshiper 2   But to the wicked, God says:

God
  (voice)   What right have you to recite my laws
  or take my covenant on your lips?
You hate my instruction
  and cast my words behind you.
When you see a thief, you join with him;
  you throw in your lot with adulterers.
You use your mouth for evil
  and harness your tongue to deceit.
You speak continually against your brother
  and slander your own mother's son.
These things you have done and I kept silent;
  you thought I was altogether like you.
But I will rebuke you
  and accuse you to your face.

Consider this, you who forget God,
  or I will tear you to pieces, with none to rescue:
He who sacrifices thank offerings honors me,
  and he prepares the way
  so that I may show him the salvation of God.

Cast: **Worshiper 1**, **Worshiper 2**, **God** (voice only)

Prayers for Forgiveness

Psalm 51:1–19

Penitent 1   Have mercy on me, O God,
  according to your unfailing love—

Sinner 1   According to your great compassion
  blot out my transgressions.

Sinner 2	Wash away all my iniquity and cleanse me from my sin.
Sinner 1	For I know my transgressions, and my sin is always before me.

Sinner 2	Against you, you only, have I sinned
	    and done what is evil in your sight,
	so that you are proved right when you speak
	    and justified when you judge.

Sinner 1	Surely I was sinful at birth, sinful from the time my mother conceived me.
Penitent 1	Surely you desire truth in the inner parts; you teach me wisdom in the inmost place.
Sinner 1	Cleanse me with hyssop, and I will be clean; wash me, and I will be whiter than snow.
Penitent 2	Let me hear joy and gladness; let the bones you have crushed rejoice.
Sinner 2	Hide your face from my sins and blot out all my iniquity.
Penitent 1	Create in me a pure heart, O God, and renew a steadfast spirit within me.
Penitent 2	Do not cast me from your presence or take your Holy Spirit from me.
Penitent 1	Restore to me the joy of your salvation and grant me a willing spirit, to sustain me.
	Then I will teach transgressors your ways, and sinners will turn back to you.

Sinner 1	Save me from bloodguilt, O God,
	    the God who saves me,
	    and my tongue will sing of your righteousness.

Penitent 1	O Lord, open my lips, and my mouth will declare your praise.
Sinner 2	You do not delight in sacrifice, or I would bring it; you do not take pleasure in burnt offerings.

Sinner 1	The sacrifices of God are a broken spirit;
	    a broken and contrite heart,
	    O God, you will not despise.

Penitent 1	In your good pleasure make Zion prosper; build up the walls of Jerusalem.

> Then there will be righteous sacrifices,
> whole burnt offerings to delight you;
> then bulls will be offered on your altar.

Cast: **Penitent 1, Sinner 1, Sinner 2, Penitent 2**

Prayer for the Help of God's Spirit

From Psalm 51:6–12 and Psalm 143:6–10 (LIT)

Leader
A (group 1)
O Lord, I spread my hands out to you:
I thirst for you like dry ground.

Leader
B (group 2)
Teach me to do your will, for you are my God:
let your good Spirit lead me in safety.

Leader
A (group 1)
You require sincerity and truth in me:
fill my mind with your wisdom.

Leader
B (group 2)
Create in me a pure heart, O God:
renew a faithful spirit in me.

Leader
A (group 1)
Do not cast me from your presence:
or take your Holy Spirit from me.

Leader
B (group 2)
Give me again the joy of your salvation:
and make me willing to obey.

All
Glory to the Father, and to the Son,
and to the Holy Spirit:
as it was in the beginning, is now,
and shall be forever. Amen.

Cast: **Leader,** A (group 1—part of congregation), B (group 2—part of congregation), All (entire congregation). *(Psalms 51 and 143 have been grouped together to provide for an occasion when the person and work of the Holy Spirit are being considered.)*

God's Judgment

Psalm 52:1–7

Psalmist
Why do you boast of evil, you mighty man?
> Why do you boast all day long,
> you who are a disgrace in the eyes of God?
Your tongue plots destruction;
> it is like a sharpened razor,
> you who practice deceit.
You love evil rather than good,
> falsehood rather than speaking the truth.

You love every harmful word,
O you deceitful tongue!

Surely God will bring you down to everlasting ruin:
He will snatch you up and tear you from your tent;
he will uproot you from the land of the living.
The righteous will see and fear;
they will laugh at him, saying:

Righteous
person 1   Here now is the man
who did not make God his stronghold—

Righteous
person 2   But trusted in his great wealth—

Righteous
person 1   And grew strong by destroying others!

Cast: **Psalmist, Righteous person 1, Righteous person 2**

Wickedness and Ignorance

Psalm 53:1–6

Psalmist   The fool says in his heart:

Fool(s)   There is no God.

Psalmist   They are corrupt, and their ways are vile;
there is no one who does good. (PAUSE)

God looks down from heaven
on the sons of men
to see if there are any who understand,
any who seek God.
Everyone has turned away,
they have together become corrupt;
there is no one who does good,
not even one. (PAUSE)
[God asks:]

God
(voice only)   Will the evildoers never learn—
those who devour my people as men eat bread
and who do not call on God?

Psalmist   There they were, overwhelmed with dread,
where there was nothing to dread.
God scattered the bones of those who attacked you;
you put them to shame, for God despised them.

79

Worshiper	Oh, that salvation for Israel would come out of Zion! When God restores the fortunes of his people, let Jacob rejoice and Israel be glad!

Cast: **Psalmist, Fool(s), God** (voice only), **Worshiper**

A Prayer for Deliverance

Psalm 60:1–12

Worshiper 1 You have rejected us, O God, and burst forth upon us;
 you have been angry—now restore us!

Worshiper 2 You have shaken the land and torn it open;
 mend its fractures, for it is quaking.

Worshiper 1 You have shown your people desperate times;
 you have given us wine that makes us stagger.

Worshiper 3 But for those who fear you, you have raised a banner
 to be unfurled against the bow.

Worshiper 2 Save us and help us with your right hand,
 that those you love may be delivered.

Worshiper 3 God has spoken from his sanctuary:

God
 (voice only) In triumph I will parcel out Shechem
 and measure off the Valley of Succoth.
 Gilead is mine, and Manasseh is mine;
 Ephraim is my helmet,
 Judah my scepter.
 Moab is my washbasin,
 upon Edom I toss my sandal;
 over Philistia I shout in triumph.

Worshiper 3 Who will bring me to the fortified city?
 Who will lead me to Edom?

Worshiper 1 Is it not you, O God, you who have rejected us
 and no longer go out with our armies?

Worshiper 2 Give us aid against the enemy,
 for the help of man is worthless.

Worshiper 3 With God we will gain the victory,
 and he will trample down our enemies.

Cast: **Worshiper 1, Worshiper 2, Worshiper 3, God** (voice only)

A Prayer for Protection

Psalm 64:1–10

Worshiper 1	Hear me, O God, as I voice my complaint; protect my life from the threat of the enemy.
Worshiper 2	Hide me from the conspiracy of the wicked, from that noisy crowd of evildoers.
Worshiper 1	They sharpen their tongues like swords and aim their words like deadly arrows.
Worshiper 2	They shoot from ambush at the innocent man; they shoot at him suddenly, without fear.
Worshiper 1	They encourage each other in evil plans, they talk about hiding their snares; they say:
Evil person(s)	Who will see them?
Worshiper 2	They plot injustice and say:
Evil person(s)	We have devised a perfect plan!
Worshiper 1 (thought-fully)	Surely the mind and heart of man are cunning. (PAUSE)
Worshiper 2	But God will shoot them with arrows; suddenly they will be struck down. He will turn their own tongues against them and bring them to ruin—
Worshiper 1	All who see them will shake their heads in scorn.
Worshiper 2	All mankind will fear; they will proclaim the works of God and ponder what he has done.
Worshiper 1	Let the righteous rejoice in the LORD and take refuge in him;
Worshipers 1 and 2	Let all the upright in heart praise him!

Cast: **Worshiper 1, Worshiper 2, Evil person(s)**

Praise for the Harvest

From Psalm 65:1–13 (LIT)

Leader 2	O God, it is right for us to praise you, because you answer our prayers:

Leader 1	You care for the land and water it:
A (group 1)	**and make it rich and fertile.**
Leader 2	You fill the running streams with water:
B (group 2)	**and irrigate the land.**
Leader 1	You soften the ground with showers:
A (group 1)	**and make the young crops grow.**
Leader 2	You crown the year with goodness:
B (group 2)	**and give us a plentiful harvest.**
Leader 1	The pastures are filled with flocks:
A (group 1)	**the hillsides are clothed with joy.**
Leader 2	The fields are covered with grain:
All	**they shout for joy and sing.**
All	**Glory to the Father, and to the Son, and to the Holy Spirit: as it was in the beginning, is now, and shall be forever. Amen.**

Cast: **Leader 2**, **Leader 1**, **A** (group 1—part of the congregation), **B** (group 2—part of the congregation), **All** (the entire congregation)

A Song of Praise and Thanksgiving

Psalm 66:1–20

Psalmist	Shout with joy to God, all the earth! Sing the glory of his name; make his praise glorious! Say to God:
Worshipers 1–3	How awesome are your deeds!
Worshiper 1	So great is your power that your enemies cringe before you. All the earth bows down to you; they sing praise to you, they sing praise to your name.
Psalmist	Come and see what God has done, how awesome his works in man's behalf! He turned the sea into dry land, they passed through the waters on foot— come, let us rejoice in him. He rules forever by his power, his eyes watch the nations— let not the rebellious rise up against him.

Praise our God, O peoples,
    let the sound of his praise be heard;
he has preserved our lives
    and kept our feet from slipping.

Worshiper 1 For you, O God, tested us;
    you refined us like silver.
You brought us into prison
    and laid burdens on our backs.
You let men ride over our heads;
    we went through fire and water,
    but you brought us to a place of abundance.

I will come to your temple with burnt offerings
    and fulfill my vows to you—
vows my lips promised and my mouth spoke
    when I was in trouble.

Worshiper 2 I will sacrifice fat animals to you
    and an offering of rams;
    I will offer bulls and goats.

Psalmist Come and listen, all you who fear God.

Worshiper 3 Let me tell you what he has done for me.
I cried out to him with my mouth;
    his praise was on my tongue.
If I had cherished sin in my heart,
    the Lord would not have listened;
but God has surely listened
    and heard my voice in prayer.

Worshiper 2 Praise be to God,
    who has not rejected my prayer
    or withheld his love from me!

Cast: **Psalmist, Worshiper 1, Worshiper 2, Worshiper 3**

A Song of Praise and Thanksgiving

From Psalm 66:1–20 (LIT)

Leader Praise your God with shouts of joy:
All **all the earth sing praise to him.**

Leader Sing the glory of his name:
A (group 1) **offer him your highest praise.**

Leader Say to him: How great you are:
B (group 2) **wonderful the things you do!**

Leader	All your enemies bow down:
C (group 3)	**all the earth sings praise to you.**

Leader	Come and see what God has done:
A (group 1)	**causing mortal men to fear—**
B (group 2)	**for he turned the sea to land,**
C (group 3)	**led his people safely through.**

Leader	We rejoice at what he does—
A (group 1)	**ruling through eternity,**
B (group 2)	**watching over all the world,**
C (group 3)	**keeping every rebel down.**

Leader	Praise our God, you nations, praise:
A (group 1)	**let the sound of praise be heard!**
B (group 2)	**God sustains our very lives:**
C (group 3)	**keeps our feet upon the way.**

Leader	Once, you tested us, O God—
A (group 1)	**silver purified by fire—**

Leader	Let us fall into a trap,
B (group 2)	**placed hard burdens on our backs—**

Leader	Sent us through the flame and flood:
C (group 3)	**now you bring us safely home.**

Leader	I will come to worship you:
A (group 1)	**bring to you my offering,**
B (group 2)	**give you what I said I would,**
C (group 3)	**when the troubles threatened me.**

Leader	All who love and honor God:
A (group 1)	**come and listen, while I tell**
B (group 2)	**what great things he did for me**
C (group 3)	**when I cried to him for help,**
A (group 1)	**when I praised him with my songs.**
B (group 2)	**When my heart was free from sin,**
C (group 3)	**then he listened to my prayer.**

Leader	Praise the Lord who heard my cry:
All	**God has shown his love to me! Amen.**

Cast: **Leader**, A (group 1—part of congregation), B (group 2—part of congregation, C (group 3—part of congregation), **All** (entire congregation)

A Song of Thanksgiving

Psalm 67:1–7 (LIT)

Leader 1	May God be gracious to us and bless us:
A (group 1)	**and make his face to shine upon us.**

Leader 2	Let your ways be known upon earth:
B (group 2)	**your saving grace to every nation.**
Leaders	
1 and **2**	Let the peoples praise you, O God:
All	**let the peoples praise you.**
Leader 1	Let the nations be glad:
A (group 1)	**and sing aloud for joy.**
Leader 2	Because you judge the peoples justly:
B (group 2)	**and guide the nations of the earth.**
Leaders	
1 and **2**	Let the peoples praise you, O God:
All	**let all the peoples praise you.**
Leader 1	Then the land will yield its harvest:
A (group 1)	**and God, our God, will bless us.**
Leader 2	God will bless us:
B (group 2)	**and people will fear him**
All	**to the ends of the earth. Amen.**
All	**Glory to the Father, and to the Son,**
	and to the Holy Spirit:
	as it was in the beginning, is now,
	and shall be forever. Amen.

Cast: **Leader 1**, **A** (group 1—part of the congregation), **Leader 2**, **B** (group 2—part of the congregation), **All** (the entire congregation)

A National Song of Triumph

From Psalm 68:1–35

Psalmist	May God arise, may his enemies be scattered;
	may his foes flee before him.
	As smoke is blown away by the wind,
	may you blow them away;
	as wax melts before the fire,
	may the wicked perish before God.
	But may the righteous be glad
	and rejoice before God;
	may they be happy and joyful.
Leader	Sing to God, sing praise to his name,
	extol him who rides on the clouds—
	his name is the LORD—
	and rejoice before him.

Psalmist	A father to the fatherless, a defender of widows,
	    is God in his holy dwelling.
	God sets the lonely in families,
	    he leads forth the prisoners with singing;
	    but the rebellious live in a sun-scorched land.

Worshiper	When you went out before your people, O God,
	    when you marched through the wasteland,
	the earth shook,
	    the heavens poured down rain,
	before God, the One of Sinai,
	    before God, the God of Israel.
	You gave abundant showers, O God;
	    you refreshed your weary inheritance.
	Your people settled in it,
	    and from your bounty, O God, you provided for the poor.
	
	The Lord announced the word,
	    and great was the company of those who proclaimed it:

Woman	Kings and armies flee in haste; in the camps men divide the plunder. . . .

Psalmist	The chariots of God are tens of thousands
	    and thousands of thousands;
	    the Lord ⌐has come⌐ from Sinai into his sanctuary.
	When you ascended on high,
	    you led captives in your train;
	    you received gifts from men,
	even from the rebellious—
	    that you, O Lord God, might dwell there.

Leader	Praise be to the Lord, to God our Savior,
	    who daily bears our burdens.
	
	Our God is a God who saves;
	    from the Sovereign Lord comes escape from death. . . .

Worshiper	Your procession has come into view, O God, the procession of my God and King into the sanctuary.
Onlooker 1	In front are the singers—
Onlooker 2	After them the musicians—
Onlooker 3	With them are the maidens playing tambourines.
Leader	Praise God in the great congregation; praise the Lord in the assembly of Israel.
Onlooker 1	There is the little tribe of Benjamin leading them—
Onlooker 2	There the great throng of Judah's princes—
Onlooker 3	And there the princes of Zebulun and of Naphtali. . . .

Leader	Sing to God, O kingdoms of the earth,
	sing praise to the Lord,
	to him who rides the ancient skies above,
	who thunders with mighty voice.
	Proclaim the power of God,
	whose majesty is over Israel,
	whose power is in the skies.
Worshiper	You are awesome, O God, in your sanctuary—
	the God of Israel gives power and strength to his people.
Cast	Praise be to God!

Cast: **Psalmist, Leader, Worshiper, Woman** (can be the same as Worshiper), **Onlooker 1, Onlooker 2, Onlooker 3**

The Prayer of an Older Person

Psalm 71:1–24

Senior person 1	In you, O Lord, I have taken refuge;
	let me never be put to shame.
Senior person 2	Rescue me and deliver me in your righteousness;
	turn your ear to me and save me.
Senior person 1	Be my rock of refuge,
	to which I can always go;
	give the command to save me,
	for you are my rock and my fortress.
Senior person 2	Deliver me, O my God, from the hand of the wicked,
	from the grasp of evil and cruel men.
	For you have been my hope, O Sovereign Lord,
	my confidence since my youth.
	From birth I have relied on you;
	you brought me forth from my mother's womb.
	I will ever praise you.
Senior person 1	I have become like a portent to many,
	but you are my strong refuge.
	My mouth is filled with your praise,
	declaring your splendor all day long.
	Do not cast me away when I am old;
	do not forsake me when my strength is gone.

For my enemies speak against me;
  those who wait to kill me conspire together.
They say:

Enemy 1 God has forsaken him—

Enemy 2 Pursue him and seize him—

Enemy 3 No one will rescue him.

Senior
  person 1 Be not far from me, O God;
  come quickly, O my God, to help me.
May my accusers perish in shame;
  may those who want to harm me
  be covered with scorn and disgrace.

But as for me, I will always have hope;
  I will praise you more and more.
My mouth will tell of your righteousness,
  of your salvation all day long,
  though I know not its measure.
I will come and proclaim your mighty acts, O Sovereign Lord;
  I will proclaim your righteousness, yours alone.

Senior
  person 2 Since my youth, O God, you have taught me,
  and to this day I declare your marvelous deeds.
Even when I am old and gray,
  do not forsake me, O God,
till I declare your power to the next generation,
  your might to all who are to come.

Senior
  person 1 Your righteousness reaches to the skies, O God,
  you who have done great things.
  Who, O God, is like you?
Though you have made me see troubles, many and bitter,
  you will restore my life again;
from the depths of the earth
  you will again bring me up.
You will increase my honor
  and comfort me once again.

Senior
  person 2 I will praise you with the harp
  for your faithfulness, O my God;
I will sing praise to you with the lyre,
  O Holy One of Israel.
My lips will shout for joy
  when I sing praise to you—
  I, whom you have redeemed.

My tongue will tell of your righteous acts
    all day long,
for those who wanted to harm me
    have been put to shame and confusion.

Cast: **Senior person 1, Senior person 2, Enemy 1, Enemy 2** (can be the same as Enemy 1), **Enemy 3**

God, the Judge

Psalm 75:1–10

Worshipers
1 and 2   We give thanks to you, O God,
        we give thanks—

Worshiper 1   Your Name is near;
        men tell of your wonderful deeds.

Worshiper 2   You say:

God
(voice only)   I choose the appointed time;
        it is I who judge uprightly.
When the earth and all its people quake,
        it is I who hold its pillars firm.

To the arrogant I say, "Boast no more,"
        and to the wicked, "Do not lift up your horns.
Do not lift your horns against heaven;
        do not speak with outstretched neck."

Worshiper 2   No one from the east or the west
        or from the desert can exalt a man.
But it is God who judges:
        He brings one down, he exalts another.

Worshiper 1   In the hand of the LORD is a cup
        full of foaming wine mixed with spices;
he pours it out, and all the wicked of the earth
        drink it down to its very dregs.

Worshiper 2   As for me, I will declare this forever;
        I will sing praise to the God of Jacob.
I will cut off the horns of all the wicked,
        but the horns of the righteous will be lifted up.

Cast: **Worshiper 1, Worshiper 2, God** (voice only)

Comfort in Time of Distress

Psalm 77:1–20

Worshiper 1   I cried out to God for help;
        I cried out to God to hear me.
    When I was in distress, I sought the Lord;
        at night I stretched out untiring hands
        and my soul refused to be comforted.

Worshiper 2   I remembered you, O God, and I groaned;
        I mused, and my spirit grew faint.
    You kept my eyes from closing;
        I was too troubled to speak.
    I thought about the former days,
        the years of long ago;
    I remembered my songs in the night.
        My heart mused and my spirit inquired:

Thinker   Will the Lord reject forever?
        Will he never show his favor again?
    Has his unfailing love vanished forever?
        Has his promise failed for all time?
    Has God forgotten to be merciful?
        Has he in anger withheld his compassion?

Worshiper 2   Then I thought:

Thinker   To this I will appeal:
        the years of the right hand of the Most High.

Worshiper 2   I will remember the deeds of the LORD;
        yes, I will remember your miracles of long ago.
    I will meditate on all your works
        and consider all your mighty deeds.

Worshiper 1   Your ways, O God, are holy.
        What god is so great as our God?
    You are the God who performs miracles;
        you display your power among the peoples.
    With your mighty arm you redeemed your people,
        the descendants of Jacob and Joseph.

Worshiper 2   The waters saw you, O God,
        the waters saw you and writhed;
        the very depths were convulsed.

Worshiper 1   The clouds poured down water,
        the skies resounded with thunder;
        your arrows flashed back and forth.

Worshiper 2	Your thunder was heard in the whirlwind,
	    your lightning lit up the world;
	    the earth trembled and quaked.

Worshiper 1	Your path led through the sea,
	    your way through the mighty waters,
	    though your footprints were not seen.

Worshiper 2	You led your people like a flock by the hand of Moses and Aaron.

Cast: **Worshiper 1, Worshiper 2, Thinker**

A Prayer for Restoration

From Psalm 80:1–19 (LIT)

Leader 1	Hear us, O Shepherd of Israel, leader of your flock.
Leader 2	Hear us from your throne above the cherubim.
Leader 3 All	Shine forth, awaken your strength, and come to save us. **Bring us back, O God, and save us, make your face to shine upon us.**
Leader 1	O Lord God Almighty, how long will you be angry with your people's prayers?
Leader 2	You have given us sorrow to eat and tears to drink.
Leader 3 All	You have made us a source of contention to our neighbors, and our enemies insult us. **Bring us back, O God, and save us, make your face to shine upon us.**
Leader 1	Return to us, O God Almighty, look down from heaven and see.
Leader 2	Look on this vine that you planted with your own hand, this child you raised for yourself.
Leader 3 All	Let you hand rest upon the people you have chosen, then we will not turn away from you; revive us, and we shall praise your name. **Bring us back, O God, and save us, make your face to shine upon us.**
All	**Glory to the Father, and to the Son, and to the Holy Spirit: as it was in the beginning, is now, and shall be forever. Amen.**

Cast: **Leader 1, Leader 2, Leader 3, All** (two or more persons/congregation)

A Song for a Festival

Psalm 81:1–16

Psalmist
Sing for joy to God our strength;
　　shout aloud to the God of Jacob!
Begin the music, strike the tambourine,
　　play the melodious harp and lyre.

Sound the ram's horn at the New Moon,
　　and when the moon is full, on the day of our Feast;
this is a decree for Israel,
　　an ordinance of the God of Jacob.
He established it as a statute for Joseph
　　when he went out against Egypt, (PAUSE)
　　where we heard a language we did not understand.

He says:

Voice of God
I removed the burden from their shoulders;
　　their hands were set free from the basket.
In your distress you called and I rescued you,
　　I answered you out of a thundercloud;
　　I tested you at the waters of Meribah.

Hear, O my people, and I will warn you—
　　if you would but listen to me, O Israel!
You shall have no foreign god among you;
　　you shall not bow down to an alien god.
I am the LORD your God,
　　who brought you up out of Egypt.
　　Open wide your mouth and I will fill it.

But my people would not listen to me;
　　Israel would not submit to me.
So I gave them over to their stubborn hearts
　　to follow their own devices.

If my people would but listen to me,
　　if Israel would follow my ways,
how quickly would I subdue their enemies
　　and turn my hand against their foes!
Those who hate the LORD would cringe before him,
　　and their punishment would last forever.
But you would be fed with the finest of wheat;
　　with honey from the rock I would satisfy you.

Cast: **Psalmist, Voice of God**

God, the Supreme Ruler

Psalm 82:1–8

Psalmist	God presides in the great assembly; he gives judgment among the "gods":

Voice of God	How long will you defend the unjust
	    and show partiality to the wicked?
	Defend the cause of the weak and fatherless;
	    maintain the rights of the poor and oppressed.
	Rescue the weak and needy;
	    deliver them from the hand of the wicked.

	They know nothing, they understand nothing. They walk about in darkness; all the foundations of the earth are shaken.

	I said, "You are 'gods';
	    you are all sons of the Most High."
	But you will die like mere men;
	    you will fall like every other ruler.

Psalmist	Rise up, O God, judge the earth, for all the nations are your inheritance.

Cast: **Psalmist, Voice of God**

A Prayer for the Defeat of Israel's Enemies

Psalm 83:1–18

Worshiper 1	O God, do not keep silent;
	    be not quiet, O God, be not still.
	See how your enemies are astir,
	    how your foes rear their heads.
	With cunning they conspire against your people;
	    they plot against those you cherish.

Enemies 1 and 2	Come, let us destroy them as a nation—
Enemy 2	That the name of Israel be remembered no more.

Worshiper 1	With one mind they plot together;
	    they form an alliance against you—
	the tents of Edom and the Ishmaelites,
	    of Moab and the Hagrites,
	Gebal, Ammon and Amalek,
	    Philistia, with the people of Tyre.

<table>
<tr><td></td><td>Even Assyria has joined them
    to lend strength to the descendants of Lot.</td></tr>
</table>

Worshiper 2   Do to them as you did to Midian,
      as you did to Sisera and Jabin at the river Kishon,
  who perished at Endor
      and became like refuse on the ground.
  Make their nobles like Oreb and Zeeb,
      all their princes like Zebah and Zalmunna,
  who said:

Zebah and
Zalmunna   Let us take possession of the pasturelands of God.

Worshiper 2   Make them like tumbleweed, O my God,
      like chaff before the wind.
  As fire consumes the forest
      or a flame sets the mountains ablaze,
  so pursue them with your tempest
      and terrify them with your storm.
  Cover their faces with shame
      so that men will seek your name, O LORD.

  May they ever be ashamed and dismayed;
      may they perish in disgrace.

Worshipers
  1 and 2   Let them know that you, whose name is the LORD—
      that you alone are the Most High over all the earth.

Cast: **Worshiper 1, Enemy 1, Enemy 2** (can be the same as Enemy 1), **Worshiper 2, Zebah, Zalmunna** (can be the same as Zebah)

Longing for God's House

Psalm 84:1–12

Worshiper 1   How lovely is your dwelling place,
      O LORD Almighty!

Worshiper 2   My soul yearns, even faints,
      for the courts of the LORD;
  my heart and my flesh cry out
      for the living God.

Worshiper 1   Even the sparrow has found a home,
      and the swallow a nest for herself,
      where she may have her young—
  a place near your altar,
      O LORD Almighty, my King and my God.

Worshiper 2   Blessed are those who dwell in your house;
      they are ever praising you.

Worshiper 1 Blessed are those whose strength is in you,
who have set their hearts on pilgrimage.
As they pass through the Valley of Baca,
they make it a place of springs;
the autumn rains also cover it with pools.
They go from strength to strength,
till each appears before God in Zion.

Worshiper 2 Hear my prayer, O LORD God Almighty;
listen to me, O God of Jacob.
Look upon our shield, O God;
look with favor on your anointed one.

Worshiper 1 Better is one day in your courts
than a thousand elsewhere;
I would rather be a doorkeeper in the house of my God
than dwell in the tents of the wicked.

Worshiper 2 For the LORD God is a sun and shield;
the LORD bestows favor and honor;
no good thing does he withhold
from those whose walk is blameless.

**Worshipers
1 and 2** O LORD Almighty,
blessed is the man who trusts in you.

Cast: **Worshiper 1, Worshiper 2**

A Prayer for the Nation's Welfare

Psalm 85:1–13

Worshiper 1 You showed favor to your land, O LORD;
you restored the fortunes of Jacob.
You forgave the iniquity of your people
and covered all their sins.
You set aside all your wrath
and turned from your fierce anger.

Worshiper 2 Restore us again, O God our Savior,
and put away your displeasure toward us.
Will you be angry with us forever?
Will you prolong your anger through all generations?
Will you not revive us again,
that your people may rejoice in you?
Show us your unfailing love, O LORD,
and grant us your salvation.

Psalmist	I will listen to what God the LORD will say;
	    he promises peace to his people, his saints—
	    but let them not return to folly.
	Surely his salvation is near those who fear him,
	    that his glory may dwell in our land.

Worshipers 1 and 2	Love and faithfulness meet together; righteousness and peace kiss each other.
Worshiper 1	Faithfulness springs forth from the earth—
Psalmist	Righteousness looks down from heaven.
Worshiper 2	The LORD will indeed give what is good, and our land will yield its harvest.
Psalmist	Righteousness goes before him and prepares the way for his steps.

Cast: **Worshiper 1, Worshiper 2, Psalmist**

In Praise of Jerusalem

Psalm 87:1–7

Psalmist	He has set his foundation on the holy mountain;
	    the LORD loves the gates of Zion
	    more than all the dwellings of Jacob.
	Glorious things are said of you,
	    O city of God:

The Lord
(voice only)
	I will record Rahab and Babylon
	    among those who acknowledge me—
	Philistia too, and Tyre, along with Cush—
	    and will say, "This one was born in Zion."

Psalmist	Indeed, of Zion it will be said,
Person	This one and that one were born in her, and the Most High himself will establish her. The LORD will write in the register of the peoples:
The Lord (voice)	This one was born in Zion. As they make music they will sing:
Singer(s)	All my fountains are in you.

Cast: **Psalmist, the Lord** (voice only), **Person, Singer(s)** (one or more; can be the same as Person)

96

A National Hymn; God's Promise to David

Psalm 89:1–52

Worshiper 1 I will sing of the LORD's great love forever;
      with my mouth I will make your faithfulness known
         through all generations.
I will declare that your love stands firm forever,
      that you established your faithfulness in heaven itself.

You said:

The Lord
(voice only) I have made a covenant with my chosen one,
      I have sworn to David my servant,
"I will establish your line forever
      and make your throne firm through all generations."

Worshiper 2 The heavens praise your wonders, O LORD,
      your faithfulness too, in the assembly of the holy ones.
For who in the skies above can compare with the LORD?
      Who is like the LORD among the heavenly beings?
In the council of the holy ones God is greatly feared;
      he is more awesome than all who surround him.

Worshiper 1 O LORD God Almighty, who is like you?
      You are mighty, O LORD, and your faithfulness surrounds you.

You rule over the surging sea;
      when its waves mount up, you still them.
You crushed Rahab like one of the slain;
      with your strong arm you scattered your enemies.
The heavens are yours, and yours also the earth;
      you founded the world and all that is in it.
You created the north and the south;
      Tabor and Hermon sing for joy at your name.
Your arm is endued with power;
      your hand is strong, your right hand exalted.

Righteousness and justice are the foundation of your throne;
      love and faithfulness go before you.

**Worshipers
1 and 2** Blessed are those who have learned to acclaim you,
      who walk in the light of your presence, O LORD.
They rejoice in your name all day long;
      they exult in your righteousness.

Worshiper 2 For you are their glory and strength,
      and by your favor you exalt our horn.
Indeed, our shield belongs to the LORD,
      our king to the Holy One of Israel.

Once you spoke in a vision,
     to your faithful people you said:

The Lord
(voice)

I have bestowed strength on a warrior;
     I have exalted a young man from among the people.
I have found David my servant;
     with my sacred oil I have anointed him.
My hand will sustain him;
     surely my arm will strengthen him.
No enemy will subject him to tribute;
     no wicked man will oppress him.
I will crush his foes before him
     and strike down his adversaries.
My faithful love will be with him,
     and through my name his horn will be exalted.
I will set his hand over the sea,
     his right hand over the rivers.
He will call out to me:

David

You are my Father,
     my God, the Rock my Savior.

The Lord
(voice)

I will also appoint him my firstborn,
     the most exalted of the kings of the earth.
I will maintain my love to him forever,
     and my covenant with him will never fail.
I will establish his line forever,
     his throne as long as the heavens endure.

If his sons forsake my law
     and do not follow my statutes,
if they violate my decrees
     and fail to keep my commands,
I will punish their sin with the rod,
     their iniquity with flogging;
but I will not take my love from him,
     nor will I ever betray my faithfulness.
I will not violate my covenant
     or alter what my lips have uttered.
Once for all, I have sworn by my holiness—
     and I will not lie to David—
that his line will continue forever
     and his throne endure before me like the sun;
it will be established forever like the moon,
     the faithful witness in the sky.

Worshiper 1

But you have rejected, you have spurned,
     you have been very angry with your anointed one.
You have renounced the covenant with your servant
     and have defiled his crown in the dust.

You have broken through all his walls
    and reduced his strongholds to ruins.
All who pass by have plundered him;
    he has become the scorn of his neighbors.
You have exalted the right hand of his foes;
    you have made all his enemies rejoice.
You have turned back the edge of his sword
    and have not supported him in battle.
You have put an end to his splendor
    and cast his throne to the ground.
You have cut short the days of his youth;
    you have covered him with a mantle of shame.

Worshiper 2   How long, O Lord? Will you hide yourself forever?
    How long will your wrath burn like fire?
Remember how fleeting is my life.
    For what futility you have created all men!
What man can live and not see death,
    or save himself from the power of the grave?

Worshiper 1   O Lord, where is your former great love,
    which in your faithfulness you swore to David?
Remember, Lord, how your servant has been mocked,
    how I bear in my heart the taunts of all the nations,
the taunts with which your enemies have mocked, O Lord,
    with which they have mocked every step of your anointed one.

Worshipers
1 and 2   Praise be to the Lord forever!

Cast/All   Amen and Amen.

Cast: **Worshiper 1**, **the Lord** (voice only), **Worshiper 2**, **David** (can be the same as the Lord)

The Sovereignty of God

Psalm 90:1–17

Worshiper 1   Lord, you have been our dwelling place
    throughout all generations.
Before the mountains were born
    or you brought forth the earth and the world,
    from everlasting to everlasting you are God.

Worshiper 2   You turn men back to dust,
    saying, "Return to dust, O sons of men."
For a thousand years in your sight
    are like a day that has just gone by,
    or like a watch in the night.

Worshiper 1   You sweep men away in the sleep of death;
        they are like the new grass of the morning—
    though in the morning it springs up new,
        by evening it is dry and withered.

Worshiper 2   We are consumed by your anger
        and terrified by your indignation.
    You have set our iniquities before you,
        our secret sins in the light of your presence.

Worshiper 1   All our days pass away under your wrath;
        we finish our years with a moan.
    The length of our days is seventy years—
        or eighty, if we have the strength;
    yet their span is but trouble and sorrow,
        for they quickly pass, and we fly away.

Worshiper 2   Who knows the power of your anger?
        For your wrath is as great as the fear that is due you.
    Teach us to number our days aright,
        that we may gain a heart of wisdom.

Worshiper 1   Relent, O LORD! How long will it be?
        Have compassion on your servants.
    Satisfy us in the morning with your unfailing love,
        that we may sing for joy and be glad all our days.

Worshiper 2   Make us glad for as many days as you have afflicted us,
        for as many years as we have seen trouble.

Worshiper 1   May your deeds be shown to your servants—

Worshiper 2   Your splendor to their children.

**Worshipers
  1 and 2**   May the favor of the Lord our God rest upon us:

Worshiper 1   Establish the work of our hands for us—
    yes, establish the work of our hands.

Cast: **Worshiper 1, Worshiper 2**

God, Our Protector

Psalm 91:1–16

Voice 1   He who dwells in the shelter of the Most High
        will rest in the shadow of the Almighty.
    I will say of the LORD:

Supplicant   He is my refuge and my fortress,
             my God, in whom I trust.

Voice 1
(to
Supplicant)   Surely he will save you from the fowler's snare
             and from the deadly pestilence.

Voice 2
(to
Supplicant)   He will cover you with his feathers,
             and under his wings you will find refuge;
             his faithfulness will be your shield and rampart.

Voice 1   You will not fear the terror of night,
             nor the arrow that flies by day,
           nor the pestilence that stalks in the darkness,
             nor the plague that destroys at midday.

Voice 2   A thousand may fall at your side,
             ten thousand at your right hand,
             but it will not come near you.
           You will only observe with your eyes
             and see the punishment of the wicked.

Voice 1   If you make the Most High your dwelling—
             even the LORD, who is my refuge—
           then no harm will befall you,
             no disaster will come near your tent.

Voice 2   For he will command his angels concerning you
             to guard you in all your ways;
           they will lift you up in their hands,
             so that you will not strike your foot against a stone.

Voice 1   You will tread upon the lion and the cobra;
             you will trample the great lion and the serpent. (PAUSE)

           [Says the LORD:]

The Lord
(voice only) Because he loves me . . . I will rescue him;
             I will protect him, for he acknowledges my name.
           He will call upon me, and I will answer him;
             I will be with him in trouble,
             I will deliver him and honor him.
           With long life will I satisfy him
             and show him my salvation.

Cast: **Voice 1, Supplicant, Voice 2, the Lord** (voice only)

God, the King

Psalm 93:1–5

Psalmist The LORD reigns, he is robed in majesty;
the LORD is robed in majesty
and is armed with strength.
The world is firmly established;
it cannot be moved.

Worshiper 1 Your throne was established long ago;
you are from all eternity.

Worshiper 2 The seas have lifted up, O LORD,
the seas have lifted up their voice;
the seas have lifted up their pounding waves.

Psalmist Mightier than the thunder of the great waters,
mightier than the breakers of the sea—
the LORD on high is mighty.

Worshiper 1 Your statutes stand firm—

**Worshipers
1 and 2** Holiness adorns your house
for endless days, O LORD.

Cast: **Psalmist, Worshiper 1. Worshiper 2** (can be the same as Worshiper 1)

God Is King

From Psalm 93:1–5 (LIT)

Leader The Lord reigns, robed in majesty:
A (group 1) **he arms himself with power.**

Leader The earth is firmly set in place:
B (group 2) **it never can be moved.**

Leader Your throne was founded long ago:
A (group 1) **before all time began.**

Leader The oceans raise their voice, O Lord:
B (group 2) **and lift their roaring waves.**

Leader The Lord is mightier than the sea:
A (group 1) **he rules supreme on high.**

Leader His laws stand firm through endless days:
B (group 2) **his praise for evermore.**

All Amen.

All	Glory to the Father, and to the Son, and to the Holy Spirit: as it was in the beginning, is now, and shall be forever. Amen.

Cast: **Leader, A** (group 1—part of congregation), **B** (group 2—part of congregation), **All** (entire congregation)

God, the Judge of All

Psalm 94:1–23

Worshiper 1   O Lᴏʀᴅ, the God who avenges,
     O God who avenges, shine forth.
Rise up, O Judge of the earth;
     pay back to the proud what they deserve.
How long will the wicked, O Lᴏʀᴅ,
     how long will the wicked be jubilant?

They pour out arrogant words;
     all the evildoers are full of boasting.
They crush your people, O Lᴏʀᴅ;
     they oppress your inheritance
They slay the widow and the alien;
     they murder the fatherless.

They say:

Evildoer   The Lᴏʀᴅ does not see;
     the God of Jacob pays no heed.

Prophet   Take heed, you senseless ones among the people;
     you fools, when will you become wise?
Does he who implanted the ear not hear?
     Does he who formed the eye not see?
Does he who disciplines nations not punish?
     Does he who teaches man lack knowledge?
The Lᴏʀᴅ knows the thoughts of man;
     he knows that they are futile.

Worshiper 2   Blessed is the man you discipline, O Lᴏʀᴅ,
     the man you teach from your law;
you grant him relief from days of trouble,
     till a pit is dug for the wicked.

Prophet   The Lᴏʀᴅ will not reject his people;
     he will never forsake his inheritance.
Judgment will again be founded on righteousness,
     and all the upright in heart will follow it.

Worshiper 1	Who will rise up for me against the wicked?
	    Who will take a stand for me against evildoers?
	Unless the Lord had given me help,
	    I would soon have dwelt in the silence of death.

	When I said:
Young worshiper	My foot is slipping.
Worshiper 2	Your love, O Lord, supported me. When anxiety was great within me, your consolation brought joy to my soul.

Worshiper 1	Can a corrupt throne be allied with you—
	    one that brings on misery by its decrees?
	They band together against the righteous
	    and condemn the innocent to death.

Worshiper 2	But the Lord has become my fortress, and my God the rock in whom I take refuge.

Prophet	He will repay them for their sins
	    and destroy them for their wickedness;
	    the Lord our God will destroy them.

Cast: **Worshiper 1, Evildoer, Prophet, Worshiper 2, Young worshiper** (can be the same as Worshiper 1)

A Song of Praise

Psalm 95:1–7 (LIT)

Leader 1	Come, let's joyfully praise our God, acclaiming the Rock of our salvation.
Leader 2	Come before him with thanksgiving, and greet him with melody.
A (group 1)	**Our God is a great God—**
B (group 2)	**a king above all other gods.**
A (group 1)	**The depths of the earth are in his hands—**
B (group 2)	**the mountain peaks belong to him.**
A (group 1)	**The sea is his—he made it!**
B (group 2)	**His own hands prepared the land.**
Leader 1	Come, bow down to worship him;
Leader 2	kneel before the Lord who made us.
A and B (groups 1 and 2)	**We are his people, the sheep of his flock.**
Leaders 1 and 2	You shall know his power today—

Leader 2	if you listen to his voice.
All	**Glory to the Father, and to the Son, and to the Holy Spirit: as it was in the beginning, is now, and shall be forever. Amen.**

Cast: **Leader 1**, **Leader 2**, **A** (group 1—part of congregation), **B** (group 2—part of congregation), **All** (entire congregation). **Leaders** may be ministers.

God, the Supreme King

Psalm 96:1–13

Leader 1	Sing to the LORD a new song—
Leader 2	Sing to the LORD, all the earth.
Leader 3	Sing to the LORD, praise his name—
Leader 1	Proclaim his salvation day after day.
Leader 2	Declare his glory among the nations—
Leader 3	His marvelous deeds among all peoples.
Worshiper 1	For great is the LORD and most worthy of praise;
Worshiper 2	He is to be feared above all gods.
Worshiper 1	For all the gods of the nations are idols, but the LORD made the heavens.
Worshipers 1 and 2	Splendor and majesty are before him; strength and glory are in his sanctuary.
Leader 1	Ascribe to the LORD, O families of nations,
Leader 2	Ascribe to the LORD glory and strength.
Leader 3	Ascribe to the LORD the glory due his name;
Leader 1	Bring an offering and come into his courts.
Leader 2	Worship the LORD in the splendor of his holiness;
Leader 3	Tremble before him, all the earth.
Leader 1	Say among the nations:
Cast/All	The LORD reigns.
Worshiper 1	The world is firmly established, it cannot be moved;
Worshiper 2	He will judge the peoples with equity.
Leader 1	Let the heavens rejoice, let the earth be glad;

From Psalm 96:1–13 (LIT)

Leader 2	Let the sea resound, and all that is in it;
Leader 3	Let the fields be jubilant, and everything in them.
Worshiper 1	Then all the trees of the forest will sing for joy;
Worshiper 2	They will sing before the LORD, for he comes, he comes to judge the earth. He will judge the world in righteousness and the peoples in his truth.

Cast: **Leader 1, Leader 2, Leader 3, Worshiper 1, Worshiper 2** (Worshipers 1 and 2 can be within or behind the congregation/audience)

God, the Supreme King

From Psalm 96:1–13 (LIT)

Leader **A (group 1)**	Sing a new song to the Lord! **Sing to the Lord, all the world!**
Leader **B (group 2)**	Sing to the Lord, and praise him! **Proclaim every day the good news that he has saved us.**
Leader **A (group 1)**	Proclaim his glory to the nations— **his mighty deeds to all peoples.**
Leader **B (group 2)**	The Lord is great and is to be highly praised. **He is to be honored more than all the gods.**
Leader **A (group 1)**	Glory and majesty surround him; **power and beauty fill his temple.**
Leader **B (group 2)**	Praise the Lord, all people on earth— **praise his glory and might.**
Leader **A (group 1)**	Give him the glory due to his name: **bring an offering into his temple.**
Leader **B (group 2)**	Worship the Lord in his beauty and holiness: **tremble before him, all the earth.**
Leader **All**	Say to the nations: **The Lord is king!**
Leader **A (group 1)**	Let the heavens rejoice and the earth be glad: **let all creation sing for joy.**
Leader **B (group 2)**	For God shall come to judge the world: **and rule the people with his truth.**
All	**Amen.**

Cast: **Leader, A** (group 1—part of the congregation), **B** (group 2—part of the congregation), **All** (the entire congregation)

God, the Supreme Ruler

From Psalm 97:1–12 (LIT)

Leader	The Lord is king:
All	**the Lord is king!**
Leader	Let the whole wide earth rejoice:
A (group 1)	**let the islands all be glad.**
Leader	Thunder clouds encircle him:
B (group 2)	**truth and justice are his throne.**
Leader	Fire shall go before the Lord:
C (group 3)	**burning up his enemies.**
Leader	Lightning strikes the darkened world:
A (group 1)	**all the people see and fear.**
Leader	Mountains melt before our God:
B (group 2)	**he is Lord of all the earth.**
Leader	Kings proclaim his righteousness:
C (group 3)	**nations see his glory now.**
Leader	Idol-worshipers are shamed:
A (group 1)	**gods bow down before the Lord.**
Leader	Let Jerusalem rejoice:
B (group 2)	**in your faithful judgments, Lord!**
Leader	Sovereign of the universe:
C (group 3)	**mightier still than all the gods!**
Leader	Yet you help your saints, O Lord:
A (group 1)	**saving them from wicked men.**
Leader	Light will shine upon the good:
B (group 2)	**gladness fill the righteous heart.**
Leader	Now recall what God has done:
C (group 3)	**Thank him,**
B (group 2)	**praise him,**
All	**and rejoice!**
All	**Glory to the Father, and to the Son, and to the Holy Spirit: as it was in the beginning, is now, and shall be forever. Amen.**

Cast: **Leader, All** (the entire congregation), **A** (group 1—part of the congregation), **B** (group 2—part of the congregation), **C** (group 3—part of the congregation)

God, the Ruler of the World

From Psalm 98:1–9 (LIT)

Leader	Sing to the Lord a new song:
All	**for he has done marvelous things.**
Leader	His right hand and his holy arm:
All	**have brought a great triumph to us.**
A (group 1)	**He lets his salvation be known:**
B (group 2)	**his righteousness shines in the world.**
A (group 1)	**To us he continues his love:**
B (group 2)	**his glory is witnessed by all.**
Leader	Shout for joy to the Lord, all the earth:
All	**and burst into jubilant song.**
A (group 1)	**Make music to God with the harp:**
B (group 2)	**with songs and the sound of your praise.**
A (group 1)	**With trumpets and blast of the horn:**
B (group 2)	**sing praises to God as your king.**
Leader	Let rivers and streams clap their hands:
All	**the mountains together sing praise.**
Leader	The Lord comes to judge the whole earth:
All	**in righteousness God rules the world. Amen.**

Cast: **Leader, All** (the entire congregation), **A** (group 1—part of the congregation), **B** (group 2—part of the congregation)

God, the Supreme King

From Psalm 99:1–9 (LIT)

Leader 1	The Lord reigns:
A (group 1)	**let the nations tremble!**
Leader 2	He sits enthroned on high:
B (group 2)	**let the earth shake!**
Leader 1	Great is the Lord our God:
All	**exalted over all the world.**
Leader 1	Let the nations praise his awesome name, and say:
A (group 1)	**God is holy!**
Leader 2	Praise the Lord our God, and worship at his feet:
B (group 2)	**God is holy!**
Leader 1	Exalt the Lord our God, and worship on his holy mountain:
All	**The Lord our God is holy!**
All	**Glory to the Father, and to the Son,**

and to the Holy Spirit:
as it was in the beginning, is now,
and shall be forever. Amen.

Cast: **Leader 1**, **A** (group 1—part of congregation), **Leader 2**, **B** (group 2—part of congregation), **All** (the entire congregation)

A Hymn of Praise

From Psalm 100:1–5 (LIT)

| Leader | Rejoice in the Lord, all the earth: |
| All | **worship the Lord with gladness.** |

| Leader | Remember the Lord is our God: |
| A (group 1) | **we are his flock and he made us.** |

| Leader | Come to his temple with praise: |
| B (group 2) | **enter his gates with thanksgiving.** |

| Leader | The love of the Lord will not fail: |
| All | **God will be faithful forever. Amen.** |

Cast: **Leader**, **All** (the entire congregation), **A** (group 1—part of the congregation), **B** (group 2—part of the congregation)

The Love of God

From Psalm 103:1–22 (LIT)

| Leader | Praise the Lord, my soul: |
| A (group 1) | **all my being, praise his holy name!** |

Leader	Praise the Lord, my soul:
B (group 2)	**and do not forget how generous he is.**
A (group 1)	**He forgives all my sins:**
B (group 2)	**and heals all my diseases.**
A (group 1)	**He keeps me from the grave:**
B (group 2)	**and blesses me with love and mercy.**

Leader	The Lord is gracious and compassionate:
A (group 1)	**slow to become angry,**
B (group 2)	**and full of constant love.**

| Leader | He does not keep on rebuking: |
| A (group 1) | **he is not angry forever.** |

| Leader | He does not punish us as we deserve: |
| B (group 2) | **or repay us for our wrongs.** |

| Leader | As far as the east is from the west: |
| A (group 1) | **so far does he remove our sins from us.** |

| Leader | As kind as a Father to his children: |
| B (group 2) | **so kind is the Lord to those who honor him.** |

| Leader | Praise the Lord, all his creation: |
| All | **praise the Lord, my soul! Amen.** |

Cast: **Leader, A** (group 1—part of the congregation), **B** (group 2—part of the congregation), **All** (the entire congregation)

In Praise of the Creator

From Psalm 104:1–4, 29–30 (LIT)

| Leader | O Lord our God, you are very great: |
| All | **you are clothed with splendor and majesty.** |

| Leader | You make winds your messengers: |
| A (group 1) | **and flashes of fire your servants.** |

| Leader | How many are your works: |
| B (group 2) | **the earth is full of your creatures!** |

| Leader | When you hide your face, they are afraid: |
| A (group 1) | **when you take away their breath, they die.** |

| Leader | When you send your Spirit they are created: |
| B (group 2) | **and you renew the face of the earth.** |

All	**Glory to the Father, and to the Son,**
	and to the Holy Spirit:
	as it was in the beginning, is now,
	and shall be forever. Amen.

Cast: **Leader, All** (the entire congregation), **A** (group 1—part of the congregation), **B** (group 2—part of the congregation)

Praise the Lord, My Soul

From Psalm 104:1–34 (choral version)

All	Praise the LORD, O my soul.
	O LORD my God, you are very great—
Light people	you are clothed with splendor and majesty.
Sky people	He wraps himself in light as with a garment;
	he stretches out the heavens like a tent
	and lays the beams of his upper chambers on their waters.

	He makes the clouds his chariot and rides on the wings of the wind.
Light people	He makes winds his messengers, flames of fire his servants.
Deep voices	He set the earth on its foundations; it can never be moved.
Water people	You covered it with the deep as with a garment; the waters stood above the mountains.
Deep voices	At your rebuke—
Water people	The waters fled.
Deep voices	At the sound of your thunder—
Water people	they took to flight. They flowed over the mountains, they went down into the valleys, to the place you assigned for them.
Deep voices	You set a boundary they cannot cross; never again will they cover the earth.
Water people	He makes springs pour water into the ravines; it flows between the mountains.
Animals	They give water to all the beasts of the field; the wild donkeys quench their thirst.
Birds	The birds of the air nest by the waters; they sing among the branches.
Sky people	He waters the mountains from his upper chambers; the earth is satisfied by the fruit of his work.
Animals	He makes grass grow for the cattle—
Man	And plants for man to cultivate— bringing forth food from the earth:
Woman	Wine that gladdens the heart of man—
Man	Oil—
Woman	To make his face shine.
Man	Bread—
Woman	That sustains his heart.
Deep voices	The trees of the LORD—
Water people	Are well watered.
Deep voices	The cedars of Lebanon that he planted.

Birds	There the birds make their nests; the stork has its home in the pine trees.
Animals	The high mountains belong to the wild goats; the crags are a refuge for the coneys.
Light people	The moon marks off the seasons, and the sun knows when to go down.
Deep voices	You bring darkness, it becomes night—
Animals	And all the beasts of the forest prowl. The lions roar for their prey and seek their food from God.
Light people	The sun rises—
Animals	And they steal away; they return and lie down in their dens.

Man and
  Woman
	Then man goes out to his work,
	    to his labor until evening.

All	How many are your works, O Lord!
	    In wisdom you made them all;
	    the earth is full of your creatures.

Water people	There is the sea, vast and spacious—
Animals	Teeming with creatures beyond number— living things both large and small.
Man	There the ships go to and fro—
Deep voices	And the leviathan—
Animals	Which you formed to frolic there.
Woman	These all look to you to give them their food at the proper time.
Man	When you give it to them, they gather it up—
All	When you open your hand, they are satisfied with good things.
Man	When you hide your face, they are terrified—
All	When you take away their breath, (PAUSE) they die—
Man	And return to the dust.
Woman	When you send your Spirit—

All	They are created—
Woman	And you renew the face of the earth.
Light people	May the glory of the LORD endure forever—
Animals	May the LORD rejoice in his works—
Deep voices	He who looks at the earth, and it trembles, who touches the mountains—
Sky and water people	And they smoke.
Man	I will sing to the LORD all my life—
Woman	I will sing praise to my God as long as I live.
All	May my meditation be pleasing to him, as [we] rejoice in the LORD.

Cast: **Light people, Sky people, Deep voices, Water people, Animals, Birds, Man, Woman.** (This reading is arranged for choral speaking. Properties—such as torches/lamps for light people, blue cloth for sky and water people, costumes for animals—can be used by children. See also short version above.)

God and His People

From Psalm 105:1–45 (LIT)

Leader 1 A (group 1)	Give thanks to the Lord, praise his name: **tell the nations what he has done.**
Leader 2 B (group 2)	Sing to him, sing praise to him: **tell of all his wonderful deeds.**
Leader 3 C (group 3)	Glory in his holy name: **let all who worship him rejoice.**
Leader 1 A (group 1)	Go to the Lord for help: **and worship him forever.**
Leader 2 B (group 2)	Remember the wonders he does: **the miracles he performs.**
Leader 3 C (group 3)	He is the Lord our God: **he judges the whole wide earth.**
Leader 1 A (group 1)	He keeps his word and covenant: **for a thousand generations.**
Leader 2 B (group 2)	The covenant he made with Abraham: **the oath he swore to Israel.**

Leader 3	He brought them out of Egypt:
C (group 3)	**and none of them was lost.**
Leader 1	He gave a cloud for covering:
A (group 1)	**a pillar of fire by night.**
Leader 2	He gave them bread from heaven:
B (group 2)	**and water from the rock.**
Leader 3	He brought his people out rejoicing:
C (group 3)	**his chosen ones with shouts of joy.**
All	**Praise the Lord!**
All	**Glory to the Father, and to the Son,** **and to the Holy Spirit:** **as it was in the beginning, is now,** **and shall be forever. Amen.**

Cast: **Leader 1**, **A** (group 1—part of the congregation), **Leader 2**, **B** (group 2—part of the congregation), **Leader 3**, **C** (part of the congregation), **All** (the entire congregation). **Leaders** may be ministers.

In Praise of God's Goodness

From Psalm 107:1–31 (LIT)

Leader	Give thanks to the Lord, for he is good:
All	**his love endures forever.**
Leader	Repeat these words in praise to the Lord:
All	**all those he has redeemed.**
Leader	Some sailed the ocean in ships:
A (group 1)	**they earned their way on the seas.**
Leader	They saw what the Lord can do:
B (group 2)	**his wonderful deeds in the deep.**
Leader	For he spoke and stirred up a storm:
A (group 1)	**and lifted high the waves.**
Leader	Their ships were thrown in the air:
B (group 2)	**and plunged into the depths.**
Leader	Their courage melted away:
A (group 1)	**they reeled like drunken men.**
Leader	They came to the end of themselves:
B (group 2)	**and cried to the Lord in their trouble.**
Leader	He brought them out of distress:
A (group 1)	**and stilled the raging storm.**

Leader B (group 2)	They were glad because of the calm: **he brought them safely to harbor.**
Leader All	Let them give thanks to the Lord: **for his unfailing love.**
All	**Glory to the Father, and to the Son, and to the Holy Spirit: as it was in the beginning, is now, and shall be forever. Amen.**

Cast: **Leader, All** (the entire congregation), **A** (group 1—part of the congregation), **B** (group 2—part of the congregation)

The Lord and His Chosen King

Psalm 110:1–7

Psalmist	The Lord says to my Lord:
The Lord (voice only)	Sit at my right hand until I make your enemies a footstool for your feet.
Psalmist	The Lord will extend your mighty scepter from Zion; [he says:]
The Lord (voice)	You will rule in the midst of your enemies.
Psalmist	Your troops will be willing on your day of battle. Arrayed in holy majesty, from the womb of the dawn you will receive the dew of your youth. The Lord has sworn and will not change his mind:
The Lord (voice)	You are a priest forever, in the order of Melchizedek.
Psalmist	The Lord is at your right hand; he will crush kings on the day of his wrath. He will judge the nations, heaping up the dead and crushing the rulers of the whole earth. He will drink from a brook beside the way; therefore he will lift up his head.

Cast: **Psalmist, the Lord** (voice only)

In Praise of the Lord

From Psalm 111:1–10 (LIT)

Leader	Praise the Lord:
All	**praise the Lord!**
Leader	With my whole heart I will thank the Lord: in the company of his people. Great are the works of the Lord:
A (group 1)	**those who wonder, seek them.**
Leader	Glorious and majestic are his deeds:
B (group 2)	**his goodness lasts forever.**
Leader	He reminds us of his works of grace:
A (group 1)	**he is merciful and kind.**
Leader	He sustains those who fear him:
B (group 2)	**he keeps his covenant always.**
Leader	All he does is right and just:
A (group 1)	**all his words are faithful.**
Leader	They will last for ever and ever:
B (group 2)	**and be kept in faith and truth.**
Leader	He provided redemption for his people, and made an eternal covenant with them:
All	**holy and awesome is his name!**
Leader	The fear of the Lord is the beginning of wisdom; he gives understanding to those who obey:
All	**to God belongs eternal praise!**
All	**Glory to the Father, and to the Son, and to the Holy Spirit: as it was in the beginning, is now, and shall be forever. Amen.**

Cast: **Leader, All** (the entire congregation), **A** (group 1—part of the congregation), **B** (group 2—part of the congregation)

In Praise of the Lord's Goodness

From Psalm 113:1–9 (LIT)

Leader 1	Praise the Lord:
All	**praise the Lord!**
Leader 2	You servants of the Lord, praise his name:
All	**the name of the Lord be praised, both now and evermore!**

Leader 1	From the rising of the sun to the place where it sets:
All	**the name of the Lord be praised!**
Leader 2	The Lord is exalted above the earth:
All	**his glory over the heavens.**
Leader 1	Who is like the Lord our God?
All	**He is throned in the heights above—**
Leader 2	Yet he bends down:
All	**yet he stoops to look at our world.**
Leader 1	He raises the poor from the dust:
All	**and lifts the needy from their sorrow.**
Leader 2	He honors the childless wife in her home:
All	**he makes her happy, the mother of children.**
Leaders 1 and 2	Praise the Lord:
All	**Amen.**

Cast: **Leader 1**, **Leader 2**, **All** (two or more persons/congregation). **Leaders** may be ministers

A Passover Song

Psalm 114:1–8

Psalmist	When Israel came out of Egypt,
	the house of Jacob from a people of foreign tongue,
	Judah became God's sanctuary,
	Israel his dominion.
Worshiper 1	The sea looked and fled,
	the Jordan turned back.
Worshiper 2	The mountains skipped like rams,
	the hills like lambs.
Enquirer 1	Why was it, O sea, that you fled?
Enquirer 2	O Jordan, that you turned back?
Enquirer 1	You mountains, that you skipped like rams?
Enquirer 2	You hills, like lambs?
Psalmist	Tremble, O earth, at the presence of the Lord,
	at the presence of the God of Jacob,
	who turned the rock into a pool,
	the hard rock into springs of water.

Cast: **Psalmist, Worshiper 1, Worshiper 2, Enquirer 1, Enquirer 2**

The One True God

Psalm 115:1–18

Psalmist   Not to us, O Lord, not to us
                       but to your name be the glory,
                       because of your love and faithfulness. (PAUSE)

Worshiper 1   Why do the nations say:

Enquirer   Where is their God?

Worshiper 1   Our God is in heaven;
                       he does whatever pleases him.
                   But their idols are silver and gold,
                       made by the hands of men.

Worshiper 2   They have mouths, but cannot speak,
                       eyes, but they cannot see.

Worshiper 1   They have ears, but cannot hear,
                       noses, but they cannot smell.

Worshiper 2   They have hands, but cannot feel,
                       feet, but they cannot walk;
                       nor can they utter a sound with their throats.

Psalmist   Those who make them will be like them,
                       and so will all who trust in them. (PAUSE)

                   O house of Israel, trust in the Lord—

**Worshipers
1 and 2**   He is their help and shield.

Psalmist   O house of Aaron, trust in the Lord—

**Priests
1 and 2**   He is their help and shield.

Psalmist   You who fear him, trust in the Lord—

**Worshipers
1 and 2**   He is their help and shield.

Psalmist   The Lord remembers us and will bless us:
                       He will bless the house of Israel,
                       he will bless the house of Aaron,
                   he will bless those who fear the Lord—
                       small and great alike.

Priest 1   May the Lord make you increase,
                       both you and your children.

Priest 2   May you be blessed by the Lord,
                       the Maker of heaven and earth.

Psalmist	The highest heavens belong to the LORD,
	    but the earth he has given to man.
	It is not the dead who praise the LORD,
	    those who go down to silence;
	it is we who extol the LORD,
	    both now and forevermore.

	Praise the LORD.

Cast: **Psalmist, Worshiper 1, Enquirer, Worshiper 2, Priest 1** (can be the same as Enquirer), **Priest 2** (can be the same as Priest 1)

A Testimony of Salvation

Psalm 116:1–19

Psalmist	I love the LORD, for he heard my voice;
	    he heard my cry for mercy.
	Because he turned his ear to me,
	    I will call on him as long as I live.

	The cords of death entangled me,
	    the anguish of the grave came upon me;
	    I was overcome by trouble and sorrow.
	Then I called on the name of the LORD:

Young psalmist	O LORD, save me!

Psalmist	The LORD is gracious and righteous;
	    our God is full of compassion.
	The LORD protects the simplehearted;
	    when I was in great need, he saved me.

	Be at rest once more, O my soul, for the LORD has been good to you.

	For you, O LORD, have delivered my soul from death,
	    my eyes from tears,
	    my feet from stumbling,
	that I may walk before the LORD
	    in the land of the living.
	I believed; therefore I said:

Young psalmist	I am greatly afflicted.
Psalmist	And in my dismay I said:

Young
    psalmist
    (bitterly)
	All men are liars.

Psalmist	How can I repay the LORD
	    for all his goodness to me?
	I will lift up the cup of salvation
	    and call on the name of the LORD.
	I will fulfill my vows to the LORD
	    in the presence of all his people. (PAUSE)

Precious in the sight of the LORD
    is the death of his saints.
O LORD, truly I am your servant;
    I am your servant, the son of your maidservant;
    you have freed me from my chains.

I will sacrifice a thank offering to you
    and call on the name of the LORD.
I will fulfill my vows to the LORD
    in the presence of all his people,
in the courts of the house of the LORD—
    in your midst, O Jerusalem.

Psalmist and
  Young
  psalmist   Praise the LORD.

Cast: **Psalmist, Young psalmist**

Praising God, Who Saves from Death

From Psalm 116:1–19 (LIT)

Leader   I love the Lord because he heard my voice:
A (group 1) **the Lord in mercy listened to my prayers.**

Leader   Because the Lord has turned his ear to me:
B (group 2) **I'll call on him as long as I shall live.**

Leader   The cords of death entangled me around:
C (group 3) **the horrors of the grave came over me.**

Leader   But then I called upon the Lord my God:
A (group 1) **I said to him: "O Lord, I beg you, save!"**

Leader   The Lord our God is merciful and good:
B (group 2) **the Lord protects the simple-hearted ones.**

Leader   The Lord saved me from death and stopped my tears:
C (group 3) **he saved me from defeat and picked me up.**

Leader   And so I walk before him all my days:
A (group 1) **and live to love and praise his holy name.**

| Leader | What shall I give the Lord for all his grace? |
| B (group 2) | **I'll take his saving cup, and pay my vows.** |

| Leader | Within the congregation of his saints: |
| C (group 3) | **I'll offer him my sacrifice of praise.** |

| Leader | Praise the Lord: |
| All | **Amen, amen!** |

Cast: **Leader, A** (group 1—part of the congregation), **B** (group 2—part of the congregation), **C** (group 3—part of the congregation), **All** (the entire congregation)

In Praise of the Lord

From Psalm 117:1–2 (LIT)

| Leader | Praise the Lord, all you nations: |
| A (group 1) | **praise him, all you people!** |

| Leader | Great is his love towards us: |
| B (group 2) | **his faithfulness shall last forever.** |

| Leader | Praise the Lord: |
| All | **Amen.** |

Cast: **Leader, A** (group 1—part of the congregation), **B** (group 2—part of the congregation), **All** (the entire congregation)

A Prayer of Thanks for Victory

Psalm 118:1–29

Leader	Give thanks to the LORD, for he is good;
	his love endures forever.
	Let Israel say:

| Worshipers | |
| 1 and 2 | His love endures forever. |

| Leader | Let the house of Aaron say: |

| Priests | |
| 1 and 2 | His love endures forever. |

| Leader | Let those who fear the LORD say: |

| Worshipers | |
| and **Priests** | His love endures forever. |

| Worshiper 1 | In my anguish I cried to the LORD, |
| | and he answered by setting me free. |

121

Worshiper 2	The LORD is with me; I will not be afraid.
	What can man do to me?
Worshiper 1	The LORD is with me; he is my helper.
	I will look in triumph on my enemies.
Worshiper 2	It is better to take refuge in the LORD
	than to trust in man.
Worshiper 1	It is better to take refuge in the LORD
	than to trust in princes.
	All the nations surrounded me—
Worshiper 2	But in the name of the LORD I cut them off.
Worshiper 1	They surrounded me on every side—
Worshiper 2	But in the name of the LORD I cut them off.
Worshiper 1	They swarmed around me like bees,
	but they died out as quickly as burning thorns.
Worshiper 2	In the name of the LORD I cut them off.
Worshiper 1	I was pushed back and about to fall—
Worshiper 2	But the LORD helped me.
Worshiper 1	The LORD is my strength and my song—
Worshiper 1 and 2	He has become my salvation. (PAUSE)
Victor (at a distance)	Shouts of joy and victory resound in the tents of the righteous:
Worshipers 1 and 2	The LORD's right hand has done mighty things!
Victor (at a distance)	The LORD's right hand is lifted high— the LORD's right hand has done mighty things!
Worshiper 1	I will not die but live, and will proclaim what the LORD has done.
Worshiper 2	The LORD has chastened me severely, but he has not given me over to death.
Victor (at a distance)	Open for me the gates of righteousness; I will enter and give thanks to the LORD.

Priest 1	This is the gate of the LORD through which the righteous may enter.
Victor (closer)	I will give you thanks, for you answered me; you have become my salvation.
Leader	The stone the builders rejected has become the capstone.
Priests **1 and 2**	The LORD has done this, and it is marvelous in our eyes.
Leader	This is the day the LORD has made; let us rejoice and be glad in it.
Worshipers **1 and 2**	O LORD, save us!
Worshipers and **Priests**	O LORD, grant us success.
Priest 1	Blessed is he who comes in the name of the LORD.
Priest 2	From the house of the LORD we bless you.
Worshipers **1 and 2**	The LORD is God, and he has made his light shine upon us.
Leader	With boughs in hand, join in the festal procession up to the horns of the altar.
Victor (near cast)	You are my God, and I will give you thanks; you are my God, and I will exalt you.
Leader	Give thanks to the LORD, for he is good—
Victor, **Worshipers** and **Priests**	His love endures forever.

Cast: **Leader, Worshiper 1, Worshiper 2, Priest 1, Priest 2, Victor.** (The Victor should begin at the back of the audience/congregation—or outside a door—and move forward in two stages as indicated.)

A Prayer of Thanks for Victory

Psalm 118:1–29 (LIT)

Minister	Give thanks to the Lord, for he is good:
All	**his love endures forever.**

| Minister | All those who fear the Lord shall say: |
| All | **his love endures forever.** |

| Worshiper | Open for me the gates of the temple; I will go in and give thanks to the Lord. |

| Minister | This is the gate of the Lord, only the righteous can come in. |

| Worshiper | I will give thanks because you heard me; you have become my salvation. |

| Choir | The stone which the builders rejected as worthless turned out to be the most important of all. |
| All | **The Lord has done this—what a wonderful sight it is!** |

| Worshiper | This is the day of the Lord's victory—let us be happy, let us celebrate: |
| All | **O Lord, save us—O Lord, grant us success.** |

| Minister | May God bless the one who comes in the name of the Lord: |
| All | **The Lord is God—he has been good to us!** |

| Choir | From the temple of the Lord, we bless you. |

| Director (matter-of-fact tone) | With branches in your hands, start the procession and march round the altar: |

| Worshiper | You are my God and I will give you thanks: |
| All | **You are my God, and I will exalt you.** |

| Minister | Give thanks to the Lord, for he is good: |
| All | **His love endures forever. Amen.** |

Cast: **Minister**, **All** (the entire congregation), **Worshiper** (from doorway, then moving through congregation), **Choir** or **chorus**, **Director**

The Lord, Our Protector

Psalm 121:1–8

| Pilgrim | I lift up my eyes to the hills— where does my help come from? (PAUSE) My help comes from the LORD, the Maker of heaven and earth. |

| Adviser 1 | He will not let your foot slip— he who watches over you will not slumber. |

| Adviser 2 | Indeed, he who watches over Israel will neither slumber nor sleep. |

| Adviser 1 | The LORD watches over you— the LORD is your shade at your right hand. |

124

Adviser 2	The sun will not harm you by day, nor the moon by night.
Adviser 1	The LORD will keep you from all harm— he will watch over your life.
Adviser 2	The LORD will watch over your coming and going both now and forevermore.

Cast: **Pilgrim, Adviser 1, Adviser 2**

In Praise of Jerusalem

From Psalm 122:1–8 (LIT)

Leader	I was glad when they said to me:
All	**let us go to the house of the Lord!**
Leader	Pray for the peace of Jerusalem:
A (group 1)	**may those who love our land be blessed.**
Leader	May there be peace in your homes:
B (group 2)	**and safety for our families.**
Leader	For the sake of those we love we say:
All	**Let there be peace!**
All	**Glory to the Father, and to the Son, and to the Holy Spirit: as it was in the beginning, is now, and shall be forever. Amen.**

Cast: **Leader, All** (the entire congregation), **A** (group 1—male voices), **B** (group 2—female voices)

God, the Protector of His People

Psalm 124:1–8

Leader	If the LORD had not been on our side— let Israel say:
Worshiper 1	If the LORD had not been on our side when men attacked us.
Worshiper 2	When their anger flared against us, they would have swallowed us alive.
Worshiper 3	The flood would have engulfed us.
Worshiper 2	The torrent would have swept over us.
Worshiper 3	The raging waters would have swept us away.

Leader	Praise be to the Lord, who has not let us be torn by their teeth.
Worshiper 1	We have escaped like a bird out of the fowler's snare.
Worshiper 2	The snare has been broken, and we have escaped.
Cast	Our help is in the name of the Lord, the Maker of heaven and earth.

Cast: **Leader, Worshiper 1, Worshiper 2, Worshiper 3**

God, the Protector of His People

Psalm 124:1–8 (LIT)

Leader	If the Lord had not been on our side—now let Israel say:
All	**If the Lord had not been on our side—**
A (group 1)	**when enemies attacked us,**
B (group 2)	**when their anger flared against us,**
C (group 3)	**they would have swallowed us alive.**
A (group 1)	**The flood would have engulfed us,**
B (group 2)	**the torrent would have swept over us,**
C (group 3)	**the waters would have drowned us.**
Leader	Praise the Lord:
A (group 1)	**who has not given us up to their teeth.**
B (group 2)	**We have escaped like a bird from the snare:**
C (group 3)	**the snare is broken and we are free.**
Leader	Our help is in the name of the Lord:
All	**who made heaven and earth. Amen.**

Cast: **Leader, All** (the entire congregation), **A** (group 1—part of the congregation), **B** (group 2—part of the congregation), **C** (group 3—part of the congregation)

A Prayer for Deliverance

Psalm 126:1–6

Worshiper 1	When the Lord brought back the captives to Zion, we were like men who dreamed.
Worshiper 2	Our mouths were filled with laughter, our tongues with songs of joy.
Worshiper 1	Then it was said among the nations:
Person(s)	The Lord has done great things for them.

Worshiper 1	The LORD has done great things for us!
Worshipers **1** and **2**	We are filled with joy.
Exile 1	Restore our fortunes, O LORD, like streams in the Negev.
Exile 2	Those who sow in tears will reap with songs of joy.

Psalmist	He who goes out weeping,
	   carrying seed to sow,
	will return with songs of joy,
	   carrying sheaves with him.

Cast: **Worshiper 1, Worshiper 2, Person(s), Exile 1, Exile 2, Psalmist** (can be the same as Worshiper 1)

A Prayer for Deliverance

From Psalm 126:1–6 (LIT)

Leader **A** (group 1)	When the Lord brought us back from slavery: **we were like those who dream.**
Leader **B** (group 2)	Our mouths were filled with laughter: **our tongues with songs of joy.**
Leader **A** (group 1)	Then those around us said, "The Lord has done great things for them": **The Lord has done great things for us,** **and we are filled with joy.**
Leader **B** (group 2)	Those who sow in tears **shall reap with songs of joy.**
All	**[Glory to the Father, and to the Son,** **and to the Holy Spirit:** **as it was in the beginning, is now,** **and shall be forever. Amen.]**

Cast: **Leader, A** (group 1—part of congregation), **B** (group 2—part of congregation), **All** (the entire congregation)

The Reward of Obedience to the Lord

Psalm 128:1–6

Psalmist	Blessed are all who fear the LORD, who walk in his ways.

Teacher 1	You will eat the fruit of your labor; blessings and prosperity will be yours.
Teacher 2	Your wife will be like a fruitful vine within your house—
Teacher 1	Your sons will be like olive shoots around your table.
Psalmist	Thus is the man blessed who fears the LORD.
Priest 1	May the LORD bless you from Zion all the days of your life.
Priest 2	May you see the prosperity of Jerusalem, and may you live to see your children's children.
Priests 1 and 2	Peace be upon Israel.

Cast: **Psalmist, Teacher 1, Teacher 2** (can be the same as Psalmist), **Priest 1, Priest 2**

The Reward of Obedience to the Lord

From Psalm 128:1–6 (LIT)

Leader	The pilgrims' song:
A (group 1)	**Blessed are those who fear the Lord,**
B (group 2)	**who walk in his ways.**
Leader	You will eat the fruit of your work; blessings and prosperity will be yours:
A (group 1)	**Blessed are those who fear the Lord,**
B (group 2)	**who walk in his ways.**
Leader	Your wife will be like a fruitful vine within your house; your children will be like young olive trees around your table:
A (group 1)	**Blessed are those who fear the Lord,**
B (group 2)	**who walk in his ways.**
Leader	May the Lord bless you all the days of your life; may you have prosperity; may you live to see your children's children:
All	**Peace be with you. Amen.**

Cast: **Leader, A** (group 1—part of the congregation), **B** (group 2—part of the congregation), **All** (the entire congregation)

A Psalm about Israel's Enemies

Psalm 129:1–8

Leader   [Israel, tell us how your enemies have persecuted you ever since you were young.]

Israel   They have greatly oppressed me from my youth,
            but they have not gained the victory over me.
        Plowmen have plowed my back
            and made their furrows long.
        But the LORD is righteous;
            he has cut me free from the cords of the wicked.

Leader   May all who hate Zion
            be turned back in shame.
        May they be like grass on the roof,
            which withers before it can grow;
        with it the reaper cannot fill his hands,
            nor the one who gathers fill his arms.
        May those who pass by not say:

Person 1   The blessing of the LORD be upon you.

Person 2   We bless you in the name of the LORD.

Cast: **Leader, Israel, Person 1, Person 2** (can be the same as Person 1)

A Prayer for Help

Psalm 130:1–8

Supplicant   Out of the depths I cry to you, O LORD;
        O Lord, hear my voice.
        Let your ears be attentive
           to my cry for mercy.

Psalmist   If you, O LORD, kept a record of sins,
           O Lord, who could stand?
        But with you there is forgiveness;
           therefore you are feared.

Supplicant   I wait for the LORD, my soul waits,
           and in his word I put my hope.
        My soul waits for the Lord
           more than watchmen wait for the morning.

Cast   More than watchmen wait for the morning.

Psalmist	O Israel, put your hope in the LORD,
	for with the LORD is unfailing love
	and with him is full redemption.
	He himself will redeem Israel
	from all their sins.

Cast: **Supplicant, Psalmist**

In Praise of the Temple

Psalm 132:1–18

Psalmist	O LORD, remember David
	and all the hardships he endured.

He swore an oath to the LORD
and made a vow to the Mighty One of Jacob.

David	I will not enter my house
	or go to my bed—

I will allow no sleep to my eyes,
no slumber to my eyelids,
till I find a place for the LORD,
a dwelling for the Mighty One of Jacob.

Psalmist	We heard it in Ephrathah,
	we came upon it in the fields of Jaar:
	[We said:]

Person 1	Let us go to his dwelling place.

Person 2	Let us worship at his footstool.

Psalmist	Arise, O LORD, and come to your resting place,
	you and the ark of your might.

May your priests be clothed with righteousness;
may your saints sing for joy.

For the sake of David your servant,
do not reject your anointed one.

The LORD swore an oath to David,
a sure oath that he will not revoke:

The Lord
(voice only) One of your own descendants
I will place on your throne—
if your sons keep my covenant
and the statutes I teach them,
then their sons will sit
on your throne for ever and ever.

Psalmist   For the L ORD has chosen Zion,
                    he has desired it for his dwelling:

The Lord
(voice)   This is my resting place for ever and ever;
                    here I will sit enthroned, for I have desired it—
                 I will bless her with abundant provisions;
                    her poor will I satisfy with food.
                 I will clothe her priests with salvation,
                    and her saints will ever sing for joy.

                 Here I will make a horn grow for David
                    and set up a lamp for my anointed one.
                 I will clothe his enemies with shame,
                    but the crown on his head will be resplendent.

Cast: **Psalmist, David, Person 1, Person 2** (can be the same as Person 1), **the Lord** (voice only)

A Call to Praise the Lord

From Psalm 134:1–3 (LIT)

Leader   You servants of the Lord,
                    who stand in his temple at night:
A (group 1) **praise the Lord!**

Leader   Lift your hands in prayer to the Lord:
B (group 2) **in his sanctuary, praise the Lord!**

Leader   May the Lord who made the heaven and earth
                    bless you from Zion:
All   **Amen!**

All   **Glory to the Father, and to the Son,**
                 and to the Holy Spirit:
                 as it was in the beginning, is now,
                 and shall be forever. Amen.

Cast: **Leader, A** (group 1—part of the congregation), **B** (group 2—part of the congregation), **All** (the entire congregation)

A Hymn of Praise

Psalm 135:1–21

Psalmist   Praise the L ORD.

131

Praise the name of the LORD;
    praise him, you servants of the LORD,
you who minister in the house of the LORD,
    in the courts of the house of our God.

Praise the LORD, for the LORD is good;
    sing praise to his name, for that is pleasant.
For the LORD has chosen Jacob to be his own,
    Israel to be his treasured possession.

Worshiper   I know that the LORD is great,
    that our Lord is greater than all gods.
The LORD does whatever pleases him,
    in the heavens and on the earth,
    in the seas and all their depths.
He makes clouds rise from the ends of the earth;
    he sends lightning with the rain
    and brings out the wind from his storehouses.

Psalmist   He struck down the firstborn of Egypt,
    the firstborn of men and animals.
He sent his signs and wonders into your midst, O Egypt,
    against Pharaoh and all his servants.
He struck down many nations
    and killed mighty kings—
Sihon king of the Amorites,
    Og king of Bashan
    and all the kings of Canaan—
and he gave their land as an inheritance,
    an inheritance to his people Israel. (PAUSE)

Worshiper   Your name, O LORD, endures forever,
    your renown, O LORD, through all generations.

Psalmist   The LORD will vindicate his people
    and have compassion on his servants.

The idols of the nations are silver and gold,
    made by the hands of men.
They have mouths, but cannot speak,
    eyes, but they cannot see;
they have ears, but cannot hear,
    nor is there breath in their mouths.

Worshiper   Those who make them will be like them,
    and so will all who trust in them.

Psalmist   O house of Israel, praise the LORD!

Worshiper   O house of Aaron, praise the LORD!

Psalmist   O house of Levi, praise the LORD!

Psalmist and
Worshiper   You who fear him, praise the LORD.

Worshiper   Praise be to the LORD from Zion,
                   to him who dwells in Jerusalem.

Psalmist and
Worshiper   Praise the LORD.

Cast: **Psalmist, Worshiper**

A Hymn of Thanksgiving

From Psalm 136:1–26 (LIT)

Leader 1   Give thanks to God, for he is good:
A (group 1)   **his love shall last forever!**

Leader 2   Give thanks to him, the God of gods:
B (group 2)   **his love shall last forever!**

Leader 3   Give thanks to him, the Lord of lords:
C (group 3)   **his love shall last forever!**

Leader 1   For God alone works miracles:
A (group 1)   **his love shall last forever!**

Leader 2   The skies were made at his command:
B (group 2)   **his love shall last forever!**

Leader 3   He spread the seas upon the earth:
C (group 3)   **his love shall last forever!**

Leader 1   He made the sun to shine by day:
A (group 1)   **his love shall last forever!**

Leader 2   He brought us out from slavery:
B (group 2)   **his love shall last forever!**

Leader 3   He leads us onward by his grace:
C (group 3)   **his love shall last forever!**

Leader 1   He saves us from our enemies:
A (group 1)   **his love shall last forever!**

Leader 2   Give thinks to God, for he is good:
B (group 2)   **his love shall last forever!**
All   **Amen!**

Cast: **Leader 1, A** (group 1—part of the congregation), **Leader 2, B** (group 2—part of the congregation), **Leader 3, C** (group 3—part of congregation), **All** (the entire congregation). This reading should not be used with a congregation unless it is divided into three parts. The congregation may read an entire stanza (i.e., the words here divided between a leader and a group).

A Lament of Israelites in Exile

From Psalm 137:1–8

Israelite 1   By the rivers of Babylon we sat and wept
    when we remembered Zion.

Israelite 2   There on the poplars
    we hung our harps.

Israelite 1   There our captors asked us for songs,
    our tormentors demanded songs of joy;
    they said:

Enemies   Sing us one of the songs of Zion!

Israelite 1   How can we sing the songs of the LORD
    while in a foreign land?

Israelite 2   If I forget you, O Jerusalem,
    may my right hand forget ⌞its skill⌟.

Israelite 1   May my tongue cling to the roof of my mouth
    if I do not remember you,
    if I do not consider Jerusalem
    my highest joy.

Israelite 2   Remember, O LORD, what the Edomites did
    on the day Jerusalem fell:

Enemies   Tear it down, . . .
    tear it down to its foundations!

**Israelites
  1 and 2**   O Daughter of Babylon!

Israelite 1   Doomed to destruction! . . .

Cast: **Israelite 1, Israelite 2, Enemies** (two or more)

Prayer for the Help of God's Spirit

From Psalm 143:6–10 and Psalm 51:6–12 (LIT)

Leader   O Lord, I spread my hands out to you:
A (group 1) **I thirst for you like dry ground.**

Leader   Teach me to do your will, for you are my God:
B (group 2) **let your good Spirit lead me in safety.**

Leader   You require sincerity and truth in me:
A (group 1) **fill my mind with your wisdom.**

Leader	Create in me a pure heart, O God:
B (group 2)	**and renew a faithful spirit in me.**
Leader	Do not cast me from your presence:
A (group 1)	**or take your Holy Spirit from me.**
Leader	Give me again the joy of your salvation:
B (group 2)	**and make me willing to obey.**
All	**Glory to the Father, and to the Son,** **and to the Holy Spirit:** **as it was in the beginning, is now,** **and shall be forever. Amen.**

Cast: **Leader**, **A** (group 1—part of the congregation), **B** (group 2—part of the congregation), **All** (the entire congregation). *(Psalms 143 and 151 have been grouped together to provide for an occasion when the person and work of the Holy Spirit are being considered.)*

In Praise of God the Almighty

From Psalm 147:1–20 (LIT)

Leader	O praise the Lord, sing out to God:
All	**such praise is right and good.**
Leader	The Lord restores Jerusalem:
A (group 1)	**he brings the exiles home.**
Leader	He heals all those with broken hearts:
B (group 2)	**he bandages their wounds.**
Leader	He counts the number of the stars:
C (group 3)	**he calls them each by name.**
Leader	How great and mighty is the Lord:
A (group 1)	**immeasurably wise!**
Leader	He raises up the humble ones:
B (group 2)	**and brings the mighty down.**
Leader	Sing hymns of triumph to his name:
C (group 3)	**make music to our God!**
Leader	He spreads the clouds across the sky:
A (group 1)	**he showers the earth with rain.**
Leader	He sends the animals their food:
B (group 2)	**he feeds the hungry birds.**
Leader	His true delight is not the strong:
C (group 3)	**but those who trust his love.**

135

Leader	Extol the Lord, Jerusalem:
A (group 1)	**Let Zion worship God!**
Leader	For God shall keep your people safe:
B (group 2)	**and bring your harvest home.**
Leader	He gives commandment to the earth:
C (group 3)	**his will is quickly done.**
Leader	He spreads like wool the falling snow:
A (group 1)	**how cold the frosty air!**
Leader	He sends the wind, the warming rain:
B (group 2)	**and melts the ice away.**
Leader	His laws he gives to Israel:
C (group 3)	**and Judah hears his word.**
Leader	He does not favor other lands:
All	**so, praise the Lord. Amen!**

Cast: **Leader, All** (the entire congregation), **A** (group 1—part of the congregation), **B** (group 2—part of the congregation), **C** (group 3—part of the congregation)

Let the Universe Praise God!

From Psalm 148:1–14 (LIT)

Leader	Praise the LORD! Praise the LORD from the heavens:
All	**praise him in the heights above.**
Leader	Praise him, all his angels:
A (group 1)	**praise him, all his heavenly hosts.**
Leader	Praise him, sun and moon:
B (group 2)	**praise him, all you shining stars. . . .**
Leader	Let them praise the name of the LORD:
All	**Praise the Lord!**
Leader	Praise the Lord from the earth:
A (group 1)	**praise him, great sea creatures.**
Leader	Praise him, storms and clouds:
B (group 2)	**praise him, mountains and hills.**
Leader	Praise him, fields and woods:
A (group 1)	**praise him, animals and birds.**
Leader	Praise him, rulers and nations:
B (group 2)	**praise him, old and young.**

| Leader | Let them praise the name of the Lord: |
| All | **Praise the Lord! Amen.** |

Cast: **Leader, All** (the entire congregation), **A** (group 1—part of the congregation), **B** (group 2—part of the congregation)

A Hymn of Praise

Psalm 149:1–9 (LIT)

| Leader | Praise the Lord: |
| All | **praise the Lord!** |

| Leader | Sing a new song to the Lord: |
| A (group 1) | **let the people shout his name!** |

| Leader | Praise your maker, Israel: |
| B (group 2) | **hail your king, Jerusalem.** |

| Leader | Sing and dance to honor him: |
| A (group 1) | **praise him with the strings and drums.** |

| Leader | God takes pleasure in his saints: |
| B (group 2) | **crowns the meek with victory.** |

| Leader | Rise, you saints, in triumph now: |
| A (group 1) | **sing the joyful night away!** |

| Leader | Shout aloud and praise your God! |
| B (group 2) | **Hold aloft the two-edged sword!** |

| Leader | Let the judgment now begin: |
| A (group 1) | **kings shall fail and tyrants die.** |

| Leader | Through his people, by his word: |
| B (group 2) | **God shall have the victory!** |

| Leader | Praise the Lord: |
| All | **praise the Lord!** |

All	**Glory to the Father, and to the Son,**
	and to the Holy Spirit:
	as it was in the beginning, is now,
	and shall be forever. Amen.

Cast: **Leader, All** (the entire congregation), **A** (group 1—part of the congregation [and ministers]), **B** (group 2—part of the congregation [and ministers])

A Hymn of Praise

Psalm 149:1–9

Cast   Praise the LORD.

Leader 1   Sing to the LORD a new song,
        his praise in the assembly of the saints.

Leader 2   Let Israel rejoice in their Maker;
        let the people of Zion be glad in their King.

Leader 1   Let them praise his name with dancing;
        and make music to him with tambourine and harp.

Psalmist   The LORD takes delight in his people;
        he crowns the humble with salvation.

Leader 1   Let the saints rejoice in this honor
        and sing for joy on their beds.

    May the praise of God be in their mouths
        and a double-edged sword in their hands,
    to inflict vengeance on the nations
        and punishment on the peoples,
    to bind their kings with fetters,
        their nobles with shackles of iron,
    to carry out the sentence written against them.

Psalmist   This is the glory of all his saints.

Cast   Praise the LORD.

Cast: **Leader 1, Leader 2, Psalmist**

Praise the Lord

Psalm 150:1–6 (LIT)

Leader   Praise the LORD!

    Praise God in his sanctuary:
All   **praise him in his mighty heavens.**

Leader   Praise him for his acts of power:
A (group 1) **praise him for his surpassing greatness.**

Leader   Praise him with the sounding of the trumpet:
B (group 2) **praise him with the harp and lyre.**

Leader   Praise him with tambourine and dancing:
A (group 1) **praise him with the strings and flute.**

Leader	Praise him with the clash of cymbals:
B (group 2)	**praise him with resounding cymbals.**
Leader	Let everything that has breath praise the LORD.
All	**Praise the Lord! [Amen.]**
All	**[Glory to the Father, and to the Son,**
	and to the Holy Spirit:
	as it was in the beginning, is now,
	and shall be forever. Amen.]

Cast: **Leader**, **All** (the entire congregation), **A** (group 1—part of the congregation), **B** (group 2—part of the congregation)

Proverbs

Prologue: Purpose and Theme

Proverbs 1:1–19

Announcer	The proverbs of Solomon son of David, king of Israel:

for attaining wisdom and discipline;
    for understanding words of insight;
for acquiring a disciplined and prudent life,
    doing what is right and just and fair;
for giving prudence to the simple,
    knowledge and discretion to the young—
let the wise listen and add to their learning,
    and let the discerning get guidance—
for understanding proverbs and parables,
    the sayings and riddles of the wise.

Teacher   The fear of the LORD is the beginning of knowledge,
    but fools despise wisdom and discipline.

Father   Listen, my son, to your father's instruction
    and do not forsake your mother's teaching.
They will be a garland to grace your head
    and a chain to adorn your neck.

My son, if sinners entice you,
    do not give in to them.
If they say:

Sinner 1   Come along with us;
    let's lie in wait for someone's blood.

Sinner 2   Let's waylay some harmless soul.

Sinner 1   Let's swallow them alive, like the grave,
    and whole, like those who go down to the pit.

Sinner 2   We will get all sorts of valuable things
    and fill our houses with plunder.

Sinner 1   Throw in your lot with us,
    and we will share a common purse.

Father   My son, do not go along with them,
    do not set foot on their paths;
for their feet rush into sin,
    they are swift to shed blood.
How useless to spread a net
    in full view of all the birds!

These men lie in wait for their own blood;
    they waylay only themselves!
Such is the end of all who go after ill-gotten gain;
    it takes away the lives of those who get it.

Cast: **Announcer, Teacher, Father, Sinner 1, Sinner 2**

Moral Benefits of Wisdom

Proverbs 1:20–2:8

Teacher

Wisdom calls aloud in the street,
    she raises her voice in the public squares;
at the head of the noisy streets she cries out,
    in the gateways of the city she makes her speech:

Wisdom
(voice only,
to audience)

How long will you simple ones love your simple ways?
    How long will mockers delight in mockery
        and fools hate knowledge?
If you had responded to my rebuke,
    I would have poured out my heart to you
    and made my thoughts known to you.
But since you rejected me when I called
    and no one gave heed when I stretched out my hand,
since you ignored all my advice
    and would not accept my rebuke,
I in turn will laugh at your disaster;
    I will mock when calamity overtakes you—
when calamity overtakes you like a storm,
    when disaster sweeps over you like a whirlwind,
    when distress and trouble overwhelm you.
Then they will call to me but I will not answer;
    they will look for me but will not find me.
Since they hated knowledge
    and did not choose to fear the LORD,
since they would not accept my advice
    and spurned my rebuke,
they will eat the fruit of their ways
    and be filled with the fruit of their schemes.

Teacher

The waywardness of the simple will kill them,
    and the complacency of fools will destroy them.

Wisdom
(voice)

Whoever listens to me will live in safety
    and be at ease, without fear of harm.

141

Father	My son, if you accept my words
	   and store up my commands within you,
	turning your ear to wisdom
	   and applying your heart to understanding,
	and if you call out for insight
	   and cry aloud for understanding,
	and if you look for it as for silver
	   and search for it as for hidden treasure,
	then you will understand the fear of the LORD
	   and find the knowledge of God.

Teacher	The LORD gives wisdom,
	   and from his mouth come knowledge and understanding.
	He holds victory in store for the upright,
	   he is a shield to those whose walk is blameless,
	for he guards the course of the just
	   and protects the way of his faithful ones.

Cast: **Teacher**, **Wisdom** (voice only), **Father**

Further Benefits of Wisdom

From Proverbs 3:5–26

Teacher	Trust in the LORD with all your heart
	   and lean not on your own understanding;
	in all your ways acknowledge him,
	   and he will make your paths straight.
	
	Do not be wise in your own eyes;
	   fear the LORD and shun evil.
	This will bring health to your body
	   and nourishment to your bones.
	
	Honor the LORD with your wealth,
	   with the firstfruits of all your crops;
	then your barns will be filled to overflowing,
	   and your vats will brim over with new wine.

Father	My son, do not despise the LORD's discipline
	   and do not resent his rebuke,
	because the LORD disciplines those he loves,
	   as a father the son he delights in.
	
	Blessed is the man who finds wisdom,
	   the man who gains understanding,
	for she is more profitable than silver
	   and yields better returns than gold. . . .

Singer(s)	By wisdom the LORD laid the earth's foundations,
	by understanding he set the heavens in place;
	by his knowledge the deeps were divided,
	and the clouds let drop the dew.

Father

My son, preserve sound judgment and discernment,
do not let them out of your sight;
they will be life for you,
an ornament to grace your neck.
Then you will go on your way in safety,
and your foot will not stumble;
when you lie down, you will not be afraid;
when you lie down, your sleep will be sweet.

Teacher

Have no fear of sudden disaster
or of the ruin that overtakes the wicked,
for the LORD will be your confidence
and will keep your foot from being snared.

Cast: **Teacher, Father, Singer(s)**

Wisdom Is Supreme

From Proverbs 4:1–27

Father

Listen, my sons, to a father's instruction;
pay attention and gain understanding.
I give you sound learning,
so do not forsake my teaching.
When I was a boy in my father's house,
still tender, and an only child of my mother,
he taught me and said:

Grandfather

Lay hold of my words with all your heart;
keep my commands and you will live.
Get wisdom, get understanding;
do not forget my words or swerve from them.
Do not forsake wisdom, and she will protect you;
love her, and she will watch over you.
Wisdom is supreme; therefore get wisdom.
Though it cost all you have, get understanding.
Esteem her, and she will exalt you;
embrace her, and she will honor you.
She will set a garland of grace on your head
and present you with a crown of splendor.

Father

Listen, my son, accept what I say,
and the years of your life will be many.
I guide you in the way of wisdom

143

and lead you along straight paths.
When you walk, your steps will not be hampered;
    when you run, you will not stumble.
Hold on to instruction, do not let it go;
    guard it well, for it is your life.
Do not set foot on the path of the wicked
    or walk in the way of evil men.
Avoid it, do not travel on it;
    turn from it and go on your way. . . .

Grandfather   The path of the righteous is like the first gleam of dawn,
    shining ever brighter till the full light of day.
But the way of the wicked is like deep darkness;
    they do not know what makes them stumble. . . .

Father   Above all else, guard your heart,
    for it is the wellspring of life.
Put away perversity from your mouth;
    keep corrupt talk far from your lips.
Let your eyes look straight ahead,
    fix your gaze directly before you.
Make level paths for your feet
    and take only ways that are firm.
Do not swerve to the right or the left;
    keep your foot from evil.

Cast: **Father, Grandfather**

Warnings against Folly

Proverbs 6:1–19

Father   My son, if you have put up security for your neighbor,
    if you have struck hands in pledge for another,
if you have been trapped by what you said,
    ensnared by the words of your mouth,
then do this, my son, to free yourself,
    since you have fallen into your neighbor's hands:
Go and humble yourself;
    press your plea with your neighbor!
Allow no sleep to your eyes,
    no slumber to your eyelids.
Free yourself, like a gazelle from the hand of the hunter,
    like a bird from the snare of the fowler.

Teacher   Go to the ant, you sluggard;
    consider its ways and be wise!
It has no commander,
    no overseer or ruler,

yet it stores its provisions in summer
    and gathers its food at harvest.

How long will you lie there, you sluggard?
    When will you get up from your sleep? [He says:]

Lazy person
(yawning) A little sleep, a little slumber,
    a little folding of the hands to rest—

Teacher
(furtively) And poverty will come on you like a bandit
    and scarcity like an armed man. (PAUSE)
(normally) A scoundrel and villain,
    who goes about with a corrupt mouth,
    who winks with his eye,
    signals with his feet
    and motions with his fingers,
    who plots evil with deceit in his heart—
    he always stirs up dissension.
Therefore disaster will overtake him in an instant;
    he will suddenly be destroyed—without remedy.

Father   There are six things the LORD hates,
    seven that are detestable to him;

Speaker 1   Haughty eyes,

Speaker 2   A lying tongue,

Speaker 3   Hands that shed innocent blood,

Speaker 1   A heart that devises wicked schemes,

Speaker 2   Feet that are quick to rush into evil,

Speaker 3   A false witness who pours out lies

Speaker 1   And a man who stirs up dissension among brothers.

Cast: **Father, Teacher, Lazy person, Speaker 1, Speaker 2, Speaker 3.** (The "Speaker" section can be mimed effectively—with up to seven persons.)

Warning against the Adulteress

Proverbs 7:4–27

Father   Say to wisdom, "You are my sister,"
    and call understanding your kinsman;
    they will keep you from the adulteress,
    from the wayward wife with her seductive words.

Storyteller	At the window of my house
	    I looked out through the lattice.
	I saw among the simple,
	    I noticed among the young men,
	    a youth who lacked judgment.
	He was going down the street near her corner,
	    walking along in the direction of her house
	at twilight, as the day was fading,
	    as the dark of night set in.
	
	Then out came a woman to meet him,
	    dressed like a prostitute and with crafty intent.

Father	(She is loud and defiant,
	    her feet never stay at home;
	now in the street, now in the squares,
	    at every corner she lurks.)

Storyteller	She took hold of him and kissed him and with a brazen face she said:

Woman
(seduc-
tively)
	I have fellowship offerings at home;
	    today I fulfilled my vows.
	So I came out to meet you;
	    I looked for you and have found you!
	I have covered my bed
	    with colored linens from Egypt.
	I have perfumed my bed
	    with myrrh, aloes and cinnamon.
	Come, let's drink deep of love till morning;
	    let's enjoy ourselves with love!
	My husband is not at home;
	    he has gone on a long journey.
	He took his purse filled with money
	    and will not be home till full moon.

Storyteller	With persuasive words she led him astray;
	    she seduced him with her smooth talk.
	All at once he followed her
	    like an ox going to the slaughter,
	like a deer stepping into a noose
	    till an arrow pierces his liver,
	like a bird darting into a snare,
	    little knowing it will cost him his life.

Father	Now then, my sons, listen to me;
	    pay attention to what I say.
	Do not let your heart turn to her ways
	    or stray into her paths.
	Many are the victims she has brought down;

her slain are a mighty throng.
Her house is a highway to the grave,
    leading down to the chambers of death.

Cast: **Father, Storyteller, Woman**

Wisdom's Call (i)

From Proverbs 8:1–21

Teacher   Does not wisdom call out?
    Does not understanding raise her voice?
On the heights along the way,
    where the paths meet, she takes her stand;
beside the gates leading into the city,
    at the entrances, she cries aloud:

Wisdom
(voice only)   To you, O men, I call out;
    I raise my voice to all mankind.
You who are simple, gain prudence;
    you who are foolish, gain understanding.
Listen, for I have worthy things to say;
    I open my lips to speak what is right.
My mouth speaks what is true,
    for my lips detest wickedness.
All the words of my mouth are just;
    none of them is crooked or perverse. . . .
Choose my instruction instead of silver,
    knowledge rather than choice gold,
for wisdom is more precious than rubies,
    and nothing you desire can compare with her. . . .

Teacher   To fear the LORD is to hate evil.

Wisdom
(voice)   I hate pride and arrogance,
    evil behavior and perverse speech.
Counsel and sound judgment are mine;
    I have understanding and power.
By me kings reign
    and rulers make laws that are just;
by me princes govern,
    and all nobles who rule on earth.
I love those who love me,
    and those who seek me find me.
With me are riches and honor,
    enduring wealth and prosperity.
My fruit is better than fine gold;

147

what I yield surpasses choice silver.
I walk in the way of righteousness,
along the paths of justice,
bestowing wealth on those who love me
and making their treasuries full.

Cast: **Teacher**, **Wisdom** (voice only)

Wisdom's Call (ii)

Proverbs 8:1–3, 22–36

Teacher Does not wisdom call out?
Does not understanding raise her voice?
On the heights along the way,
where the paths meet, she takes her stand;
beside the gates leading into the city,
at the entrances, she cries aloud: . . .

Wisdom The LORD brought me forth as the first of his works,
before his deeds of old;
I was appointed from eternity,
from the beginning, before the world began.
When there were no oceans, I was given birth,
when there were no springs abounding with water;
before the mountains were settled in place,
before the hills, I was given birth,
before he made the earth or its fields
or any of the dust of the world.
I was there when he set the heavens in place,
when he marked out the horizon on the face of the deep,
when he established the clouds above
and fixed securely the fountains of the deep,
when he gave the sea its boundary
so the waters would not overstep his command,
and when he marked out the foundations of the earth.
Then I was the craftsman at his side.
I was filled with delight day after day,
rejoicing always in his presence,
rejoicing in his whole world
and delighting in mankind.

Now then, my sons, listen to me;
blessed are those who keep my ways.
Listen to my instruction and be wise;
do not ignore it.
Blessed is the man who listens to me,
watching daily at my doors,

waiting at my doorway.
For whoever finds me finds life
  and receives favor from the LORD.
But whoever fails to find me harms himself;
  all who hate me love death.

Cast: **Teacher, Wisdom**

Invitations of Wisdom and Folly

Proverbs 9:1–18

Teacher Wisdom has built her house;
  she has hewn out its seven pillars.
She has prepared her meat and mixed her wine;
  she has also set her table.
She has sent out her maids, and she calls
  from the highest point of the city.

Wisdom
(voice only,
kindly) Let all who are simple come in here! . . .
Come, eat my food
  and drink the wine I have mixed.
Leave your simple ways and you will live;
  walk in the way of understanding. (PAUSE)

Teacher Whoever corrects a mocker invites insult;
  whoever rebukes a wicked man incurs abuse.
Do not rebuke a mocker or he will hate you;
  rebuke a wise man and he will love you.
Instruct a wise man and he will be wiser still;
  teach a righteous man and he will add to his learning.

Wisdom
(voice) The fear of the LORD is the beginning of wisdom,
  and knowledge of the Holy One is understanding.
For through me your days will be many,
  and years will be added to your life.

Teacher If you are wise, your wisdom will reward you;
  if you are a mocker, you alone will suffer. (PAUSE)

The woman Folly is loud;
  she is undisciplined and without knowledge.
She sits at the door of her house,
  on a seat at the highest point of the city,
calling out to those who pass by,

who go straight on their way.
[She says to those who lack judgment:]

Folly Let all who are simple come in here! . . .

Teacher [To the foolish man she says:]

Folly Stolen water is sweet;
    food eaten in secret is delicious!

Teacher But little do they know that the dead are there,
    that her guests are in the depths of the grave.

Cast: **Teacher, Wisdom** (voice only), **Folly**

Epilogue: The Wife of Noble Character

Proverbs 31:10–31

Man A wife of noble character who can find?

Woman 1 She is worth far more than rubies.

Man Her husband has full confidence in her
    and lacks nothing of value.
She brings him good, not harm,
    all the days of her life.

Woman 2 She selects wool and flax
    and works with eager hands.

Woman 1 She is like the merchant ships,
    bringing her food from afar.

Woman 2 She gets up while it is still dark;
    she provides food for her family
    and portions for her servant girls.

Woman 1 She considers a field and buys it;
    out of her earnings she plants a vineyard.

Woman 2 She sets about her work vigorously;
    her arms are strong for her tasks.

Woman 1 She sees that her trading is profitable,
    and her lamp does not go out at night.

Woman 2 In her hand she holds the distaff
    and grasps the spindle with her fingers.

Woman 1	She opens her arms to the poor and extends her hands to the needy.
Child	When it snows, she has no fear for her household; for all of them are clothed in scarlet.
Woman 2	She makes coverings for her bed; she is clothed in fine linen and purple.
Man	Her husband is respected at the city gate, where he takes his seat among the elders of the land.
Woman 1	She makes linen garments and sells them, and supplies the merchants with sashes.
Woman 2	She is clothed with strength and dignity; she can laugh at the days to come.
Woman 1	She speaks with wisdom, and faithful instruction is on her tongue.
Woman 2	She watches over the affairs of her household and does not eat the bread of idleness.
Child	Her children arise and call her blessed.
Woman 1	Her husband also, and he praises her:
Man	Many women do noble things, but you surpass them all.
Woman 2	Charm is deceptive, and beauty is fleeting; but a woman who fears the Lord is to be praised.
Man	Give her the reward she has earned.
Cast	And let her works bring her praise at the city gate.

Cast: **Man, Woman 1, Woman 2, Child**

Ecclesiastes

Life Is Useless

Ecclesiastes 1:1–18

Announcer   The words of the Teacher, son of David, king in Jerusalem:

Teacher
(protesting) Meaningless! Meaningless! . . .
Utterly meaningless!
  Everything is meaningless.

What does man gain from all his labor
  at which he toils under the sun?
Generations come and generations go,
  but the earth remains forever.
The sun rises and the sun sets,
  and hurries back to where it rises.
The wind blows to the south
  and turns to the north;
round and round it goes,
  ever returning on its course.
All streams flow into the sea,
  yet the sea is never full.
To the place the streams come from,
  there they return again.
All things are wearisome,
  more than one can say.
The eye never has enough of seeing,
  nor the ear its fill of hearing.
What has been will be again,
  what has been done will be done again;
  there is nothing new under the sun.
Is there anything of which one can say:

Person   "Look! This is something new"?

Teacher   It was here already, long ago;
  it was here before our time.
There is no remembrance of men of old,
  and even those who are yet to come
will not be remembered
  by those who follow. (PAUSE)

(deliber-
ately)   I, the Teacher, was king over Israel in Jerusalem. I devoted myself to study and to explore by wisdom all that is done under heaven. What a heavy burden God has laid on men! I have seen all the things that

152

are done under the sun; all of them are meaningless, a chasing after the wind.

What is twisted cannot be straightened;
    what is lacking cannot be counted. (PAUSE)

I thought to myself:

Young teacher
  (thinking) "Look, I have grown and increased in wisdom more than anyone who has ruled over Jerusalem before me; I have experienced much of wisdom and knowledge."

Teacher Then I applied myself to the understanding of wisdom, and also of madness and folly, but I learned that this, too, is a chasing after the wind.

For with much wisdom comes much sorrow;
    the more knowledge, the more grief.

Cast: **Announcer, Teacher, Person, Young teacher**

Work and Worry

Ecclesiastes 2:11–17 [18–26]

Teacher When I surveyed all that my hands had done
    and what I had toiled to achieve,
everything was meaningless, a chasing after the wind;
    nothing was gained under the sun. . . .

What more can the king's successor do
    than what has already been done?
[Then I saw that]

**Young
  teacher** Wisdom is better than folly,
    just as light is better than darkness.
The wise man has eyes in his head,
    while the fool walks in the darkness;

Teacher But I came to realize
    that the same fate overtakes them both.

Then I thought in my heart,

Young teacher
  (thinking) The fate of the fool will overtake me also.
    What then do I gain by being wise? . . . (PAUSE)
    This too is meaningless.

153

> For the wise man, like the fool, will not be long remembered;
>   in days to come both will be forgotten.
> Like the fool, the wise man too must die!

Teacher	So I hated life, because the work that is done under the sun was grievous to me. All of it is meaningless, a chasing after the wind. (PAUSE) [I hated all the things I had toiled for under the sun, because I must leave them to the one who comes after me.
Young teacher	Who knows whether he will be a wise man or a fool? Yet he will have control over all the work into which I have poured my effort and skill under the sun.
Teacher	This too is meaningless. So my heart began to despair over all my toilsome labor under the sun.
Young teacher	A man may do his work with wisdom, knowledge and skill, and then he must leave all he owns to someone who has not worked for it.
Teacher	This too is meaningless and a great misfortune.
Young teacher	What does a man get for all the toil and anxious striving with which he labors under the sun? All his days his work is pain and grief; even at night his mind does not rest.
Teacher	This too is meaningless.
Young teacher	A man can do nothing better than to eat and drink and find satisfaction in his work.
Teacher	This too, I see, is from the hand of God, for without him, who can eat or find enjoyment?
Young teacher	To the man who pleases him, God gives wisdom, knowledge and happiness, but to the sinner he gives the task of gathering and storing up wealth to hand it over to the one who pleases God.
Teacher	This too is meaningless, a chasing after the wind.]

Cast: **Teacher, Young teacher**

A Time for Everything

Ecclesiastes 3:1–15

Philosopher	There is a time for everything, and a season for every activity under heaven:

Singer 1	A time to be born
Singer 1A	and a time to die,
Singer 2	a time to plant
Singer 2A	and a time to uproot,
Singer 3	a time to kill
Singer 3A	and a time to heal
Singer 4	a time to tear down
Singer 4A	and a time to build.
[Philosopher	[He sets . . .]]
Singer 1	a time to weep
Singer 1A	and a time to laugh,
Singer 2	a time to mourn
Singer 2A	and a time to dance,
Singer 3	a time to scatter stones
Singer 3A	and a time to gather them,
Singer 4	a time to embrace
Singer 4A	and a time to refrain.
[Philosopher	[He sets . . .]]
Singer 1	a time to search
Singer 1A	and a time to give up,
Singer 2	a time to keep
Singer 2A	and a time to throw away,
Singer 3	a time to tear
Singer 3A	and a time to mend,
Singer 4	a time to be silent
Singer 4A	and a time to speak.
[Philosopher	[He sets . . .]]
Singer 1	a time to love
Singer 1A	and a time to hate,
Singer 2	a time for war
Singer 2A	and a time for peace.

Philosopher What does the worker gain from his toil? I have seen the burden God has laid on men. He has made everything beautiful in its time. He has also set eternity in the hearts of men; yet they cannot fathom what God has done from beginning to end. I know that there is nothing better for men than to be happy and do good while they live. That everyone may eat and drink, and find satisfaction in all his toil—this is the gift of God. (PAUSE) I know that everything God does will endure forever; nothing can be added to it and nothing taken from it. God does it so that men will revere him.

Whatever is has already been,
  and what will be has been before;
  and God will call the past to account.

Cast: **Philosopher, Singer 1, Singer 1A, Singer 2, Singer 2A, Singer 3, Singer 3A, Singer 4, Singer 4A.** (Singers 1, 1A; 2, 2A; 3, 3A; 4, 4A should have contrasting voices, and the other numbers men's voices.)

Song of Songs

The First Song

Song of Songs 1:1–2:7

Announcer   Solomon's Song of Songs.

The Woman
(to
audience)   Let him kiss me with the kisses of his mouth—

(to
The Man)   Your love is more delightful than wine.
Pleasing is the fragrance of your perfumes;
    your name is like perfume poured out.
    No wonder the maidens love you!
Take me away with you—let us hurry!
    Let the king bring me into his chambers.

Friend 1   We rejoice and delight in you;

Friend 2   We will praise your love more than wine.

The Woman
(to
The Man)   How right they are to adore you!

(to
audience)   Dark am I, yet lovely,
    O daughters of Jerusalem,
    dark like the tents of Kedar,
    like the tent curtains of Solomon.
Do not stare at me because I am dark,
    because I am darkened by the sun.
My mother's sons were angry with me
    and made me take care of the vineyards;
    my own vineyard I have neglected.

(to
The Man)   Tell me, you whom I love, where you graze your flock
    and where you rest your sheep at midday.
Why should I be like a veiled woman
    beside the flocks of your friends?

The Man
(to The
Woman)   If you do not know, most beautiful of women,
    follow the tracks of the sheep
and graze your young goats
    by the tents of the shepherds.

(musing)	I liken you, my darling, to a mare
	    harnessed to one of the chariots of Pharaoh.
	Your cheeks are beautiful with earrings,
	    your neck with strings of jewels.

Friend 1	We will make you earrings of gold,
Friend 2	Studded with silver.

The Woman
(to
audience)
	While the king was at his table,
	    my perfume spread its fragrance.
	My lover is to me a sachet of myrrh
	    resting between my breasts.
	My lover is to me a cluster of henna blossoms
	    from the vineyards of En Gedi.

The Man
(to **The**
Woman)
	How beautiful you are, my darling!
	    Oh, how beautiful!
	    Your eyes are doves.

The Woman
(to
The Man)
	How handsome you are, my lover!
	    Oh, how charming!
	    And our bed is verdant.

The Man	The beams of our house are cedars; our rafters are firs.
The Woman	I am a rose of Sharon, a lily of the valleys.
The Man (to The Woman)	Like a lily among thorns is my darling among the maidens.

The Woman
(to
audience)
	Like an apple tree among the trees of the forest
	    is my lover among the young men.
	I delight to sit in his shade,
	    and his fruit is sweet to my taste.
	He has taken me to the banquet hall,
	    and his banner over me is love.

(to the
Friends)
	Strengthen me with raisins,
	    refresh me with apples,
	    for I am faint with love.

(to the
audience)   His left arm is under my head,
        and his right arm embraces me.

(to the
Friends)   Daughters of Jerusalem, I charge you
        by the gazelles and by the does of the field:
    Do not arouse or awaken love
        until it so desires.

Cast: **Announcer, the Woman, Friend 1, Friend 2** (the Friends are probably women companions),
the Man

The Second Song

Song of Songs 2:8–3:5

The Woman
(to
audience)   Listen! My lover!
        Look! Here he comes,
    leaping across the mountains,
        bounding over the hills.
    My lover is like a gazelle or a young stag.
        Look! There he stands behind our wall,
    gazing through the windows,
        peering through the lattice.
    My lover spoke and said to me:

The Man
(calling
to The
Woman)   Arise, my darling,
        my beautiful one, and come with me.
    See! The winter is past;
        the rains are over and gone.
    Flowers appear on the earth;
        the season of singing has come,
    the cooing of doves
        is heard in our land.
    The fig tree forms its early fruit;
        the blossoming vines spread their fragrance.
    Arise, come, my darling;
        my beautiful one, come with me.

    My dove in the clefts of the rock,
        in the hiding places on the mountainside,
    show me your face,
        let me hear your voice;

for your voice is sweet,
and your face is lovely.

Friends
1 and **2**
(voices
only)

Catch for us the foxes,
the little foxes
that ruin the vineyards,
our vineyards that are in bloom.

The Woman
(to
audience)

My lover is mine and I am his;
he browses among the lilies.
Until the day breaks
and the shadows flee.

(to
The Man)

Turn, my lover,
and be like a gazelle
or like a young stag
on the rugged hills.

(to
audience)

All night long on my bed
I looked for the one my heart loves;
I looked for him but did not find him.
I will get up now and go about the city,
through its streets and squares;
I will search for the one my heart loves.
So I looked for him but did not find him.
The watchmen found me
as they made their rounds in the city.

(calling)

"Have you seen the one my heart loves?" (PAUSE)

(to
audience)

Scarcely had I passed them
when I found the one my heart loves.
I held him and would not let him go
till I had brought him to my mother's house,
to the room of the one who conceived me.

(to the Friends,
OR to
audience)

Daughters of Jerusalem, I charge you
by the gazelles and by the does of the field:
Do not arouse or awaken love
until it so desires.

Cast: **The Woman, the Man, Friend 1, Friend 2** (voices only; the Friends are probably women companions)

The Third Song

Song of Songs 3:6–5:1

The Woman
(to
audience)   Who is this coming up from the desert
    like a column of smoke,
perfumed with myrrh and incense
    made from all the spices of the merchant?
Look! It is *Solomon's* carriage,
    escorted by sixty warriors,
    the noblest of Israel,
all of them wearing the sword,
    all experienced in battle,
each with his sword at his side,
    prepared for the terrors of the night.
King Solomon made for himself the carriage;
    he made it of wood from Lebanon.
Its posts he made of silver,
    its base of gold.
Its seat was upholstered with purple,
    its interior lovingly inlaid
    by the daughters of Jerusalem.

(to the
Friends)   Come out, you daughters of Zion,
    and look at King Solomon wearing the crown,
    the crown with which his mother crowned him
on the day of his wedding,
    the day his heart rejoiced.

The Man
(to The
Woman)   How beautiful you are, my darling!
    Oh, how beautiful!
    Your eyes behind your veil are doves.
Your hair is like a flock of goats
    descending from Mount Gilead.
Your teeth are like a flock of sheep just shorn,
    coming up from the washing.
Each has its twin;
    not one of them is alone.
Your lips are like a scarlet ribbon;
    your mouth is lovely.
Your temples behind your veil
    are like the halves of a pomegranate.
Your neck is like the tower of David,
    built with elegance;
on it hang a thousand shields,

all of them shields of warriors.
Your two breasts are like two fawns,
  like twin fawns of a gazelle
  that browse among the lilies.

(musing)   Until the day breaks
  and the shadows flee,
I will go to the mountain of myrrh
  and to the hill of incense.

(to The
Woman)   All beautiful you are, my darling;
  there is no flaw in you.

Come with me from Lebanon, my bride,
  come with me from Lebanon.
Descend from the crest of Amana,
  from the top of Senir, the summit of Hermon,
from the lions' dens
  and the mountain haunts of the leopards.

(confiding
to
audience)   You have stolen my heart, my sister, my bride;
  you have stolen my heart
with one glance of your eyes,
  with one jewel of your necklace.
How delightful is your love, my sister, my bride!
  How much more pleasing is your love than wine,
  and the fragrance of your perfume than any spice!
Your lips drop sweetness as the honeycomb, my bride;
  milk and honey are under your tongue.
  The fragrance of your garments is like that of Lebanon.

(to The
Woman)   You are a garden locked up, my sister, my bride;
  you are a spring enclosed, a sealed fountain.
Your plants are an orchard of pomegranates
  with choice fruits,
  with henna and nard,
  nard and saffron,
  calamus and cinnamon,
  with every kind of incense tree,
  with myrrh and aloes
  and all the finest spices.
You are a garden fountain,
  a well of flowing water
  streaming down from Lebanon.

The Woman
  (calling)   Awake, north wind,
  and come, south wind!

Blow on my garden,
　　that its fragrance may spread abroad.

(to The
Man)　　　Let my lover come into his garden
　　　　　and taste its choice fruits.

The Man
(to The
Woman)　　I have come into my garden, my sister, my bride;
　　　　　I have gathered my myrrh with my spice.
　　　　I have eaten my honeycomb and my honey;
　　　　　I have drunk my wine and my milk.

Friend 1　　Eat, O friends, and drink.

Friend 2　　Drink your fill, O lovers.

Cast: **The Woman, the Man, Friend 1, Friend 2** (can be the same as Friend 1; the Friends are probably women companions)

The Fourth Song

Song of Songs 5:2–6:3

The Woman
(to
audience)　　I slept but my heart was awake.
　　　　　Listen! My lover is knocking:

The Man
(voice only)　Open to me, my sister, my darling,
　　　　　my dove, my flawless one.
　　　　My head is drenched with dew,
　　　　　my hair with the dampness of the night.

The Woman
(to The
Man)　　　I have taken off my robe—
　　　　　must I put it on again?
　　　　I have washed my feet—
　　　　　must I soil them again?

(to
audience)　　My lover thrust his hand through the latch-opening;
　　　　　my heart began to pound for him.
　　　　I arose to open for my lover,
　　　　　and my hands dripped with myrrh,
　　　　my fingers with flowing myrrh,
　　　　　on the handles of the lock.
　　　　I opened for my lover, (PAUSE)

but my lover had left; he was gone.
My heart sank at his departure.
I looked for him but did not find him.
I called him but he did not answer.
The watchmen found me
as they made their rounds in the city.
They beat me, they bruised me;
they took away my cloak,
those watchmen of the walls!

(to Friends
1 and 2)   O daughters of Jerusalem, I charge you—
if you find my lover,
what will you tell him?
Tell him I am faint with love.

Friend 1   How is your beloved better than others,
most beautiful of women?

Friend 2   How is your beloved better than others,
that you charge us so?

The Woman
(to the
audience)   My lover is radiant and ruddy,
outstanding among ten thousand.
His head is purest gold;
his hair is wavy
and black as a raven.
His eyes are like doves
by the water streams,
washed in milk,
mounted like jewels.
His cheeks are like beds of spice
yielding perfume.
His lips are like lilies
dripping with myrrh.
His arms are rods of gold
set with chrysolite.
His body is like polished ivory
decorated with sapphires.
His legs are pillars of marble
set on bases of pure gold.
His appearance is like Lebanon,
choice as its cedars.
His mouth is sweetness itself;
he is altogether lovely.

(to the
Friends)   This is my lover, this my friend,
O daughters of Jerusalem.

Friend 1
(to The
Woman)   Where has your lover gone,
                  most beautiful of women?

Friend 2
(to The
Woman)   Which way did your lover turn,
                  that we may look for him with you?

The Woman
(to the
Friends)   My lover has gone down to his garden,
                  to the beds of spices,
               to browse in the gardens
                  and to gather lilies.

(to
audience)   I am my lover's and my lover is mine;
                  he browses among the lilies.

Cast: **The Woman, the Man, Friend 1, Friend 2** (the Friends are probably women companions)

The Fifth Song

Songs of Songs 6:4–8:4

The Man
(to The
Woman)   You are beautiful, my darling, as Tirzah,
                  lovely as Jerusalem,
                  majestic as troops with banners.
               Turn your eyes from me;
                  they overwhelm me.
               Your hair is like a flock of goats
                  descending from Gilead.
               Your teeth are like a flock of sheep
                  coming up from the washing.
               Each has its twin,
                  not one of them is alone.
               Your temples behind your veil
                  are like the halves of a pomegranate.

(to
audience)   Sixty queens there may be,
                  and eighty concubines,
                  and virgins beyond number;
               but my dove, my perfect one, is unique,
                  the only daughter of her mother,

165

the favorite of the one who bore her.
The maidens saw her and called her blessed;
  the queens and concubines praised her.

Friend 1   Who is this that appears like the dawn,

Friend 2   fair as the moon, bright as the sun,

Friend 1   majestic as the stars in procession?

The Man
(to
audience)   I went down to the grove of nut trees
  to look at the new growth in the valley,
to see if the vines had budded
  or the pomegranates were in bloom.
Before I realized it,
  my desire set me among the royal chariots of my people.

Friend 1   Come back, come back, O Shulammite—

Friend 2   Come back, come back, that we may gaze on you!

The Woman   Why would you gaze on the Shulammite
  as on the dance of Mahanaim?

The Man
(to the
audience)   How beautiful your sandaled feet,
  O prince's daughter!
Your graceful legs are like jewels,
  the work of a craftsman's hands.
Your navel is a rounded goblet
  that never lacks blended wine.
Your waist is a mound of wheat
  encircled by lilies.
Your breasts are like two fawns,
  twins of a gazelle.
Your neck is like an ivory tower.
Your eyes are the pools of Heshbon
  by the gate of Bath Rabbim.
Your nose is like the tower of Lebanon
  looking toward Damascus.
Your head crowns you like Mount Carmel.
  Your hair is like royal tapestry;
  the king is held captive by its tresses.
How beautiful you are and how pleasing,
  O love, with your delights!
Your stature is like that of the palm,
  and your breasts like clusters of fruit.

(musing)	I said, "I will climb the palm tree; I will take hold of its fruit."
(to The Woman)	May your breasts be like the clusters of the vine, the fragrance of your breath like apples, and your mouth like the best wine.

The Woman

(to The Man)	May the wine go straight to my lover, flowing gently over lips and teeth.
(to the audience)	I belong to my lover, and his desire is for me.
(to The Man)	Come, my lover, let us go to the countryside, let us spend the night in the villages. Let us go early to the vineyards to see if the vines have budded, if their blossoms have opened, and if the pomegranates are in bloom— there I will give you my love. The mandrakes send out their fragrance, and at our door is every delicacy, both new and old, that I have stored up for you, my lover.
(musing)	If only you were to me like a brother, who was nursed at my mother's breasts! Then, if I found you outside, I would kiss you, and no one would despise me. I would lead you and bring you to my mother's house— she who has taught me. I would give you spiced wine to drink, the nectar of my pomegranates. (PAUSE)
(to audience)	His left arm is under my head and his right arm embraces me.
(to the Friends)	Daughters of Jerusalem, I charge you: Do not arouse or awaken love until it so desires.

Cast: **The Man, Friend 1, Friend 2** (the Friends are probably women companions), **the Woman**

The Sixth Song

Song of Songs 8:5–14

Friend 1

(to Friend 2
OR to
audience)   Who is this coming up from the desert
　　　　　　leaning on her lover?

The Woman

(to The
Man)   Under the apple tree I roused you;
　　　　　there your mother conceived you,
　　　　　there she who was in labor gave you birth.
　　　　Place me like a seal over your heart,
　　　　　like a seal on your arm.

(to
audience)   Love is as strong as death,
　　　　　its jealousy unyielding as the grave.
　　　　It burns like blazing fire,
　　　　　like a mighty flame.
　　　　Many waters cannot quench love;
　　　　　rivers cannot wash it away.
　　　　If one were to give
　　　　　all the wealth of his house for love,
　　　　　it would be utterly scorned.

Friend 1

(to
audience)   We have a young sister,
　　　　　and her breasts are not yet grown.

Friend 2

(to
audience)   What shall we do for our sister
　　　　　for the day she is spoken for?

Friend 1

(to
audience)   If she is a wall,
　　　　　we will build towers of silver on her.

Friend 2

(to
audience)   If she is a door,
　　　　　we will enclose her with panels of cedar.

The Woman

(to
audience)   I am a wall,

168

and my breasts are like towers.
Thus I have become in his eyes
    like one bringing contentment.
Solomon had a vineyard in Baal Hamon;
    he let out his vineyard to tenants.
Each was to bring for its fruit
    a thousand shekels of silver.
But my own vineyard is mine to give;
    the thousand shekels are for you, O Solomon,
    and two hundred are for those who tend its fruit.

The Man
    You who dwell in the gardens
        with friends in attendance,
        let me hear your voice!*

The Woman
(to The
  Man)
    Come away, my lover,
        and be like a gazelle
  or like a young stag
        on the spice-laden mountains.

Cast: **Friend 1, the Woman, Friend 2, the Man.** (*At this point, the Woman and the Man can back out on opposite sides.)

Full cast for The Song of Songs: **Announcer, the Woman, the Man, Friend 1, Friend 2** (the Friends are probably women companions)

Isaiah

God Reprimands His People

Isaiah 1:1–9

Narrator   The vision concerning Judah and Jerusalem that Isaiah son of Amoz saw during the reigns of Uzziah, Jotham, Ahaz and Hezekiah, kings of Judah.

Isaiah   Hear, O heavens! Listen, O earth!
    For the LORD has spoken:

The Lord
(voice only) I reared children and brought them up,
    but they have rebelled against me.
The ox knows his master,
    the donkey his owner's manger,
but Israel does not know,
    my people do not understand.

Isaiah   Ah, sinful nation,
    a people loaded with guilt,
a brood of evildoers,
    children given to corruption!
They have forsaken the LORD;
    they have spurned the Holy One of Israel
    and turned their backs on him.
Why should you be beaten anymore?
    Why do you persist in rebellion?
Your whole head is injured,
    your whole heart afflicted.
From the sole of your foot to the top of your head
    there is no soundness—
only wounds and welts
    and open sores,
not cleansed or bandaged
    or soothed with oil.

Your country is desolate,
    your cities burned with fire;
your fields are being stripped by foreigners
    right before you,
    laid waste as when overthrown by strangers.
The Daughter of Zion is left
    like a shelter in a vineyard,
like a hut in a field of melons,
    like a city under siege.
Unless the LORD Almighty
    had left us some survivors,

we would have become like Sodom,
we would have been like Gomorrah.

Cast: **Narrator, Isaiah, the Lord** (voice only)

God Reprimands His City

Isaiah 1:10–20

Isaiah   Hear the word of the LORD,
        you rulers of Sodom;
    listen to the law of our God,
        you people of Gomorrah!
    [The LORD says:]

The Lord
(voice only)   The multitude of your sacrifices—
        what are they to me? . . .
    I have more than enough of burnt offerings,
        of rams and the fat of fattened animals;
    I have no pleasure
        in the blood of bulls and lambs and goats.
    When you come to appear before me,
        who has asked this of you,
        this trampling of my courts?
    Stop bringing meaningless offerings!
        Your incense is detestable to me.
    New Moons, Sabbaths and convocations—
        I cannot bear your evil assemblies.
    Your New Moon festivals and your appointed feasts
        my soul hates.
    They have become a burden to me;
        I am weary of bearing them.
    When you spread out your hands in prayer,
        I will hide my eyes from you;
    even if you offer many prayers,
        I will not listen.
    Your hands are full of blood;
        wash and make yourselves clean.
    Take your evil deeds
        out of my sight!
    Stop doing wrong,
        learn to do right!
    Seek justice,
        encourage the oppressed.
    Defend the cause of the fatherless,
        plead the case of the widow.

Isaiah   [The LORD says:]

The Lord
(voice)   Come now, let us reason together. . . .
             Though your sins are like scarlet,
                 they shall be as white as snow;
             though they are red as crimson,
                 they shall be like wool.
             If you are willing and obedient,
                 you will eat the best from the land;
             but if you resist and rebel,
                 you will be devoured by the sword. (PAUSE)

Isaiah   The mouth of the LORD has spoken.

Cast: **Isaiah, the Lord** (voice only)

The Sinful City

Isaiah 1:21–31

Isaiah   See how the faithful city
                 has become a harlot!
             She once was full of justice;
                 righteousness used to dwell in her—
                 but now murderers!
             Your silver has become dross,
                 your choice wine is diluted with water.
             Your rulers are rebels,
                 companions of thieves;
             they all love bribes
                 and chase after gifts.
             They do not defend the cause of the fatherless;
                 the widow's case does not come before them.
             Therefore the Lord, the LORD Almighty,
                 the Mighty One of Israel, declares:

The Lord
(voice only) Ah, I will get relief from my foes
                 and avenge myself on my enemies.
             I will turn my hand against you;
                 I will thoroughly purge away your dross
                 and remove all your impurities.
             I will restore your judges as in days of old,
                 your counselors as at the beginning.
             Afterward you will be called
                 the City of Righteousness,
                 the Faithful City.

Isaiah   Zion will be redeemed with justice,
                 her penitent ones with righteousness.

But rebels and sinners will both be broken,
   and those who forsake the LORD will perish.

You will be ashamed because of the sacred oaks
   in which you have delighted;
you will be disgraced because of the gardens
   that you have chosen.
You will be like an oak with fading leaves,
   like a garden without water.
The mighty man will become tinder
   and his work a spark;
both will burn together,
   with no one to quench the fire.

Cast: **Isaiah, the Lord** (voice only)

The Mountain of the Lord

Isaiah 2:1–5

Narrator   This is what Isaiah son of Amoz saw concerning Judah and Jerusalem:

Isaiah   In the last days

the mountain of the LORD's temple will be established
   as chief among the mountains;
it will be raised above the hills,
   and all nations will stream to it.

Many peoples will come and say,

Person 1   Come, let us go up to the mountain of the LORD,
   to the house of the God of Jacob.

Person 2   He will teach us his ways,
   so that we may walk in his paths.

Isaiah   The law will go out from Zion,
   the word of the LORD from Jerusalem.
He will judge between the nations
   and will settle disputes for many peoples.
They will beat their swords into plowshares
   and their spears into pruning hooks.
Nation will not take up sword against nation,
   nor will they train for war anymore.

Come, O house of Jacob,
   let us walk in the light of the LORD.

Cast: **Narrator, Isaiah, Person 1, Person 2**

The Day of the Lord

Isaiah 2:6–22

Voice 1   You have abandoned your people,
     the house of Jacob.

Voice 2   They are full of superstitions from the East—

Voice 3   They practice divination like the Philistines
     and clasp hands with pagans.

Voice 1   Their land is full of silver and gold;
     there is no end to their treasures.

Voice 2   Their land is full of horses;
     there is no end to their chariots.

Voice 3   Their land is full of idols;
     they bow down to the work of their hands,
     to what their fingers have made.

Voice 1   So man will be brought low
     and mankind humbled—

Voices 1–3   Do not forgive them.

Voice 1   Go into the rocks,
     hide in the ground
    from dread of the LORD
     and the splendor of his majesty!

Voice 2   The eyes of the arrogant man will be humbled
     and the pride of men brought low.

Voice 3   The LORD alone will be exalted in that day.

Voice 1   The LORD Almighty has a day in store
     for all the proud and lofty.

Voice 2   For all that is exalted . . .
     For all the cedars of Lebanon, tall and lofty,
     and all the oaks of Bashan.

Voice 3   For all the towering mountains
     and all the high hills.

Voice 1   For every lofty tower
     and every fortified wall.

Voice 2   For every trading ship
     and every stately vessel.

Voice 3	The arrogance of man will be brought low and the pride of men humbled;
Voices 1–3	The LORD alone will be exalted in that day, and the idols will totally disappear.

Voice 1	Men will flee to caves in the rocks
	    and to holes in the ground
	from dread of the LORD
	    and the splendor of his majesty,
	    when he rises to shake the earth.

Voice 2	In that day men will throw away
	    to the rodents and bats
	their idols of silver and idols of gold,
	    which they made to worship.

Voice 3	They will flee to caverns in the rocks
	    and to the overhanging crags
	from dread of the LORD
	    and the splendor of his majesty,
	    when he rises to shake the earth.

Voices 1–3	Stop trusting in man,
Voice 1	who is but a breath in his nostrils.
Voice 2	Of what account is he?

Cast: **Voice 1, Voice 2, Voice 3**

Judgment on Jerusalem and Judah

Isaiah 3:1–15

Isaiah	See now, the Lord,
	    the LORD Almighty,
	is about to take from Jerusalem and Judah
	    both supply and support:
	all supplies of food and all supplies of water,
	    the hero and warrior,
	    the judge and prophet,
	        the soothsayer and elder,
	    the captain of fifty and man of rank,
	        the counselor, skilled craftsman and clever enchanter.
	
	I will make boys their officials;
	    mere children will govern them.
	People will oppress each other—

man against man, neighbor against neighbor.
The young will rise up against the old,
   the base against the honorable.

A man will seize one of his brothers
   at his father's home, and say:

Man   You have a cloak, you be our leader;
   take charge of this heap of ruins!

Isaiah   But in that day he will cry out:

Brother   I have no remedy.
I have no food or clothing in my house;
   do not make me the leader of the people.

Isaiah   Jerusalem staggers,
   Judah is falling;
their words and deeds are against the Lord,
   defying his glorious presence.
The look on their faces testifies against them;
   they parade their sin like Sodom;
   they do not hide it.
Woe to them!
   They have brought disaster upon themselves.

The Lord
(voice only) Tell the righteous it will be well with them,
   for they will enjoy the fruit of their deeds.
Woe to the wicked! Disaster is upon them!
   They will be paid back for what their hands have done.

The Lord
(voice only) Youths oppress my people,
   women rule over them.
O my people, your guides lead you astray;
   they turn you from the path. (PAUSE)

Isaiah   The Lord takes his place in court;
   he rises to judge the people.
The Lord enters into judgment
   against the elders and leaders of his people.
         [Declares the Lord, the Lord Almighty:]

The Lord
(voice)   It is you who have ruined my vineyard;
   the plunder from the poor is in your houses.
What do you mean by crushing my people
   and grinding the faces of the poor? . . .

Cast: **Isaiah, Man, Brother, the Lord** (voice only)

A Warning to the Women of Zion

Isaiah 3:16–4:1

Isaiah　　　　The LORD says,

The Lord
　(voice only)　The women of Zion are haughty,
　　　　　　　walking along with outstretched necks,
　　　　　　　　　flirting with their eyes,
　　　　　　　tripping along with mincing steps,
　　　　　　　　　with ornaments jingling on their ankles.

Isaiah　　　　Therefore the Lord will bring sores on the heads
　　　　　　　　　of the women of Zion;
　　　　　　　　　the LORD will make their scalps bald.

　　　　　　　In that day the Lord will snatch away their finery: the bangles and head-
　　　　　　　bands and crescent necklaces, the earrings and bracelets and veils, the
　　　　　　　headdresses and ankle chains and sashes, the perfume bottles and
　　　　　　　charms, the signet rings and nose rings, the fine robes and the capes and
　　　　　　　cloaks, the purses and mirrors, and the linen garments and tiaras and
　　　　　　　shawls.

　　　　　　　Instead of fragrance there will be a stench;
　　　　　　　　instead of a sash, a rope;
　　　　　　　instead of well-dressed hair, baldness;
　　　　　　　　instead of fine clothing, sackcloth;
　　　　　　　　instead of beauty, branding.

The Lord
　(voice)　　　Your men will fall by the sword,
　　　　　　　　your warriors in battle.
　　　　　　　The gates of Zion will lament and mourn;
　　　　　　　　destitute, she will sit on the ground.

Isaiah　　　　In that day seven women
　　　　　　　　will take hold of one man
　　　　　　　and say:

Woman 1　　We will eat our own food
　　　　　　　　and provide our own clothes—

Woman 2　　Only let us be called by your name.

Women 1
　and 2　　　Take away our disgrace!

Cast: **Isaiah**, the Lord (voice only), **Woman 1**, **Woman 2**

The Song of the Vineyard

Isaiah 5:1–7

Isaiah   I will sing for the one I love
           a song about his vineyard:
        My loved one had a vineyard
           on a fertile hillside.
        He dug it up and cleared it of stones
           and planted it with the choicest vines.
        He built a watchtower in it
           and cut out a winepress as well.
        Then he looked for a crop of good grapes,
           but it yielded only bad fruit.

Owner   Now you dwellers in Jerusalem and men of Judah,
           judge between me and my vineyard.
        What more could have been done for my vineyard
           than I have done for it?
        When I looked for good grapes,
           why did it yield only bad?
        Now I will tell you
           what I am going to do to my vineyard:
        I will take away its hedge,
           and it will be destroyed;
        I will break down its wall,
           and it will be trampled.
        I will make it a wasteland,
           neither pruned nor cultivated,
           and briers and thorns will grow there.
        I will command the clouds
           not to rain on it.

Isaiah   The vineyard of the LORD Almighty
           is the house of Israel,
        and the men of Judah
           are the garden of his delight.
        And he looked for justice, but saw bloodshed;
           for righteousness, but heard cries of distress.

Cast: **Isaiah, Owner**

Woes and Judgments

Isaiah 5:8–30

Isaiah   Woe to you who add house to house
           and join field to field

till no space is left
and you live alone in the land.

The LORD Almighty has declared in my hearing:

The Lord
(voice only) Surely the great houses will become desolate,
the fine mansions left without occupants.
A ten-acre vineyard will produce only a bath of wine,
a homer of seed only an ephah of grain.

Isaiah Woe to those who rise early in the morning
to run after their drinks,
who stay up late at night
till they are inflamed with wine.
They have harps and lyres at their banquets,
tambourines and flutes and wine,
but they have no regard for the deeds of the LORD,
no respect for the work of his hands.

The Lord
(voice) Therefore my people will go into exile
for lack of understanding;
their men of rank will die of hunger
and their masses will be parched with thirst.
Therefore the grave enlarges its appetite
and opens its mouth without limit;
into it will descend their nobles and masses
with all their brawlers and revelers.

Isaiah So man will be brought low
and mankind humbled,
the eyes of the arrogant humbled.
But the LORD Almighty will be exalted by his justice,
and the holy God will show himself holy by his righteousness.
Then sheep will graze as in their own pasture;
lambs will feed among the ruins of the rich.

Woe to those who draw sin along with cords of deceit,
and wickedness as with cart ropes. (PAUSE)

To those who say:

Person 1 Let God hurry.

Person 2 Let him hasten his work
so we may see it.

Person 1 Let it approach,
let the plan of the Holy One of Israel come,
so we may know it.

Isaiah

Woe to those who call evil good
   and good evil,
who put darkness for light
   and light for darkness,
who put bitter for sweet
   and sweet for bitter.

Woe to those who are wise in their own eyes
   and clever in their own sight.

Woe to those who are heroes at drinking wine
   and champions at mixing drinks,
who acquit the guilty for a bribe,
   but deny justice to the innocent.
Therefore, as tongues of fire lick up straw
   and as dry grass sinks down in the flames,
so their roots will decay
   and their flowers blow away like dust;
for they have rejected the law of the Lord Almighty
   and spurned the word of the Holy One of Israel.
Therefore the Lord's anger burns against his people;
   his hand is raised and he strikes them down.
The mountains shake,
   and the dead bodies are like refuse in the streets.

Yet for all this, his anger is not turned away,
   his hand is still upraised.

He lifts up a banner for the distant nations,
   he whistles for those at the ends of the earth.
Here they come,
   swiftly and speedily!
Not one of them grows tired or stumbles,
   not one slumbers or sleeps;
not a belt is loosened at the waist,
   not a sandal thong is broken.
Their arrows are sharp,
   all their bows are strung;
their horses' hoofs seem like flint,
   their chariot wheels like a whirlwind.
Their roar is like that of the lion,
   they roar like young lions;
they growl as they seize their prey
   and carry it off with no one to rescue.
In that day they will roar over it
   like the roaring of the sea.
And if one looks at the land,

he will see darkness and distress;
even the light will be darkened by the clouds.

Cast: **Isaiah, the Lord** (voice only), **Person 1, Person 2** (can be the same as Person 1)

Isaiah's Commission

Isaiah 6:1–8 [9–12]

Isaiah	In the year that King Uzziah died, I saw the Lord seated on a throne, high and exalted, and the train of his robe filled the temple. Above him were seraphs, each with six wings: With two wings they covered their faces, with two they covered their feet, and with two they were flying. And they were calling to one another:
Seraph 1	Holy,
Seraph 2	Holy,
Seraph 3	Holy, is the LORD Almighty—
Seraphs 1–3	The whole earth is full of his glory.
Isaiah	At the sound of their voices the doorposts and thresholds shook and the temple was filled with smoke.
	[I cried:]
Young Isaiah	Woe to me! . . . I am ruined! For I am a man of unclean lips, and I live among a people of unclean lips, and my eyes have seen the King, the LORD Almighty.
Isaiah	Then one of the seraphs flew to me with a live coal in his hand, which he had taken with tongs from the altar. With it he touched my mouth and said:
Seraph 1	See, this has touched your lips; your guilt is taken away and your sin atoned for.
Isaiah	Then I heard the voice of the Lord saying:
The Lord (voice only)	Whom shall I send? And who will go for us?
Isaiah	And I said:
Young Isaiah	Here am I. Send me!
[Isaiah	He said,
The Lord (voice)	Go and tell this people:

181

> "Be ever hearing, but never understanding;
>   be ever seeing, but never perceiving."
> Make the heart of this people calloused;
>   make their ears dull
>   and close their eyes.
> Otherwise they might see with their eyes,
>   hear with their ears,
>   understand with their hearts,
> and turn and be healed.

Isaiah	Then I said,
Young Isaiah	For how long, O Lord?
Isaiah	And he answered:

The Lord (voice)	Until the cities lie ruined
	    and without inhabitant,
	until the houses are left deserted
	    and the fields ruined and ravaged,
	until the LORD has sent everyone far away
	    and the land is utterly forsaken.]

Cast: **Isaiah, Seraph 1, Seraph 2, Seraph 3, Young Isaiah, the Lord** (voice only)

A Message for King Ahaz

Isaiah 7:1–9

Narrator	When Ahaz son of Jotham, the son of Uzziah, was king of Judah, King Rezin of Aram and Pekah son of Remaliah king of Israel marched up to fight against Jerusalem, but they could not overpower it. (PAUSE) Now the house of David was told:
Spy	Aram has allied itself with Ephraim.
Narrator	So the hearts of Ahaz and his people were shaken, as the trees of the forest are shaken by the wind. Then the LORD said to Isaiah,
The Lord (voice only)	Go out, you and your son Shear-Jashub, to meet Ahaz at the end of the aqueduct of the Upper Pool, on the road to the Washerman's Field. Say to him, "Be careful, keep calm and don't be afraid. Do not lose heart because of these two smoldering stubs of firewood—because of the fierce anger of Rezin and Aram and of the son of Remaliah. Aram, Ephraim and Remaliah's son have plotted your ruin, saying, 'Let us invade Judah; let us tear it apart and divide it among ourselves, and make the son of Tabeel king over it.'"

Narrator	Yet this is what the Sovereign Lᴏʀᴅ says:

The Lord
(voice)
	It will not take place,
	    it will not happen,
	for the head of Aram is Damascus,
	    and the head of Damascus is only Rezin.
	Within sixty-five years
	    Ephraim will be too shattered to be a people.
	The head of Ephraim is Samaria,
	    and the head of Samaria is only Remaliah's son.

(deliber- ately)	If you do not stand firm in your faith, you will not stand at all.

Cast: **Narrator, Spy, the Lord** (voice only)

The Sign of Immanuel

Isaiah 7:10–14

Narrator	Again the Lᴏʀᴅ spoke to Ahaz.
The Lord (voice only)	Ask the Lᴏʀᴅ your God for a sign, whether in the deepest depths or in the highest heights.
Narrator	But Ahaz said:
Ahaz	I will not ask; I will not put the Lᴏʀᴅ to the test.
Narrator	Then Isaiah said:
Isaiah	Hear now, you house of David! Is it not enough to try the patience of men? Will you try the patience of my God also? Therefore the Lord himself will give you a sign:
The Lord (voice)	The virgin will be with child and will give birth to a son, and will call him Immanuel.

Cast: **Narrator, the Lord** (voice only), **Ahaz, Isaiah.** (See also Appendix: Christmas Readings, New Testament page 416.)

Isaiah's Son as a Sign to the People

Isaiah 8:1–4

Isaiah	The Lᴏʀᴅ said to me:

The Lord

(voice only) Take a large scroll and write on it with an ordinary pen: Maher-Shalal-Hash-Baz. And I will call in Uriah the priest and Zechariah son of Jeberekiah as reliable witnesses for me.

Isaiah Then I went to the prophetess, and she conceived and gave birth to a son. And the LORD said to me:

The Lord

(voice) Name him Maher-Shalal-Hash-Baz. Before the boy knows how to say "My father" or "My mother," the wealth of Damascus and the plunder of Samaria will be carried off by the king of Assyria.

Cast: **Isaiah, the Lord** (voice only)

Assyria, the Lord's Instrument

Isaiah 8:5–10

Isaiah The LORD spoke to me again:

The Lord

(voice only) Because this people has rejected
the gently flowing waters of Shiloah
and rejoices over Rezin
and the son of Remaliah,
therefore the Lord is about to bring against them
the mighty floodwaters of the River—
the king of Assyria with all his pomp.
It will overflow all its channels,
run over all its banks
and sweep on into Judah, swirling over it,
passing through it and reaching up to the neck.
Its outspread wings will cover the breadth of your land,
O Immanuel!

Isaiah Raise the war cry, you nations, and be shattered!
Listen, all you distant lands.
Prepare for battle, and be shattered!
Prepare for battle, and be shattered!
Devise your strategy, but it will be thwarted;
propose your plan, but it will not stand,
for God is with us.

Cast: **Isaiah, the Lord** (voice only)

Fear God

Isaiah 8:11–15

Isaiah   The LORD spoke to me with his strong hand upon me, warning me not to follow the way of this people. [He said:]

The Lord
(voice only) Do not call conspiracy
    everything that these people call conspiracy;
do not fear what they fear,
    and do not dread it.
The LORD Almighty is the one you are to regard as holy,
    he is the one you are to fear,
    he is the one you are to dread,
and he will be a sanctuary;
    but for both houses of Israel he will be
a stone that causes men to stumble
    and a rock that makes them fall.
And for the people of Jerusalem he will be
    a trap and a snare.
Many of them will stumble;
    they will fall and be broken,
    they will be snared and captured.

Cast: **Isaiah, the Lord** (voice only)

Isaiah's Warning against Consulting the Dead

Isaiah 8:16–20

Isaiah   Bind up the testimony
    and seal up the law among my disciples.
I will wait for the LORD,
    who is hiding his face from the house of Jacob.
I will put my trust in him.
Here am I, and the children the LORD has given me. We are signs and symbols in Israel from the LORD Almighty, who dwells on Mount Zion.

When men tell you to consult mediums and spiritists, who whisper and mutter:

Spiritist   Should not a people inquire of their God?

Isaiah   Why consult the dead on behalf of the living? To the law and to the testimony! If they do not speak according to this word, they have no light of dawn.

Cast: **Isaiah, Spiritist**

185

To Us a Child Is Born

Isaiah 9:2–7

Voice 1   The people walking in darkness
    have seen a great light—

Voice 2   On those living in the land of the shadow of death
    a light has dawned.

Voice 3   You have enlarged the nation
    and increased their joy—

Voice 1   They rejoice before you
    as people rejoice at the harvest—

Voice 2   As men rejoice
    when dividing the plunder.

Voice 3   For as in the day of Midian's defeat,
    you have shattered
the yoke that burdens them,
    the bar across their shoulders,
    the rod of their oppressor.

Voice 1   Every warrior's boot used in battle
    and every garment rolled in blood
will be destined for burning,
    will be fuel for the fire. (PAUSE)

Voice 2   For to us a child is born—

Voice 3   To us a son is given—

Voice 1   The government will be on his shoulders.

Voice 2   He will be called
    Wonderful Counselor,

Voice 3   Mighty God,

Voice 1   Everlasting Father,

Voice 2   Prince of Peace.

Voice 3   Of the increase of his government and peace
    there will be no end.

Voice 1   He will reign on David's throne
    and over his kingdom,
establishing and upholding it

> with justice and righteousness
> from that time on and forever.

Voices 1–3
(with
flourish)   The zeal of the Lord Almighty
> will accomplish this.

Cast: **Voice 1**, **Voice 2**, **Voice 3**. (See also Appendix: Christmas Readings, New Testament page 416.)

The Lord's Anger against Israel

From Isaiah 9:8–10:3

Isaiah   The Lord has sent a message against Jacob;
> it will fall on Israel.
> All the people will know it—
>> Ephraim and the inhabitants of Samaria—
> who say with pride
>> and arrogance of heart:

Person 1   The bricks have fallen down,
> but we will rebuild with dressed stone;

Person 2   The fig trees have been felled,
> but we will replace them with cedars.

Isaiah   But the Lord has strengthened Rezin's foes against them
> and has spurred their enemies on.
> Arameans from the east and Philistines from the west
> have devoured Israel with open mouth.

Yet for all this, his anger is not turned away,
> his hand is still upraised.

But the people have not returned to him who struck them,
> nor have they sought the Lord Almighty.
> So the Lord will cut off from Israel both head and tail,
> both palm branch and reed in a single day;
> the elders and prominent men are the head,
> the prophets who teach lies are the tail.
> Those who guide this people mislead them,
> and those who are guided are led astray. . . .

The Lord
(voice only)   Woe to those who make unjust laws,
> to those who issue oppressive decrees,
> to deprive the poor of their rights
>> and withhold justice from the oppressed of my people,
> making widows their prey
>> and robbing the fatherless.

> What will you do on the day of reckoning,
> > when disaster comes from afar?
> To whom will you run for help?
> > Where will you leave your riches?

Cast: **Isaiah, Person 1, Person 2, the Lord** (voice only)

God's Judgment on Assyria

Isaiah 10:5–19

The Lord

(voice only) Woe to the Assyrian, the rod of my anger,
> in whose hand is the club of my wrath!
I send him against a godless nation,
> I dispatch him against a people who anger me,
to seize loot and snatch plunder,
> and to trample them down like mud in the streets.
But this is not what he intends,
> this is not what he has in mind;
his purpose is to destroy,
> to put an end to many nations. [He says:]

Assyrian

(boastfully) Are not my commanders all kings? . . .
> Has not Calno fared like Carchemish?
Is not Hamath like Arpad,
> and Samaria like Damascus?
As my hand seized the kingdoms of the idols,
> kingdoms whose images excelled those of Jerusalem and
> > Samaria—
shall I not deal with Jerusalem and her images
> as I dealt with Samaria and her idols?

Isaiah When the Lord has finished all his work against Mount Zion and Jerusalem, he will say:

The Lord

(voice) I will punish the king of Assyria for the willful pride of his heart and the haughty look in his eyes.

Isaiah For he says:

Assyrian

(boastfully) By the strength of my hand I have done this,
> and by my wisdom, because I have understanding.
I removed the boundaries of nations,
> I plundered their treasures;
> like a mighty one I subdued their kings.
As one reaches into a nest,
> so my hand reached for the wealth of the nations;

as men gather abandoned eggs,
   so I gathered all the countries;
not one flapped a wing,
   or opened its mouth to chirp.

Isaiah   Does the ax raise itself above him who swings it,
   or the saw boast against him who uses it?
As if a rod were to wield him who lifts it up,
   or a club brandish him who is not wood!
Therefore, the Lord, the LORD Almighty,
   will send a wasting disease upon his sturdy warriors;
under his pomp a fire will be kindled
   like a blazing flame.
The Light of Israel will become a fire,
   their Holy One a flame;
in a single day it will burn and consume
   his thorns and his briers.
The splendor of his forests and fertile fields
   it will completely destroy,
   as when a sick man wastes away.
And the remaining trees of his forests will be so few
   that a child could write them down.

Cast: **The Lord** (voice only), **Assyrian**, **Isaiah**

The Remnant of Israel

Isaiah 10:20–27

Isaiah   In that day the remnant of Israel,
   the survivors of the house of Jacob,
will no longer rely on him
   who struck them down
but will truly rely on the LORD,
   the Holy One of Israel.
A remnant will return, a remnant of Jacob
   will return to the Mighty God.
Though your people, O Israel, be like the sand by the sea,
   only a remnant will return.
Destruction has been decreed,
   overwhelming and righteous.
The Lord, the LORD Almighty, will carry out
   the destruction decreed upon the whole land.

Therefore, this is what the Lord, the LORD Almighty, says:

The Lord
(voice only) O my people who live in Zion,
   do not be afraid of the Assyrians,

who beat you with a rod
    and lift up a club against you, as Egypt did.
Very soon my anger against you will end
    and my wrath will be directed to their destruction.

Isaiah   The Lord Almighty will lash them with a whip,
    as when he struck down Midian at the rock of Oreb;
and he will raise his staff over the waters,
    as he did in Egypt.
In that day their burden will be lifted from your shoulders,
    their yoke from your neck;
the yoke will be broken
    because you have grown so fat.

Cast: **Isaiah, the Lord** (voice only)

A Branch from Jesse

Isaiah 11:1–9

Isaiah   A shoot will come up from the stump of Jesse;
    from his roots a Branch will bear fruit.
The Spirit of the Lord will rest on him—

Singer 1   The Spirit of wisdom and of understanding,
    the Spirit of counsel and of power,
    the Spirit of knowledge and of the fear of the Lord—

Singer 2   And he will delight in the fear of the Lord.

Singer 1   He will not judge by what he sees with his eyes,
    or decide by what he hears with his ears.

Singer 2   With righteousness he will judge the needy,
    with justice he will give decisions for the poor of the earth.

Singer 1   He will strike the earth with the rod of his mouth;

Singer 2   with the breath of his lips he will slay the wicked.

**Singers 1
and 2**   Righteousness will be his belt
    and faithfulness the sash around his waist. (PAUSE)

Singer 1   The wolf will live with the lamb—

Singer 2   The leopard will lie down with the goat—

Singer 1   The calf and the lion and the yearling together;

**Singers 1
and 2**   and a little child will lead them.

Singer 2	The cow will feed with the bear, their young will lie down together—
Singer 1	The lion will eat straw like the ox.
Singer 2	The infant will play near the hole of the cobra.
Singer 1	The young child put his hand into the viper's nest.
Singer 2	They will neither harm nor destroy on all my holy mountain—

Singers 1
    and 2
	For the earth will be full of the knowledge of the LORD
	    as the waters cover the sea.

Cast: **Isaiah, Singer 1, Singer 2**

Songs of Praise

Isaiah 12:1–6

Isaiah	In that day you will say:

Singer 1	I will praise you, O LORD.
	    Although you were angry with me,
	your anger has turned away
	    and you have comforted me.

Singer 2	Surely God is my salvation; I will trust and not be afraid.
Singer 3	The LORD, the LORD, is my strength and my song; he has become my salvation.
Singers 1–3	With joy you will draw water from the wells of salvation.
Isaiah	In that day you will say:
Singer 1	Give thanks to the LORD, call on his name:
Singer 2	Make known among the nations what he has done, and proclaim that his name is exalted.
Singer 3	Sing to the LORD, for he has done glorious things—
Singer 1	Let this be known to all the world.
Singer 2	Shout aloud and sing for joy, people of Zion.
Singer 3	For great is the Holy One of Israel among you.

Cast: **Isaiah, Singer 1, Singer 2, Singer 3**

The Day of the Lord

Isaiah 13:6–13

Isaiah   Wail, for the day of the LORD is near;
      it will come like destruction from the Almighty.
     Because of this, all hands will go limp,
      every man's heart will melt.
     Terror will seize them,
      pain and anguish will grip them;
      they will writhe like a woman in labor.
     They will look aghast at each other,
      their faces aflame.

     See, the day of the LORD is coming
      —a cruel day, with wrath and fierce anger—
     to make the land desolate
      and destroy the sinners within it.
     The stars of heaven and their constellations
      will not show their light.
     The rising sun will be darkened
      and the moon will not give its light.

The Lord
(voice only) I will punish the world for its evil,
      the wicked for their sins.
     I will put an end to the arrogance of the haughty
      and will humble the pride of the ruthless.
     I will make man scarcer than pure gold,
      more rare than the gold of Ophir.
     Therefore I will make the heavens tremble;
      and the earth will shake from its place
     at the wrath of the LORD Almighty,
      in the day of his burning anger.

Cast: **Isaiah, the Lord** (voice only)

The Return from Exile

Isaiah 14:1–21

Isaiah   The LORD will have compassion on Jacob;
      once again he will choose Israel
      and will settle them in their own land.
     Aliens will join them
      and unite with the house of Jacob.
     Nations will take them
      and bring them to their own place.
     And the house of Israel will possess the nations

as menservants and maidservants in the LORD's land.
They will make captives of their captors
   and rule over their oppressors.

On the day the LORD gives you relief from suffering and turmoil and cruel bondage, you will take up this taunt against the king of Babylon:

Israelite 1
  (mocking)   How the oppressor has come to an end!

Israelite 2
  (mocking)   How his fury has ended!

Isaiah   The LORD has broken the rod of the wicked,
   the scepter of the rulers,
which in anger struck down peoples
   with unceasing blows,
and in fury subdued nations
   with relentless aggression.

Israelite 1   All the lands are at rest and at peace;
   they break into singing.

Israelite 2   Even the pine trees and the cedars of Lebanon
   exult over you and say.

Voice 1   Now that you have been laid low,
   no woodsman comes to cut us down.

Israelite 1   The grave below is all astir
   to meet you at your coming:

Israelite 2   It rouses the spirits of the departed to greet you—

Israelite 1   All those who were leaders in the world;
it makes them rise from their thrones—

Israelite 2   All those who were kings over the nations.
They will all respond,
   they will say to you:

Voice 2   You also have become weak, as we are:

Voices
  1 and 2   You have become like us.

Voice 3   All your pomp has been brought down to the grave,
   along with the noise of your harps:

Voice   Maggots are spread out beneath you
   and worms cover you.

Isaiah   How you have fallen from heaven,
   O morning star, son of the dawn!
You have been cast down to the earth,
   you who once laid low the nations!
You said in your heart:

Israelite 1	I will ascend to heaven;
Israelite 2	I will raise my throne above the stars of God;
Israelite 1	I will sit enthroned on the mount of assembly, on the utmost heights of the sacred mountain. I will ascend above the tops of the clouds.
Israelites 1 and 2	I will make myself like the Most High.

Isaiah	But you are brought down to the grave,
	    to the depths of the pit.
	
	Those who see you stare at you,
	    they ponder your fate:

Voice 2	Is this the man who shook the earth and made kingdoms tremble:

Voice 3	The man who made the world a desert,
	    who overthrew its cities
	    And would not let his captives go home?

Isaiah	All the kings of the nations lie in state,
	    each in his own tomb.
	But you are cast out of your tomb
	    like a rejected branch:
	you are covered with the slain,
	    with those pierced by the sword,
	    those who descend to the stones of the pit.
	Like a corpse trampled underfoot,
	    you will not join them in burial,
	for you have destroyed your land
	    and killed your people.
	
	The offspring of the wicked
	    will never be mentioned again.
	Prepare a place to slaughter his sons
	    for the sins of their forefathers;
	they are not to rise to inherit the land
	    and cover the earth with their cities.

Cast: **Isaiah, Israelite 1, Israelite 2, Voice 1, Voice 2, Voice 3**

A Prophecy against Babylon

Isaiah 14:22–27

Isaiah	[The Lord Almighty declares:]

The Lord
(voice only)   I will rise up against them. . . .
I will cut off from Babylon her name and survivors,
    her offspring and descendants. . . .
I will turn her into a place for owls
    and into swampland;
I will sweep her with the broom of destruction. . . .

Isaiah   The LORD Almighty has sworn:

The Lord
(voice)   Surely, as I have planned, so it will be,
    and as I have purposed, so it will stand.
I will crush the Assyrian in my land;
    on my mountains I will trample him down.
His yoke will be taken from my people,
    and his burden removed from their shoulders.

Isaiah   This is the plan determined for the whole world;
    this is the hand stretched out over all nations.
For the LORD Almighty has purposed, and who can thwart him?
    His hand is stretched out, and who can turn it back?

Cast: **Isaiah, the Lord** (voice only)

A Prophecy against Moab

From Isaiah 16:2–14

Isaiah   Like fluttering birds
    pushed from the nest,
so are the women of Moab
    at the fords of the Arnon.

Moabitess 1   Give us counsel.

Moabitess 2   Render a decision.

Moabitess 1   Make your shadow like night—

Moabitess 2   At high noon.

Moabitess 1   Hide the fugitives.

Moabitess 2   Do not betray the refugees.

Moabitess 1   Let the Moabite fugitives stay with you.

Moabitesses
1 and 2   Be their shelter from the destroyer.

Isaiah	The oppressor will come to an end,
	    and destruction will cease;
	    the aggressor will vanish from the land.
	In love a throne will be established;
	    in faithfulness a man will sit on it—
	    one from the house of David—
	one who in judging seeks justice
	    and speeds the cause of righteousness.

Judean 1	We have heard of Moab's pride—
Judean 2	Her overweening pride and conceit—
Judean 1	Her pride and her insolence—
Judean 2	But her boasts are empty. . . .
Isaiah	This is the word the LORD has already spoken concerning Moab. But now the LORD says:
The Lord (voice only)	Within three years, as a servant bound by contract would count them, Moab's splendor and all her many people will be despised, and her survivors will be very few and feeble.

Cast: **Isaiah, Moabitess 1, Moabitess 2, Judean 1, Judean 2, the Lord** (voice only)

An Oracle against Damascus

From Isaiah 17:1–11

Isaiah	An oracle concerning Damascus:

The Lord
(voice only)
	See, Damascus will no longer be a city
	    but will become a heap of ruins.
	The cities of Aroer will be deserted
	    and left to flocks, which will lie down,
	    with no one to make them afraid.
	The fortified city will disappear from Ephraim,
	    and royal power from Damascus;
	the remnant of Aram will be
	    like the glory of the Israelites. . . .
	
	In that day the glory of Jacob will fade;
	    the fat of his body will waste away.
	It will be as when a reaper gathers the standing grain
	    and harvests the grain with his arm—
	as when a man gleans heads of grain
	    in the Valley of Rephaim.
	Yet some gleanings will remain,

as when an olive tree is beaten,
   leaving two or three olives on the topmost branches,
     four or five on the fruitful boughs. . . .

Isaiah In that day men will look to their Maker
   and turn their eyes to the Holy One of Israel.
They will not look to the altars,
   the work of their hands,
and they will have no regard for the Asherah poles
   and the incense altars their fingers have made.

In that day their strong cities, which they left because of the Israelites, will be like places abandoned to thickets and undergrowth. And all will be desolation.

You have forgotten God your Savior;
   you have not remembered the Rock, your fortress.
Therefore, though you set out the finest plants
   and plant imported vines,
though on the day you set them out, you make them grow,
   and on the morning when you plant them, you bring them to bud,
yet the harvest will be as nothing
   in the day of disease and incurable pain.

Cast: **Isaiah, the Lord** (voice only)

A Prophecy against Cush

Isaiah 18:1–7

Isaiah Woe to the land of whirring wings
   along the rivers of Cush,
which sends envoys by sea
   in papyrus boats over the water.

Go, swift messengers,
to a people tall and smooth-skinned,
   to a people feared far and wide,
an aggressive nation of strange speech,
   whose land is divided by rivers.

All you people of the world,
   you who live on the earth,
when a banner is raised on the mountains,
   you will see it,
and when a trumpet sounds,
   you will hear it.
This is what the LORD says to me:

The Lord
(voice only)   I will remain quiet and will look on from my dwelling place,
  like shimmering heat in the sunshine,
   like a cloud of dew in the heat of harvest.
  For, before the harvest, when the blossom is gone
   and the flower becomes a ripening grape,
  he will cut off the shoots with pruning knives,
   and cut down and take away the spreading branches.
  They will all be left to the mountain birds of prey
   and to the wild animals;
  the birds will feed on them all summer,
   the wild animals all winter.

Isaiah   At that time gifts will be brought to the Lord Almighty

  from a people tall and smooth-skinned,
   from a people feared far and wide,
  an aggressive nation of strange speech,
   whose land is divided by rivers—

  the gifts will be brought to Mount Zion, the place of the Name of the
Lord Almighty.

Cast: **Isaiah, the Lord** (voice only)

A Prophecy about Egypt

Isaiah 19:1–12

Isaiah   An oracle concerning Egypt:

  See, the Lord rides on a swift cloud
   and is coming to Egypt.
  The idols of Egypt tremble before him,
   and the hearts of the Egyptians melt within them,
       [declares the Lord, the Lord Almighty].

The Lord
(voice only) I will stir up Egyptian against Egyptian—
  brother will fight against brother,
  neighbor against neighbor,
  city against city,
  kingdom against kingdom.
  The Egyptians will lose heart,
   and I will bring their plans to nothing;
  they will consult the idols and the spirits of the dead,
   the mediums and the spiritists.
  I will hand the Egyptians over
   to the power of a cruel master,
  and a fierce king will rule over them. . . .

Isaiah	The waters of the river will dry up, 　and the riverbed will be parched and dry. The canals will stink; 　the streams of Egypt will dwindle and dry up. The reeds and rushes will wither, 　also the plants along the Nile, 　at the mouth of the river. Every sown field along the Nile 　will become parched, will blow away and be no more. The fishermen will groan and lament, 　all who cast hooks into the Nile; those who throw nets on the water 　will pine away. Those who work with combed flax will despair, 　the weavers of fine linen will lose hope. The workers in cloth will be dejected, 　and all the wage earners will be sick at heart. The officials of Zoan are nothing but fools; 　the wise counselors of Pharaoh give senseless advice. How can you say to Pharaoh,
Wise man	I am one of the wise men, 　a disciple of the ancient kings.
Isaiah	Where are your wise men now? 　Let them show you and make known what the Lord Almighty 　has planned against Egypt.

Cast: **Isaiah, the Lord** (voice only), **Wise man**

A Prophecy against Babylon

Isaiah 21:1–10

Isaiah	An oracle concerning the Desert by the Sea: Like whirlwinds sweeping through the southland, 　an invader comes from the desert, 　from a land of terror. A dire vision has been shown to me: 　The traitor betrays, the looter takes loot.
Commander	Elam, attack! Media, lay siege! 　I will bring to an end all the groaning she caused.
Isaiah	At this my body is racked with pain, 　pangs seize me, like those of a woman in labor; I am staggered by what I hear,

I am bewildered by what I see.
My heart falters,
  fear makes me tremble;
the twilight I longed for
  has become a horror to me.

They set the tables,
  they spread the rugs,
  they eat, they drink!

Commander Get up, you officers,
  oil the shields!

Isaiah This is what the Lord says to me:

The Lord
  (voice only) Go, post a lookout
  and have him report what he sees.
When he sees chariots
  with teams of horses,
riders on donkeys
  or riders on camels,
let him be alert,
  fully alert.

Isaiah And the lookout shouted:

Lookout Day after day, my lord, I stand on the watchtower;
  every night I stay at my post.

Isaiah Look, here comes a man in a chariot
  with a team of horses.
And he gives back the answer:

Lookout Babylon has fallen, has fallen!
All the images of its gods
  lie shattered on the ground!

Isaiah O my people, crushed on the threshing floor,
  I tell you what I have heard
from the Lord Almighty,
  from the God of Israel.

Cast: **Isaiah**, **Commander**, **the Lord** (voice only), **Lookout**

Prophecies against Edom, Arabia, and Jerusalem

Isaiah 21:11–22:4, 12–14

Announcer An oracle concerning Dumah:

Isaiah Someone calls to me from Seir:

Seirite	Watchman, what is left of the night? Watchman, what is left of the night?
Isaiah	The watchman replies,
Watchman	Morning is coming, but also the night. If you would ask, then ask; and come back yet again. (PAUSE)
Announcer	An oracle concerning Arabia:

Isaiah	You caravans of Dedanites,
	    who camp in the thickets of Arabia,
	    bring water for the thirsty;
	you who live in Tema,
	    bring food for the fugitives.
	They flee from the sword,
	    from the drawn sword,
	from the bent bow
	    and from the heat of battle.
	
	This is what the Lord says to me:

The Lord (voice only)	Within one year, as a servant bound by contract would count it, all the pomp of Kedar will come to an end. The survivors of the bowmen, the warriors of Kedar, will be few. The Lord, the God of Israel, has spoken. (PAUSE)
Announcer	An oracle concerning the Valley of Vision:

Isaiah	What troubles you now,
	    that you have all gone up on the roofs,
	O town full of commotion,
	    O city of tumult and revelry?
	Your slain were not killed by the sword,
	    nor did they die in battle.
	All your leaders have fled together;
	    they have been captured without using the bow.
	All you who were caught were taken prisoner together,
	    having fled while the enemy was still far away. . . .

Young Isaiah	Turn away from me;
	    let me weep bitterly.
	Do not try to console me
	    over the destruction of my people. . . .

Isaiah	The Lord, the LORD Almighty,
	    called you on that day
	to weep and to wail,
	    to tear out your hair and put on sackcloth.
	But see, there is joy and revelry,

slaughtering of cattle and killing of sheep,
eating of meat and drinking of wine! [You say:]

Jew 1   Let us eat and drink.

Jew 2   For tomorrow we die!

Isaiah   The LORD Almighty has revealed this in my hearing:

The Lord   Till your dying day this sin will not be atoned for. . . .

Cast: **Announcer, Isaiah** (can be the same as Announcer), **Seirite, Watchman, the Lord** (voice only), **Young Isaiah** (can be the same as Isaiah), **Jew 1, Jew 2** (can be the same as Jew 1)

Praise to the Lord

Isaiah 25:1–5

Singer 1   O LORD, you are my God;
I will exalt you and praise your name.

Singer 2   For in perfect faithfulness
you have done marvelous things,
things planned long ago.

Singer 1   You have made the city a heap of rubble,
the fortified town a ruin.

Singer 2   The foreigners' stronghold a city no more;
it will never be rebuilt.

Singer 1   Therefore strong peoples will honor you;
cities of ruthless nations will revere you.

Singer 2   You have been a refuge for the poor,
a refuge for the needy in his distress.

Singer 1   A shelter from the storm
and a shade from the heat.

Singer 2   For the breath of the ruthless
is like a storm driving against a wall
and like the heat of the desert.

Singer 1   You silence the uproar of foreigners;
as heat is reduced by the shadow of a cloud,
so the song of the ruthless is stilled.

Cast: **Singer 1, Singer 2**

God Prepares a Banquet

Isaiah 25:6–9

Isaiah   On this mountain the Lord Almighty will prepare
    a feast of rich food for all peoples,
a banquet of aged wine—
    the best of meats and the finest of wines.
On this mountain he will destroy
    the shroud that enfolds all peoples,
the sheet that covers all nations;
    he will swallow up death forever.
The Sovereign Lord will wipe away the tears
    from all faces;
he will remove the disgrace of his people
    from all the earth.
The Lord has spoken.

In that day they will say:

**Believers
1 and 2**   Surely this is our God.

Believer 1   We trusted in him, and he saved us.

**Believers
1 and 2**   This is the Lord, we trusted in him.

Believer 2   Let us rejoice and be glad in his salvation.

Cast: **Isaiah, Believer 1, Believer 2**

A Song of Praise

Isaiah 26:1–8

Isaiah   In that day this song will be sung in the land of Judah:

Singer 1   We have a strong city;
    God makes salvation
    its walls and ramparts.

Singer 2   Open the gates
    that the righteous nation may enter,
    the nation that keeps faith.

Singer 3   You will keep in perfect peace
    him whose mind is steadfast,
    because he trusts in you.

Singer 1	Trust in the L<small>ORD</small> forever, for the L<small>ORD</small>, the L<small>ORD</small>, is the Rock eternal.
Singer 2	He humbles those who dwell on high, he lays the lofty city low; he levels it to the ground and casts it down to the dust.
Singer 3	Feet trample it down— the feet of the oppressed, the footsteps of the poor.
Singer 1	The path of the righteous is level; O upright One, you make the way of the righteous smooth.
Singers 2 and 3	Yes, L<small>ORD</small>, walking in the way of your laws, we wait for you; your name and renown are the desire of our hearts.

Cast: **Isaiah, Singer 1, Singer 2, Singer 3**

Deliverance of Israel

Isaiah 27:2–6

Isaiah	. . . Sing about a fruitful vineyard:
The Lord (voice only)	I, the L<small>ORD</small>, watch over it; I water it continually. I guard it day and night so that no one may harm it. I am not angry. If only there were briers and thorns confronting me! I would march against them in battle; I would set them all on fire. Or else let them come to me for refuge; let them make peace with me, yes, let them make peace with me.
Isaiah	In days to come Jacob will take root, Israel will bud and blossom and fill all the world with fruit.

Cast: **Isaiah, the Lord** (voice only)

Isaiah and the Drunken Prophets of Judah

Isaiah 28:7–13

Isaiah	And these also stagger from wine
	   and reel from beer:
	Priests and prophets stagger from beer
	   and are befuddled with wine;
	they reel from beer,
	   they stagger when seeing visions,
	   they stumble when rendering decisions.
	All the tables are covered with vomit
	   and there is not a spot without filth.

Priest 1	Who is it he is trying to teach?
Priest 2	To whom is he explaining his message?
Priest 1	To children weaned from their milk, to those just taken from the breast?
Priest 2	. . . Do and do, do and do.
Priest 1	Rule on rule, rule on rule.
Priest 2	A little here, a little there.
Isaiah	Very well then, with foreign lips and strange tongues God will speak to this people. . . .
The Lord (voice only)	This is the resting place, let the weary rest. This is the place of repose—

Isaiah	But they would not listen.
	So then, the word of the LORD to them will become:
	   Do and do, do and do,
	   rule on rule, rule on rule;
	   a little here, a little there—
	so that they will go and fall backward,
	   be injured and snared and captured.

Cast: **Isaiah, Priest 1, Priest 2, the Lord** (voice only)

A Cornerstone for Zion

Isaiah 28:14–22

Isaiah	Therefore hear the word of the LORD, you scoffers who rule this people in Jerusalem. You boast:

Ruler 1	We have entered into a covenant with death.
Ruler 2	With the grave we have made an agreement.

Ruler 1	When an overwhelming scourge sweeps by,
	  it cannot touch us,
	for we have made a lie our refuge
	  and falsehood our hiding place.

Isaiah	So this is what the Sovereign Lord says:

The Lord
(voice only)
	See, I lay a stone in Zion,
	  a tested stone,
	a precious cornerstone for a sure foundation;
	  the one who trusts will never be dismayed.
	I will make justice the measuring line
	  and righteousness the plumb line;
	hail will sweep away your refuge, the lie,
	  and water will overflow your hiding place.
	Your covenant with death will be annulled;
	  your agreement with the grave will not stand.
	When the overwhelming scourge sweeps by,
	  you will be beaten down by it.
	As often as it comes it will carry you away;
	  morning after morning, by day and by night,
	it will sweep through.

Isaiah	The understanding of this message
	  will bring sheer terror.
	The bed is too short to stretch out on,
	  the blanket too narrow to wrap around you.
	The Lord will rise up as he did at Mount Perazim,
	  he will rouse himself as in the Valley of Gibeon—
	to do his work, his strange work,
	  and perform his task, his alien task.
	Now stop your mocking,
	  or your chains will become heavier;
	the Lord, the Lord Almighty, has told me
	  of the destruction decreed against the whole land.

Cast: **Isaiah, Ruler 1, Ruler 2, the Lord** (voice only)

Woe to David's City

Isaiah 29:9–14

Isaiah	Be stunned and amazed, blind yourselves and be sightless;

be drunk, but not from wine,
    stagger, but not from beer.
The LORD has brought over you a deep sleep:

(to Prophet)   He has sealed your eyes . . .

(to Seer)   he has covered your heads. . . .

For you this whole vision is nothing but words sealed in a scroll. And if you give the scroll to someone who can read, and say to him:

Prophet   Read this, please,

Isaiah   He will answer,

Person 1   I can't; it is sealed.

Isaiah   Or if you give the scroll to someone who cannot read, and say:

Seer   Read this, please,

Isaiah   He will answer,

Person 2   I don't know how to read.

Isaiah   The Lord says:

The Lord
(voice only)   These people come near to me with their mouth
                    and honor me with their lips,
                    but their hearts are far from me.
                Their worship of me
                    is made up only of rules taught by men.
                Therefore once more I will astound these people
                    with wonder upon wonder;
                the wisdom of the wise will perish,
                    the intelligence of the intelligent will vanish.

Cast: **Isaiah, Prophet, Person 1, Seer, Person 2, the Lord** (voice only)

Hope for the Future

Isaiah 29:15–24

Isaiah   Woe to those who go to great depths
                    to hide their plans from the LORD,
                who do their work in darkness and think:

Person 1   Who sees us?

Person 2   Who will know?

Isaiah	You turn things upside down, as if the potter were thought to be like the clay! Shall what is formed say to him who formed it:
Pot	He did not make me.
Isaiah	Can the pot say of the potter:
Pot	He knows nothing.

Isaiah	In a very short time, will not Lebanon be turned into a fertile field
	    and the fertile field seem like a forest?
	In that day the deaf will hear the words of the scroll,
	    and out of gloom and darkness
	    the eyes of the blind will see.
	Once more the humble will rejoice in the LORD;
	    the needy will rejoice in the Holy One of Israel.
	The ruthless will vanish,
	    the mockers will disappear,
	    and all who have an eye for evil will be cut down—
	those who with a word make a man out to be guilty,
	    who ensnare the defender in court
	    and with false testimony deprive the innocent of justice.
	
	Therefore this is what the LORD, who redeemed Abraham, says to the house of Jacob:

The Lord	

(voice only)	No longer will Jacob be ashamed;
	    no longer will their faces grow pale.
	When they see among them their children,
	    the work of my hands,
	they will keep my name holy;
	    they will acknowledge the holiness of the Holy One of Jacob,
	    and will stand in awe of the God of Israel.
	Those who are wayward in spirit will gain understanding;
	    those who complain will accept instruction.

Cast: **Isaiah, Person 1, Person 2, Pot, the Lord** (voice only)

Woe to the Obstinate Nation

From Isaiah 30:8–18

Isaiah	Go now, write it on a tablet for them,
	    inscribe it on a scroll,
	that for the days to come
	    it may be an everlasting witness.
	These are rebellious people, deceitful children,

children unwilling to listen to the LORD's instruction.
They say to the seers [and to the prophets:]

Person 1 See no more visions!

Person 2 Give us no more visions of what is right!

Person 1 Tell us pleasant things,
   prophesy illusions.

Person 2 Leave this way—
   get off this path.

Person 1 Stop confronting us
   with the Holy One of Israel!

Isaiah Therefore, this is what the Holy One of Israel says:

The Lord
(voice only) Because you have rejected this message,
   relied on oppression
   and depended on deceit,
this sin will become for you
   like a high wall, cracked and bulging,
   that collapses suddenly, in an instant.
It will break in pieces like pottery,
   shattered so mercilessly
that among its pieces not a fragment will be found
   for taking coals from a hearth
   or scooping water out of a cistern.

Isaiah This is what the Sovereign LORD, the Holy One of Israel, says:

The Lord
(voice) In repentance and rest is your salvation,
   in quietness and trust is your strength,
   but you would have none of it. . . .

Isaiah Yet the LORD longs to be gracious to you;
   he rises to show you compassion.
For the LORD is a God of justice.
   Blessed are all who wait for him!

Cast: **Isaiah, Person 1, Person 2, the Lord** (voice only)

God Will Bless His People

Isaiah 30:19–26

Isaiah O people of Zion, who live in Jerusalem, you will weep no more. How gracious [the Lord] will be when you cry for help! As soon as he hears, he will answer you. Although the Lord gives you the bread of adversity and the water of affliction, your teachers will be hidden no more; with your own eyes you will see them. Whether you turn to the right or to the left, your ears will hear a voice behind you, saying:

The Lord
(voice only) This is the way; walk in it.

Isaiah Then you will defile your idols overlaid with silver and your images covered with gold; you will throw them away . . . and say to them:

Person Away with you!

Isaiah He will also send you rain for the seed you sow in the ground, and the food that comes from the land will be rich and plentiful. In that day your cattle will graze in broad meadows. The oxen and donkeys that work the soil will eat fodder and mash, spread out with fork and shovel. In the day of great slaughter, when the towers fall, streams of water will flow on every high mountain and every lofty hill. The moon will shine like the sun, and the sunlight will be seven times brighter, like the light of seven full days, when the LORD binds up the bruises of his people and heals the wounds he inflicted.

Cast: **Isaiah, the Lord** (voice only), **Person**

Woe to Those Who Rely on Egypt

Isaiah 31:1–9

Isaiah Woe to those who go down to Egypt for help,
   who rely on horses,
who trust in the multitude of their chariots
   and in the great strength of their horsemen,
but do not look to the Holy One of Israel,
   or seek help from the LORD.
Yet he too is wise and can bring disaster;
   he does not take back his words.
He will rise up against the house of the wicked,
   against those who help evildoers.
But the Egyptians are men and not God;
   their horses are flesh and not spirit.
When the LORD stretches out his hand,
   he who helps will stumble,
   he who is helped will fall;
   both will perish together.

This is what the LORD says to me:

The Lord
(voice only) As a lion growls,
   a great lion over his prey—
and though a whole band of shepherds

	is called together against him,
	he is not frightened by their shouts
	or disturbed by their clamor—
	so the Lord Almighty will come down
	to do battle on Mount Zion and on its heights.
	Like birds hovering overhead,
	the Lord Almighty will shield Jerusalem;
	he will shield it and deliver it,
	he will "pass over" it and will rescue it.

Isaiah   [The Lord,
             whose fire is in Zion,
             whose furnace is in Jerusalem, declares:]

The Lord
  (voice)   Return to him you have so greatly revolted against, O Israelites. For in that day every one of you will reject the idols of silver and gold your sinful hands have made.

         Assyria will fall by a sword that is not of man;
           a sword, not of mortals, will devour them.
         They will flee before the sword
           and their young men will be put to forced labor.
         Their stronghold will fall because of terror;
           at sight of the battle standard their commanders will panic

Cast: **Isaiah, the Lord** (voice only)

Distress and Help

Isaiah 33:10–16

Isaiah   [The Lord says:]

The Lord
  (voice only) Now will I arise. . . .
         Now will I be exalted;
         now will I be lifted up.
      You conceive chaff,
         you give birth to straw;
         your breath is a fire that consumes you.
      The peoples will be burned as if to lime;
         like cut thornbushes they will be set ablaze.

      You who are far away, hear what I have done;
         you who are near, acknowledge my power!

Isaiah   The sinners in Zion are terrified;
         trembling grips the godless:

Jew 1   Who of us can dwell with the consuming fire?

Jew 2	Who of us can dwell with everlasting burning?

Isaiah	He who walks righteously
	    and speaks what is right,
	who rejects gain from extortion
	    and keeps his hand from accepting bribes,
	who stops his ears against plots of murder
	    and shuts his eyes against contemplating evil—
	this is the man who will dwell on the heights,
	    whose refuge will be the mountain fortress.
	His bread will be supplied,
	    and water will not fail him.

Cast: **Isaiah, the Lord** (voice only), **Jew 1, Jew 2**

Joy of the Redeemed

Isaiah 35:1–10

Voice 1	The desert and the parched land will be glad; the wilderness will rejoice and blossom.

Voice 2	Like the crocus, it will burst into bloom;
	    it will rejoice greatly and shout for joy.
	The glory of Lebanon will be given to it,
	    the splendor of Carmel and Sharon.

Voice 3	They will see the glory of the LORD, the splendor of our God.
Voice 1	Strengthen the feeble hands, steady the knees that give way.
Voice 2	Say to those with fearful hearts:

Voice 3	Be strong, do not fear;
	your God will come,
	    he will come with vengeance;
	with divine retribution
	    he will come to save you.

Voice 1	Then will the eyes of the blind be opened and the ears of the deaf unstopped.
Voice 2	Then will the lame leap like a deer, and the mute tongue shout for joy.
Voice 1	Water will gush forth in the wilderness and streams in the desert.
Voice 2	The burning sand will become a pool—

Voice 3	The thirsty ground bubbling springs.
Voice 1	In the haunts where jackals once lay—
Voice 2	Grass and reeds and papyrus will grow.
Voice 3	And a highway will be there; it will be called—
Voices 1–3 (strongly)	The Way of Holiness.
Voice 2	The unclean will not journey on it—
Voice 3	It will be for those who walk in that Way;
Voice 1	Wicked fools will not go about on it.
Voice 2	No lion will be there.
Voice 3	Nor will any ferocious beast get up on it.
Voice 1	They will not be found there.
Voice 2	But only the redeemed will walk there.
Voice 3	And the ransomed of the LORD will return.
Voice 1	They will enter Zion with singing; everlasting joy will crown their heads.
Voice 2	Gladness and joy will overtake them—
Voice 3	And sorrow and sighing will flee away.

Cast: **Voice 1, Voice 2, Voice 3**

Sennacherib Threatens Jerusalem

Isaiah 36:1–22

Narrator	In the fourteenth year of King Hezekiah's reign, Sennacherib king of Assyria attacked all the fortified cities of Judah and captured them. Then the king of Assyria sent his field commander with a large army from Lachish to King Hezekiah at Jerusalem. When the commander stopped at the aqueduct of the Upper Pool, on the road to the Washerman's Field, Eliakim son of Hilkiah the palace administrator, Shebna the secretary, and Joah son of Asaph the recorder went out to him. (PAUSE) The field commander said to them:
Commander	Tell Hezekiah, This is what the great king, the king of Assyria, says:
King	On what are you basing this confidence of yours? You say you have strategy and military strength—but you speak only empty words. On whom

213

are you depending, that you rebel against me? Look now, you are depending on Egypt, that splintered reed of a staff, which pierces a man's hand and wounds him if he leans on it! Such is Pharaoh king of Egypt to all who depend on him.

Commander   And if you say to me:

Person   We are depending on the LORD our God—

Commander   Isn't he the one whose high places and altars Hezekiah removed, saying to Judah and Jerusalem, "You must worship before this altar"?

Come now, make a bargain with my master, the king of Assyria: I will give you two thousand horses—if you can put riders on them! How then can you repulse one officer of the least of my master's officials, even though you are depending on Egypt for chariots and horsemen? Furthermore, have I come to attack and destroy this land without the LORD? The LORD himself told me to march against this country and destroy it.

Narrator   Then Eliakim, Shebna and Joah said to the field commander:

Eliakim   Please speak to your servants in Aramaic, since we understand it. Don't speak to us in Hebrew in the hearing of the people on the wall.

Narrator   But the commander replied:

Commander   Was it only to your master and you that my master sent me to say these things, and not to the men sitting on the wall . . . ?

Narrator   Then the commander stood and called out in Hebrew:

Commander   Hear the words of the great king, the king of Assyria! This is what the king says:

King   Do not let Hezekiah deceive you. He cannot deliver you! Do not let Hezekiah persuade you to trust in the LORD when he says, "The LORD will surely deliver us; this city will not be given into the hand of the king of Assyria."

Do not listen to Hezekiah.

Commander   This is what the king of Assyria says:

King   Make peace with me and come out to me. Then every one of you will eat from his own vine and fig tree and drink water from his own cistern, until I come and take you to a land like your own—a land of grain and new wine, a land of bread and vineyards.

Commander   Do not let Hezekiah mislead you when he says, "The LORD will deliver us." Has the god of any nation ever delivered his land from the hand of the king of Assyria? Where are the gods of Hamath and Arpad? Where are the gods of Sepharvaim? Have they rescued Samaria from my hand? Who of all the gods of these countries has been able to save his land from me? How then can the LORD deliver Jerusalem from my hand?

Narrator	But the people remained silent and said nothing in reply, because the king had commanded, "Do not answer him."
	Then Eliakim son of Hilkiah the palace administrator, Shebna the secretary, and Joah son of Asaph the recorder went to Hezekiah, with their clothes torn, and told him what the field commander had said.

Cast: **Narrator, Commander, King, Person, Eliakim**

The King Asks Isaiah's Advice

Isaiah 37:1–7

Narrator	When King Hezekiah heard [what the field commander had said], he tore his clothes and put on sackcloth and went into the temple of the LORD. He sent Eliakim the palace administrator, Shebna the secretary, and the leading priests, all wearing sackcloth, to the prophet Isaiah son of Amoz. They told him, "This is what Hezekiah says":
Hezekiah	This day is a day of distress and rebuke and disgrace, as when children come to the point of birth and there is no strength to deliver them. It may be that the LORD your God will hear the words of the field commander, whom his master, the king of Assyria, has sent to ridicule the living God, and that he will rebuke him for the words the LORD your God has heard. Therefore pray for the remnant that still survives.
Narrator	When King Hezekiah's officials came to Isaiah, Isaiah said to them:
Isaiah	Tell your master, "This is what the LORD says: Do not be afraid of what you have heard—those words with which the underlings of the king of Assyria have blasphemed me. Listen! I am going to put a spirit in him so that when he hears a certain report, he will return to his own country, and there I will have him cut down with the sword."

Cast: **Narrator, Hezekiah, Isaiah**

Hezekiah's Prayer

Isaiah 37:8–20

Narrator	When the field commander heard that the king of Assyria had left Lachish, he withdrew and found the king fighting against Libnah.
	Now Sennacherib received a report that Tirhakah, the Cushite king ⌐of Egypt¬, was marching out to fight against him. When he heard it, he sent messengers to Hezekiah with this word: "Say to Hezekiah king of Judah":

Sennacherib	Do not let the god you depend on deceive you when he says, "Jerusalem will not be handed over to the king of Assyria." Surely you have heard what the kings of Assyria have done to all the countries, destroying them completely. And will you be delivered? Did the gods of the nations that were destroyed by my forefathers deliver them—the gods of Gozan, Haran, Rezeph and the people of Eden who were in Tel Assar? Where is the king of Hamath, the king of Arpad, the king of the city of Sepharvaim, or of Hena or Ivvah?
Narrator	Hezekiah received the letter from the messengers and read it. Then he went up to the temple of the LORD and spread it out before the LORD. And Hezekiah prayed to the LORD:
Hezekiah	O LORD Almighty, God of Israel, enthroned between the cherubim, you alone are God over all the kingdoms of the earth. You have made heaven and earth. Give ear, O LORD, and hear; open your eyes, O LORD, and see; listen to all the words Sennacherib has sent to insult the living God.
	It is true, O LORD, that the Assyrian kings have laid waste all these peoples and their lands. They have thrown their gods into the fire and destroyed them, for they were not gods but only wood and stone, fashioned by human hands. Now, O LORD our God, deliver us from his hand, so that all kingdoms on earth may know that you alone, O LORD, are God.

Cast: **Narrator, Sennacherib, Hezekiah**

Sennacherib's Fall

Isaiah 37:21–35

Narrator	Then Isaiah son of Amoz sent a message to Hezekiah: . . .

Isaiah	The Daughter of Jerusalem
	   tosses her head as you flee.
	Who is it you have insulted and blasphemed?
	   Against whom have you raised your voice
	and lifted your eyes in pride?
	   Against the Holy One of Israel!
	By your messengers
	   you have heaped insults on the Lord.
	And you have said:

King of Assyria	With my many chariots
	I have ascended the heights of the mountains,
	   the utmost heights of Lebanon.
	I have cut down its tallest cedars,
	   the choicest of its pines.
	I have reached its remotest heights,

the finest of its forests.
I have dug wells in foreign lands
   and drunk the water there.
With the soles of my feet
   I have dried up all the streams of Egypt.

The Lord
(voice only) Have you not heard?
   Long ago I ordained it.
In days of old I planned it;
   now I have brought it to pass,
that you have turned fortified cities
   into piles of stone.
Their people, drained of power,
   are dismayed and put to shame.
They are like plants in the field,
   like tender green shoots,
like grass sprouting on the roof,
   scorched before it grows up.

But I know where you stay
   and when you come and go
   and how you rage against me.
Because you rage against me
   and because your insolence has reached my ears,
I will put my hook in your nose
   and my bit in your mouth,
and I will make you return
   by the way you came.

Isaiah This will be the sign for you, O Hezekiah:

This year you will eat what grows by itself,
   and the second year what springs from that.
But in the third year sow and reap,
   plant vineyards and eat their fruit.
Once more a remnant of the house of Judah
   will take root below and bear fruit above.
For out of Jerusalem will come a remnant,
   and out of Mount Zion a band of survivors.
The zeal of the LORD Almighty
   will accomplish this.

Therefore this is what the LORD says concerning the king of Assyria:

The Lord
(voice) He will not enter this city
   or shoot an arrow here.
He will not come before it with shield
   or build a siege ramp against it.
By the way that he came he will return;
   he will not enter this city. . . .

> I will defend this city and save it,
>> for my sake and for the sake of David my servant!

Cast: **Narrator, Isaiah, King of Assyria, the Lord** (voice only)

King Hezekiah's Illness

Isaiah 38:1–8 [9–20]

Narrator   In those days Hezekiah became ill and was at the point of death. The prophet Isaiah son of Amoz went to him and said:

Isaiah   This is what the LORD says:

The Lord
   (voice only) Put your house in order, because you are going to die; you will not recover.

Narrator   Hezekiah turned his face to the wall and prayed to the LORD:

Hezekiah   Remember, O LORD, how I have walked before you faithfully and with wholehearted devotion and have done what is good in your eyes.

Narrator   And Hezekiah wept bitterly.

   Then the word of the LORD came to Isaiah: "Go and tell Hezekiah: 'This is what the LORD, the God of your father David, says'":

The Lord
   (voice) I have heard your prayer and seen your tears; I will add fifteen years to your life. And I will deliver you and this city from the hand of the king of Assyria. I will defend this city.

Isaiah   This is the LORD's sign to you that the LORD will do what he has promised:

The Lord
   (voice) I will make the shadow cast by the sun go back the ten steps it has gone down on the stairway of Ahaz.

Narrator   So the sunlight went back the ten steps it had gone down. (PAUSE)

   [A writing of Hezekiah king of Judah after his illness and recovery: . . .

Hezekiah
   (to
   audience) In the prime of my life
      must I go through the gates of death
      and be robbed of the rest of my years?
   I will not again see the LORD,
      the LORD, in the land of the living;
   no longer will I look on mankind,
      or be with those who now dwell in this world.
   Like a shepherd's tent my house
      has been pulled down and taken from me.
   Like a weaver I have rolled up my life,
      and he has cut me off from the loom;

day and night you made an end of me.
I waited patiently till dawn,
    but like a lion he broke all my bones;
    day and night you made an end of me.
I cried like a swift or thrush,
    I moaned like a mourning dove.
My eyes grew weak as I looked to the heavens.

(praying)   I am troubled; O Lord, come to my aid!

(to
audience)   But what can I say?
    He has spoken to me, and he himself has done this.
I will walk humbly all my years
    because of this anguish of my soul.

(praying)   Lord, by such things men live;
    and my spirit finds life in them too.
You restored me to health
    and let me live.
Surely it was for my benefit
    that I suffered such anguish.
In your love you kept me
    from the pit of destruction;
you have put all my sins
    behind your back.
For the grave cannot praise you,
    death cannot sing your praise;
those who go down to the pit
    cannot hope for your faithfulness.
The living, the living—they praise you,
    as I am doing today;
fathers tell their children
    about your faithfulness.

(to
audience)   The LORD will save me,
    and we will sing with stringed instruments
all the days of our lives
    in the temple of the LORD.]

Cast: **Narrator, Isaiah, the Lord** (voice only; can be the same as Isaiah), **Hezekiah**

Envoys from Babylon

Isaiah 39:1–8

Narrator   Merodach-Baladan son of Baladan king of Babylon sent Hezekiah letters and a gift, because he had heard of his illness and recovery. Hezekiah received the envoys gladly and showed them what was in his storehouses—the silver, the gold, the spices, the fine oil, his entire armory and everything found among his treasures. There was nothing in his palace or in all his kingdom that Hezekiah did not show them.

Then Isaiah the prophet went to King Hezekiah [and asked:]

Isaiah What did those men say, and where did they come from?

[Narrator [Hezekiah replied:]]

Hezekiah From a distant land. They came to me from Babylon.

Isaiah What did they see in your palace?

Hezekiah
(proudly) They saw everything in my palace. There is nothing among my treasures that I did not show them.

[Narrator Then Isaiah said to Hezekiah:]

Isaiah
(severely) Hear the word of the LORD Almighty:

The Lord
(voice only) The time will surely come when everything in your palace, and all that your fathers have stored up until this day, will be carried off to Babylon.

Isaiah Nothing will be left, says the LORD. And some of your descendants, your own flesh and blood who will be born to you, will be taken away, and they will become eunuchs in the palace of the king of Babylon.

Hezekiah The word of the LORD you have spoken is good.

Narrator For he thought:

Hezekiah There will be peace and security in my lifetime.

Cast: **Narrator, Isaiah, Hezekiah, the Lord** (voice only, or can be the same as Isaiah)

Comfort for God's People

Isaiah 40:1–11

The Lord
(voice only) Comfort, comfort my people—

Isaiah
(with
flourish) Says your God.

The Lord
(voice) Speak tenderly to Jerusalem,
  and proclaim to her
that her hard service has been completed,
  that her sin has been paid for,

	that she has received from the LORD's hand double for all her sins.
Isaiah	A voice of one calling:
Voice	"In the desert prepare the way for the LORD; make straight in the wilderness a highway for our God. Every valley shall be raised up, every mountain and hill made low; the rough ground shall become level, the rugged places a plain. And the glory of the LORD will be revealed, and all mankind together will see it. For the mouth of the LORD has spoken."
Isaiah	A voice says:
Voice	Cry out.
Isaiah	What shall I cry?
Voice	"All men are like grass, and all their glory is like the flowers of the field. The grass withers and the flowers fall, because the breath of the LORD blows on them. Surely the people are grass.
Isaiah	"The grass withers and the flowers fall, but the word of our God stands forever."
Voice	You who bring good tidings to Zion, go up on a high mountain. You who bring good tidings to Jerusalem, lift up your voice with a shout, lift it up, do not be afraid; say to the towns of Judah, "Here is your God!"
Isaiah	See, the Sovereign LORD comes with power, and his arm rules for him. See, his reward is with him, and his recompense accompanies him. He tends his flock like a shepherd: He gathers the lambs in his arms and carries them close to his heart; he gently leads those that have young.

Cast: **The Lord** (voice only), **Isaiah**, **Voice**

Israel's Incomparable God

Isaiah 40:12–31

Voice 1   Who has measured the waters in the hollow of his hand,
    or with the breadth of his hand marked off the heavens?

Voice 2   Who has held the dust of the earth in a basket,
    or weighed the mountains on the scales
    and the hills in a balance?

Voice 3   Who has understood the mind of the Lord—

Voice 1   Or instructed him as his counselor?

Voice 2   Whom did the Lord consult to enlighten him,
    and who taught him the right way?

Voice 3   Who was it that taught him knowledge
    or showed him the path of understanding?

Voice 1   Surely the nations are like a drop in a bucket;
    they are regarded as dust on the scales;
    he weighs the islands as though they were fine dust.

Voice 2   Lebanon is not sufficient for altar fires,
    nor its animals enough for burnt offerings.

Voice 3   Before him all the nations are as nothing;
    they are regarded by him as worthless
    and less than nothing.

Voice 1   To whom, then, will you compare God?

Voice 2   What image will you compare him to?

Voice 3   As for an idol, a craftsman casts it,
    and a goldsmith overlays it with gold
    and fashions silver chains for it.
    A man too poor to present such an offering
    selects wood that will not rot.
    He looks for a skilled craftsman
    to set up an idol that will not topple.

Voice 1   Do you not know?

Voice 2   Have you not heard?

Voice 3   Has it not been told you from the beginning?

Voice 1   Have you not understood since the earth was founded?

Voice 2   He sits enthroned above the circle of the earth,
    and its people are like grasshoppers.

Voice 3	He stretches out the heavens like a canopy, and spreads them out like a tent to live in.
Voice 1	He brings princes to naught and reduces the rulers of this world to nothing.

Voice 2	No sooner are they planted,
	    no sooner are they sown,
	    no sooner do they take root in the ground,
	than he blows on them and they wither,
	    and a whirlwind sweeps them away like chaff.

Voice 3	[The Holy One says:]

The Lord
(voice only)
	To whom will you compare me?
	    Or who is my equal? . . .
	Lift your eyes and look to the heavens:
	    Who created all these?

Voice 3	He who brings out the starry host one by one,
	    and calls them each by name.
	Because of his great power and mighty strength,
	    not one of them is missing.
	
	Why do you say, O Jacob,
	    and complain, O Israel,

Person	My way is hidden from the LORD; my cause is disregarded by my God.

Voice 3	Do you not know?
	    Have you not heard?
	The LORD is the everlasting God,
	    the Creator of the ends of the earth.

Voice 1	He will not grow tired or weary, and his understanding no one can fathom.
Voice 2	He gives strength to the weary and increases the power of the weak.
Voice 3	Even youths grow tired and weary—
Voice 1	And young men stumble and fall.
Voice 2	But those who hope in the LORD will renew their strength.
Voice 3	They will soar on wings like eagles.
Voice 2	They will run and not grow weary.
Voice 1	They will walk and not be faint.

Cast: **Voice 1, Voice 2, Voice 3**, the **Lord** (voice only), **Person**

223

The Servant of the Lord

Isaiah 42:1–9

[Isaiah [The Lord says:]**]**

The Lord
 (voice only) Here is my servant, whom I uphold,
    my chosen one in whom I delight;
  I will put my Spirit on him
    and he will bring justice to the nations.
  He will not shout or cry out,
    or raise his voice in the streets.
  A bruised reed he will not break,
    and a smoldering wick he will not snuff out.
  In faithfulness he will bring forth justice;
    he will not falter or be discouraged
  till he establishes justice on earth.
    In his law the islands will put their hope.

Isaiah This is what God the Lord says—
  he who created the heavens and stretched
    them out,
    who spread out the earth and all that comes
    out of it,
  who gives breath to its people,
    and life to those who walk on it:

The Lord
 (voice) I, the Lord, have called you in righteousness;
    I will take hold of your hand.
  I will keep you and will make you
    to be a covenant for the people
    and a light for the Gentiles,
  to open eyes that are blind,
    to free captives from prison
    and to release from the dungeon those who
    sit in darkness.

  I am the Lord; that is my name!
    I will not give my glory to another
    or my praise to idols.
  See, the former things have taken place,
    and new things I declare;
  before they spring into being
    I announce them to you.

Cast: **Isaiah, the Lord** (voice only)

God's Mercy

Isaiah 43:14–21

Isaiah	This is what the LORD says— your Redeemer, the Holy One of Israel:

The Lord
(voice only)
	For your sake I will send to Babylon
	        and bring down as fugitives all the Babylonians,
	        in the ships in which they took pride.
	    I am the LORD, your Holy One,
	        Israel's Creator, your King.

Isaiah	This is what the LORD says—
	    he who made a way through the sea,
	        a path through the mighty waters,
	    who drew out the chariots and horses,
	        the army and reinforcements together,
	    and they lay there, never to rise again,
	        extinguished, snuffed out like a wick:

The Lord
(voice)
	Forget the former things;
	        do not dwell on the past.
	    See, I am doing a new thing!
	        Now it springs up; do you not perceive it?
	    I am making a way in the desert
	        and streams in the wasteland.
	    The wild animals honor me,
	        the jackals and the owls,
	    because I provide water in the desert
	        and streams in the wasteland,
	    to give drink to my people, my chosen,
	        the people I formed for myself
	        that they may proclaim my praise.

Cast: **Isaiah, the Lord** (voice only)

The Lord, Not Idols

Isaiah 44:1–8

Isaiah	But now listen, O Jacob, my servant,
	        Israel, whom I have chosen.
	    This is what the LORD says—
	        he who made you, who formed you in the womb,
	        and who will help you:

225

The Lord
(voice only)
	Do not be afraid, O Jacob, my servant,
	    Jeshurun, whom I have chosen.
	For I will pour water on the thirsty land,
	    and streams on the dry ground;
	I will pour out my Spirit on your offspring,
	    and my blessing on your descendants.
	They will spring up like grass in a meadow,
	    like poplar trees by flowing streams.

Isaiah	One will say:
Person 1	I belong to the LORD.
Isaiah	Another will call himself by the name of Jacob; still another will write on his hand:
Person 2 (slowly, writing)	"The LORD's"
Isaiah	and will take the name Israel.
Person 2	This is what the LORD says—
Isaiah	Israel's King and Redeemer, the LORD Almighty:

The Lord
(voice)
	I am the first and I am the last;
	    apart from me there is no God.
	Who then is like me? Let him proclaim it.
	    Let him declare and lay out before me
	what has happened since I established my ancient people,
	    and what is yet to come—
	    yes, let him foretell what will come.
	Do not tremble, do not be afraid.
	    Did I not proclaim this and foretell it long ago?
	You are my witnesses. Is there any God besides me?
	    No, there is no other Rock; I know not one.

Cast: **Isaiah, the Lord** (voice only), **Person 1**, **Person 2** (can be the same as the Lord)

Idolatry Is Ridiculed

Isaiah 44:9–20

Isaiah	All who make idols are nothing,
	    and the things they treasure are worthless.
	Those who would speak up for them are blind;
	    they are ignorant, to their own shame.
	Who shapes a god and casts an idol,

which can profit him nothing?
He and his kind will be put to shame;
   craftsmen are nothing but men.
Let them all come together and take their stand;
   they will be brought down to terror and infamy.

The blacksmith takes a tool
   and works with it in the coals;
he shapes an idol with hammers,
   he forges it with the might of his arm.
He gets hungry and loses his strength;
   he drinks no water and grows faint.
The carpenter measures with a line
   and makes an outline with a marker;
he roughs it out with chisels
   and marks it with compasses.
He shapes it in the form of man,
   of man in all his glory,
   that it may dwell in a shrine.
He cut down cedars,
   or perhaps took a cypress or oak.
He let it grow among the trees of the forest,
   or planted a pine, and the rain made it grow.
It is man's fuel for burning;
   some of it he takes and warms himself,
   he kindles a fire and bakes bread.
But he also fashions a god and worships it;
   he makes an idol and bows down to it.

(with irony)
Half of the wood he burns in the fire;
   over it he prepares his meal,
   he roasts his meat and eats his fill.
He also warms himself and says:

Idol worshiper
Ah! I am warm; I see the fire.

Isaiah (with irony)
From the rest he makes a god, his idol;
   he bows down to it and worships.
He prays to it and says:

Idol worshiper (stupidly)
Save me; you are my god.

Isaiah
They know nothing, they understand nothing;
   their eyes are plastered over so they cannot see,
   and their minds closed so they cannot understand.

227

No one stops to think,
    no one has the knowledge or understanding to say:

Wiser person
  (reflec-
    tively)   Half of it I used for fuel;
      I even baked bread over its coals,
      I roasted meat and I ate.
    Shall I make a detestable thing from what is left?
      Shall I bow down to a block of wood?

Isaiah   He feeds on ashes, a deluded heart misleads him;
      he cannot save himself, or say:

Wiser person   Is not this thing in my right hand a lie?

Cast: **Isaiah, Idol worshiper, Wiser person**

The Lord, the Creator and Savior

Isaiah 44:21–25 [26–28]

[Isaiah   [The Lord says:]]

The Lord
  (voice only) Remember these things, O Jacob,
      for you are my servant, O Israel.
    I have made you, you are my servant;
      O Israel, I will not forget you.
    I have swept away your offenses like a cloud,
      your sins like the morning mist.
    Return to me,
      for I have redeemed you.

Isaiah   Sing for joy, O heavens, for the LORD has done this;
      shout aloud, O earth beneath.
    Burst into song, you mountains,
      you forests and all your trees,
    for the LORD has redeemed Jacob,
      he displays his glory in Israel.

    This is what the LORD says—
      your Redeemer, who formed you in the womb:

The Lord
  (voice)   I am the LORD,
    who has made all things,
    who alone stretched out the heavens,
    who spread out the earth by myself,

    who foils the signs of false prophets
      and makes fools of diviners,
    who overthrows the learning of the wise

and turns it into nonsense
[who carries out the words of his servants
    and fulfills the predictions of his messengers,

who says of Jerusalem, "It shall be inhabited,"
    of the towns of Judah, "They shall be built,"
    and of their ruins, "I will restore them,"
who says to the watery deep, "Be dry,
    and I will dry up your streams,"
who says of Cyrus, "He is my shepherd
    and will accomplish all that I please;
    he will say of Jerusalem:

Cyrus   'Let it be rebuilt,'

The Lord
  (voice)   and of the temple:

Cyrus   'Let its foundations be laid.'"]

Cast: **Isaiah, the Lord** (voice only), **[Cyrus]**

The Lord Appoints Cyrus

Isaiah 45:1–8

Isaiah   This is what the LORD says to his anointed,
    to Cyrus, whose right hand I take hold of
to subdue nations before him
    and to strip kings of their armor,
to open doors before him
    so that gates will not be shut:

The Lord
  (voice only) I will go before you
    and will level the mountains;
I will break down gates of bronze
    and cut through bars of iron.
I will give you the treasures of darkness,
    riches stored in secret places,
so that you may know that I am the LORD,
    the God of Israel, who summons you by name.
For the sake of Jacob my servant,
    of Israel my chosen,
I summon you by name
    and bestow on you a title of honor,
    though you do not acknowledge me.
I am the LORD, and there is no other;
    apart from me there is no God.
I will strengthen you,

though you have not acknowledged me,
so that from the rising of the sun
    to the place of its setting
men may know there is none besides me.
    I am the LORD, and there is no other.
I form the light and create darkness,
    I bring prosperity and create disaster;
    I, the LORD, do all these things.

You heavens above, rain down righteousness;
    let the clouds shower it down.
Let the earth open wide,
    let salvation spring up,
let righteousness grow with it;
    I, the LORD, have created it.

Cast: **Isaiah, the Lord** (voice only)

The Lord of Creation and History

Isaiah 45:9–19

Isaiah Woe to him who quarrels with his Maker,
    to him who is but a potsherd among the potsherds on the ground.
Does the clay say to the potter,
    "What are you making?"
Does your work say,
    "He has no hands"? (PAUSE)
Woe to him who says to his father [or to his mother:]

Child
(impu-
dently) What have you begotten?
What have you brought to birth?

Isaiah This is what the LORD says—
    the Holy One of Israel, and its Maker:

The Lord
(voice only) Concerning things to come,
    do you question me about my children,
    or give me orders about the work of my hands?
It is I who made the earth
    and created mankind upon it.
My own hands stretched out the heavens;
    I marshaled their starry hosts.
I will raise up Cyrus in my righteousness:
    I will make all his ways straight.
He will rebuild my city
    and set my exiles free,

	but not for a price or reward, says the Lord Almighty.
Isaiah	This is what the Lord says:

The Lord
 (voice)
	The products of Egypt and the merchandise of Cush,
	   and those tall Sabeans—
	 they will come over to you
	   and will be yours;
	 they will trudge behind you,
	   coming over to you in chains.
	 They will bow down before you
	   and plead with you, saying:

Sabean	Surely God is with you, and there is no other;
	   there is no other god.
	
	 Truly you are a God who hides himself,
	   O God and Savior of Israel.

Isaiah	All the makers of idols will be put to shame and disgraced;
	   they will go off into disgrace together.
	 But Israel will be saved by the Lord
	   with an everlasting salvation;
	 you will never be put to shame or disgraced,
	   to ages everlasting.
	
	 For this is what the Lord says—
	 he who created the heavens,
	   he is God;
	 he who fashioned and made the earth,
	   he founded it;
	 he did not create it to be empty,
	   but formed it to be inhabited—
	 he says:

The Lord
 (voice)
	I am the Lord,
	   and there is no other.
	 I have not spoken in secret,
	   from somewhere in a land of darkness;
	 I have not said to Jacob's descendants,
	   "Seek me in vain."
	 I, the Lord, speak the truth;
	   I declare what is right.

Cast: **Isaiah, Child, the Lord** (voice only), **Sabean**

Stubborn Israel

From Isaiah 48:1–11

Isaiah

Listen to this, O house of Jacob,
you who are called by the name of Israel
and come from the line of Judah,
you who take oaths in the name of the Lord
and invoke the God of Israel—
but not in truth or righteousness—
you who call yourselves citizens of the holy city
and rely on the God of Israel—
the Lord Almighty is his name:

The Lord
(voice only) I foretold the former things long ago,
my mouth announced them and I made them known;
then suddenly I acted, and they came to pass.
For I knew how stubborn you were;
the sinews of your neck were iron,
your forehead was bronze.
Therefore I told you these things long ago;
before they happened I announced them to you
so that you could not say,
"My idols did them;
my wooden image and metal god ordained them." . . .
For my own name's sake I delay my wrath;
for the sake of my praise I hold it back from you,
so as not to cut you off.
See, I have refined you, though not as silver;
I have tested you in the furnace of affliction.
For my own sake, for my own sake, I do this.
How can I let myself be defamed?
I will not yield my glory to another.

Cast: **Isaiah, the Lord** (voice only)

Israel Freed

Isaiah 48:17–22

Isaiah

This is what the Lord says—
your Redeemer, the Holy One of Israel:

The Lord
(voice only) I am the Lord your God,
who teaches you what is best for you,
who directs you in the way you should go.
If only you had paid attention to my commands,

                your peace would have been like a river,
                    your righteousness like the waves of the sea.
                Your descendants would have been like the sand,
                    your children like its numberless grains;
                their name would never be cut off
                    nor destroyed from before me.

Isaiah   Leave Babylon,
                    flee from the Babylonians!
                Announce this with shouts of joy
                    and proclaim it.
                Send it out to the ends of the earth;
                    say:

Herald
(calling)   The Lord has redeemed his servant Jacob.

Isaiah   They did not thirst when he led them through the deserts;
                he made water flow for them from the rock;
                he split the rock
                    and water gushed out.

The Lord
(voice,
slowly)   There is no peace . . . for the wicked.

Isaiah
(with
flourish)   [Says the Lord.]

Cast: **Isaiah, the Lord** (voice only), **Herald**

The Servant of the Lord

Isaiah 49:1–7

The Servant Listen to me, you islands;
                hear this, you distant nations:
            Before I was born the Lord called me;
                from my birth he has made mention of my name.
            He made my mouth like a sharpened sword,
                in the shadow of his hand he hid me;
            he made me into a polished arrow
                and concealed me in his quiver.
            He said to me:

The Lord
(voice only) You are my servant,
                Israel, in whom I will display my splendor.

The Servant But I said:

Young
servant
     I have labored to no purpose;
       I have spent my strength in vain and for nothing.
     Yet what is due me is in the LORD's hand,
       and my reward is with my God.

The Servant
     And now the LORD says—
       he who formed me in the womb to be his servant
     to bring Jacob back to him
       and gather Israel to himself,
     for I am honored in the eyes of the LORD
       and my God has been my strength—
     he says:

The Lord
(voice)
     It is too small a thing for you to be my servant
       to restore the tribes of Jacob
       and bring back those of Israel I have kept.
     I will also make you a light for the Gentiles,
       that you may bring my salvation to the ends of the earth.

Isaiah
     This is what the LORD says—
       the Redeemer and Holy One of Israel—
     to him who was despised and abhorred by the nation,
       to the servant of rulers:

The Lord
(voice)
     Kings will see you and rise up,
       princes will see and bow down,
     because of the LORD, who is faithful,
       the Holy One of Israel, who has chosen you.

Cast: **The Servant, the Lord** (voice only), **Young servant** (can be the same as the Servant), **Isaiah**

The Restoration of Israel

Isaiah 49:8–16

Isaiah
     This is what the LORD says:

The Lord
(voice only)
     In the time of my favor I will answer you,
       and in the day of salvation I will help you;
     I will keep you and will make you
       to be a covenant for the people,
     to restore the land
       and to reassign its desolate inheritances,
     to say to the captives, "Come out,"
       and to those in darkness, "Be free!"

Isaiah	They will feed beside the roads
	   and find pasture on every barren hill.
	They will neither hunger nor thirst,
	   nor will the desert heat or the sun beat upon them.
	He who has compassion on them will guide them
	   and lead them beside springs of water.

The Lord
(voice)
	I will turn all my mountains into roads,
	   and my highways will be raised up.
	See, they will come from afar—
	   some from the north, some from the west,
	   some from the region of Aswan.

Isaiah	Shout for joy, O heavens;
	   rejoice, O earth;
	   burst into song, O mountains!
	For the LORD comforts his people
	   and will have compassion on his afflicted ones. (PAUSE)
	But Zion said:

Person(s)	The LORD has forsaken me, the Lord has forgotten me.

The Lord
(voice)
	Can a mother forget the baby at her breast
	   and have no compassion on the child she has borne?
	Though she may forget,
	   I will not forget you!
	See, I have engraved you on the palms of my hands;
	   your walls are ever before me.

Cast: **Isaiah**, **the Lord** (voice only), **Person(s)**

Everlasting Salvation for Zion

Isaiah 51:4–16

The Lord
(voice only) Listen to me, my people;
   hear me, my nation:
The law will go out from me;
   my justice will become a light to the nations.
My righteousness draws near speedily,
   my salvation is on the way,
   and my arm will bring justice to the nations.
The islands will look to me
   and wait in hope for my arm.
Lift up your eyes to the heavens,
   look at the earth beneath;

the heavens will vanish like smoke,
    the earth will wear out like a garment
    and its inhabitants die like flies.
But my salvation will last forever,
    my righteousness will never fail.

Hear me, you who know what is right,
    you people who have my law in your hearts:
Do not fear the reproach of men
    or be terrified by their insults.
For the moth will eat them up like a garment;
    the worm will devour them like wool.
But my righteousness will last forever,
    my salvation through all generations.

Isaiah

Awake, awake! Clothe yourself with strength,
    O arm of the Lord;
awake, as in days gone by,
    as in generations of old.
Was it not you who cut Rahab to pieces,
    who pierced that monster through?
Was it not you who dried up the sea,
    the waters of the great deep,
who made a road in the depths of the sea
    so that the redeemed might cross over?
The ransomed of the Lord will return.
    They will enter Zion with singing;
    everlasting joy will crown their heads.
Gladness and joy will overtake them,
    and sorrow and sighing will flee away.

The Lord
(voice)

I, even I, am he who comforts you.
    Who are you that you fear mortal men,
    the sons of men, who are but grass,
that you forget the Lord your Maker,
    who stretched out the heavens
    and laid the foundations of the earth,
that you live in constant terror every day
    because of the wrath of the oppressor,
    who is bent on destruction?
For where is the wrath of the oppressor?
    The cowering prisoners will soon be set free;
they will not die in their dungeon,
    nor will they lack bread.
For I am the Lord your God,
    who churns up the sea so that its waves roar—
    the Lord Almighty is his name.
I have put my words in your mouth
    and covered you with the shadow of my hand—

I who set the heavens in place,
  who laid the foundations of the earth,
  and who say to Zion, "You are my people."

Cast: **The Lord** (voice only), **Isaiah**

The Cup of the Lord's Wrath

Isaiah 51:17–23

| Isaiah | Awake, awake!
Rise up, O Jerusalem,
you who have drunk from the hand of the Lord
  the cup of his wrath,
you who have drained to its dregs
  the goblet that makes men stagger.
Of all the sons she bore
  there was none to guide her;
of all the sons she reared
  there was none to take her by the hand.
These double calamities have come upon you—
  who can comfort you? —
ruin and destruction, famine and sword—
  who can console you?
Your sons have fainted;
  they lie at the head of every street,
  like antelope caught in a net.
They are filled with the wrath of the Lord
  and the rebuke of your God.

Therefore hear this, you afflicted one,
  made drunk, but not with wine.
This is what your Sovereign Lord says,
  your God, who defends his people: |

The Lord
(voice only) See, I have taken out of your hand
  the cup that made you stagger;
from that cup, the goblet of my wrath,
  you will never drink again.
I will put it into the hands of your tormentors,
  who said to you,
  "Fall prostrate that we may walk over you."
And you made your back like the ground,
  like a street to be walked over.

Cast: **Isaiah, the Lord** (voice only)

237

God Will Rescue Jerusalem

Isaiah 52:1–12

Isaiah   Awake, awake, O Zion,
                 clothe yourself with strength.
            Put on your garments of splendor,
                 O Jerusalem, the holy city.
            The uncircumcised and defiled
                 will not enter you again.
            Shake off your dust;
                 rise up, sit enthroned, O Jerusalem.
            Free yourself from the chains on your neck,
                 O captive Daughter of Zion.

           For this is what the LORD says:

The Lord
(voice only) You were sold for nothing,
                 and without money you will be redeemed. . . .

           At first my people went down to Egypt to live;
                 lately, Assyria has oppressed them.

           And now what do I have here? . . .

           For my people have been taken away for nothing,
                 and those who rule them mock. . . .
           And all day long
                 my name is constantly blasphemed.
           Therefore my people will know my name;
                 therefore in that day they will know
           that it is I who foretold it.
                 Yes, it is I.

Isaiah   How beautiful on the mountains
                 are the feet of those who bring good news,
           who proclaim peace,
                 who bring good tidings,
                 who proclaim salvation,
           who say to Zion:

Messenger
(calling)   Your God reigns!

Isaiah   Listen! Your watchmen lift up their voices;
                 together they shout for joy.
           When the LORD returns to Zion,
                 they will see it with their own eyes.
           Burst into songs of joy together,
                 you ruins of Jerusalem,
           for the LORD has comforted his people,
                 he has redeemed Jerusalem.

The LORD will lay bare his holy arm
in the sight of all the nations,
and all the ends of the earth will see
the salvation of our God.

Depart, depart, go out from there!
Touch no unclean thing!
Come out from it and be pure,
you who carry the vessels of the LORD.
But you will not leave in haste
or go in flight;
for the LORD will go before you,
the God of Israel will be your rear guard.

Cast: **Isaiah, the Lord** (voice only), **Messenger**

The Suffering and Glory of the Servant

Isaiah 52:13–53:12

The Lord
(voice only) See, my servant will act wisely;
he will be raised and lifted up and highly exalted.
Just as there were many who were appalled at him—
his appearance was so disfigured beyond that of any man
and his form marred beyond human likeness—
so will he sprinkle many nations,
and kings will shut their mouths because of him.
For what they were not told, they will see,
and what they have not heard, they will understand.

Person 1 Who has believed our message
to whom has the arm of the LORD been revealed?

Person 2 He grew up before him like a tender shoot,
and like a root out of dry ground.

Person 1 He had no beauty or majesty to attract us to him—

Person 2 Nothing in his appearance that we should desire him.

Person 1 He was despised and rejected by men—

Person 2 A man of sorrows, and familiar with suffering.

Person 1 Like one from whom men hide their faces—
he was despised, and we esteemed him not.

Person 2 Surely he took up our infirmities
and carried our sorrows—

Person 1	Yet we considered him stricken by God, smitten by him, and afflicted.
Person 2	But he was pierced for our transgressions—
Person 3	He was crushed for our iniquities:
Person 1	The punishment that brought us peace was upon him—
Person 2	And by his wounds we are healed.
Persons 1–3	We all, like sheep, have gone astray—
Person 2	Each of us has turned to his own way:
Persons 1–2	And the Lord has laid on him the iniquity of us all.
Person 1	He was oppressed and afflicted—
Person 3	Yet he did not open his mouth;
Person 1	He was led like a lamb to the slaughter—
Person 2	And as a sheep before her shearers is silent—
Person 3	So he did not open his mouth.
Person 1	By oppression and judgment he was taken away.
Person 2	And who can speak of his descendants?
Person 3	For he was cut off from the land of the living;
Person 1 (slowly)	For the transgression of my people he was stricken.
Person 2	He was assigned a grave with the wicked—
Person 3	And with the rich in his death—
Person 1	Though he had done no violence—
Person 3	Nor was any deceit in his mouth.

Isaiah	Yet it was the Lord's will to crush him and cause him to suffer,
	    and though the Lord makes his life a guilt offering,
	he will see his offspring and prolong his days,
	    and the will of the Lord will prosper in his hand.

The Lord
  (voice)
	After the suffering of his soul,
	    he will see the light ⌞of life⌟ and be satisfied;
	by his knowledge my righteous servant will justify many,
	    and he will bear their iniquities.
	Therefore I will give him a portion among the great,
	    and he will divide the spoils with the strong,
	because he poured out his life unto death,
	    and was numbered with the transgressors.

240

For he bore the sin of many,
> and made intercession for the transgressors.

Cast: **The Lord** (voice only), **Person 1, Person 2, Person 3** (Persons 1–3 can be the same), **Isaiah**

The Lord's Love for Israel

Isaiah 54:6–10

Isaiah
> The LORD will call you back
>> as if you were a wife deserted and distressed in spirit—
> a wife who married young,
>> only to be rejected, says your God.

The Lord
(voice only) For a brief moment I abandoned you,
>> but with deep compassion I will bring you back.
> In a surge of anger
>> I hid my face from you for a moment,
> but with everlasting kindness
>> I will have compassion on you.

Isaiah
(with
flourish) Says the LORD your Redeemer.

The Lord To me this is like the days of Noah,
>> when I swore that the waters of Noah would never again
>>> cover the earth.
> So now I have sworn not to be angry with you,
>> never to rebuke you again.
> Though the mountains be shaken
>> and the hills be removed,
> yet my unfailing love for you will not be shaken
>> nor my covenant of peace be removed,
>> says the LORD, who has compassion on you.

Cast: **Isaiah, the Lord** (voice only)

Invitation to the Thirsty

Isaiah 55:1–11 [12–13]

Isaiah [The Lord says:]

The Lord
(voice only) Come, all you who are thirsty,
>> come to the waters;
> and you who have no money,

come, buy and eat!
Come, buy wine and milk
　　without money and without cost.
Why spend money on what is not bread,
　　and your labor on what does not satisfy?
Listen, listen to me, and eat what is good,
　　and your soul will delight in the richest of fare.
Give ear and come to me;
　　hear me, that your soul may live.
I will make an everlasting covenant with you,
　　my faithful love promised to David.
See, I have made him a witness to the peoples,
　　a leader and commander of the peoples.

Isaiah　　Surely you will summon nations you know not,
　　and nations that do not know you will hasten to you,
because of the LORD your God,
　　the Holy One of Israel,
　　for he has endowed you with splendor.

(urgently)　Seek the LORD while he may be found;
　　call on him while he is near.
Let the wicked forsake his way
　　and the evil man his thoughts.
Let him turn to the LORD, and he will have mercy on him,
　　and to our God, for he will freely pardon.
[The LORD declares:]

The Lord
(voice,
with
dignity)　My thoughts are not your thoughts,
　　neither are your ways my ways. . . .
As the heavens are higher than the earth,
　　so are my ways higher than your ways
　　and my thoughts than your thoughts.
As the rain and the snow
　　come down from heaven,
and do not return to it
　　without watering the earth
and making it bud and flourish,
　　so that it yields seed for the sower and bread for the eater,
so is my word that goes out from my mouth:
　　It will not return to me empty,
but will accomplish what I desire
　　and achieve the purpose for which I sent it.

[Isaiah　You will go out in joy
　　and be led forth in peace;
the mountains and hills
　　will burst into song before you,

242

and all the trees of the field
   will clap their hands.
Instead of the thornbush will grow the pine tree,
   and instead of briers the myrtle will grow.
This will be for the LORD's renown,
   for an everlasting sign,
   which will not be destroyed.]

Cast: **Isaiah, the Lord** (voice only)

Salvation for Others

From Isaiah 56:1–8

Isaiah   This is what the LORD says:

The Lord
  (voice only) Maintain justice
      and do what is right,
  for my salvation is close at hand
      and my righteousness will soon be revealed.
  Blessed is the man who does this,
      the man who holds it fast,
  who keeps the Sabbath without desecrating it,
      and keeps his hand from doing any evil.

Isaiah   Let no foreigner who has bound himself to the LORD say,
      "The LORD will surely exclude me from his people." . . .
  And foreigners who bind themselves to the LORD
      to serve him,
  to love the name of the LORD,
      and to worship him,
  all who keep the Sabbath without desecrating it
      and who hold fast to my covenant—

The Lord
  (voice)   These I will bring to my holy mountain
      and give them joy in my house of prayer.
  Their burnt offerings and sacrifices
      will be accepted on my altar;
  for my house will be called
      a house of prayer for all nations.

Isaiah   The Sovereign LORD declares—
      he who gathers the exiles of Israel:

The Lord
  (voice)   I will gather still others to them
      besides those already gathered.

Cast: **Isaiah, the Lord** (voice only)

True Fasting

Isaiah 58:1–9

The Lord

(voice only) Shout it aloud, do not hold back.
  Raise your voice like a trumpet.
Declare to my people their rebellion
  and to the house of Jacob their sins.
For day after day they seek me out;
  they seem eager to know my ways,
as if they were a nation that does what is right
  and has not forsaken the commands of its God.
They ask me for just decisions
  and seem eager for God to come near them.

Isaiah [They say:]

Person 1 Why have we fasted, . . .
  and you have not seen it?

Person 2 Why have we humbled ourselves,
  and you have not noticed?

The Lord

(voice) Yet on the day of your fasting, you do as you please
  and exploit all your workers.
Your fasting ends in quarreling and strife,
  and in striking each other with wicked fists.
You cannot fast as you do today
  and expect your voice to be heard on high.
Is this the kind of fast I have chosen,
  only a day for a man to humble himself?
Is it only for bowing one's head like a reed
  and for lying on sackcloth and ashes?
Is that what you call a fast,
  a day acceptable to the Lord?

Is not this the kind of fasting I have chosen:
to loose the chains of injustice
  and untie the cords of the yoke,
to set the oppressed free
  and break every yoke?
Is it not to share your food with the hungry
  and to provide the poor wanderer with shelter—
when you see the naked, to clothe him,
  and not to turn away from your own flesh and blood?

Isaiah Then your light will break forth like the dawn,
  and your healing will quickly appear;
then your righteousness will go before you,
  and the glory of the Lord will be your rear guard.

Then you will call, and the LORD will answer;
   you will cry for help, and he will say: Here am I.

Cast: **The Lord** (voice only), **Isaiah, Person 1, Person 2**

Sin, Confession, and Redemption

Isaiah 59:1–19

Isaiah   Surely the arm of the LORD is not too short to save,
       nor his ear too dull to hear.
    But your iniquities have separated
       you from your God;
    your sins have hidden his face from you,
       so that he will not hear.
    For your hands are stained with blood,
       your fingers with guilt.
    Your lips have spoken lies,
       and your tongue mutters wicked things.
    No one calls for justice;
       no one pleads his case with integrity.
    They rely on empty arguments and speak lies;
       they conceive trouble and give birth to evil.
    They hatch the eggs of vipers
       and spin a spider's web.
    Whoever eats their eggs will die,
       and when one is broken, an adder is hatched.
    Their cobwebs are useless for clothing;
       they cannot cover themselves with what they make.
    Their deeds are evil deeds,
       and acts of violence are in their hands.
    Their feet rush into sin;
       they are swift to shed innocent blood.
    Their thoughts are evil thoughts;
       ruin and destruction mark their ways.
    The way of peace they do not know;
       there is no justice in their paths.
    They have turned them into crooked roads;
       no one who walks in them will know peace.

Person 1   So justice is far from us,
       and righteousness does not reach us.

Person 2   We look for light, but all is darkness;
       for brightness, but we walk in deep shadows.
    Like the blind we grope along the wall,
       feeling our way like men without eyes.

245

Person 3	At midday we stumble as if it were twilight; among the strong, we are like the dead.
Person 4	We all growl like bears; we moan mournfully like doves.
Person 1	We look for justice, but find none; for deliverance, but it is far away.
Person 2	For our offenses are many in your sight, and our sins testify against us. Our offenses are ever with us, and we acknowledge our iniquities.
Person 3	Rebellion and treachery against the LORD, turning our backs on our God—
Person 4	Fomenting oppression and revolt, uttering lies our hearts have conceived.
Person 3	So justice is driven back, and righteousness stands at a distance; truth has stumbled in the streets, honesty cannot enter.
Person 1	Truth is nowhere to be found, and whoever shuns evil becomes a prey.
Isaiah	The LORD looked and was displeased that there was no justice. He saw that there was no one, he was appalled that there was no one to intervene; so his own arm worked salvation for him, and his own righteousness sustained him. He put on righteousness as his breastplate, and the helmet of salvation on his head; he put on the garments of vengeance and wrapped himself in zeal as in a cloak. According to what they have done, so will he repay wrath to his enemies and retribution to his foes; he will repay the islands their due. From the west, men will fear the name of the LORD, and from the rising of the sun, they will revere his glory. For he will come like a pent-up flood that the breath of the LORD drives along.

Cast: **Isaiah**, **Person 1** (practical), **Person 2** (educated), **Person 3** (poetic), **Person 4** (conscientious). (Persons 1–4 can be the same.)

The Glory of Zion

Isaiah 60:1–6

Voice 1   Arise, shine, for your light has come:

Voice 2   And the glory of the Lord rises upon you.

Voice 1   See, darkness covers the earth
              and thick darkness is over the peoples.

Voice 2   But the Lord rises upon you
              and his glory appears over you.

Voice 3   Nations will come to your light,
              and kings to the brightness of your dawn.

Voice 1   Lift up your eyes and look about you:
              All assemble and come to you.

Voice 2   Your sons come from afar—

Voice 3   And your daughters are carried on the arm.

Voice 1   Then you will look and be radiant.

Voice 2   Your heart will throb and swell with joy.

Voice 3   The wealth on the seas will be brought to you,
              to you the riches of the nations will come.

Voice 1   Herds of camels will cover your land,
              young camels of Midian and Ephah.

Voice 2   And all from Sheba will come—

Voice 3   Bearing gold and incense
              and proclaiming the praise of the Lord.

Cast: **Voice 1, Voice 2, Voice 3**

The Year of the Lord's Favor

Isaiah 61:1–11

Isaiah   The Spirit of the Sovereign Lord is on me,
              because the Lord has anointed me
              to preach good news to the poor.
           He has sent me to bind up the brokenhearted,
              to proclaim freedom for the captives
              and release from darkness for the prisoners,
           to proclaim the year of the Lord's favor
              and the day of vengeance of our God,
           to comfort all who mourn,

and provide for those who grieve in Zion—
to bestow on them a crown of beauty
   instead of ashes,
the oil of gladness
   instead of mourning,
and a garment of praise
   instead of a spirit of despair.
They will be called oaks of righteousness,
   a planting of the LORD
   for the display of his splendor.

They will rebuild the ancient ruins
   and restore the places long devastated;
they will renew the ruined cities
   that have been devastated for generations.
Aliens will shepherd your flocks;
   foreigners will work your fields and vineyards.
And you will be called priests of the LORD,
   you will be named ministers of our God.
You will feed on the wealth of nations,
   and in their riches you will boast.

Instead of their shame
   my people will receive a double portion,
and instead of disgrace
   they will rejoice in their inheritance;
and so they will inherit a double portion in their land,
   and everlasting joy will be theirs.

The Lord
  (voice only) I, the LORD, love justice;
   I hate robbery and iniquity.
In my faithfulness I will reward them
   and make an everlasting covenant with them.
Their descendants will be known among the nations
   and their offspring among the peoples.
All who see them will acknowledge
   that they are a people the LORD has blessed.

Isaiah   I delight greatly in the LORD;
   my soul rejoices in my God.
For he has clothed me with garments of salvation
   and arrayed me in a robe of righteousness,
as a bridegroom adorns his head like a priest,
   and as a bride adorns herself with her jewels.
For as the soil makes the sprout come up
   and a garden causes seeds to grow,
so the Sovereign LORD will make righteousness and praise
   spring up before all nations.

Cast: **Isaiah, the Lord** (voice only)

Zion's New Name

From Isaiah 62:1–12

Isaiah	For Zion's sake I will not keep silent,
	    for Jerusalem's sake I will not remain quiet,
	till her righteousness shines out like the dawn,
	    her salvation like a blazing torch.
	The nations will see your righteousness,
	    and all kings your glory;
	you will be called by a new name
	    that the mouth of the LORD will bestow.
	You will be a crown of splendor in the LORD's hand,
	    a royal diadem in the hand of your God.
	No longer will they call you:

Sad voice	Deserted.
Isaiah	Or name your land:
Sad voice	Desolate.
Isaiah	But you will be called:
Joyful voice	Hephzibah,
Isaiah	and your land—
Joyful voice	Beulah.

Isaiah	For the LORD will take delight in you,
	    and your land will be married.
	As a young man marries a maiden,
	    so will your sons marry you;
	as a bridegroom rejoices over his bride,
	    so will your God rejoice over you.
	
	I have posted watchmen on your walls, O Jerusalem;
	    they will never be silent day or night.
	You who call on the LORD,
	    give yourselves no rest,
	and give him no rest till he establishes Jerusalem
	    and makes her the praise of the earth. . . .
	
	Pass through, pass through the gates!
	    Prepare the way for the people.
	Build up, build up the highway!
	    Remove the stones.
	Raise a banner for the nations.
	
	The LORD has made proclamation
	    to the ends of the earth:

The Lord (voice only)	Say to the Daughter of Zion,

"See, your Savior comes!
See, his reward is with him,
and his recompense accompanies him."

Isaiah   They will be called—

Joyful voice   The Holy People,
the Redeemed of the LORD.

Isaiah   And you will be called:

Joyful voice   Sought After, the City No Longer Deserted.

Cast: **Isaiah, Sad voice, Joyful voice, the Lord** (voice only)

God's Day of Vengeance and Redemption

Isaiah 63:1–6

Person 1   Who is this coming from Edom,
from Bozrah, with his garments stained crimson?

Person 2   Who is this, robed in splendor,
striding forward in the greatness of his strength?

The Lord
(voice only)   It is I, speaking in righteousness,
mighty to save.

Person 1   Why are your garments red—

Person 2   Like those of one treading the winepress?

The Lord
(voice)   I have trodden the winepress alone;
from the nations no one was with me.
I trampled them in my anger
and trod them down in my wrath;
their blood spattered my garments,
and I stained all my clothing.
For the day of vengeance was in my heart,
and the year of my redemption has come.
I looked, but there was no one to help,
I was appalled that no one gave support;
so my own arm worked salvation for me,
and my own wrath sustained me.
I trampled the nations in my anger;
in my wrath I made them drunk
and poured their blood on the ground.

Cast: **Person 1, Person 2, the Lord** (voice only)

Praise and Prayer

Isaiah 63:7–14

Isaiah
I will tell of the kindnesses of the LORD,
   the deeds for which he is to be praised,
   according to all the LORD has done for us—
yes, the many good things he has done
   for the house of Israel,
   according to his compassion and many kindnesses.
He said:

The Lord
(voice only) Surely they are my people,
   sons who will not be false to me.

Isaiah
   And so he became their Savior.
In all their distress he too was distressed,
   and the angel of his presence saved them.
In his love and mercy he redeemed them;
   he lifted them up and carried them
   all the days of old.
Yet they rebelled
   and grieved his Holy Spirit.
So he turned and became their enemy
   and he himself fought against them.

   Then his people recalled the days of old,
   the days of Moses and his people:

Person 1
Where is he who brought them through the sea,
   with the shepherd of his flock?

Person 2
Where is he who set
   his Holy Spirit among them?

Person 1
[Where is he] who sent his glorious arm of power
   to be at Moses' right hand?

Person 2
[Where is he] who divided the waters before them,
   to gain for himself everlasting renown?

Person 1
[Where is he] who led them through the depths?

Isaiah
Like a horse in open country,
   they did not stumble;
like cattle that go down to the plain,
   they were given rest by the Spirit of the LORD.

(praying)
This is how you guided your people
   to make for yourself a glorious name.

Cast: **Isaiah**, **the Lord** (voice only), **Person 1**, **Person 2**

Jeremiah

The Call of Jeremiah

Jeremiah 1:1–10

Narrator	The words of Jeremiah son of Hilkiah, one of the priests at Anathoth in the territory of Benjamin. (PAUSE) The word of the LORD came to him in the thirteenth year of the reign of Josiah son of Amon king of Judah, and through the reign of Jehoiakim son of Josiah king of Judah, down to the fifth month of the eleventh year of Zedekiah son of Josiah king of Judah, when the people of Jerusalem went into exile.
Jeremiah	The word of the LORD came to me, saying:
The Lord (voice only)	Before I formed you in the womb I knew you, before you were born I set you apart; I appointed you as a prophet to the nations.
Jeremiah	[I said:]
Young Jeremiah	Ah, Sovereign LORD, I do not know how to speak; I am only a child.
Jeremiah	But the LORD said to me:
The Lord (voice)	Do not say, "I am only a child." You must go to everyone I send you to and say whatever I command you. Do not be afraid of them, for I am with you and will rescue you. . . .
Jeremiah	Then the LORD reached out his hand and touched my mouth and said to me:
The Lord (voice)	Now, I have put my words in your mouth. See, today I appoint you over nations and kingdoms to uproot and tear down, to destroy and overthrow, to build and to plant.

Cast: **Narrator, Jeremiah, the Lord** (voice only), **Young Jeremiah**

Jeremiah's Two Visions

Jeremiah 1:11–19

Jeremiah	The word of the LORD came to me:
The Lord (voice only)	What do you see, Jeremiah?

Young Jeremiah	I see the branch of an almond tree.
Jeremiah	The LORD said to me:
The Lord (voice)	You have seen correctly, for I am watching to see that my word is fulfilled. (PAUSE)
Jeremiah	The word of the LORD came to me again:
The Lord (voice)	What do you see?
Young Jeremiah	I see a boiling pot, tilting away from the north.
Jeremiah	The LORD said to me:
The Lord (voice)	From the north disaster will be poured out on all who live in the land. I am about to summon all the peoples of the northern kingdoms. . . .

Their kings will come and set up their thrones
   in the entrance of the gates of Jerusalem;
they will come against all her surrounding walls
   and against all the towns of Judah.
I will pronounce my judgments on my people
   because of their wickedness in forsaking me,
in burning incense to other gods
   and in worshiping what their hands have made.

Get yourself ready! Stand up and say to them whatever I command you. Do not be terrified by them, or I will terrify you before them. Today I have made you a fortified city, an iron pillar and a bronze wall to stand against the whole land—against the kings of Judah, its officials, its priests and the people of the land. They will fight against you but will not overcome you, for I am with you and will rescue you. . . .

Cast: **Jeremiah, the Lord** (voice only), **Young Jeremiah**

Israel Forsakes God

Jeremiah 2:1–13

Jeremiah	The word of the LORD came to me:
The Lord (voice only)	Go and proclaim in the hearing of Jerusalem:

"I remember the devotion of your youth,
   how as a bride you loved me
and followed me through the desert,
   through a land not sown.

Israel was holy to the L\ord,
  the firstfruits of his harvest;
all who devoured her were held guilty,
  and disaster overtook them." . . .

Jeremiah   Hear the word of the L\ord, O house of Jacob,
  all you clans of the house of Israel.

This is what the L\ord says:

The Lord
  (voice)   What fault did your fathers find in me,
  that they strayed so far from me?
They followed worthless idols
  and became worthless themselves.
They did not ask, "Where is the L\ord,
  who brought us up out of Egypt
and led us through the barren wilderness,
  through a land of deserts and rifts,
a land of drought and darkness,
  a land where no one travels and no one lives?"
I brought you into a fertile land
  to eat its fruit and rich produce.
But you came and defiled my land
  and made my inheritance detestable.
The priests did not ask,
  "Where is the L\ord?"
Those who deal with the law did not know me;
  the leaders rebelled against me.
The prophets prophesied by Baal,
  following worthless idols.

Therefore I bring charges against you again. . . .
  And I will bring charges against your children's children.

  (urgently)   Cross over to the coasts of Kittim and look,
  send to Kedar and observe closely;
  see if there has ever been anything like this:
Has a nation ever changed its gods?

Jeremiah   (Yet they are not gods at all.)

The Lord
  (voice)   But my people have exchanged their Glory
  for worthless idols.

  (severely)   Be appalled at this, O heavens,
  and shudder with great horror. . . .
My people have committed two sins:
They have forsaken me,
  the spring of living water,

and have dug their own cisterns,
    broken cisterns that cannot hold water.

Cast: **Jeremiah, the Lord** (voice only)

Israel Refuses to Worship the Lord

From Jeremiah 2:20–25

Jeremiah [The LORD Almighty declares:]

The Lord
(voice only) Long ago you broke off your yoke
    and tore off your bonds;
    you said:

Person I will not serve you!

The Lord
(voice) Indeed, on every high hill
    and under every spreading tree
    you lay down as a prostitute.
I had planted you like a choice vine
    of sound and reliable stock.
How then did you turn against me
    into a corrupt, wild vine?
Although you wash yourself with soda
    and use an abundance of soap,
    the stain of your guilt is still before me. . . .
How can you say, "I am not defiled;
    I have not run after the Baals"?
See how you behaved in the valley;
    consider what you have done. . . .
You said:

Person It's no use!
    I love foreign gods,
    and I must go after them.

Cast: **Jeremiah, the Lord** (voice only), **Person**

Israel Deserves to Be Punished

From Jeremiah 2:31–3:5

Jeremiah You of this generation, consider the word of the LORD:

The Lord
(voice only) Have I been a desert to Israel
    or a land of great darkness?

	Why do my people say, "We are free to roam; we will come to you no more"? Does a maiden forget her jewelry, a bride her wedding ornaments? Yet my people have forgotten me, days without number. . . . In spite of all this you say:
Person 1	I am innocent.
Person 2	He is not angry with me.
The Lord (voice)	But I will pass judgment on you because you say:
Person 1	I have not sinned.
The Lord (voice)	Why do you go about so much, changing your ways? You will be disappointed by Egypt as you were by Assyria. You will also leave that place with your hands on your head, for the LORD has rejected those you trust; you will not be helped by them. . . . Have you not just called to me:
Person 1	My Father, my friend from my youth, will you always be angry?
Person 2	Will your wrath continue forever?
The Lord	This is how you talk, but you do all the evil you can.

Cast: **Jeremiah, the Lord** (voice only), **Person 1, Person 2** (can be the same as Person 1)

Unfaithful Israel

From Jeremiah 3:11–22a

Jeremiah	The LORD said to me:
The Lord (voice only)	Faithless Israel is more righteous than unfaithful Judah. Go, proclaim this message toward the north:

"Return, faithless Israel," . . .
"I will frown on you no longer,
for I am merciful," . . .
"I will not be angry forever.
Only acknowledge your guilt—
    you have rebelled against the LORD your God,
you have scattered your favors to foreign gods
    under every spreading tree,
and have not obeyed me."

Return, faithless people, . . . for I am your husband. I will choose you—
one from a town and two from a clan—and bring you to Zion. . . .

Jeremiah	[The Lord declares:]

The Lord	How gladly would I treat you like sons
	    and give you a desirable land,
	    the most beautiful inheritance of any nation.
	I thought you would call me "Father"
	    and not turn away from following me.
	But like a woman unfaithful to her husband,
	    so you have been unfaithful to me, O house of Israel. . . .

Jeremiah	A cry is heard on the barren heights,
	    the weeping and pleading of the people of Israel,
	because they have perverted their ways
	    and have forgotten the LORD their God.

The Lord (voice)	Return, faithless people; I will cure you of backsliding.

Cast: **Jeremiah, the Lord** (voice only)

The Idolatry of God's People

Jeremiah 3:19–4:4

[Jeremiah	[The Lord himself says:]]

The Lord
(voice only)
	How gladly would I treat you like sons
	    and give you a desirable land,
	    the most beautiful inheritance of any nation.
	I thought you would call me "Father"
	    and not turn away from following me.
	But like a woman unfaithful to her husband,
	    so you have been unfaithful to me, O house of Israel. . . .

Jeremiah	A cry is heard on the barren heights,
	    the weeping and pleading of the people of Israel,
	because they have perverted their ways
	    and have forgotten the Lord their God.

The Lord (voice)	Return, faithless people; I will cure you of backsliding.
Person 1	Yes, we will come to you, for you are the Lord our God.
Person 2 (sadly)	Surely the ⌞idolatrous⌟ commotion on the hills and mountains is a deception:
Person 1	Surely in the Lord our God is the salvation of Israel.

Person 2	From our youth shameful gods have consumed
	    the fruits of our fathers' labor—
	their flocks and herds,
	    their sons and daughters.

Person 1	Let us lie down in our shame, and let our disgrace cover us.

Person 2	We have sinned against the Lord our God,
	    both we and our fathers;
	from our youth till this day
	    we have not obeyed the Lord our God.

Jeremiah	[The Lord declares:]

The Lord
(voice)
	If you will return, O Israel,
	    return to me, . . .
	If you put your detestable idols out of my sight
	    and no longer go astray,

Jeremiah	and if in a truthful, just and righteous way
	    you swear, "As surely as the Lord lives,"
	then the nations will be blessed by him
	    and in him they will glory.
	
	This is what the Lord says to the men of Judah and to Jerusalem:

The Lord
(voice)
	Break up your unplowed ground
	    and do not sow among thorns.
	Circumcise yourselves to the Lord,
	    circumcise your hearts,
	    you men of Judah and people of Jerusalem,

> or my wrath will break out and burn like fire
> > because of the evil you have done—
> > burn with no one to quench it.

Cast: **Jeremiah, the Lord** (voice only), **Person 1, Person 2.** (This reading overlaps with the previous one.)

A Call to Repentance

Jeremiah 4:1–4

Jeremiah [The Lord declares:]

The Lord
  (voice only) If you will return, O Israel,
> > return to me, . . .
> If you put your detestable idols out of my sight
> > and no longer go astray,
> and if in a truthful, just and righteous way
> > you swear, "As surely as the LORD lives,"
> then the nations will be blessed by him
> > and in him they will glory.

Jeremiah This is what the LORD says to the men of Judah and to Jerusalem:

The Lord
  (voice) Break up your unplowed ground
> > and do not sow among thorns.
> Circumcise yourselves to the LORD,
> > circumcise your hearts,
> > you men of Judah and people of Jerusalem,
> or my wrath will break out and burn like fire
> > because of the evil you have done—
> > burn with no one to quench it.

Cast: **Jeremiah, the Lord** (voice only). (This reading is included in the previous one.)

Disaster from the North

From Jeremiah 4:5–18

The Lord
  (voice only) Announce in Judah and proclaim in Jerusalem and say:

Herald 1 Sound the trumpet throughout the land!

The Lord
  (voice) Cry aloud and say:

Herald 2	Gather together!
Herald 1	Let us flee to the fortified cities!
Herald 2	Raise the signal to go to Zion!
Herald 1	Flee for safety without delay!
The Lord (voice)	For I am bringing disaster from the north, even terrible destruction.

Jeremiah

A lion has come out of his lair;
  a destroyer of nations has set out.
He has left his place
  to lay waste your land.
Your towns will lie in ruins
  without inhabitant.
So put on sackcloth,
  lament and wail,
for the fierce anger of the LORD
  has not turned away from us.

[The LORD declares:]

The Lord (voice)

In that day, . . .
  the king and the officials will lose heart,
the priests will be horrified,
  and the prophets will be appalled.

Jeremiah   Then I said:

Young Jeremiah   Ah, Sovereign LORD, how completely you have deceived this people and Jerusalem by saying, "You will have peace," when the sword is at our throats.

Jeremiah   At that time this people and Jerusalem will be told:

The Lord (voice)   A scorching wind from the barren heights in the desert blows toward my people, but not to winnow or cleanse; a wind too strong for that comes from me. Now I pronounce my judgments against them.

Herald 1   Look! He advances like the clouds.

Herald 2   His chariots come like a whirlwind.

Herald 1   His horses are swifter than eagles.
     Woe to us!

Heralds 1 and 2   We are ruined!

Jeremiah   O Jerusalem, wash the evil from your heart and be saved.
    How long will you harbor wicked thoughts? . . .

Your own conduct and actions
  have brought this upon you.
This is your punishment.
  How bitter it is!
  How it pierces to the heart!

Cast: **The Lord** (voice only), **Herald 1, Herald 2, Jeremiah, Young Jeremiah**

Jeremiah's Sorrow for His People

Jeremiah 4:19–22

Jeremiah   Oh, my anguish, my anguish!
  I writhe in pain.
Oh, the agony of my heart!
  My heart pounds within me,
  I cannot keep silent.
For I have heard the sound of the trumpet;
  I have heard the battle cry.
Disaster follows disaster;
  the whole land lies in ruins.
In an instant my tents are destroyed,
  my shelter in a moment.
How long must I see the battle standard
  and hear the sound of the trumpet?

The Lord
(voice only)   My people are fools;
  they do not know me.
They are senseless children;
  they have no understanding.
They are skilled in doing evil;
  they know not how to do good.

Cast: **Jeremiah, the Lord** (voice only). (This reading can be linked with the previous one, or with the next.)

Jeremiah's Vision of the Coming Destruction

Jeremiah 4:23–31

Voice 1   I looked at the earth,
  and it was formless and empty;
and at the heavens,
  and their light was gone.

Voice 2	I looked at the mountains,
	    and they were quaking;
	    all the hills were swaying.

Voice 3	I looked, and there were no people; every bird in the sky had flown away.

Voices 1–3	I looked, and the fruitful land was a desert;
	    all its towns lay in ruins
	    before the Lord, before his fierce anger.

Voice 3	This is what the Lord says:

The Lord
(voice only)
	The whole land will be ruined,
	    though I will not destroy it completely.
	Therefore the earth will mourn
	    and the heavens above grow dark.
	Because I have spoken and will not relent.
	    I have decided and will not turn back.

Voice 1	At the sound of horsemen and archers every town takes to flight.
Voice 2	Some go into the thickets.
Voice 1	Some climb up among the rocks.
Voice 2	All the towns are deserted.
Voice 3	No one lives in them.
Voice 1	What are you doing, O devastated one?
Voice 2	Why dress yourself in scarlet and put on jewels of gold?
Voice 1	Why shade your eyes with paint?
Voice 2	You adorn yourself in vain.
Voice 1	Your lovers despise you; they seek your life.

Voice 2	I hear a cry as of a woman in labor,
	    a groan as of one bearing her first child—
	the cry of the Daughter of Zion gasping for breath,
	    stretching out her hands and saying:

Voice 3	"Alas! I am fainting; my life is given over to murderers."

Cast: **Voice 1** (preferably male), **Voice 2**, **Voice 3** (preferably female), **the Lord** (voice only)

No One Is Upright

Jeremiah 5:1–11

Jeremiah	Go up and down the streets of Jerusalem,
	    look around and consider,
	    search through her squares.
	If you can find but one person
	    who deals honestly and seeks the truth,
	    I will forgive this city.
	Although they say:

Person	As surely as the LORD lives,
Jeremiah	still they are swearing falsely.

(praying)	O LORD, do not your eyes look for truth?
	    You struck them, but they felt no pain;
	    you crushed them, but they refused correction.
	They made their faces harder than stone
	    and refused to repent.

(to audience)	I thought:

Young Jeremiah	These are only the poor;
	    they are foolish,
	for they do not know the way of the LORD,
	    the requirements of their God.
	So I will go to the leaders
	    and speak to them;
	surely they know the way of the LORD,
	    the requirements of their God.

Jeremiah	But with one accord they too had broken off the yoke
	    and torn off the bonds.
	Therefore a lion from the forest will attack them,
	    a wolf from the desert will ravage them,
	a leopard will lie in wait near their towns
	    to tear to pieces any who venture out,
	for their rebellion is great
	    and their backslidings many.

The Lord (voice only)	Why should I forgive you?
	    Your children have forsaken me
	    and sworn by gods that are not gods.
	I supplied all their needs,
	    yet they committed adultery
	    and thronged to the houses of prostitutes.
	They are well-fed, lusty stallions,

> each neighing for another man's wife.
> Should I not punish them for this? . . .
> Should I not avenge myself
>   on such a nation as this?

Young
Jeremiah Go through her vineyards and ravage them,
>   but do not destroy them completely.
> Strip off her branches,
>   for these people do not belong to the LORD.

Jeremiah [The LORD declares:]

The Lord
(voice) The house of Israel and the house of Judah
>   have been utterly unfaithful to me. . . .

Cast: **Jeremiah**, **Person**, **Young Jeremiah**, **the Lord** (voice only)

The Lord Rejects Israel

Jeremiah 5:12–19

Jeremiah They have lied about the LORD;
>   they said:

Person 1 He will do nothing!

Person 2 No harm will come to us:

Person 1 We will never see sword or famine.

Person 2 The prophets are but wind
>   and the word is not in them.

Person 1 So let what they say be done to them.

Jeremiah Therefore this is what the LORD God Almighty says:

The Lord
(voice only) Because the people have spoken these words,
>   I will make my words in your mouth a fire
>   and these people the wood it consumes.
> O house of Israel, . . .
>   I am bringing a distant nation against you—
> an ancient and enduring nation,
>   a people whose language you do not know,
>   whose speech you do not understand.
> Their quivers are like an open grave;
>   all of them are mighty warriors.
> They will devour your harvests and food,
>   devour your sons and daughters;
> they will devour your flocks and herds,

devour your vines and fig trees.
With the sword they will destroy
    the fortified cities in which you trust.

Yet even in those days . . . I will not destroy you completely. And when the people ask,

Person 2
(anxiously)   Why has the LORD our God done all this to us?

The Lord
(voice)   You will tell them, "As you have forsaken me and served foreign gods in your own land, so now you will serve foreigners in a land not your own."

Cast: **Jeremiah, Person 1, Person 2** (can be the same as Person 1), **the Lord** (voice only)

Jerusalem under Siege

Jeremiah 6:1–8

Jeremiah   Flee for safety, people of Benjamin!
    Flee from Jerusalem!
Sound the trumpet in Tekoa!
    Raise the signal over Beth Hakkerem!
For disaster looms out of the north,
    even terrible destruction.

The Lord
(voice only) I will destroy the Daughter of Zion,
    so beautiful and delicate.
Shepherds with their flocks will come against her;
    they will pitch their tents around her,
    each tending his own portion.

Shepherd 1   Prepare for battle against her!

Shepherd 2   Arise, let us attack at noon!

Shepherd 3   But, alas, the daylight is fading,
    and the shadows of evening grow long.

Shepherd 2   So arise, let us attack at night—

Shepherd 1   And destroy her fortresses!

Jeremiah   This is what the LORD Almighty says:

The Lord
(voice only,
to
Jeremiah)   Cut down the trees
    and build siege ramps against Jerusalem.

           This city must be punished;
              it is filled with oppression.
           As a well pours out its water,
              so she pours out her wickedness.
           Violence and destruction resound in her;
              her sickness and wounds are ever before me.

(calling)   Take warning, O Jerusalem,
              or I will turn away from you
           and make your land desolate
              so no one can live in it.

Cast: **Jeremiah, the Lord** (voice only), **Shepherd 1, Shepherd 2, Shepherd 3**

Rebellious Israel

Jeremiah 6:9–15

Jeremiah   This is what the LORD Almighty says:

The Lord
(voice only) Let them glean the remnant of Israel
              as thoroughly as a vine;
           pass your hand over the branches again,
              like one gathering grapes.

Jeremiah
(petulantly) To whom can I speak and give warning?
              Who will listen to me?
           Their ears are closed
              so they cannot hear.
           The word of the LORD is offensive to them;
              they find no pleasure in it.

(angrily)   But I am full of the wrath of the LORD,
              and I cannot hold it in.

The Lord
(voice)   Pour it out on the children in the street
              and on the young men gathered together;
           both husband and wife will be caught in it,
              and the old, those weighed down with years.
           Their houses will be turned over to others,
              together with their fields and their wives,
           when I stretch out my hand
              against those who live in the land. . . .
           From the least to the greatest,
              all are greedy for gain;
           prophets and priests alike,
              all practice deceit.

They dress the wound of my people
    as though it were not serious.

[They say:]

A prophet
(compla-
cently)   Peace, peace . . .

The Lord
(voice)   When there is no peace. (PAUSE)
Are they ashamed of their loathsome conduct?
    No, they have no shame at all;
    they do not even know how to blush.
So they will fall among the fallen;
    they will be brought down when I punish them. (PAUSE)
[I, the Lord, have spoken!]

Cast: **Jeremiah, the Lord** (voice only), **A prophet**

Israel Rejects God's Way

Jeremiah 6:16–21

Jeremiah   This is what the LORD says:

The Lord
(voice only) Stand at the crossroads and look;
    ask for the ancient paths,
    ask where the good way is, and walk in it,
    and you will find rest for your souls.

Jeremiah   But you said:

Persons
1 and 2   We will not walk in it.

The Lord
(voice)   I appointed watchmen over you and said:
    "Listen to the sound of the trumpet!"

Jeremiah   But you said:

Persons
1 and 2   We will not listen.

The Lord
(voice)   Therefore hear, O nations;
    observe, O witnesses,
    what will happen to them.
Hear, O earth:
I am bringing disaster on this people,
    the fruit of their schemes,

because they have not listened to my words
and have rejected my law.
What do I care about incense from Sheba
or sweet calamus from a distant land?
Your burnt offerings are not acceptable;
your sacrifices do not please me.

Jeremiah   Therefore this is what the LORD says:

The Lord
(voice)   I will put obstacles before this people.
Fathers and sons alike will stumble over them;
neighbors and friends will perish.

Cast: **Jeremiah, the Lord** (voice only), **Person 1, Person 2**

Invasion from the North

Jeremiah 6:22–30

Jeremiah   This is what the LORD says:

The Lord
(voice only) Look, an army is coming
from the land of the north;
a great nation is being stirred up
from the ends of the earth.
They are armed with bow and spear;
they are cruel and show no mercy.
They sound like the roaring sea
as they ride on their horses;
they come like men in battle formation
to attack you, O Daughter of Zion.

Person 1   We have heard reports about them.

Person 2   Our hands hang limp.

Person 1   Anguish has gripped us—

Person 2   Pain like that of a woman in labor.

Person 1   Do not go out to the fields
or walk on the roads.

Person 2   For the enemy has a sword.

Person 1   There is terror on every side.

Jeremiah   O my people, put on sackcloth
and roll in ashes;
mourn with bitter wailing
as for an only son,

> for suddenly the destroyer
> will come upon us.

The Lord
(voice, to
Jerusalem)   I have made you a tester of metals
> and my people the ore,
> that you may observe
> and test their ways.

Jeremiah   They are all hardened rebels,
> going about to slander.
> They are bronze and iron;
> they all act corruptly.
> The bellows blow fiercely
> to burn away the lead with fire,
> but the refining goes on in vain;
> the wicked are not purged out.
> They are called rejected silver,
> because the LORD has rejected them.

Cast: **Jeremiah, the Lord** (voice only), **Person 1** (strong voice), **Person 2** (timid voice)

False Religion Worthless

Jeremiah 7:1–15

Jeremiah   This is the word that came to Jeremiah from the LORD:

The Lord
(voice only)   Stand at the gate of the LORD's house and there proclaim this message:

Jeremiah
(calling)   Hear the word of the LORD, all you people of Judah who come through these gates to worship the LORD. This is what the LORD Almighty, the God of Israel, says:

The Lord
(voice)   Reform your ways and your actions, and I will let you live in this place. Do not trust in deceptive words and say:

Person 1
(proudly)   This is the temple of the LORD.

Person 2   The temple of the LORD.

**Persons 1
and 2**   The temple of the LORD!

The Lord
(voice)   If you really change your ways and your actions and deal with each other justly, if you do not oppress the alien, the fatherless or the widow and do not shed innocent blood in this place, and if you do not follow other

gods to your own harm, then I will let you live in this place, in the land I gave your forefathers for ever and ever. But look, you are trusting in deceptive words that are worthless.

Will you steal and murder, commit adultery and perjury, burn incense to Baal and follow other gods you have not known, and then come and stand before me in this house, which bears my Name, and say:

Persons 1
and **2** (com-
placently)   We are safe—safe to do all these detestable things.

The Lord
(voice)   Has this house, which bears my Name, become a den of robbers to you? But I have been watching! . . .

Go now to the place in Shiloh where I first made a dwelling for my Name, and see what I did to it because of the wickedness of my people Israel.

Jeremiah   [The LORD declares:]

The Lord
(voice)   While you were doing all these things, . . . I spoke to you again and again, but you did not listen; I called you, but you did not answer. Therefore, what I did to Shiloh I will now do to the house that bears my Name, the temple you trust in, the place I gave to you and your fathers. I will thrust you from my presence, just as I did all your brothers, the people of Ephraim.

Cast: **Jeremiah, the Lord** (voice only), **Person 1, Person 2** (can be the same as Person 1)

Sin and Punishment

Jeremiah 8:4–13 [14–17]

Jeremiah   This is what the LORD says:

The Lord
(voice only) When men fall down, do they not get up?
         When a man turns away, does he not return?
      Why then have these people turned away?
         Why does Jerusalem always turn away?
      They cling to deceit;
         they refuse to return.
      I have listened attentively,
         but they do not say what is right.
      No one repents of his wickedness,
         saying:

Person 1
(penitently) What *have* I done?

Jeremiah	Each pursues his own course
	like a horse charging into battle. (PAUSE)
	Even the stork in the sky
	knows her appointed seasons,
	and the dove, the swift and the thrush
	observe the time of their migration.
	But my people do not know
	the requirements of the LORD.
	How can you say:
Person 1	We are wise—
Person 2	For we have the law of the LORD,
Jeremiah	when actually the lying pen of the scribes
	has handled it falsely? (PAUSE)
	The wise will be put to shame;
	they will be dismayed and trapped.
	Since they have rejected the word of the LORD,
	what kind of wisdom do they have?
The Lord (voice)	Therefore I will give their wives to other men
	and their fields to new owners.
	From the least to the greatest,
	all are greedy for gain;
	prophets and priests alike,
	all practice deceit.
	They dress the wound of my people
	as though it were not serious. [They say:]
Person 1 (complacently)	Peace—
Person 2 (complacently)	Peace (PAUSE)
The Lord (voice)	when there is *no* peace.
	Are they ashamed of their loathsome conduct?
	No, they have no shame at all;
	they do not even know how to blush.
	So they will fall among the fallen;
	they will be brought down when they are punished. . . .
Jeremiah	[The LORD declares:]
The Lord (voice)	I will take away their harvest . . .
	There will be no grapes on the vine.
	There will be no figs on the tree,

271

and their leaves will wither.
What I have given them
will be taken from them.

[Person 1   Why are we sitting here?

Person 2   Gather together!

Person 1   Let us flee to the fortified cities
and perish there!

Person 2   The LORD our God has doomed us to perish
and given us poisoned water to drink,
because we have sinned against him.

Person 1   We hoped for peace
but no good has come—

Person 2   For a time of healing
but there was only terror.

Person 1   The snorting of the enemy's horses
is heard from Dan;
at the neighing of their stallions
the whole land trembles.

Person 2   They have come to devour
the land and everything in it,
the city and all who live there.

The Lord
(voice)   See, I will send venomous snakes among you,
vipers that cannot be charmed,
and they will bite you. . . .]

Cast: **Jeremiah, the Lord** (voice only), **Person 1, Person 2**

Jeremiah's Sorrow for His People

Jeremiah 8:18–9:16

Jeremiah
(praying)   O my Comforter in sorrow,
my heart is faint within me.
Listen to the cry of my people
from a land far away:

Person 1   Is the LORD not in Zion?

Person 2   Is her King no longer there? (PAUSE)

The Lord
(voice only)   Why have they provoked me to anger with their images,
with their worthless foreign idols?

Person 1	The harvest is past.
Person 2	The summer has ended.
Persons **1** and **2**	And we are not saved.

Jeremiah	Since my people are crushed, I am crushed;
	    I mourn, and horror grips me.
	Is there no balm in Gilead?
	    Is there no physician there?
	Why then is there no healing
	    for the wound of my people?
	Oh, that my head were a spring of water
	    and my eyes a fountain of tears!
	I would weep day and night
	    for the slain of my people.
	Oh, that I had in the desert
	    a lodging place for travelers,
	so that I might leave my people
	    and go away from them;
	for they are all adulterers,
	    a crowd of unfaithful people.

The Lord
  (voice)
	They make ready their tongue
	    like a bow, to shoot lies;
	it is not by truth
	    that they triumph in the land.
	They go from one sin to another;
	    they do not acknowledge me. . . .

Jeremiah	Beware of your friends;
	    do not trust your brothers.
	For every brother is a deceiver,
	    and every friend a slanderer.
	Friend deceives friend,
	    and no one speaks the truth.
	They have taught their tongues to lie;
	    they weary themselves with sinning.
	[The LORD declares:]

The Lord
  (voice)
	You live in the midst of deception;
	    in their deceit they refuse to acknowledge me. . . .

Jeremiah	Therefore this is what the LORD Almighty says:

The Lord
  (voice)
	See, I will refine and test them,
	    for what else can I do
	    because of the sin of my people?
	Their tongue is a deadly arrow;
	    it speaks with deceit.

With his mouth each speaks cordially to his neighbor,
    but in his heart he sets a trap for him.
Should I not punish them for this? . . .
Should I not avenge myself
    on such a nation as this?

Jeremiah   I will weep and wail for the mountains
    and take up a lament concerning the desert pastures.
They are desolate and untraveled,
    and the lowing of cattle is not heard.
The birds of the air have fled
    and the animals are gone.

The Lord
(voice)   I will make Jerusalem a heap of ruins,
    a haunt of jackals;
and I will lay waste the towns of Judah
    so no one can live there.

Jeremiah   What man is wise enough to understand this? Who has been instructed by the LORD and can explain it? Why has the land been ruined and laid waste like a desert that no one can cross?

The LORD said:

The Lord
(voice)   It is because they have forsaken my law, which I set before them; they have not obeyed me or followed my law. Instead, they have followed the stubbornness of their hearts; they have followed the Baals, as their fathers taught them.

Jeremiah   Therefore, this is what the LORD Almighty, the God of Israel, says:

The Lord
(voice)   See, I will make this people eat bitter food and drink poisoned water. I will scatter them among nations that neither they nor their fathers have known, and I will pursue them with the sword until I have destroyed them.

Cast: **Jeremiah, Person 1, Person 2** (can be the same as Person 1), **the Lord** (voice only)

The People of Jerusalem Cry Out for Help

Jeremiah 9:17–24

Jeremiah   This is what the LORD Almighty says:

The Lord
(voice only) Consider now! Call for the wailing women to come;
    send for the most skillful of them.

Person 1   Let them come quickly
    and wail over us

Person 2	Till our eyes overflow with tears and water streams from our eyelids.
Jeremiah	The sound of wailing is heard from Zion:
Person 2	How ruined we are!
Person 1	How great is our shame!
Person 2	We must leave our land because our houses are in ruins.

Jeremiah	Now, O women, hear the word of the Lord;
	    open your ears to the words of his mouth.
	Teach your daughters how to wail;
	    teach one another a lament.

Person 1	Death has climbed in through our windows and has entered our fortresses.
Person 2	It has cut off the children from the streets and the young men from the public squares.
Jeremiah	This is what the Lord declares:

The Lord
  (voice)
	The dead bodies of men will lie
	    like refuse on the open field,
	like cut grain behind the reaper,
	    with no one to gather them.

Jeremiah	This is what the Lord says:

The Lord
  (voice)
	Let not the wise man boast of his wisdom
	    or the strong man boast of his strength
	    or the rich man boast of his riches,
	but let him who boasts boast about this:
	    that he understands and knows me,
	that I am the Lord, who exercises kindness,
	    justice and righteousness on earth,
	    for in these I delight. . . .

Cast: **Jeremiah, the Lord** (voice only), **Person 1, Person 2** (preferably women's voices)

God and Idols

Jeremiah 10:1–11

Jeremiah	Hear what the Lord says to you, O house of Israel. This is what the Lord says:
The Lord (voice only)	Do not learn the ways of the nations

or be terrified by signs in the sky,
   though the nations are terrified by them.
For the customs of the peoples are worthless;
   they cut a tree out of the forest,
   and a craftsman shapes it with his chisel.
They adorn it with silver and gold;
   they fasten it with hammer and nails
   so it will not totter.
Like a scarecrow in a melon patch,
   their idols cannot speak;
they must be carried
   because they cannot walk.
Do not fear them;
   they can do no harm
   nor can they do any good.

Jeremiah
(to
The Lord)   No one is like you, O Lord;
   you are great,
   and your name is mighty in power.
Who should not revere you,
   O King of the nations?
   This is your due.
Among all the wise men of the nations
   and in all their kingdoms,
   there is no one like you.

(to
audience)   They are all senseless and foolish;
   they are taught by worthless wooden idols.
Hammered silver is brought from Tarshish
   and gold from Uphaz.
What the craftsman and goldsmith have made
   is then dressed in blue and purple—
   all made by skilled workers.
But the Lord is the true God;
   he is the living God, the eternal King.
When he is angry, the earth trembles;
   the nations cannot endure his wrath.

(emphatic-
ally)   . . .These gods, who did not make the heavens and the earth, will perish from the earth and from under the heavens.

Cast: **Jeremiah, the Lord** (voice only)

A Hymn of Praise to God

Jeremiah 10:12–16

Voice 1   God made the earth by his power;
he founded the world by his wisdom
and stretched out the heavens by his understanding.

Voice 2   When he thunders, the waters in the heavens roar;
he makes clouds rise from the ends of the earth.

Voice 1   He sends lightning with the rain
and brings out the wind from his storehouses.

Voice 2   Everyone is senseless and without knowledge;
every goldsmith is shamed by his idols.
His images are a fraud;
they have no breath in them.

Voice 1   They are worthless, the objects of mockery;
when their judgment comes, they will perish.

Voice 3   He who is the Portion of Jacob is not like these,
for he is the Maker of all things,
including Israel, the tribe of his inheritance—

Voices 1–3   The Lord Almighty is his name.

Cast: **Voice 1, Voice 2, Voice 3**

Coming Destruction

Jeremiah 10:17–25

Jeremiah   Gather up your belongings to leave the land,
you who live under siege.
For this is what the Lord says:

The Lord
(voice only)   At this time I will hurl out
those who live in this land;
I will bring distress on them
so that they may be captured.

Person 1   Woe to me because of my injury!

Person 2   My wound is incurable!

Jeremiah   Yet I said to myself:

Young Jeremiah	This is my sickness, and I must endure it.
Person 2	My tent is destroyed; all its ropes are snapped.
Person 1	My sons are gone from me and are no more.
Voice 1	No one is left now to pitch my tent—
Voice 2	Or to set up my shelter.
Jeremiah	[I answered:]

Young Jeremiah
(to Voices 1 and 2)
	The shepherds are senseless
	    and do not inquire of the LORD;
	so they do not prosper
	    and all their flock is scattered. (PAUSE)

(to audience)	Listen! The report is coming—
	    a great commotion from the land of the north!
	It will make the towns of Judah desolate,
	    a haunt of jackals.

Jeremiah
(praying)
	I know, O LORD, that a man's life is not his own;
	    it is not for man to direct his steps.
	Correct me, LORD, but only with justice—
	    not in your anger,
	    lest you reduce me to nothing.
	Pour out your wrath on the nations
	    that do not acknowledge you,
	    on the peoples who do not call on your name.
	For they have devoured Jacob;
	    they have devoured him completely
	    and destroyed his homeland.

Cast: **Jeremiah**, **the Lord** (voice only), **Person 1**, **Person 2**, **Voice 1**, **Voice 2**, **Young Jeremiah**

The Covenant Is Broken

Jeremiah 11:1–17

Announcer	This is the word that came to Jeremiah from the LORD:
Jeremiah	Listen to the terms of this covenant and tell them to the people of Judah and to those who live in Jerusalem. Tell them that this is what the LORD, the God of Israel, says:

The Lord
(voice only)   Cursed is the man who does not obey the terms of this covenant—the terms I commanded your forefathers when I brought them out of Egypt, out of the iron-smelting furnace. I said, "Obey me and do everything I command you, and you will be my people, and I will be your God. Then I will fulfill the oath I swore to your forefathers, to give them a land flowing with milk and honey"—the land you possess today.

Jeremiah   I answered, "Amen, Lord."

The Lord said to me: "Proclaim all these words in the towns of Judah and in the streets of Jerusalem":

The Lord
(voice)   Listen to the terms of this covenant and follow them. From the time I brought your forefathers up from Egypt until today, I warned them again and again, saying, "Obey me." But they did not listen or pay attention; instead, they followed the stubbornness of their evil hearts. So I brought on them all the curses of the covenant I had commanded them to follow but that they did not keep.

Jeremiah   Then the Lord said to me:

The Lord
(voice)   There is a conspiracy among the people of Judah and those who live in Jerusalem. They have returned to the sins of their forefathers, who refused to listen to my words. They have followed other gods to serve them. Both the house of Israel and the house of Judah have broken the covenant I made with their forefathers.

Jeremiah   Therefore this is what the Lord says:

The Lord
(voice)   I will bring on them a disaster they cannot escape. Although they cry out to me, I will not listen to them. The towns of Judah and the people of Jerusalem will go and cry out to the gods to whom they burn incense, but they will not help them at all when disaster strikes.

Jeremiah   You have as many gods as you have towns, O Judah; and the altars you have set up to burn incense to that shameful god Baal are as many as the streets of Jerusalem.

The Lord
(voice, to
Jeremiah)   Do not pray for this people nor offer any plea or petition for them, because I will not listen when they call to me in the time of their distress.

What is my beloved *doing* in my temple
   as she works out her evil schemes with many?

Jeremiah
(to
audience)   Can consecrated *meat* avert ⸢your punishment⸣?
When you engage in your wickedness,
   then you rejoice.

The LORD called you a thriving olive tree
  with fruit beautiful in form.
But with the roar of a mighty storm
  he will set it on fire,
  and its branches will be broken.

The LORD Almighty, who planted you, has decreed disaster for you, because the house of Israel and the house of Judah have done evil and provoked me to anger by burning incense to Baal.

Cast: **Announcer, Jeremiah, the Lord** (voice only)

Plot against Jeremiah

Jeremiah 11:18–23

Jeremiah Because the LORD revealed their plot to me, I knew it, for at that time he showed me what they were doing. I had been like a gentle lamb led to the slaughter; I did not realize that they had plotted against me, saying:

Enemy 1
(mali-
ciously) Let us destroy the tree and its fruit!

Enemy 2 Let us cut him off from the land of the living,
  that his name be remembered no more.

Jeremiah
(praying) O LORD Almighty, you who judge righteously
  and test the heart and mind,
let me see your vengeance upon them,
  for to you I have committed my cause.

(to
audience) Therefore this is what the LORD says about the men of Anathoth who are seeking your life and saying,

Enemy 1 Do not prophesy in the name of the LORD

Enemy 2 Or you will die by our hands.

Jeremiah Therefore this is what the LORD Almighty says:

The Lord
(voice only) I will punish them. Their young men will die by the sword, their sons and daughters by famine. Not even a remnant will be left to them, because I will bring disaster on the men of Anathoth in the year of their punishment.

Cast: **Jeremiah, Enemy 1, Enemy 2** (can be the same as Enemy 1), **the Lord** (voice only)

Jeremiah's Complaint

Jeremiah 12:1–6

Jeremiah
(to
The Lord)   You are always righteous, O LORD,
      when I bring a case before you.
    Yet I would speak with you about your justice:
      Why does the way of the wicked prosper?
      Why do all the faithless live at ease?
    You have planted them, and they have taken root;
      they grow and bear fruit.
    You are always on their lips
      but far from their hearts.
    Yet you know me, O LORD;
      you see me and test my thoughts about you.
    Drag them off like sheep to be butchered!
      Set them apart for the day of slaughter!

(musing)   How long will the land lie parched
      and the grass in every field be withered?
    Because those who live in it are wicked,
      the animals and birds have perished.
    Moreover, the people are saying:

Person(s)   He will not see what happens to us. (PAUSE)

The Lord
(voice only) If you have raced with men on foot
      and they have worn you out,
      how can you compete with horses?
    If you stumble in safe country,
      how will you manage in the thickets by the Jordan?
    Your brothers, your own family—
      even they have betrayed you;
      they have raised a loud cry against you.
    Do not trust them,
      though they speak well of you.

Cast: **Jeremiah, Person(s), the Lord** (voice only)

A Linen Belt

Jeremiah 13:1–11

Jeremiah   This is what the LORD said to me:

The Lord
(voice only) Go and buy a linen belt and put it around your waist, but do not let it
touch water.

281

Jeremiah	So I bought a belt, as the L<small>ORD</small> directed, and put it around my waist.
	Then the word of the L<small>ORD</small> came to me a second time:
The Lord (voice)	Take the belt you bought and are wearing around your waist, and go now to Perath and hide it there in a crevice in the rocks.
Jeremiah	So I went and hid it at Perath, as the L<small>ORD</small> told me. (PAUSE)
	Many days later the L<small>ORD</small> said to me:
The Lord (voice)	Go now to Perath and get the belt I told you to hide there.
Jeremiah	So I went to Perath and dug up the belt and took it from the place where I had hidden it, but now it was ruined and completely useless.
	Then the word of the L<small>ORD</small> came to me: This is what the L<small>ORD</small> says:
The Lord (voice)	In the same way I will ruin the pride of Judah and the great pride of Jerusalem. These wicked people, who refuse to listen to my words, who follow the stubbornness of their hearts and go after other gods to serve and worship them, will be like this belt—completely useless! For as a belt is bound around a man's waist, so I bound the whole house of Israel and the whole house of Judah to me . . . to be my people for my renown and praise and honor. But they have not listened.

Cast: **Jeremiah, the Lord** (voice only)

Threat of Captivity

Jeremiah 13:15–25

Jeremiah	Hear and pay attention,
	do not be arrogant,
	for the L<small>ORD</small> has spoken.
	Give glory to the L<small>ORD</small> your God
	before he brings the darkness,
	before your feet stumble
	on the darkening hills.
	You hope for light,
	but he will turn it to thick darkness
	and change it to deep gloom.
	But if you do not listen,
	I will weep in secret
	because of your pride;
	my eyes will weep bitterly,
	overflowing with tears,
	because the L<small>ORD</small>'s flock will be taken captive.

Say to the king and to the queen mother:

Person 1   Come down from your thrones,
for your glorious crowns
    will fall from your heads.

Jeremiah   The cities in the Negev will be shut up,
    and there will be no one to open them.
All Judah will be carried into exile,
    carried completely away.

Lift up your eyes and see
    those who are coming from the north.
Where is the flock that was entrusted to you,
    the sheep of which you boasted?
What will you say when ⌞the Lord⌟ sets over you
    those you cultivated as your special allies?
Will not pain grip you
    like that of a woman in labor?
And if you ask yourself:

Person 2   Why has this happened to me?

Jeremiah   It is because of your many sins
    that your skirts have been torn off
    and your body mistreated.
Can the Ethiopian change his skin
    or the leopard its spots?
Neither can you do good
    who are accustomed to doing evil.

[The Lord declares:]

The Lord
(voice)   I will scatter you like chaff
    driven by the desert wind.
This is your lot,
    the portion I have decreed for you . . .
because you have forgotten me
    and trusted in false gods.

Cast: **Jeremiah**, **Person 1**, **Person 2** (can be the same as Person 1), **the Lord** (voice only)

The Terrible Drought

Jeremiah 14:1–18

Jeremiah   This is the word of the Lord to Jeremiah concerning the drought:

The Lord
(voice only) Judah mourns,
    her cities languish;

they wail for the land,
and a cry goes up from Jerusalem.
The nobles send their servants for water;
they go to the cisterns
but find no water.
They return with their jars unfilled;
dismayed and despairing,
they cover their heads.
The ground is cracked
because there is no rain in the land;
the farmers are dismayed
and cover their heads.
Even the doe in the field
deserts her newborn fawn
because there is no grass.
Wild donkeys stand on the barren heights
and pant like jackals;
their eyesight fails
for lack of pasture.

Person 1   Although our sins testify against us,
O LORD, do something for the sake of your name.

Person 2   Our backsliding is great;
we have sinned against you.

Person 3   O Hope of Israel,
its Savior in times of distress,
why are you like a stranger in the land,
like a traveler who stays only a night?

Person 1   Why are you like a man taken by surprise,
like a warrior powerless to save?

Person 2   You are among us, O LORD,
and we bear your name;
do not forsake us!

Jeremiah   This is what the LORD says about this people:

The Lord
(voice)   They greatly love to wander;
they do not restrain their feet.

Jeremiah   So the LORD does not accept them;
he will now remember their wickedness
and punish them for their sins.

Then the LORD said to me:

The Lord
(voice)   Do not pray for the well-being of this people. Although they fast, I will
not listen to their cry; though they offer burnt offerings and grain offer-

ings, I will not accept them. Instead, I will destroy them with the sword, famine and plague.

Jeremiah   But I said, "Ah, Sovereign LORD, the prophets keep telling them, 'You will not see the sword or suffer famine. Indeed, I will give you lasting peace in this place.'"

[Then the LORD said to me:]

The Lord
(voice)   The prophets are prophesying lies in my name. I have not sent them or appointed them or spoken to them. They are prophesying to you false visions, divinations, idolatries and the delusions of their own minds.

Jeremiah   Therefore, this is what the LORD says about the prophets who are prophesying in [his] name:

The Lord
(voice)   I did not send them, yet they are saying, "No sword or famine will touch this land." Those same prophets will perish by sword and famine. And the people they are prophesying to will be thrown out into the streets of Jerusalem because of the famine and sword. There will be no one to bury them or their wives, their sons or their daughters. I will pour out on them the calamity they deserve.

Speak this word to them:

"Let my eyes overflow with tears
    night and day without ceasing;
for my virgin daughter—my people—
    has suffered a grievous wound,
    a crushing blow.
If I go into the country,
    I see those slain by the sword;
if I go into the city,
    I see the ravages of famine.
Both prophet and priest
    have gone to a land they know not."

Cast: **Jeremiah, the Lord** (voice only), **Person 1, Person 2, Person 3**

The People Plead with the Lord

Jeremiah 14:19–22

Voice 1   Have you rejected Judah completely?

Voice 2   Do you despise Zion?

Voice 3   Why have you afflicted us
    so that we cannot be healed?

Voice 1	We hoped for peace but no good has come.
Voice 2	For a time of healing but there is only terror.

Voice 3	O LORD, we acknowledge our wickedness
	    and the guilt of our fathers;
	    we have indeed sinned against you.

Voice 1	For the sake of your name do not despise us; do not dishonor your glorious throne.
Voice 2	Remember your covenant with us and do not break it.
Voice 3	Do any of the worthless idols of the nations bring rain?
Voice 1	Do the skies themselves send down showers?
Voice 2	No, it is you, O LORD our God.
Voice 3	Therefore our hope is in you, for you are the one who does all this.

Cast: **Voice 1**, **Voice 2**, **Voice 3**

Doom for the People of Judah

Jeremiah 15:1–4

Jeremiah	Then the LORD said to me:
The Lord (voice only)	Even if Moses and Samuel were to stand before me, my heart would not go out to this people. Send them away from my presence! Let them go! And if they ask you:
Person	Where shall we go?
The Lord (voice)	Tell them, "This is what the LORD says":
Voice 1	Those destined for death,
Voice 2	To death.
Voice 1	Those for the sword—
Voice 2	To the sword.
Voice 2	Those for starvation—
Voice 1	To starvation.

Voices
1 and **2**   Those for captivity, to captivity.

The Lord
(voice)   I will send four kinds of destroyers against them. . . .

Voice 1   The sword

Voice 2   To kill.

Voice 1   The dogs

Voice 2   To drag away.

Voice 1   The birds of the air—and the beasts of the earth—

Voice 2   To devour and destroy.

The Lord
(voice)   I will make them abhorrent to all the kingdoms of the earth because of what Manasseh son of Hezekiah king of Judah did in Jerusalem.

Cast: **Jeremiah, the Lord** (voice only), **Person, Voice 1, Voice 2** (can be the same as Voice 1; Voices speak God's words)

Jeremiah Complains to the Lord

Jeremiah 15:10–21

Jeremiah
(meditating) Alas, my mother, that you gave me birth,
        a man with whom the whole land strives and contends!
    I have neither lent nor borrowed,
        yet everyone curses me.

(to
audience)   The Lord said:

The Lord
(voice only) Surely I will deliver you for a good purpose;
        surely I will make your enemies plead with you
        in times of disaster and times of distress.

    Can a man break iron—
        iron from the north—or bronze?
    Your wealth and your treasures
        I will give as plunder, without charge,
    because of all your sins
        throughout your country.
    I will enslave you to your enemies
        in a land you do not know,
    for my anger will kindle a fire
        that will burn against you.

Jeremiah
(praying)   You understand, O LORD;
remember me and care for me.
Avenge me on my persecutors.
You are long-suffering—do not take me away;
think of how I suffer reproach for your sake.
When your words came, I ate them;
they were my joy and my heart's delight,
for I bear your name,
O LORD God Almighty.
I never sat in the company of revelers,
never made merry with them;
I sat alone because your hand was on me
and you had filled me with indignation.
Why is my pain unending
and my wound grievous and incurable?
Will you be to me like a deceptive brook,
like a spring that fails?

Therefore this is what the LORD says:

The Lord
(voice)   If you repent, I will restore you
that you may serve me;
if you utter worthy, not worthless, words,
you will be my spokesman.
Let this people turn to you,
but you must not turn to them.
I will make you a wall to this people,
a fortified wall of bronze;
they will fight against you
but will not overcome you,
for I am with you
to rescue and save you, . . .
I will save you from the hands of the wicked
and redeem you from the grasp of the cruel.

Cast: **Jeremiah, the Lord** (voice only)

Jeremiah's Prayer of Confidence in the Lord

Jeremiah 16:19–21

Jeremiah
(praying)   O LORD, my strength and my fortress,
my refuge in time of distress,
to you the nations will come
from the ends of the earth and say:

Person 1	Our fathers possessed nothing but false gods—
Person 2	Worthless idols that did them no good.
Person 1	Do men make their own gods?
Person 2	Yes, but they are *not* gods!

The Lord
(voice only)
	Therefore I will teach them—
	    this time I will teach them
	    my power and might.
	Then they will know
	    that my name is the LORD.

Cast: **Jeremiah**, **Person 1**, **Person 2** (can be the same as Person 1), **the Lord** (voice only)

Various Sayings

Jeremiah 17:5–17

Jeremiah	This is what the LORD says:

The Lord
(voice only)
	Cursed is the one who trusts in man,
	    who depends on flesh for his strength
	    and whose heart turns away from the LORD.
	He will be like a bush in the wastelands;
	    he will not see prosperity when it comes.
	He will dwell in the parched places of the desert,
	    in a salt land where no one lives.
	
	But blessed is the man who trusts in the LORD,
	    whose confidence is in him.
	He will be like a tree planted by the water
	    that sends out its roots by the stream.
	It does not fear when heat comes;
	    its leaves are always green.
	It has no worries in a year of drought
	    and never fails to bear fruit.

Jeremiah	The heart is deceitful above all things
	    and beyond cure.
	    Who can understand it?

The Lord
(voice)
	I the LORD search the heart
	    and examine the mind,
	to reward a man according to his conduct,
	    according to what his deeds deserve.

Jeremiah (to audience)	Like a partridge that hatches eggs it did not lay

	is the man who gains riches by unjust means.

           is the man who gains riches by unjust means.
     When his life is half gone, they will desert him,
           and in the end he will prove to be a fool.

     A glorious throne, exalted from the beginning,
           is the place of our sanctuary.

(praying)   O LORD, the hope of Israel,
           all who forsake you will be put to shame.
     Those who turn away from you will be written in the dust
           because they have forsaken the LORD,
           the spring of living water.

     Heal me, O LORD, and I will be healed;
           save me and I will be saved,
           for you are the one I praise.
     They keep saying to me:

Person 1   Where is the word of the LORD?

Person 2   Let it now be fulfilled!

Jeremiah
(praying)   I have not run away from being your shepherd;
           you know I have not desired the day of despair.
           What passes my lips is open before you.
     Do not be a terror to me;
           you are my refuge in the day of disaster.

Cast: **Jeremiah, the Lord** (voice only), **Person 1, Person 2** (can be the same as Person 1)

At the Potter's House

Jeremiah 18:1–17

Narrator   This is the word that came to Jeremiah from the LORD:

The Lord
(voice only) Go down to the potter's house, and there I will give you my message.

Jeremiah   So I went down to the potter's house, and I saw him working at the wheel. But the pot he was shaping from the clay was marred in his hands; so the potter formed it into another pot, shaping it as seemed best to him.

     Then the word of the LORD came to me:

The Lord
(voice)   O house of Israel, can I not do with you as this potter does? . . . Like clay in the hand of the potter, so are you in my hand, O house of Israel. If at any time I announce that a nation or kingdom is to be uprooted, torn down and destroyed, and if that nation I warned repents of its evil, then I will relent and not inflict on it the disaster I had planned. And if at another time I announce that a nation or kingdom is to be built up and

planted, and if it does evil in my sight and does not obey me, then I will reconsider the good I had intended to do for it.

Now therefore say to the people of Judah and those living in Jerusalem, "This is what the LORD says: Look! I am preparing a disaster for you and devising a plan against you. So turn from your evil ways, each one of you, and reform your ways and your actions." But they will reply:

Person 1 It's no use.

Person 2 We will continue with our own plans:

Person 1 Each of us will follow the stubbornness of his evil heart.

Jeremiah Therefore this is what the LORD says:

The Lord
(voice)

    Inquire among the nations:
      Who has ever heard anything like this?
    A most horrible thing has been done
      by Virgin Israel.
    Does the snow of Lebanon
      ever vanish from its rocky slopes?
    Do its cool waters from distant sources
      ever cease to flow?
    Yet my people have forgotten me,
      they burn incense to worthless idols,
    which made them stumble in their ways
      and in the ancient paths.
    They made them walk in bypaths
      and on roads not built up.
    Their land will be laid waste,
      an object of lasting scorn;
    all who pass by will be appalled
      and will shake their heads.
    Like a wind from the east,
      I will scatter them before their enemies;
    I will show them my back and not my face
      in the day of their disaster.

Cast: **Narrator**, the Lord (voice only), **Jeremiah, Person 1, Person 2**

A Plot against Jeremiah

Jeremiah 18:18–19:11

[**Jeremiah** They said:]

Person 1 Come, let's make plans against Jeremiah.

Person 2	For the teaching of the law by the priest will not be lost, nor will counsel from the wise, nor the word from the prophets.
Person 1	So come, let's attack him with our tongues—
Person 2	And pay no attention to anything he says.

Jeremiah
(praying)

Listen to me, O LORD;
   hear what my accusers are saying!
Should good be repaid with evil?
   Yet they have dug a pit for me.
Remember that I stood before you
   and spoke in their behalf
   to turn your wrath away from them.
So give their children over to famine;
   hand them over to the power of the sword.
Let their wives be made childless and widows;
   let their men be put to death,
   their young men slain by the sword in battle.
Let a cry be heard from their houses
   when you suddenly bring invaders against them,
for they have dug a pit to capture me
   and have hidden snares for my feet.
But you know, O LORD,
   all their plots to kill me.
Do not forgive their crimes
   or blot out their sins from your sight.
Let them be overthrown before you;
   deal with them in the time of your anger.

This is what the LORD says:

The Lord
(voice only) Go and buy a clay jar from a potter. Take along some of the elders of the people and of the priests and go out to the Valley of Ben Hinnom, near the entrance of the Potsherd Gate. There proclaim the words I tell you, and say: "Hear the word of the LORD, O kings of Judah and people of Jerusalem."

Jeremiah   This is what the LORD Almighty, the God of Israel, says:

The Lord
(voice)

Listen! I am going to bring a disaster on this place that will make the ears of everyone who hears of it tingle. They have forsaken me and made this a place of foreign gods; they have burned sacrifices in it to gods that neither they nor their fathers nor the kings of Judah ever knew, and they have filled this place with the blood of the innocent. They have built the high places of Baal to burn their sons in the fire as offerings to Baal—something I did not command or mention, nor did it enter my mind.

Jeremiah	So beware, the days are coming, declares the LORD, when people will no longer call this place Topheth or the Valley of Ben Hinnom, but the Valley of Slaughter.
The Lord (voice)	In this place I will ruin the plans of Judah and Jerusalem. I will make them fall by the sword before their enemies, at the hands of those who seek their lives, and I will give their carcasses as food to the birds of the air and the beasts of the earth. I will devastate this city and make it an object of scorn; all who pass by will be appalled and will scoff because of all its wounds. I will make them eat the flesh of their sons and daughters, and they will eat one another's flesh during the stress of the siege imposed on them by the enemies who seek their lives.
	Break the jar while those who go with you are watching, and say to them:
The Lord (voice)	This is what the LORD Almighty says: I will smash this nation and this city just as this potter's jar is smashed and cannot be repaired. They will bury the dead in Topheth until there is no more room.

Cast: **Jeremiah, Person 1, Person 2** (can be the same as Person 1), **the Lord** (voice only)

The Clay Jar

Jeremiah 19:11–15

Jeremiah (breaking a jar)	[This is what the LORD Almighty says:]
The Lord (voice only)	I will smash this nation and this city just as this potter's jar is smashed and cannot be repaired. They will bury the dead in Topheth until there is no more room. This is what I will do to this place and to those who live here.
Jeremiah	[The LORD declares:]
The Lord (voice)	I will make this city like Topheth. The houses in Jerusalem and those of the kings of Judah will be defiled like this place, Topheth—all the houses where they burned incense on the roofs to all the starry hosts and poured out drink offerings to other gods.
Jeremiah	[I] then returned from Topheth, where the LORD had sent [me] to prophesy, and stood in the court of the LORD's temple and said to all the people, "This is what the LORD Almighty, the God of Israel, says":
The Lord (voice)	Listen! I am going to bring on this city and the villages around it every

disaster I pronounced against them, because they were stiff-necked and would not listen to my words.

Cast: **Jeremiah, the Lord** (voice only). (Note: This reading overlaps with the previous one.)

Jeremiah and Pashhur

Jeremiah 20:1–6

Narrator When the priest Pashhur son of Immer, the chief officer in the temple of the Lord, heard Jeremiah prophesying these things, he had Jeremiah the prophet beaten and put in the stocks at the Upper Gate of Benjamin at the Lord's temple. The next day, when Pashhur released him from the stocks, Jeremiah said to him:

Jeremiah The Lord's name for you is not Pashhur, but Magor-Missabib. For this is what the Lord says:

The Lord
(voice only) I will make you a terror to yourself and to all your friends; with your own eyes you will see them fall by the sword of their enemies. I will hand all Judah over to the king of Babylon, who will carry them away to Babylon or put them to the sword. I will hand over to their enemies all the wealth of this city—all its products, all its valuables and all the treasures of the kings of Judah. They will take it away as plunder and carry it off to Babylon. And you, Pashhur, and all who live in your house will go into exile to Babylon. There you will die and be buried, you and all your friends to whom you have prophesied lies.

Cast: **Narrator, Jeremiah, the Lord** (voice only)

Jeremiah's Complaint

Jeremiah 20:7–13

Jeremiah
(praying) O Lord, you deceived me, and I was deceived;
　　you overpowered me and prevailed.
I am ridiculed all day long;
　　everyone mocks me.
Whenever I speak, I cry out
　　proclaiming:

Voice Violence! And destruction!

Jeremiah
(to
audience) So the word of the Lord has brought me
　　insult and reproach all day long.
But if I say:

294

Voice	I will not mention him or speak any more in his name—

Jeremiah	His word is in my heart like a fire,
	    a fire shut up in my bones.
	I am weary of holding it in;
	    indeed, I cannot.
	I hear many whispering:

Person 1	Terror on every side!
Person 2	Report him!
Person 1	Let's report him!
Jeremiah	All my friends are waiting for me to slip, saying:
Friend 1	Perhaps he will be deceived:
Friend 2	Then we will prevail over him.
Friend 1	And take our revenge on him.

Jeremiah
(to
audience)
	But the LORD is with me like a mighty warrior;
	    so my persecutors will stumble and not prevail.
	They will fail and be thoroughly disgraced;
	    their dishonor will never be forgotten.

(praying)	O LORD Almighty, you who examine the righteous
	    and probe the heart and mind,
	let me see your vengeance upon them,
	    for to you I have committed my cause.

(to
audience)
	Sing to the LORD!
	    Give praise to the LORD!
	He rescues the life of the needy
	    from the hands of the wicked.

Cast: **Jeremiah, Voice** (can be the same as Jeremiah), **Person 1, Person 2, Friend 1, Friend 2** (Friends 1 and 2 can be the same as Persons 1 and 2)

God Rejects Zedekiah's Request

Jeremiah 21:1–10

Narrator	The word came to Jeremiah from the LORD when King Zedekiah sent to him Pashhur son of Malkijah and the priest Zephaniah son of Maaseiah. They said:

Pashhur	Inquire now of the LORD for us because Nebuchadnezzar king of Babylon is attacking us.
Zephaniah	Perhaps the LORD will perform wonders for us as in times past so that he will withdraw from us.
Narrator	But Jeremiah answered them:
Jeremiah	Tell Zedekiah, "This is what the LORD, the God of Israel, says":
The Lord (voice only)	I am about to turn against you the weapons of war that are in your hands, which you are using to fight the king of Babylon and the Babylonians who are outside the wall besieging you. And I will gather them inside this city. I myself will fight against you with an outstretched hand and a mighty arm in anger and fury and great wrath. I will strike down those who live in this city—both men and animals—and they will die of a terrible plague. After that . . . , I will hand over Zedekiah king of Judah, his officials and the people in this city who survive the plague, sword and famine, to Nebuchadnezzar king of Babylon and to their enemies who seek their lives. He will put them to the sword; he will show them no mercy or pity or compassion.
Jeremiah	Furthermore, tell the people, "This is what the LORD says":
The Lord (voice)	See, I am setting before you the way of life and the way of death. Whoever stays in this city will die by the sword, famine or plague. But whoever goes out and surrenders to the Babylonians who are besieging you will live; he will escape with his life. I have determined to do this city harm and not good. . . . It will be given into the hands of the king of Babylon, and he will destroy it with fire.

Cast: **Narrator, Pashhur, Zephaniah, Jeremiah, the Lord** (voice only)

Judgment on the Royal House of Judah and Evil Kings

Jeremiah 21:11–22:9

Jeremiah	. . . Hear the word of the LORD; O house of David, this is what the LORD says:
The Lord (voice only)	Administer justice every morning;

      rescue from the hand of his oppressor
      the one who has been robbed,
or my wrath will break out and burn like fire
      because of the evil you have done—
      burn with no one to quench it.

Jeremiah	[The LORD declares:]

The Lord
(voice)

I am against you, Jerusalem,
   you who live above this valley
   on the rocky plateau, . . .
You who say:

Person 1   Who can come against us?

Person 2   Who can enter our refuge?

The Lord
(voice)

I will punish you as your deeds deserve, . . .
I will kindle a fire in your forests
   that will consume everything around you.

Jeremiah   This is what the Lord says:

The Lord
(voice)

Go down to the palace of the king of Judah and proclaim this message there:

Jeremiah   Hear the word of the Lord, O king of Judah, you who sit on David's throne—you, your officials and your people who come through these gates. This is what the Lord says:

The Lord
(voice)

Do what is just and right. Rescue from the hand of his oppressor the one who has been robbed. Do no wrong or violence to the alien, the fatherless or the widow, and do not shed innocent blood in this place. For if you are careful to carry out these commands, then kings who sit on David's throne will come through the gates of this palace, riding in chariots and on horses, accompanied by their officials and their people. But if you do not obey these commands . . . I swear by myself that this palace will become a ruin.

Jeremiah   For this is what the Lord says about the palace of the king of Judah:

The Lord
(voice)

Though you are like Gilead to me,
   like the summit of Lebanon,
I will surely make you like a desert,
   like towns not inhabited.
I will send destroyers against you,
   each man with his weapons,
and they will cut up your fine cedar beams
   and throw them into the fire.

People from many nations will pass by this city and will ask one another:

Person 1   Why has the Lord done such a thing to this great city?

Jeremiah   And the answer will be:

| Person 2 | Because they have forsaken the covenant of the LORD their God and have worshiped and served other gods. |

Cast: **Jeremiah, the Lord** (voice only), **Person 1, Person 2**

Jeremiah's Message Concerning the King of Judah

Jeremiah 22:10–19

| Jeremiah | Do not weep for the dead ⸢king⸣ or mourn his loss;
   rather, weep bitterly for him who is exiled,
because he will never return
   nor see his native land again. |

For this is what the LORD says about Shallum son of Josiah, who succeeded his father as king of Judah but has gone from this place:

| The Lord
(voice only) | He will never return. He will die in the place where they have led him captive; he will not see this land again. |

| Jeremiah | Woe to him who builds his palace by unrighteousness,
   his upper rooms by injustice,
making his countrymen work for nothing,
   not paying them for their labor.
He says: |

| Jehoiakim
(pretentiously) | I will build myself a great palace
   with spacious upper rooms. |

| Jeremiah | So he makes large windows in it,
   panels it with cedar
   and decorates it in red. |

[The LORD declares:]

| The Lord
(voice) | Does it make you a king
   to have more and more cedar?
Did not your father have food and drink?
   He did what was right and just,
   so all went well with him.
He defended the cause of the poor and needy,
   and so all went well.
Is that not what it means to know me? . . .
But your eyes and your heart
   are set only on dishonest gain,
on shedding innocent blood
   and on oppression and extortion. |

Jeremiah	Therefore this is what the LORD says about Jehoiakim son of Josiah king of Judah:
The Lord (voice)	They will not mourn for him:
Person 1 (cynically)	Alas, my brother!
Person 2 (cynically)	Alas, my sister!
The Lord (voice)	They will not mourn for him:
Person 1 (cynically)	Alas, my master!
Person 2 (cynically)	Alas, his splendor!
The Lord (voice)	He will have the burial of a donkey— dragged away and thrown outside the gates of Jerusalem.

Cast: **Jeremiah**, **the Lord** (voice only), **Jehoiakim, Person 1, Person 2**

God's Judgment on Jehoiachin

Jeremiah 22:24–30

Jeremiah	[The Lord declares:]
The Lord (voice only)	As surely as I live . . . even if you, Jehoiachin son of Jehoiakim king of Judah, were a signet ring on my right hand, I would still pull you off. I will hand you over to those who seek your life, those you fear—to Nebuchadnezzar king of Babylon and to the Babylonians. I will hurl you and the mother who gave you birth into another country, where neither of you was born, and there you both will die. You will never come back to the land you long to return to.

Jeremiah	Is this man Jehoiachin a despised, broken pot,
	    an object no one wants?
	Why will he and his children be hurled out,
	    cast into a land they do not know?
	O land, land, land,
	    hear the word of the LORD!
	This is what the LORD says:

The Lord (voice)	Record this man as if childless, a man who will not prosper in his lifetime,

for none of his offspring will prosper,
   none will sit on the throne of David
   or rule anymore in Judah.

Cast: **Jeremiah, the Lord** (voice only)

The Righteous Branch

Jeremiah 23:1–6 [7–8]

Jeremiah   [The LORD declares:]

The Lord
  (voice only)   Woe to the shepherds who are destroying and scattering the sheep of
                 my pasture! . . .

Jeremiah   Therefore this is what the LORD, the God of Israel, says to the shepherds
                 who tend my people:

The Lord
  (voice)   Because you have scattered my flock and driven them away and have
                 not bestowed care on them, I will bestow punishment on you for the
                 evil you have done. . . . I myself will gather the remnant of my flock out
                 of all the countries where I have driven them and will bring them back
                 to their pasture, where they will be fruitful and increase in number. I
                 will place shepherds over them who will tend them, and they will no
                 longer be afraid or terrified, nor will any be missing. . . .

Jeremiah   [The Lord declares:]

The Lord   The days are coming . . .
                    when I will raise up to David a righteous Branch,
                 a King who will reign wisely
                    and do what is just and right in the land.
                 In his days Judah will be saved
                    and Israel will live in safety.
                 This is the name by which he will be called:

Persons
  1 and 2   The LORD Our Righteousness.

Jeremiah   [The Lord declares:]

[The Lord
  (voice)   So then, the days are coming . . . when people will no longer say:

Person 1   As surely as the LORD lives, who brought the Israelites up out of Egypt!

The Lord
  (voice)   But they will say:

300

Person 2	As surely as the Lord lives, who brought the descendants of Israel up out of the land of the north and out of all the countries where he had banished them!
The Lord (voice)	Then they will live in their own land.]

Cast: **Jeremiah, the Lord** (voice only), **Person 1, Person 2.** (See also Appendix: Christmas Readings, New Testament, page 416.)

Lying Prophets

Jeremiah 23:9–15

Jeremiah	Concerning the prophets:

My heart is broken within me;
   all my bones tremble.
I am like a drunken man,
   like a man overcome by wine,
because of the Lord
   and his holy words.
The land is full of adulterers;
   because of the curse the land lies parched
   and the pastures in the desert are withered.
The ⌊prophets⌋ follow an evil course
   and use their power unjustly.

The Lord
(voice only) Both prophet and priest are godless;
   even in my temple I find their wickedness. . . .
Therefore their path will become slippery;
   they will be banished to darkness
   and there they will fall.
I will bring disaster on them
   in the year they are punished. . . . (PAUSE)

Among the prophets of Samaria
   I saw this repulsive thing:
They prophesied by Baal
   and led my people Israel astray.
And among the prophets of Jerusalem
   I have seen something horrible:
   They commit adultery and live a lie.
They strengthen the hands of evildoers,
   so that no one turns from his wickedness.
They are all like Sodom to me;
   the people of Jerusalem are like Gomorrah.

Jeremiah	Therefore, this is what the Lord Almighty says concerning the prophets:

The Lord
(voice)   I will make them eat bitter food
                  and drink poisoned water,
              because from the prophets of Jerusalem
                  ungodliness has spread throughout the land.

Cast: **Jeremiah, the Lord** (voice only)

Two Baskets of Figs

Jeremiah 24:1–10

Jeremiah   After Jehoiachin son of Jehoiakim king of Judah and the officials, the craftsmen and the artisans of Judah were carried into exile from Jerusalem to Babylon by Nebuchadnezzar king of Babylon, the LORD showed me two baskets of figs placed in front of the temple of the LORD. One basket had very good figs, like those that ripen early; the other basket had very poor figs, so bad they could not be eaten.

Then the LORD asked me:

The Lord
(voice only) What do you see, Jeremiah?

Jeremiah
(to
the Lord)   Figs. . . . The good ones are very good, but the poor ones are so bad they cannot be eaten.

(to
audience)   Then the word of the LORD came to me: "This is what the LORD, the God of Israel, says":

The Lord
(voice)   Like these good figs, I regard as good the exiles from Judah, whom I sent away from this place to the land of the Babylonians. My eyes will watch over them for their good, and I will bring them back to this land. I will build them up and not tear them down; I will plant them and not uproot them. I will give them a heart to know me, that I am the LORD. They will be my people, and I will be their God, for they will return to me with all their heart.

              But like the poor figs, which are so bad they cannot be eaten, so will I deal with Zedekiah king of Judah, his officials and the survivors from Jerusalem, whether they remain in this land or live in Egypt. I will make them abhorrent and an offense to all the kingdoms of the earth, a reproach and a byword, an object of ridicule and cursing, wherever I banish them. I will send the sword, famine and plague against them until they are destroyed from the land I gave to them and their fathers.

Cast: **Jeremiah, the Lord** (voice only)

302

The Cup of God's Wrath

Jeremiah 25:15–31

Jeremiah This is what the LORD, the God of Israel, said to me:

The Lord
(voice only) Take from my hand this cup filled with the wine of my wrath and make all the nations to whom I send you drink it. When they drink it, they will stagger and go mad because of the sword I will send among them.

Jeremiah So I took the cup from the LORD's hand and made all the nations to whom he sent me drink it: Jerusalem and the towns of Judah, its kings and officials, to make them a ruin and an object of horror and scorn and cursing, as they are today:

Reader 1 Pharaoh king of Egypt.

Reader 2 His attendants,
his officials and all his people—
and all the foreign people there.

Reader 1 All the kings of Uz.

Reader 2 All the kings of the Philistines—
(those of Ashkelon, Gaza, Ekron,
and the people left at Ashdod).

Reader 1 Edom, Moab and Ammon;
all the kings of Tyre and Sidon;
the kings of the coastlands across the sea—

Reader 2 Dedan, Tema, Buz and all who are in distant places.

Reader 1 All the kings of Arabia—

Reader 2 And all the kings of the foreign people
who live in the desert.

Reader 1 All the kings of Zimri, Elam and Media.

Reader 2 And all the kings of the north, near and far—

**Readers
1 and 2** One after the other.

Reader 1 All the kingdoms on the face of the earth.

Reader 2 And after all of them, the king of Sheshach will drink it too. . . .

Jeremiah This is what the LORD Almighty, the God of Israel, says:

The Lord
(voice) Drink, get drunk and vomit, and fall to rise no more because of the sword I will send among you. But if they refuse to take the cup from your hand and drink, tell them, "This is what the LORD Almighty says: You must

	drink it! See, I am beginning to bring disaster on the city that bears my Name, and will you indeed go unpunished?"
Jeremiah	[The LORD declares:]
The Lord (voice)	You will not go unpunished, for I am calling down a sword upon all who live on the earth. . . .
	Now prophesy all these words against them and say to them:
Jeremiah	The LORD will roar from on high;

       he will thunder from his holy dwelling
       and roar mightily against his land.
He will shout like those who tread the grapes,
       shout against all who live on the earth.
The tumult will resound to the ends of the earth,
       for the LORD will bring charges against the nations;
he will bring judgment on all mankind
       and put the wicked to the sword,

                      declares the LORD.

Cast: **Jeremiah, the Lord** (voice only), **Reader 1, Reader 2**

Jeremiah Threatened with Death

Jeremiah 26:1–16

Jeremiah	Early in the reign of Jehoiakim son of Josiah king of Judah, this word came from the LORD: "This is what the LORD says":
The Lord (voice only)	Stand in the courtyard of the LORD's house and speak to all the people of the towns of Judah who come to worship in the house of the LORD. Tell them everything I command you; do not omit a word. Perhaps they will listen and each will turn from his evil way. Then I will relent and not bring on them the disaster I was planning because of the evil they have done.
Jeremiah	Say to them: "This is what the LORD says":
The Lord (voice)	If you do not listen to me and follow my law, which I have set before you, and if you do not listen to the words of my servants the prophets, whom I have sent to you again and again—
Jeremiah	(though you have not listened)—
The Lord (voice)	then I will make this house like Shiloh and this city an object of cursing among all the nations of the earth.

304

Narrator	The priests, the prophets and all the people heard Jeremiah speak these words in the house of the LORD. But as soon as Jeremiah finished telling all the people everything the LORD had commanded him to say, the priests, the prophets and all the people seized him and said:
Priest	You must die!
Prophet	Why do you prophesy in the LORD's name that this house will be like Shiloh—
Priest	And this city will be desolate and deserted?
Narrator	And all the people crowded around Jeremiah in the house of the LORD. (PAUSE)
	When the officials of Judah heard about these things, they went up from the royal palace to the house of the LORD and took their places at the entrance of the New Gate of the LORD's house. Then the priests and the prophets said to the officials and all the people:
Priest	This man should be sentenced to death because he has prophesied against this city.
Prophet	You have heard it with your own ears!
Narrator	Then Jeremiah said to all the officials and all the people:
Jeremiah	The LORD sent me to prophesy against this house and this city all the things you have heard. Now reform your ways and your actions and obey the LORD your God. Then the LORD will relent and not bring the disaster he has pronounced against you. As for me, I am in your hands; do with me whatever you think is good and right. Be assured, however, that if you put me to death, you will bring the guilt of innocent blood on yourselves and on this city and on those who live in it, for in truth the LORD has sent me to you to speak all these words in your hearing.
Narrator	Then the officials and all the people said to the priests and the prophets:
Official	This man should not be sentenced to death! He has spoken to us in the name of the LORD our God.

Cast: **Jeremiah, the Lord** (voice only), **Narrator, Priest, Prophet** (can be the same as Priest), **Official** (can be the same as Priest)

Judah to Serve Nebuchadnezzar

Jeremiah 27:1–22

Jeremiah	Early in the reign of Zedekiah son of Josiah king of Judah, this word came to [me] from the LORD: This is what the LORD said to me:
The Lord (voice only)	Make a yoke out of straps and crossbars and put it on your neck. Then

305

send word to the kings of Edom, Moab, Ammon, Tyre and Sidon through the envoys who have come to Jerusalem to Zedekiah king of Judah. Give them a message for their masters. . .

Jeremiah

This is what the LORD Almighty, the God of Israel, says: "Tell this to your masters":

The Lord
(voice)

With my great power and outstretched arm I made the earth and its people and the animals that are on it, and I give it to anyone I please. Now I will hand all your countries over to my servant Nebuchadnezzar king of Babylon; I will make even the wild animals subject to him. All nations will serve him and his son and his grandson until the time for his land comes; then many nations and great kings will subjugate him.

Jeremiah

[The LORD declares:]

The Lord
(voice)

If, however, any nation or kingdom will not serve Nebuchadnezzar king of Babylon or bow its neck under his yoke, I will punish that nation with the sword, famine and plague . . . until I destroy it by his hand. So do not listen to your prophets, your diviners, your interpreters of dreams, your mediums or your sorcerers who tell you:

Prophet

You will not serve the king of Babylon.

The Lord
(voice)

They prophesy lies to you that will only serve to remove you far from your lands; I will banish you and you will perish.

Jeremiah

[The LORD declares:]

The Lord
(voice)

If any nation will bow its neck under the yoke of the king of Babylon and serve him, I will let that nation remain in its own land to till it and to live there. . . .

Jeremiah

I gave the same message to Zedekiah king of Judah. I said: "Bow your neck under the yoke of the king of Babylon; serve him and his people, and you will live. Why will you and your people die by the sword, famine and plague with which the LORD has threatened any nation that will not serve the king of Babylon? Do not listen to the words of the prophets who say to you:

Prophet

You will not serve the king of Babylon—

Jeremiah

They are prophesying lies to you.

The Lord
(voice)

I have not sent them. . . . They are prophesying lies in my name. Therefore, I will banish you and you will perish, both you and the prophets who prophesy to you.

Jeremiah

Then I said to the priests and all these people, "This is what the LORD says":

306

The Lord (voice)	Do not listen to the prophets who say:
Prophet	Very soon now the articles from the Lord's house will be brought back from Babylon.
The Lord (voice)	They are prophesying lies to you. Do not listen to them.
Jeremiah	Serve the king of Babylon, and you will live. Why should this city become a ruin? If they are prophets and have the word of the Lord, let them plead with the Lord Almighty that the furnishings remaining in the house of the Lord and in the palace of the king of Judah and in Jerusalem not be taken to Babylon. For this is what the Lord Almighty says about the pillars, the Sea, the movable stands and the other furnishings that are left in this city, which Nebuchadnezzar king of Babylon did not take away when he carried Jehoiachin son of Jehoiakim king of Judah into exile from Jerusalem to Babylon, along with all the nobles of Judah and Jerusalem—yes, this is what the Lord Almighty, the God of Israel, says about the things that are left in the house of the Lord and in the palace of the king of Judah and in Jerusalem:
The Lord (voice)	They will be taken to Babylon and there they will remain until the day I come for them.
Jeremiah	Declares the Lord.
The Lord (voice)	Then I will bring them back and restore them to this place.

Cast: **Jeremiah**, **the Lord** (voice only), **Prophet**

The False Prophet Hananiah

Jeremiah 28:1–17

Jeremiah	In the fifth month of that same year, the fourth year, early in the reign of Zedekiah king of Judah, the prophet Hananiah son of Azzur, who was from Gibeon, said to me in the house of the Lord in the presence of the priests and all the people:
Hananiah	This is what the Lord Almighty, the God of Israel, says: "I will break the yoke of the king of Babylon. Within two years I will bring back to this place all the articles of the Lord's house that Nebuchadnezzar king of Babylon removed from here and took to Babylon. I will also bring back to this place Jehoiachin son of Jehoiakim king of Judah and all the other exiles from Judah who went to Babylon," declares the Lord, "for I will break the yoke of the king of Babylon."

307

Narrator	Then the prophet Jeremiah replied to the prophet Hananiah before the priests and all the people who were standing in the house of the LORD. He said:
Jeremiah (to Hananiah)	Amen! May the LORD do so! May the LORD fulfill the words you have prophesied by bringing the articles of the LORD's house and all the exiles back to this place from Babylon. Nevertheless, listen to what I have to say in your hearing and in the hearing of all the people: From early times the prophets who preceded you and me have prophesied war, disaster and plague against many countries and great kingdoms. But the prophet who prophesies peace will be recognized as one truly sent by the LORD only if his prediction comes true.
Narrator	Then the prophet Hananiah took the yoke off the neck of the prophet Jeremiah and broke it, and he said before all the people:
Hananiah	This is what the LORD says: "In the same way will I break the yoke of Nebuchadnezzar king of Babylon off the neck of all the nations within two years."
Narrator	At this, the prophet Jeremiah went on his way. (PAUSE)
	Shortly after the prophet Hananiah had broken the yoke off the neck of the prophet Jeremiah, the word of the LORD came to Jeremiah:
The Lord (voice only)	Go and tell Hananiah, "This is what the LORD says: You have broken a wooden yoke, but in its place you will get a yoke of iron. This is what the LORD Almighty, the God of Israel, says: I will put an iron yoke on the necks of all these nations to make them serve Nebuchadnezzar king of Babylon, and they will serve him. I will even give him control over the wild animals."
Narrator	Then Jeremiah said to Hananiah the prophet:
Jeremiah (to Hananiah)	Listen, Hananiah! The LORD has not sent you, yet you have persuaded this nation to trust in lies. Therefore, this is what the LORD says:
The Lord (voice)	I am about to remove you from the face of the earth. This very year you are going to die, because you have preached rebellion against the LORD.
Narrator	In the seventh month of that same year, Hananiah the prophet died.

Cast: **Jeremiah, Hananiah, Narrator, the Lord** (voice only)

A Letter to the Exiles

Jeremiah 29:1–23

Narrator	This is the text of the letter that the prophet Jeremiah sent from Jerusalem to the surviving elders among the exiles and to the priests, the prophets and all the other people Nebuchadnezzar had carried into exile from Jerusalem to Babylon. (This was after King Jehoiachin and the queen mother, the court officials and the leaders of Judah and Jerusalem, the craftsmen and the artisans had gone into exile from Jerusalem.) He entrusted the letter to Elasah son of Shaphan and to Gemariah son of Hilkiah, whom Zedekiah king of Judah sent to King Nebuchadnezzar in Babylon. It said:
Jeremiah	This is what the LORD Almighty, the God of Israel, says to all those I carried into exile from Jerusalem to Babylon:
The Lord (voice only)	Build houses and settle down; plant gardens and eat what they produce. Marry and have sons and daughters; find wives for your sons and give your daughters in marriage, so that they too may have sons and daughters. Increase in number there, do not decrease. Also, seek the peace and prosperity of the city to which I have carried you into exile.
Jeremiah	Pray to the LORD for it, because if it prospers, you too will prosper. Yes, this is what the LORD Almighty, the God of Israel, says:
The Lord (voice)	Do not let the prophets and diviners among you deceive you. Do not listen to the dreams you encourage them to have. They are prophesying lies to you in my name. I have not sent them. . . .
Jeremiah	This is what the LORD says:
The Lord (voice)	When seventy years are completed for Babylon, I will come to you and fulfill my gracious promise to bring you back to this place. For I know the plans I have for you . . . plans to prosper you and not to harm you, plans to give you hope and a future. Then you will call upon me and come and pray to me, and I will listen to you. You will seek me and find me when you seek me with all your heart. I will be found by you . . . and will bring you back from captivity. I will gather you from all the nations and places where I have banished you . . . and will bring you back to the place from which I carried you into exile.
Jeremiah	You may say:
Person	The LORD has raised up prophets for us in Babylon.
Jeremiah	But this is what the LORD says about the king who sits on David's throne and all the people who remain in this city, your countrymen who did not go with you into exile—yes, this is what the LORD Almighty says:

The Lord (voice)	I will send the sword, famine and plague against them and I will make them like poor figs that are so bad they cannot be eaten. I will pursue them with the sword, famine and plague and will make them abhorrent to all the kingdoms of the earth and an object of cursing and horror, of scorn and reproach, among all the nations where I drive them. For they have not listened to my words . . . words that I sent to them again and again by my servants the prophets.
Jeremiah	And you exiles have not listened either. . . . Therefore, hear the word of the LORD, all you exiles whom I have sent away from Jerusalem to Babylon. This is what the LORD Almighty, the God of Israel, says about Ahab son of Kolaiah and Zedekiah son of Maaseiah:
The Lord (voice)	[they] are prophesying lies to you in my name: I will hand them over to Nebuchadnezzar king of Babylon, and he will put them to death before your very eyes. Because of them, all the exiles from Judah who are in Babylon will use this curse:
Person	"The LORD treat you like Zedekiah and Ahab, whom the king of Babylon burned in the fire."
The Lord (voice)	For they have done outrageous things in Israel; they have committed adultery with their neighbors' wives and in my name have spoken lies, which I did not tell them to do.
Jeremiah	[The LORD declares:]
The Lord (voice)	I know it and am a witness to it. . . .

Cast: **Narrator, Jeremiah, the Lord** (voice only), **Person**

Message to Shemaiah

Jeremiah 29:24–32

Jeremiah	Tell Shemaiah the Nehelamite, "This is what the LORD Almighty, the God of Israel, says":
The Lord (voice only)	You sent letters in your own name to all the people in Jerusalem, to Zephaniah son of Maaseiah the priest, and to all the other priests. You said to Zephaniah:
Shemaiah	The LORD has appointed you priest in place of Jehoiada to be in charge of the house of the LORD; you should put any madman who acts like a prophet into the stocks and neck-irons. So why have you not reprimanded

Jeremiah from Anathoth, who poses as a prophet among you? He has sent this message to us in Babylon:

Jeremiah   It will be a long time. Therefore build houses and settle down; plant gardens and eat what they produce.

Narrator   Zephaniah the priest, however, read the letter to Jeremiah the prophet. Then the word of the LORD came to Jeremiah:

Jeremiah   Send this message to all the exiles: "This is what the LORD says about Shemaiah the Nehelamite: Because Shemaiah has prophesied to you, even though I did not send him, and has led you to believe a lie, this is what the LORD says":

The Lord
(voice)   I will surely punish Shemaiah the Nehelamite and his descendants. He will have no one left among this people, nor will he see the good things I will do for my people . . . because he has preached rebellion against me.

Cast: **Jeremiah, the Lord** (voice only), **Shemaiah, Narrator**

Restoration of Israel (i)

Jeremiah 30:1–11

Narrator   This is the word that came to Jeremiah from the LORD:

Jeremiah   This is what the LORD, the God of Israel, says:

The Lord
(voice only)   Write in a book all the words I have spoken to you. The days are coming . . . when I will bring my people Israel and Judah back from captivity and restore them to the land I gave their forefathers to possess. . . .

Narrator   These are the words the LORD spoke concerning Israel and Judah:

Jeremiah   This is what the LORD says:

The Lord
(voice)   Cries of fear are heard—
          terror, not peace.
      Ask and see:
          Can a man bear children?
      Then why do I see every strong man
          with his hands on his stomach like a woman in labor,
          every face turned deathly pale?
      How awful that day will be!
          None will be like it.
      It will be a time of trouble for Jacob,
          but he will be saved out of it.

Jeremiah   [The LORD Almighty declares:]

The Lord
(voice)

In that day, . . .
I will break the yoke off their necks
and will tear off their bonds;
no longer will foreigners enslave them.
Instead, they will serve the Lord their God
and David their king,
whom I will raise up for them.

So do not fear, O Jacob my servant;
do not be dismayed, O Israel . . .
I will surely save you out of a distant place,
your descendants from the land of their exile.
Jacob will again have peace and security,
and no one will make him afraid.
I am with you and will save you . . .
Though I completely destroy all the nations
among which I scatter you,
I will not completely destroy you.
I will discipline you but only with justice;
I will not let you go entirely unpunished.

Cast: **Narrator, Jeremiah, the Lord** (voice only)

Restoration of Israel (ii)

Jeremiah 30:18–24

Jeremiah

This is what the Lord says:

The Lord
(voice only)

I will restore the fortunes of Jacob's tents
and have compassion on his dwellings;
the city will be rebuilt on her ruins,
and the palace will stand in its proper place.
From them will come songs of thanksgiving
and the sound of rejoicing.
I will add to their numbers,
and they will not be decreased;
I will bring them honor,
and they will not be disdained.
Their children will be as in days of old,
and their community will be established before me;
I will punish all who oppress them.
Their leader will be one of their own;
their ruler will arise from among them.
I will bring him near and he will come close to me,
for who is he who will devote himself
to be close to me? . . .

	So you will be my people, and I will be your God.

Jeremiah	See, the storm of the LORD
	  will burst out in wrath,
	a driving wind swirling down
	  on the heads of the wicked.
	The fierce anger of the LORD will not turn back
	  until he fully accomplishes
	  the purposes of his heart.
	In days to come
	  you will understand this.

Cast: **Jeremiah, the Lord** (voice only)

Israel's Return Home

Jeremiah 31:1–14

Jeremiah	[The LORD declares:]
The Lord (voice only)	At that time . . . I will be the God of all the clans of Israel, and they will be my people
Jeremiah	This is what the LORD says:

The Lord
(voice)
	The people who survive the sword
	  will find favor in the desert;
	  I will come to give rest to Israel.

Jeremiah
The Lord
(voice)
	The LORD appeared to us in the past, saying:
	
	I have loved you with an everlasting love;
	  I have drawn you with loving-kindness.
	I will build you up again
	  and you will be rebuilt, O Virgin Israel.
	Again you will take up your tambourines
	  and go out to dance with the joyful.
	Again you will plant vineyards
	  on the hills of Samaria;
	the farmers will plant them
	  and enjoy their fruit.
	There will be a day when watchmen cry out
	  on the hills of Ephraim:

Watchman 1	Come, let us go up to Zion—
Watchman 2	To the LORD our God.
Jeremiah	This is what the LORD says:

313

The Lord
  (voice)   Sing with joy for Jacob;
                shout for the foremost of the nations.
            Make your praises heard, and say:

Person
  (praying)   O Lᴏʀᴅ, save your people,
            the remnant of Israel.

The Lord
  (voice)   See, I will bring them from the land of the north
                and gather them from the ends of the earth.
            Among them will be the blind and the lame,
                expectant mothers and women in labor;
                a great throng will return.
            They will come with weeping;
                they will pray as I bring them back.
            I will lead them beside streams of water
                on a level path where they will not stumble,
            because I am Israel's father,
                and Ephraim is my firstborn son.

Jeremiah   Hear the word of the Lᴏʀᴅ, O nations;
                proclaim it in distant coastlands:

The Lord
  (voice)   He who scattered Israel will gather them
                and will watch over his flock like a shepherd.

Jeremiah   For the Lᴏʀᴅ will ransom Jacob
                and redeem them from the hand of those
                    stronger than they.
            They will come and shout for joy on
                    the heights of Zion;
                they will rejoice in the bounty of the Lᴏʀᴅ—
            the grain, the new wine and the oil,
                the young of the flocks and herds.
            They will be like a well-watered garden,
                and they will sorrow no more.
            Then maidens will dance and be glad,
                young men and old as well.

The Lord
  (voice)   I will turn their mourning into gladness;
                I will give them comfort and joy instead of sorrow.
            I will satisfy the priests with abundance,
                and my people will be filled with my bounty. . . .

Cast: **Jeremiah, the Lord** (voice only), **Watchman 1, Watchman 2** (can be the same as Watchman 1), **Person**

The Lord's Mercy on Israel

Jeremiah 31:15–22

Jeremiah	This is what the LORD says:

The Lord
(voice only)
	A voice is heard in Ramah,
	    mourning and great weeping,
	Rachel weeping for her children
	    and refusing to be comforted,
	    because her children are no more.

Jeremiah	This is what the LORD says:

The Lord
(voice)
	Restrain your voice from weeping
	    and your eyes from tears,
	for your work will be rewarded . . . .
	    They will return from the land of the enemy.
	So there is hope for your future. . . .
	    Your children will return to their own land. (PAUSE)
	
	I have surely heard Ephraim's moaning.

Person 1 (praying)	You disciplined me like an unruly calf, and I have been disciplined.
Person 2 (praying)	Restore me, and I will return, because you are the LORD my God.
Person 1 (to audience)	After I strayed, I repented.
Person 2 (to audience)	After I came to understand, I beat my breast.
Person 1	I was ashamed and humiliated because I bore the disgrace of my youth.

The Lord
(voice)
	Is not Ephraim my dear son,
	    the child in whom I delight?
	Though I often speak against him,
	    I still remember him.
	Therefore my heart yearns for him;
	    I have great compassion for him. . . .

Jeremiah (urgently)	Set up road signs;

          put up guideposts.
          Take note of the highway,
             the road that you take.

The Lord
  (voice)   Return, O Virgin Israel,
            return to your towns.
          How long will you wander,
            O unfaithful daughter? . . .

Cast: **Jeremiah, the Lord** (voice only), **Person 1, Person 2** (Persons 1 and 2 can be the same)

The Future Prosperity of God's People

Jeremiah 31:23–37 [38–40]

Jeremiah   This is what the LORD Almighty, the God of Israel, says:

The Lord
  (voice only) When I bring them back from captivity, the people in the land of Judah and in its towns will once again use these words:

Persons
  1 and 2   The LORD bless you—

Person 1   O righteous dwelling—

Person 2   O sacred mountain.

The Lord
  (voice)   People will live together in Judah and all its towns—farmers and those who move about with their flocks. I will refresh the weary and satisfy the faint.

Jeremiah   At this I awoke and looked around. My sleep had been pleasant to me.

The Lord
  (voice)   The days are coming . . . when I will plant the house of Israel and the house of Judah with the offspring of men and of animals. Just as I watched over them to uproot and tear down, and to overthrow, destroy and bring disaster, so I will watch over them to build and to plant. . . . In those days people will no longer say:

Person 1   The fathers have eaten sour grapes,
           and the children's teeth are set on edge.

The Lord
  (voice)   Instead, everyone will die for his *own* sin; whoever eats sour grapes—his *own* teeth will be set on edge.

Jeremiah   [The LORD declares:]

The Lord
  (voice)   The time is coming, . . . ,

when I will make a new covenant
with the house of Israel
and with the house of Judah.
It will not be like the covenant
I made with their forefathers
when I took them by the hand
to lead them out of Egypt,
because they broke my covenant,
though I was a husband to them. . . .
This is the covenant I will make with the house of Israel
after that time. . . .
I will put my law in their minds
and write it on their hearts.
I will be their God,
and they will be my people.
No longer will a man teach his neighbor,
or a man his brother, saying:

Person 2
(proudly)   Know the LORD!

The Lord
(voice)   Because they will all know me,
from the least of them to the greatest. . . .
For I will forgive their wickedness
and will remember their sins no more.

Jeremiah   This is what the LORD says:

He who appoints the sun
to shine by day,
who decrees the moon and stars
to shine by night,
who stirs up the sea
so that its waves roar—
the LORD Almighty is his name:

The Lord
(voice)   Only if these decrees vanish from my sight . . .
will the descendants of Israel ever cease
to be a nation before me.

Jeremiah   This is what the LORD says:

The Lord
(voice)   Only if the heavens above can be measured
and the foundations of the earth below be searched out
will I reject all the descendants of Israel
because of all they have done. . . .

[The days are coming . . . when this city will be rebuilt for me from the Tower of Hananel to the Corner Gate.

Jeremiah	The measuring line will stretch from there straight to the hill of Gareb and then turn to Goah. The whole valley where dead bodies and ashes are thrown, and all the terraces out to the Kidron Valley on the east as far as the corner of the Horse Gate, will be holy to the Lord. The city will never again be uprooted or demolished.]

Cast: **Jeremiah, the Lord** (voice only), **Person 1, Person 2**

Jeremiah Buys a Field

Jeremiah 32:1–15

Narrator	This is the word that came to Jeremiah from the Lord in the tenth year of Zedekiah king of Judah, which was the eighteenth year of Nebuchadnezzar. The army of the king of Babylon was then besieging Jerusalem, and Jeremiah the prophet was confined in the courtyard of the guard in the royal palace of Judah.
	Now Zedekiah king of Judah had imprisoned him there, saying:
Zedekiah	Why do you prophesy as you do? You say:
Jeremiah	This is what the Lord says:
The Lord (voice only)	I am about to hand this city over to the king of Babylon, and he will capture it. Zedekiah king of Judah will not escape out of the hands of the Babylonians but will certainly be handed over to the king of Babylon, and will speak with him face to face and see him with his own eyes. He will take Zedekiah to Babylon, where he will remain until I deal with him.
Jeremiah	Declares the Lord, If you fight against the Babylonians, you will not succeed.
	The word of the Lord came to me:
The Lord (voice)	Hanamel son of Shallum your uncle is going to come to you and say:
Hanamel (voice only)	Buy my field at Anathoth, because as nearest relative it is your right and duty to buy it.
Jeremiah	Then, just as the Lord had said, my cousin Hanamel came to me in the courtyard of the guard and said:
Hanamel (in person)	Buy my field at Anathoth in the territory of Benjamin. Since it is your right to redeem it and possess it, buy it for yourself.
Jeremiah	I knew that this was the word of the Lord; so I bought the field at Anathoth from my cousin Hanamel and weighed out for him seventeen

shekels of silver. I signed and sealed the deed, had it witnessed, and weighed out the silver on the scales. I took the deed of purchase—the sealed copy containing the terms and conditions, as well as the unsealed copy—and I gave this deed to Baruch son of Neriah, the son of Mahseiah, in the presence of my cousin Hanamel and of the witnesses who had signed the deed and of all the Jews sitting in the courtyard of the guard.

In their presence I gave Baruch these instructions: "This is what the LORD Almighty, the God of Israel, says":

The Lord
(voice)   Take these documents, both the sealed and unsealed copies of the deed of purchase, and put them in a clay jar so they will last a long time.

Jeremiah   For this is what the LORD Almighty, the God of Israel, says:

The Lord
(voice)   Houses, fields and vineyards will again be bought in this land.

Cast: **Narrator, Zedekiah, Jeremiah, the Lord** (voice only), **Hanamel**

Jeremiah's Prayer

Jeremiah 32:16–35

Narrator   After [Jeremiah] had given the deed of purchase to Baruch son of Neriah, [he] prayed to the LORD:

Jeremiah
(praying)   Ah, Sovereign LORD, you have made the heavens and the earth by your great power and outstretched arm. Nothing is too hard for you. You show love to thousands but bring the punishment for the fathers' sins into the laps of their children after them. O great and powerful God, whose name is the LORD Almighty, great are your purposes and mighty are your deeds. Your eyes are open to all the ways of men; you reward everyone according to his conduct and as his deeds deserve. You performed miraculous signs and wonders in Egypt and have continued them to this day, both in Israel and among all mankind, and have gained the renown that is still yours. You brought your people Israel out of Egypt with signs and wonders, by a mighty hand and an outstretched arm and with great terror. You gave them this land you had sworn to give their forefathers, a land flowing with milk and honey. They came in and took possession of it, but they did not obey you or follow your law; they did not do what you commanded them to do. So you brought all this disaster upon them.

See how the siege ramps are built up to take the city. Because of the sword, famine and plague, the city will be handed over to the Babylonians who are attacking it. What you said has happened, as you now see. And though the city will be handed over to the Babylonians, you,

O Sovereign LORD, say to me, "Buy the field with silver and have the transaction witnessed."

Narrator Then the word of the LORD came to Jeremiah:

The Lord
(voice only) I am the LORD, the God of all mankind. Is anything too hard for me?

Jeremiah Therefore, this is what the LORD says:

The Lord
(voice) I am about to hand this city over to the Babylonians and to Nebuchad-nezzar king of Babylon, who will capture it. The Babylonians who are attacking this city will come in and set it on fire; they will burn it down, along with the houses where the people provoked me to anger by burning incense on the roofs to Baal and by pouring out drink offerings to other gods.

The people of Israel and Judah have done nothing but evil in my sight from their youth; indeed, the people of Israel have done nothing but provoke me with what their hands have made. . . . From the day it was built until now, this city has so aroused my anger and wrath that I must remove it from my sight. The people of Israel and Judah have provoked me by all the evil they have done—they, their kings and officials, their priests and prophets, the men of Judah and the people of Jerusalem. They turned their backs to me and not their faces; though I taught them again and again, they would not listen or respond to discipline. They set up their abominable idols in the house that bears my Name and defiled it. They built high places for Baal in the Valley of Ben Hinnom to sacrifice their sons and daughters to Molech, though I never commanded, nor did it enter my mind, that they should do such a detestable thing and so make Judah sin.

Cast: **Narrator, Jeremiah, the Lord** (voice only)

Promise of Restoration

Jeremiah 33:1–11

Narrator While Jeremiah was still confined in the courtyard of the guard, the word of the LORD came to him a second time:

Jeremiah This is what the LORD says, he who made the earth, the LORD who formed it and established it—the LORD is his name:

The Lord
(voice only) Call to me and I will answer you and tell you great and unsearchable things you do not know.

Jeremiah This is what the LORD, the God of Israel, says about the houses in this city and the royal palaces of Judah that have been torn down to be used against the siege ramps and the sword in the fight with the Babylonians:

The Lord
(voice)

They will be filled with the dead bodies of the men I will slay in my anger and wrath. I will hide my face from this city because of all its wickedness.

Nevertheless, I will bring health and healing to it; I will heal my people and will let them enjoy abundant peace and security. I will bring Judah and Israel back from captivity and will rebuild them as they were before. I will cleanse them from all the sin they have committed against me and will forgive all their sins of rebellion against me. Then this city will bring me renown, joy, praise and honor before all nations on earth that hear of all the good things I do for it; and they will be in awe and will tremble at the abundant prosperity and peace I provide for it.

Jeremiah

This is what the LORD says:

The Lord
(voice)

You say about this place:

Person 1

It is a desolate waste—

Person 2

Without men or animals.

The Lord
(voice)

Yet in the towns of Judah and the streets of Jerusalem that are deserted, inhabited by neither men nor animals, there will be heard once more the sounds of joy and gladness, the voices of bride and bridegroom, and the voices of those who bring thank offerings to the house of the LORD, saying:

Person 1

Give thanks to the LORD Almighty!

Person 2

For the LORD is good—

**Persons
1 and 2**

His love endures forever.

The Lord
(voice)

For I will restore the fortunes of the land as they were before. . . .

Cast: **Narrator, Jeremiah, the Lord** (voice only), **Person 1, Person 2** (can be the same as Person 1)

The Coming King

Jeremiah 33:1–2, 14–26

Narrator

While Jeremiah was still confined in the courtyard of the guard, the word of the LORD came to him a second time:

Jeremiah

This is what the LORD says, he who made the earth, the LORD who formed it and established it—the LORD is his name:

The Lord
(voice only)

The days are coming . . . when I will fulfill the gracious promise I made to the house of Israel and to the house of Judah.

321

In those days and at that time
I will make a righteous Branch sprout from David's line;
he will do what is just and right in the land.
In those days Judah will be saved
and Jerusalem will live in safety.
This is the name by which it will be called:

Herald
(calling)   The LORD Our Righteousness.

Jeremiah   For this is what the LORD says:

The Lord
(voice)   David will never fail to have a man to sit on the throne of the house of Israel, nor will the priests, who are Levites, ever fail to have a man to stand before me continually to offer burnt offerings, to burn grain offerings and to present sacrifices.

Narrator   The word of the LORD came to Jeremiah:

Jeremiah   This is what the LORD says:

The Lord
(voice)   If you can break my covenant with the day and my covenant with the night, so that day and night no longer come at their appointed time, then my covenant with David my servant—and my covenant with the Levites who are priests ministering before me—can be broken and David will no longer have a descendant to reign on his throne. I will make the descendants of David my servant and the Levites who minister before me as countless as the stars of the sky and as measureless as the sand on the seashore.

Narrator   The word of the LORD came to Jeremiah:

The Lord
(voice)   Have you not noticed that these people are saying:

Person   The LORD has rejected the two kingdoms he chose.

The Lord
(voice)   So they despise my people and no longer regard them as a nation.

Jeremiah   This is what the LORD says:

The Lord
(voice)   If I have not established my covenant with day and night and the fixed laws of heaven and earth, then I will reject the descendants of Jacob and David my servant and will not choose one of his sons to rule over the descendants of Abraham, Isaac and Jacob. For I will restore their fortunes and have compassion on them.

Cast: **Narrator, Jeremiah, the Lord** (voice only), **Herald, Person**

Warning to Zedekiah

Jeremiah 34:1–7

Narrator	While Nebuchadnezzar king of Babylon and all his army and all the kingdoms and peoples in the empire he ruled were fighting against Jerusalem and all its surrounding towns, this word came to Jeremiah from the LORD:
Jeremiah	This is what the LORD, the God of Israel, says:
The Lord (voice only)	Go to Zedekiah king of Judah and tell him, This is what the LORD says: I am about to hand this city over to the king of Babylon, and he will burn it down. You will not escape from his grasp but will surely be captured and handed over to him. You will see the king of Babylon with your own eyes, and he will speak with you face to face. And you will go to Babylon.
Jeremiah	Yet hear the promise of the LORD, O Zedekiah king of Judah. This is what the LORD says concerning you:
The Lord (voice)	You will not die by the sword; you will die peacefully. As people made a funeral fire in honor of your fathers, the former kings who preceded you, so they will make a fire in your honor and lament·
Mourner(s)	Alas, O master!
Jeremiah	[The LORD declares:]
The Lord (voice, slowly)	I myself make this promise. . . .
Narrator	Then Jeremiah the prophet told all this to Zedekiah king of Judah, in Jerusalem, while the army of the king of Babylon was fighting against Jerusalem and the other cities of Judah that were still holding out— Lachish and Azekah. These were the only fortified cities left in Judah.

Cast: **Narrator, Jeremiah, the Lord** (voice only), **Mourners** (preferably two)

Freedom for Slaves

Jeremiah 34:8–22

Narrator	The word came to Jeremiah from the LORD after King Zedekiah had made a covenant with all the people in Jerusalem to proclaim freedom for the slaves. Everyone was to free his Hebrew slaves, both male and female; no one was to hold a fellow Jew in bondage. So all the officials and people who entered into this covenant agreed that they would free their male and female slaves and no longer hold them in bondage. They agreed, and

set them free. But afterward they changed their minds and took back the slaves they had freed and enslaved them again.

Then the word of the LORD came to Jeremiah:

Jeremiah   This is what the LORD, the God of Israel, says:

The Lord

(voice only)   I made a covenant with your forefathers when I brought them out of Egypt, out of the land of slavery. I said, "Every seventh year each of you must free any fellow Hebrew who has sold himself to you. After he has served you six years, you must let him go free." Your fathers, however, did not listen to me or pay attention to me. Recently you repented and did what is right in my sight: Each of you proclaimed freedom to his countrymen. You even made a covenant before me in the house that bears my Name. But now you have turned around and profaned my name; each of you has taken back the male and female slaves you had set free to go where they wished. You have forced them to become your slaves again.

Jeremiah   Therefore, this is what the LORD says:

The Lord

(voice)   You have not obeyed me; you have not proclaimed freedom for your fellow countrymen. So I now proclaim "freedom" for you . . .

(severely)   "freedom" to fall by the sword, plague and famine. I will make you abhorrent to all the kingdoms of the earth. The men who have violated my covenant and have not fulfilled the terms of the covenant they made before me, I will treat like the calf they cut in two and then walked between its pieces. The leaders of Judah and Jerusalem, the court officials, the priests and all the people of the land who walked between the pieces of the calf, I will hand over to their enemies who seek their lives. Their dead bodies will become food for the birds of the air and the beasts of the earth.

I will hand Zedekiah king of Judah and his officials over to their enemies who seek their lives, to the army of the king of Babylon, which has withdrawn from you.

Jeremiah   [The LORD declares:]

The Lord

(voice)   I am going to give the order . . . and I will bring them back to this city. They will fight against it, take it and burn it down. And I will lay waste the towns of Judah so no one can live there.

Cast: **Narrator, Jeremiah, the Lord** (voice only)

The Recabites

Jeremiah 35:1–19

Narrator   This is the word that came to Jeremiah from the LORD during the reign of Jehoiakim son of Josiah king of Judah:

The Lord

(voice only) Go to the Recabite family and invite them to come to one of the side rooms of the house of the Lord and give them wine to drink.

Jeremiah So I went to get Jaazaniah son of Jeremiah, the son of Habazziniah, and his brothers and all his sons—the whole family of the Recabites. I brought them into the house of the Lord, into the room of the sons of Hanan son of Igdaliah the man of God. It was next to the room of the officials, which was over that of Maaseiah son of Shallum the doorkeeper. Then I set bowls full of wine and some cups before the men of the Recabite family and said to them:

**Young
Jeremiah** Drink some wine.

[Jeremiah But they replied:]

**Recabites 1
and 2** We do not drink wine—

Recabite 1 Because our forefather Jonadab son of Recab gave us this command: "Neither you nor your descendants must ever drink wine.

Recabite 2 "Also you must never build houses, sow seed or plant vineyards.

Recabite 1 "You must never have any of these things, but must always live in tents. Then you will live a long time in the land where you are nomads."

Recabite 2 We have obeyed everything our forefather Jonadab son of Recab commanded us.

Recabite 1 Neither we nor our wives nor our sons and daughters have ever drunk wine.

Recabite 2 Or built houses to live in or had vineyards, fields or crops.

Recabite 1 We have lived in tents and have fully obeyed everything our forefather Jonadab commanded us. But when Nebuchadnezzar king of Babylon invaded this land, we said, "Come, we must go to Jerusalem to escape the Babylonian and Aramean armies."

Recabite 2 So we have remained in Jerusalem.

Narrator Then the word of the Lord came to Jeremiah, saying:

Jeremiah This is what the Lord Almighty, the God of Israel, says: Go and tell the men of Judah and the people of Jerusalem:

The Lord
(voice) Will you not learn a lesson and obey my words? . . .

Narrator Jonadab son of Recab ordered his sons not to drink wine and this command has been kept. To this day they do not drink wine, because they obey their forefather's command. But I have spoken to you again and again, yet you have not obeyed me. Again and again I sent all my servants the prophets to you. They said:

325

Young	
Jeremiah	Each of you must turn from your wicked ways and reform your actions; do not follow other gods to serve them. Then you will live in the land I have given to you and your fathers.
The Lord (voice)	But you have not paid attention or listened to me. The descendants of Jonadab son of Recab have carried out the command their forefather gave them, but these people have not obeyed me.
Jeremiah	Therefore, this is what the LORD God Almighty, the God of Israel, says:
The Lord (voice)	Listen! I am going to bring on Judah and on everyone living in Jerusalem every disaster I pronounced against them. I spoke to them, but they did not listen; I called to them, but they did not answer.
Narrator	Then Jeremiah said to the family of the Recabites:
Jeremiah	This is what the LORD Almighty, the God of Israel, says:
The Lord (voice)	You have obeyed the command of your forefather Jonadab and have followed all his instructions and have done everything he ordered.
Jeremiah	Therefore, this is what the LORD Almighty, the God of Israel, says:
The Lord (voice)	Jonadab son of Recab will never fail to have a man to serve me.

Cast: **Narrator**, **the Lord** (voice only), **Jeremiah**, **Young Jeremiah**, **Recabite 1**, **Recabite 2**

Baruch Reads the Scroll in the Temple

Jeremiah 36:1–10

Narrator	In the fourth year of Jehoiakim son of Josiah king of Judah, this word came to Jeremiah from the LORD:
The Lord (voice only)	Take a scroll and write on it all the words I have spoken to you concerning Israel, Judah and all the other nations from the time I began speaking to you in the reign of Josiah till now. Perhaps when the people of Judah hear about every disaster I plan to inflict on them, each of them will turn from his wicked way; then I will forgive their wickedness and their sin.
Narrator	So Jeremiah called Baruch son of Neriah, and while Jeremiah dictated all the words the LORD had spoken to him, Baruch wrote them on the scroll. Then Jeremiah told Baruch:
Jeremiah	I am restricted; I cannot go to the LORD's temple. So *you* go to the house of the LORD on a day of fasting and read to the people from the scroll the

words of the LORD that you wrote as I dictated. Read them to all the people of Judah who come in from their towns. Perhaps they will bring their petition before the LORD, and each will turn from his wicked ways, for the anger and wrath pronounced against this people by the LORD are great.

Narrator   Baruch son of Neriah did everything Jeremiah the prophet told him to do; at the LORD's temple he read the words of the LORD from the scroll. (PAUSE) In the ninth month of the fifth year of Jehoiakim son of Josiah king of Judah, a time of fasting before the LORD was proclaimed for all the people in Jerusalem and those who had come from the towns of Judah. From the room of Gemariah son of Shaphan the secretary, which was in the upper courtyard at the entrance of the New Gate of the temple, Baruch read to all the people at the LORD's temple the words of Jeremiah from the scroll. (PAUSE)

Cast: **Narrator, the Lord** (voice only), **Jeremiah**

The Scroll Is Read to the Officials

Jeremiah 36:11–19

Narrator   When Micaiah son of Gemariah, the son of Shaphan, heard all the words of the LORD from the scroll, he went down to the secretary's room in the royal palace, where all the officials were sitting: Elishama the secretary, Delaiah son of Shemaiah, Elnathan son of Acbor, Gemariah son of Shaphan, Zedekiah son of Hananiah, and all the other officials. After Micaiah told them everything he had heard Baruch read to the people from the scroll, all the officials sent Jehudi son of Nethaniah, the son of Shelemiah, the son of Cushi, to say to Baruch:

Jehudi   Bring the scroll from which you have read to the people and come.

Narrator   So Baruch son of Neriah went to them with the scroll in his hand. They said to him:

Official 1   Sit down, please.

Official 2   And read it to us.

Narrator   So Baruch read it to them. When they heard all these words, they looked at each other in fear and said to Baruch:

Official 2
(to
Official 1)   We must report all these words to the king. . . .

Official 1
(to Baruch)   Tell us, how did you come to write all this? Did *Jeremiah* dictate it?

Baruch   Yes, . . . , he dictated all these words to me, and I wrote them in ink on the scroll.

327

Narrator	Then the officials said to Baruch:
Official 1	You and Jeremiah, go and hide.
Official 2	Don't let anyone know where you are.

Cast: **Narrator, Jehudi, Official 1, Official 2** (can be the same as Official 1), **Baruch**

Jehoiakim Burns Jeremiah's Scroll

Jeremiah 36:20–32

Narrator   After they put the scroll in the room of Elishama the secretary, they went to the king in the courtyard and reported everything to him. The king sent Jehudi to get the scroll, and Jehudi brought it from the room of Elishama the secretary and read it to the king and all the officials standing beside him. (PAUSE) It was the ninth month and the king was sitting in the winter apartment, with a fire burning in the firepot in front of him. Whenever Jehudi had read three or four columns of the scroll, the king cut them off with a scribe's knife and threw them into the firepot, until the entire scroll was burned in the fire. The king and all his attendants who heard all these words showed no fear, nor did they tear their clothes. Even though Elnathan, Delaiah and Gemariah urged the king not to burn the scroll, he would not listen to them. Instead, the king commanded Jerahmeel, a son of the king, Seraiah son of Azriel and Shelemiah son of Abdeel to arrest Baruch the scribe and Jeremiah the prophet. (PAUSE) But the LORD had hidden them. (PAUSE)

After the king burned the scroll containing the words that Baruch had written at Jeremiah's dictation, the word of the LORD came to Jeremiah:

Jeremiah   Take another scroll and write on it all the words that were on the first scroll, which Jehoiakim king of Judah burned up. Also tell Jehoiakim king of Judah, "This is what the LORD says: You burned that scroll and said, 'Why did you write on it that the king of Babylon would certainly come and destroy this land and cut off both men and animals from it?' Therefore, this is what the LORD says about Jehoiakim king of Judah":

The Lord
(voice only)   He will have no one to sit on the throne of David; his body will be thrown out and exposed to the heat by day and the frost by night. I will punish him and his children and his attendants for their wickedness; I will bring on them and those living in Jerusalem and the people of Judah every disaster I pronounced against them, because they have not listened.

Narrator   So Jeremiah took another scroll and gave it to the scribe Baruch son of Neriah, and as Jeremiah dictated, Baruch wrote on it all the words of the scroll that Jehoiakim king of Judah had burned in the fire. And many similar words were added to them.

Cast: **Narrator, Jeremiah, the Lord** (voice only)

Jeremiah Receives Zedekiah's Request

Jeremiah 37:1–10

Narrator	Zedekiah son of Josiah was made king of Judah by Nebuchadnezzar king of Babylon; he reigned in place of Jehoiachin son of Jehoiakim. Neither he nor his attendants nor the people of the land paid any attention to the words the LORD had spoken through Jeremiah the prophet.
	King Zedekiah, however, sent Jehucal son of Shelemiah with the priest Zephaniah son of Maaseiah to Jeremiah the prophet with this message:
Jehucal	Please pray to the LORD our God for us.
Narrator	Now Jeremiah was free to come and go among the people, for he had not yet been put in prison. Pharaoh's army had marched out of Egypt, and when the Babylonians who were besieging Jerusalem heard the report about them, they withdrew from Jerusalem.
Jeremiah	Then the word of the LORD came to Jeremiah: "This is what the LORD, the God of Israel, says":
The Lord (voice only)	Tell the king of Judah, who sent you to inquire of me, "Pharaoh's army, which has marched out to support you, will go back to its own land, to Egypt. Then the Babylonians will return and attack this city; they will capture it and burn it down."
Jeremiah	This is what the LORD says:
The Lord (voice)	Do not deceive yourselves, thinking:
Jehucal (thinking)	The Babylonians will surely leave us.
The Lord (voice)	They will not! Even if you were to defeat the entire Babylonian army that is attacking you and only wounded men were left in their tents, they would come out and burn this city down.

Cast: **Narrator, Jehucal, Narrator, Jeremiah, the Lord** (voice only)

Jeremiah in Prison

Jeremiah 37:11–21

Narrator	After the Babylonian army had withdrawn from Jerusalem because of Pharaoh's army, Jeremiah started to leave the city to go to the territory of Benjamin to get his share of the property among the people there. But when he reached the Benjamin Gate, the captain of the guard, whose name was Irijah son of Shelemiah, the son of Hananiah, arrested him and said:
Irijah	You are deserting to the Babylonians!

Narrator	Jeremiah said:
Jeremiah	That's not true! I am not deserting to the Babylonians.
Narrator	But Irijah would not listen to him; instead, he arrested Jeremiah and brought him to the officials. They were angry with Jeremiah and had him beaten and imprisoned in the house of Jonathan the secretary, which they had made into a prison.
	Jeremiah was put into a vaulted cell in a dungeon, where he remained a long time. Then King Zedekiah sent for him and had him brought to the palace, where he asked him privately:
Zedekiah	Is there any word from the LORD?
Jeremiah	Yes . . . you will be handed over to the king of Babylon.
Narrator	Then Jeremiah said to King Zedekiah:
Jeremiah	What crime have I committed against you or your officials or this people, that you have put me in prison? Where are your prophets who prophesied to you:
Prophet	The king of Babylon will not attack you or this land.
Jeremiah	But now, my lord the king, please listen. Let me bring my petition before you: Do not send me back to the house of Jonathan the secretary, or I will die there.
Narrator	King Zedekiah then gave orders for Jeremiah to be placed in the courtyard of the guard and given bread from the street of the bakers each day until all the bread in the city was gone. So Jeremiah remained in the courtyard of the guard.

Cast: **Narrator, Irijah, Jeremiah, Zedekiah, Prophet** (can be the same as Irijah)

Jeremiah Thrown into a Cistern

Jeremiah 38:1–13; 39:15–18

Narrator	Shephatiah son of Mattan, Gedaliah son of Pashhur, Jehucal son of Shelemiah, and Pashhur son of Malkijah heard what Jeremiah was telling all the people when he said:
Jeremiah	This is what the LORD says:
The Lord (voice only)	Whoever stays in this city will die by the sword, famine or plague, but whoever goes over to the Babylonians will live. He will escape with his life; he will live.
Jeremiah	And this is what the LORD says:

The Lord (voice)	This city will certainly be handed over to the army of the king of Babylon, who will capture it.
Jeremiah	Then the officials said to the king:
Officials 1 and 2 (to Zedekiah)	This man should be put to death.
Official 1	He is discouraging the soldiers who are left in this city, as well as all the people, by the things he is saying to them.
Official 2	This man is not seeking the good of these people but their ruin.
Zedekiah (to Officials)	He is in your hands. . . . The king can do nothing to oppose you.
Narrator	So they took Jeremiah and put him into the cistern of Malkijah, the king's son, which was in the courtyard of the guard. They lowered him by ropes into the cistern; it had no water in it, only mud, and he sank down into the mud.
	But Ebed-Melech, a Cushite, an official in the royal palace, heard that they had put Jeremiah into the cistern. While the king was sitting in the Benjamin Gate, Ebed-Melech went out of the palace and said to him:
Ebed-Melech (to Zedekiah)	My lord the king, these men have acted wickedly in all they have done to Jeremiah the prophet. They have thrown him into a cistern, where he will starve to death when there is no longer any bread in the city.
Narrator	Then the king commanded Ebed-Melech the Cushite:
Zedekiah	Take thirty men from here with you and lift Jeremiah the prophet out of the cistern before he dies.
Jeremiah	So Ebed-Melech took the men with him and went to a room under the treasury in the palace. He took some old rags and worn-out clothes from there and let them down with ropes to [me] in the cistern. Ebed-Melech the Cushite said to [me]:
Ebed-Melech	Put these old rags and worn-out clothes under your arms to pad the ropes.
Narrator	Jeremiah did so, and they pulled him up with the ropes and lifted him out of the cistern. And Jeremiah remained in the courtyard of the guard. . . . (PAUSE)
	While Jeremiah had been confined in the courtyard of the guard, the word of the LORD came to him:
Jeremiah	Go and tell Ebed-Melech the Cushite, "This is what the LORD Almighty, the God of Israel, says":

331

The Lord
(voice)   I am about to fulfill my words against this city through disaster, not prosperity. At that time they will be fulfilled before your eyes.

Jeremiah   [The LORD declares:] But I will rescue you on that day . . . you will not be handed over to those you fear. I will save you; you will not fall by the sword but will escape with your life, because you trust in me. . . .

Cast: **Narrator, Jeremiah, the Lord** (voice only), **Official 1, Official 2, Zedekiah, Ebed-Melech**

Zedekiah Questions Jeremiah Again

Jeremiah 38:14–28

Narrator   Then King Zedekiah sent for Jeremiah and had him brought to the third entrance to the temple of the LORD.

Zedekiah
(to
Jeremiah)   I am going to ask you something. . . . Do not hide anything from me.

Narrator   Jeremiah said to Zedekiah:

Jeremiah
(to
Zedekiah)   If I give you an answer, will you not kill me? Even if I did give you counsel, you would not listen to me.

Narrator   But King Zedekiah swore this oath secretly to Jeremiah:

Zedekiah   As surely as the LORD lives, who has given us breath, I will neither kill you nor hand you over to those who are seeking your life.

Narrator   Then Jeremiah said to Zedekiah:

Jeremiah   This is what the LORD God Almighty, the God of Israel, says:

The Lord
(voice only) If you surrender to the officers of the king of Babylon, your life will be spared and this city will not be burned down; you and your family will live. But if you will not surrender to the officers of the king of Babylon, this city will be handed over to the Babylonians and they will burn it down; you yourself will not escape from their hands.

Narrator   King Zedekiah said to Jeremiah:

Zedekiah   I am afraid of the Jews who have gone over to the Babylonians, for the Babylonians may hand me over to them and they will mistreat me.

Jeremiah   They will not hand you over. . . . Obey the LORD by doing what I tell you. Then it will go well with you, and your life will be spared. But if you refuse to surrender, this is what the LORD has revealed to me:

The Lord (voice)	All the women left in the palace of the king of Judah will be brought out to the officials of the king of Babylon.
Jeremiah	Those women will say to you:
Woman 1	They misled you and overcame you— those trusted friends of yours.
Woman 2	Your feet are sunk in the mud; your friends have deserted you.
The Lord (voice)	All your wives and children will be brought out to the Babylonians. You yourself will not escape from their hands but will be captured by the king of Babylon; and this city will be burned down.
Narrator	Then Zedekiah said to Jeremiah:
Zedekiah	Do not let anyone know about this conversation, or you may die. If the officials hear that I talked with you, and they come to you and say, "Tell us what you said to the king and what the king said to you; do not hide it from us or we will kill you," then tell them, "I was pleading with the king not to send me back to Jonathan's house to die there."
Narrator	All the officials did come to Jeremiah and question him, and he told them everything the king had ordered him to say. So they said no more to him, for no one had heard his conversation with the king.

And Jeremiah remained in the courtyard of the guard until the day Jerusalem was captured. |

Cast: **Narrator, Zedekiah, Jeremiah, the Lord** (voice only), **Woman 1, Woman 2**

Jeremiah Freed

Jeremiah 39:11–14; 40:1–6

Narrator	Now Nebuchadnezzar king of Babylon had given these orders about Jeremiah through Nebuzaradan commander of the imperial guard:
Nebuchad-nezzar	Take him and look after him; don't harm him but do for him whatever he asks.
Narrator	So Nebuzaradan the commander of the guard, Nebushazban a chief officer, Nergal-Sharezer a high official and all the other officers of the king of Babylon sent and had Jeremiah taken out of the courtyard of the guard. They turned him over to Gedaliah son of Ahikam, the son of Shaphan, to take him back to his home. So he remained among his own people. . . . (PAUSE)

The word came to Jeremiah from the LORD after Nebuzaradan com- |

	mander of the imperial guard had released him at Ramah. He had found Jeremiah bound in chains among all the captives from Jerusalem and Judah who were being carried into exile to Babylon. When the commander of the guard found Jeremiah, he said to him:
Nebuzaradan	The LORD your God decreed this disaster for this place. And now the LORD has brought it about; he has done just as he said he would. All this happened because you people sinned against the LORD and did not obey him. But today I am freeing you from the chains on your wrists. Come with me to Babylon, if you like, and I will look after you; but if you do not want to, then don't come. Look, the whole country lies before you; go wherever you please.
Narrator	However, before Jeremiah turned to go, Nebuzaradan added:
Nebuzaradan	Go back to Gedaliah son of Ahikam, the son of Shaphan, whom the king of Babylon has appointed over the towns of Judah, and live with him among the people, or go anywhere else you please.
Narrator	Then the commander gave [Jeremiah] provisions and a present and let him go. So Jeremiah went to Gedaliah son of Ahikam at Mizpah and stayed with him among the people who were left behind in the land.

Cast: **Narrator, Nebuchadnezzar, Nebuzaradan**

Gedaliah, Governor of Judah

Jeremiah 40:7–12

Narrator	When all the army officers and their men who were still in the open country heard that the king of Babylon had appointed Gedaliah son of Ahikam as governor over the land and had put him in charge of the men, women and children who were the poorest in the land and who had not been carried into exile to Babylon, they came to Gedaliah at Mizpah—Ishmael son of Nethaniah, Johanan and Jonathan the sons of Kareah, Seraiah son of Tanhumeth, the sons of Ephai the Netophathite, and Jaazaniah the son of the Maacathite, and their men. Gedaliah son of Ahikam, the son of Shaphan, took an oath to reassure them and their men.
Gedaliah	Do not be afraid to serve the Babylonians. Settle down in the land and serve the king of Babylon, and it will go well with you. I myself will stay at Mizpah to represent you before the Babylonians who come to us, but you are to harvest the wine, summer fruit and oil, and put them in your storage jars, and live in the towns you have taken over.
Narrator	When all the Jews in Moab, Ammon, Edom and all the other countries heard that the king of Babylon had left a remnant in Judah and had appointed Gedaliah son of Ahikam, the son of Shaphan, as governor over

them, they all came back to the land of Judah, to Gedaliah at Mizpah, from all the countries where they had been scattered. And they harvested an abundance of wine and summer fruit.

Cast: **Narrator, Gedaliah**

Gedaliah Assassinated

Jeremiah 40:13–41:18

Narrator   Johanan son of Kareah and all the army officers still in the open country came to Gedaliah at Mizpah and said to him:

Johanan   Don't you know that Baalis king of the Ammonites has sent Ishmael son of Nethaniah to take your life?

Narrator   But Gedaliah son of Ahikam did not believe them.

Then Johanan son of Kareah said privately to Gedaliah in Mizpah:

Johanan
(to
Gedaliah)   Let me go and kill Ishmael son of Nethaniah, and no one will know it. Why should he take your life and cause all the Jews who are gathered around you to be scattered and the remnant of Judah to perish?

Narrator   But Gedaliah son of Ahikam said to Johanan son of Kareah:

Gedaliah
(to
Johanan)   Don't do such a thing! What you are saying about Ishmael is not true.

Narrator   In the seventh month Ishmael son of Nethaniah, the son of Elishama, who was of royal blood and had been one of the king's officers, came with ten men to Gedaliah son of Ahikam at Mizpah. While they were eating together there, Ishmael son of Nethaniah and the ten men who were with him got up and struck down Gedaliah son of Ahikam, the son of Shaphan, with the sword, killing the one whom the king of Babylon had appointed as governor over the land. Ishmael also killed all the Jews who were with Gedaliah at Mizpah, as well as the Babylonian soldiers who were there.

The day after Gedaliah's assassination, before anyone knew about it, eighty men who had shaved off their beards, torn their clothes and cut themselves came from Shechem, Shiloh and Samaria, bringing grain offerings and incense with them to the house of the LORD. Ishmael son of Nethaniah went out from Mizpah to meet them, weeping as he went. When he met them, he said:

Ishmael   Come to Gedaliah son of Ahikam.

Narrator	When they went into the city, Ishmael son of Nethaniah and the men who were with him slaughtered them and threw them into a cistern. But ten of them said to Ishmael:
Man 1	Don't kill us!
Man 2	We have wheat and barley, oil and honey, hidden in a field.
Narrator	So he let them alone and did not kill them with the others. Now the cistern where he threw all the bodies of the men he had killed along with Gedaliah was the one King Asa had made as part of his defense against Baasha king of Israel. Ishmael son of Nethaniah filled it with the dead.
	Ishmael made captives of all the rest of the people who were in Mizpah—the king's daughters along with all the others who were left there, over whom Nebuzaradan commander of the imperial guard had appointed Gedaliah son of Ahikam. Ishmael son of Nethaniah took them captive and set out to cross over to the Ammonites.
	When Johanan son of Kareah and all the army officers who were with him heard about all the crimes Ishmael son of Nethaniah had committed, they took all their men and went to fight Ishmael son of Nethaniah. They caught up with him near the great pool in Gibeon. When all the people Ishmael had with him saw Johanan son of Kareah and the army officers who were with him, they were glad. All the people Ishmael had taken captive at Mizpah turned and went over to Johanan son of Kareah. But Ishmael son of Nethaniah and eight of his men escaped from Johanan and fled to the Ammonites.
	Then Johanan son of Kareah and all the army officers who were with him led away all the survivors from Mizpah whom he had recovered from Ishmael son of Nethaniah after he had assassinated Gedaliah son of Ahikam: the soldiers, women, children and court officials he had brought from Gibeon. And they went on, stopping at Geruth Kimham near Bethlehem on their way to Egypt to escape the Babylonians. They were afraid of them because Ishmael son of Nethaniah had killed Gedaliah son of Ahikam, whom the king of Babylon had appointed as governor over the land.

Cast: **Narrator, Johanan, Gedaliah, Ishmael, Man 1, Man 2**

The People Ask Jeremiah to Pray for Them

Jeremiah 42:1–22

Narrator	All the army officers, including Johanan son of Kareah and Jezaniah son of Hoshaiah, and all the people from the least to the greatest approached Jeremiah the prophet and said to him:
Officer 1	Please hear our petition and pray to the LORD your God for this entire remnant.

Officer 2	For as you now see, though we were once many, now only a few are left.
Officer 1	Pray that the LORD your God will tell us where we should go and what we should do.
Narrator	[Jeremiah replied:]
Jeremiah	I have heard you. . . . I will certainly pray to the LORD your God as you have requested; I will tell you everything the LORD says and will keep nothing back from you.
Officer 1	. . .May the LORD be a true and faithful witness against us if we do not act in accordance with everything the LORD your God sends you to tell us.
Officer 2	Whether it is favorable or unfavorable, we will obey the LORD our God, to whom we are sending you, so that it will go well with us.
Officer 1	We *will* obey the LORD our God.
Narrator	Ten days later the word of the LORD came to Jeremiah. So he called together Johanan son of Kareah and all the army officers who were with him and all the people from the least to the greatest. He said to them:
Jeremiah	This is what the LORD, the God of Israel, to whom you sent me to present your petition, says:
The Lord (voice only)	If you stay in this land, I will build you up and not tear you down; I will plant you and not uproot you, for I am grieved over the disaster I have inflicted on you. Do not be afraid of the king of Babylon, whom you now fear.
Jeremiah	[The LORD declares:]
The Lord (voice)	Do not be afraid of him . . . for I am with you and will save you and deliver you from his hands. I will show you compassion so that he will have compassion on you and restore you to your land.
Jeremiah	However, if you say:
Officer 1	We will not stay in this land—
Jeremiah	And so disobey the LORD your God, and if you say:
Officer 2	No, we will go and live in Egypt, where we will not see war or hear the trumpet or be hungry for bread.
Jeremiah	Then hear the word of the LORD, O remnant of Judah. This is what the LORD Almighty, the God of Israel, says:
The Lord (voice)	If you are determined to go to Egypt and you do go to settle there, then the sword you fear will overtake you there, and the famine you dread will follow you into Egypt, and there you will die. Indeed, all who are determined to go to Egypt to settle there will die by the sword, famine

337

	and plague; not one of them will survive or escape the disaster I will bring on them.
Jeremiah	This is what the LORD Almighty, the God of Israel, says:
The Lord (voice)	As my anger and wrath have been poured out on those who lived in Jerusalem, so will my wrath be poured out on you when you go to Egypt. You will be an object of cursing and horror, of condemnation and reproach; you will never see this place again.
Jeremiah	O remnant of Judah, the LORD has told you, "Do not go to Egypt." Be sure of this: I warn you today that you made a fatal mistake when you sent me to the LORD your God and said, "Pray to the LORD our God for us; tell us everything he says and we will do it." I have told you today, but you still have not obeyed the LORD your God in all he sent me to tell you. So now, be sure of this: You will die by the sword, famine and plague in the place where you want to go to settle.

Cast: **Narrator, Officer 1, Officer 2, Jeremiah, the Lord** (voice only)

Jeremiah Is Taken to Egypt

Jeremiah 43:1–13

Narrator	When Jeremiah finished telling the people all the words of the LORD their God—everything the LORD had sent him to tell them—Azariah son of Hoshaiah and Johanan son of Kareah and all the arrogant men said to Jeremiah:
Azariah	You are lying! The LORD our God has not sent you to say, "You must not go to Egypt to settle there." But Baruch son of Neriah is inciting you against us to hand us over to the Babylonians, so they may kill us or carry us into exile to Babylon.
Narrator	So Johanan son of Kareah and all the army officers and all the people disobeyed the LORD's command to stay in the land of Judah. (PAUSE) Instead, Johanan son of Kareah and all the army officers led away all the remnant of Judah who had come back to live in the land of Judah from all the nations where they had been scattered. They also led away all the men, women and children and the king's daughters whom Nebuzaradan commander of the imperial guard had left with Gedaliah son of Ahikam, the son of Shaphan, and Jeremiah the prophet and Baruch son of Neriah. So they entered Egypt in disobedience to the LORD and went as far as Tahpanhes.
	In Tahpanhes the word of the LORD came to Jeremiah:
The Lord (voice only)	While the Jews are watching, take some large stones with you and bury them in clay in the brick pavement at the entrance to Pharaoh's palace in Tahpanhes. Then say to them:

Jeremiah	This is what the LORD Almighty, the God of Israel, says: I will send for my servant Nebuchadnezzar king of Babylon, and I will set his throne over these stones I have buried here; he will spread his royal canopy above them.
The Lord (voice)	He will come and attack Egypt, bringing death to those destined for death, captivity to those destined for captivity, and the sword to those destined for the sword. He will set fire to the temples of the gods of Egypt; he will burn their temples and take their gods captive. As a shepherd wraps his garment around him, so will he wrap Egypt around himself and depart from there unscathed. There in the temple of the sun in Egypt he will demolish the sacred pillars and will burn down the temples of the gods of Egypt.

Cast: **Narrator**, **Azariah**, **the Lord** (voice only), **Jeremiah**

Disaster Because of Idolatry

Jeremiah 44:1–30

Narrator	This word came to Jeremiah concerning all the Jews living in Lower Egypt—in Migdol, Tahpanhes and Memphis—and in Upper Egypt.
Jeremiah	This is what the LORD Almighty, the God of Israel, says:
The Lord (voice only)	You saw the great disaster I brought on Jerusalem and on all the towns of Judah. Today they lie deserted and in ruins because of the evil they have done. They provoked me to anger by burning incense and by worshiping other gods that neither they nor you nor your fathers ever knew. Again and again I sent my servants the prophets, who said:
Prophet	Do not do this detestable thing that I hate!
The Lord (voice)	But they did not listen or pay attention; they did not turn from their wickedness or stop burning incense to other gods. Therefore, my fierce anger was poured out; it raged against the towns of Judah and the streets of Jerusalem and made them the desolate ruins they are today.
Jeremiah	Now this is what the LORD God Almighty, the God of Israel, says:
The Lord (voice)	Why bring such great disaster on yourselves by cutting off from Judah the men and women, the children and infants, and so leave yourselves without a remnant? Why provoke me to anger with what your hands have made, burning incense to other gods in Egypt, where you have come to live? You will destroy yourselves and make yourselves an object of cursing and reproach among all the nations on earth. Have you forgotten the wickedness committed by your fathers and by the kings and

queens of Judah and the wickedness committed by you and your wives in the land of Judah and the streets of Jerusalem? To this day they have not humbled themselves or shown reverence, nor have they followed my law and the decrees I set before you and your fathers.

Jeremiah   Therefore, this is what the Lord Almighty, the God of Israel, says:

The Lord
(voice)   I am determined to bring disaster on you and to destroy all Judah. I will take away the remnant of Judah who were determined to go to Egypt to settle there. They will all perish in Egypt; they will fall by the sword or die from famine. From the least to the greatest, they will die by sword or famine. They will become an object of cursing and horror, of condemnation and reproach. I will punish those who live in Egypt with the sword, famine and plague, as I punished Jerusalem. None of the remnant of Judah who have gone to live in Egypt will escape or survive to return to the land of Judah, to which they long to return and live; none will return except a few fugitives.

Narrator   Then all the men who knew that their wives were burning incense to other gods, along with all the women who were present—a large assembly— and all the people living in Lower and Upper Egypt, said to Jeremiah:

Man   We will not listen to the message you have spoken to us in the name of the Lord!

Woman   We will certainly do everything we said we would: We will burn incense to the Queen of Heaven and will pour out drink offerings to her just as we and our fathers, our kings and our officials did in the towns of Judah and in the streets of Jerusalem.

Man   At that time we had plenty of food and were well off and suffered no harm.

Woman   But ever since we stopped burning incense to the Queen of Heaven and pouring out drink offerings to her, we have had nothing and have been perishing by sword and famine.

Narrator   The women added:

Woman   When we burned incense to the Queen of Heaven and poured out drink offerings to her, did not our husbands know that we were making cakes like her image and pouring out drink offerings to her?

Narrator   Then Jeremiah said to all the people, both men and women, who were answering him:

Jeremiah   Did not the Lord remember and think about the incense burned in the towns of Judah and the streets of Jerusalem by you and your fathers, your kings and your officials and the people of the land? When the Lord could no longer endure your wicked actions and the detestable things you did, your land became an object of cursing and a desolate waste without inhabitants, as it is today. Because you have burned incense and have sinned against the Lord and have not obeyed him or followed his law or his decrees or his stipulations, this disaster has come upon you, as you now see.

Narrator	Then Jeremiah said to all the people, including the women, "Hear the word of the Lord, all you people of Judah in Egypt."
Jeremiah	This is what the Lord Almighty, the God of Israel, says:
The Lord (voice)	You and your wives have shown by your actions what you promised when you said, "We will certainly carry out the vows we made to burn incense and pour out drink offerings to the Queen of Heaven." Go ahead then, do what you promised! Keep your vows!
Jeremiah	But hear the word of the Lord, all Jews living in Egypt:
The Lord (voice)	I swear by my great name . . . that no one from Judah living anywhere in Egypt will ever again invoke my name or swear, "As surely as the Sovereign Lord lives." For I am watching over them for harm, not for good; the Jews in Egypt will perish by sword and famine until they are all destroyed. Those who escape the sword and return to the land of Judah from Egypt will be very few. Then the whole remnant of Judah who came to live in Egypt will know whose word will stand—mine or theirs.
Jeremiah	[The Lord declares.]
The Lord (voice)	This will be the sign to you that I will punish you in this place . . . so that you will know that my threats of harm against you will surely stand.
Jeremiah	This is what the Lord says:
The Lord (voice)	I am going to hand Pharaoh Hophra king of Egypt over to his enemies who seek his life, just as I handed Zedekiah king of Judah over to Nebuchadnezzar king of Babylon, the enemy who was seeking his life.

Cast: **Narrator, Jeremiah, the Lord** (voice only), **Prophet, Man, Woman**

A Message to Baruch

Jeremiah 45:1–5

Narrator	This is what Jeremiah the prophet told Baruch son of Neriah in the fourth year of Jehoiakim son of Josiah king of Judah, after Baruch had written on a scroll the words Jeremiah was then dictating:
Jeremiah	This is what the Lord, the God of Israel, says to you, Baruch: You said:
Baruch	Woe to me! The Lord has added sorrow to my pain; I am worn out with groaning and find no rest.

341

Jeremiah	Say this to him: This is what the LORD says:
The Lord (voice only)	I will overthrow what I have built and uproot what I have planted, throughout the land. Should you then seek great things for yourself? Seek them not.
Jeremiah	[The LORD declares:]
The Lord (voice)	For I will bring disaster on all people . . . but wherever you go I will let you escape with your life.

Cast: **Narrator, Jeremiah, Baruch, the Lord** (voice only)

A Message about Egypt

Jeremiah 46:1–10

Narrator 1	This is the word of the LORD that came to Jeremiah the prophet concerning the nations:
Jeremiah	Concerning Egypt:
	This is the message against the army of Pharaoh Neco king of Egypt, which was defeated at Carchemish on the Euphrates River by Nebuchadnezzar king of Babylon in the fourth year of Jehoiakim son of Josiah king of Judah:
Officer 1	Prepare your shields, both large and small.
Officer 2	March out for battle!
Officer 1	Harness the horses, mount the steeds!
Officer 2	Take your positions with helmets on!
Officer 1	Polish your spears, put on your armor!
Jeremiah	What do I see?
Narrator 1	They are terrified, they are retreating.
Narrator 2	Their warriors are defeated.
Narrator 1	They flee in haste without looking back.
Narrator 2	There is terror on every side. . . .

342

Narrator 1	The swift cannot flee nor the strong escape.
Narrator 2	In the north by the River Euphrates they stumble and fall.
Narrator 1	Who is this that rises like the Nile, like rivers of surging waters?
Narrator 2	Egypt rises like the Nile, like rivers of surging waters.
Egyptian	I will rise and cover the earth; I will destroy cities and their people.
Officer 1	Charge, O horses! Drive furiously, O charioteers!

Officer 2	March on, O warriors—
	   men of Cush and Put who carry shields,
	   men of Lydia who draw the bow.

Jeremiah	But that day belongs to the Lord, the L{ORD} Almighty—
	   a day of vengeance, for vengeance on his foes.
	The sword will devour till it is satisfied,
	   till it has quenched its thirst with blood.
	For the Lord, the L{ORD} Almighty, will offer sacrifice
	   in the land of the north by the River Euphrates.

Cast: **Narrator 1, Jeremiah, Officer 1, Officer 2, Narrator 2, Egyptian** (at a distance)

The Coming of Nebuchadnezzar

From Jeremiah 46:13–28

Narrator	This is the message the L{ORD} spoke to Jeremiah the prophet about the coming of Nebuchadnezzar king of Babylon to attack Egypt:
The Lord (voice only)	Announce this in Egypt, and proclaim it in Migdol; proclaim it also in Memphis and Tahpanhes:
Herald (calling)	Take your positions and get ready, for the sword devours those around you.

The Lord
(voice)
	Why will your warriors be laid low?
	   They cannot stand, for the L{ORD} will push them down.
	They will stumble repeatedly;
	   they will fall over each other.
	They will say:

Soldier Get up, let us go back
    to our own people and our native lands,
    away from the sword of the oppressor.

The Lord
(voice) There they will exclaim:

Soldier Pharaoh king of Egypt is only a loud noise;
    he has missed his opportunity.

Jeremiah . . . Declares the King,
    whose name is the LORD Almighty:

The Lord
(voice) [As surely as I live,]
one will come who is like Tabor among the mountains,
    like Carmel by the sea.
Pack your belongings for exile,
    you who live in Egypt,
for Memphis will be laid waste
    and lie in ruins without inhabitant.

Jeremiah Egypt is a beautiful heifer,
    but a gadfly is coming
    against her from the north.
The mercenaries in her ranks
    are like fattened calves.
They too will turn and flee together,
    they will not stand their ground,
for the day of disaster is coming upon them,
    the time for them to be punished.
Egypt will hiss like a fleeing serpent
    as the enemy advances in force;
they will come against her with axes,
    like men who cut down trees.
They will chop down her forest . . .
    dense though it be.
They are more numerous than locusts,
    they cannot be counted.
The Daughter of Egypt will be put to shame,
    handed over to the people of the north.

The Lord
(voice) . . . I am about to bring punishment on Amon god of Thebes, on
Pharaoh, on Egypt and her gods and her kings, and on those who rely
on Pharaoh. I will hand them over to those who seek their lives, to
Nebuchadnezzar king of Babylon and his officers. Later, however,
Egypt will be inhabited as in times past. . . .

Do not fear, O Jacob my servant;
    do not be dismayed, O Israel.
I will surely save you out of a distant place,

your descendants from the land of their exile.
Jacob will again have peace and security,
    and no one will make him afraid.
Do not fear, O Jacob my servant,
    for I am with you. . . .
Though I completely destroy all the nations
    among which I scatter you,
    I will not completely destroy you.
I will discipline you but only with justice;
    I will not let you go entirely unpunished.

Cast: **Narrator, the Lord** (voice only), **Herald, Soldier, Jeremiah**

A Message about the Philistines and Moab

Jeremiah 47:1–48:9

Narrator This is the word of the LORD that came to Jeremiah the prophet concerning the Philistines before Pharaoh attacked Gaza:

Jeremiah This is what the LORD says:

The Lord
(voice only) See how the waters are rising in the north,
    they will become an overflowing torrent.
They will overflow the land and everything in it,
    the towns and those who live in them.
The people will cry out;
    all who dwell in the land will wail
at the sound of the hoofs of galloping steeds,
    at the noise of enemy chariots
    and the rumble of their wheels.
Fathers will not turn to help their children;
    their hands will hang limp.
For the day has come
    to destroy all the Philistines
and to cut off all survivors
    who could help Tyre and Sidon.

Jeremiah The LORD is about to destroy the Philistines,
    the remnant from the coasts of Caphtor.
Gaza will shave her head in mourning;
    Ashkelon will be silenced.

The Lord
(voice) O remnant on the plain,
    how long will you cut yourselves?

Victim Ah, sword of the LORD . . .
    how long till you rest?

	Return to your scabbard; cease and be still.

Jeremiah	But how can it rest
	  when the LORD has commanded it,
	when he has ordered it
	  to attack Ashkelon and the coast?

	Concerning Moab:
	This is what the LORD Almighty, the God of Israel, says:

The Lord	Woe to Nebo, for it will be ruined.
	  Kiriathaim will be disgraced and captured;
	  the stronghold will be disgraced and shattered.
	Moab will be praised no more;
	  in Heshbon men will plot her downfall:

Man (craftily)	Come, let us put an end to that nation.

The Lord
  (voice)
	You too, O Madmen, will be silenced;
	  the sword will pursue you.

Jeremiah	Listen to the cries from Horonaim,
	  cries of great havoc and destruction.
	Moab will be broken;
	  her little ones will cry out.
	They go up the way to Luhith,
	  weeping bitterly as they go;
	on the road down to Horonaim
	  anguished cries over the destruction are heard.

Moabite	Flee! Run for your lives; become like a bush in the desert.

The Lord
  (voice)
	Since you trust in your deeds and riches,
	  you too will be taken captive,
	and Chemosh will go into exile,
	  together with his priests and officials.

Jeremiah	The destroyer will come against every town,
	  and not a town will escape.
	The valley will be ruined
	  and the plateau destroyed,
	  because the LORD has spoken.
	Put salt on Moab,
	  for she will be laid waste;
	her towns will become desolate,
	  with no one to live in them.

Cast: **Narrator, Jeremiah, the Lord** (voice only), **Victim, Man** (can be the same as Moabite), **Moabite**

The Cities of Moab Are Destroyed

From Jeremiah 48:11–25

Jeremiah Moab has been at rest from youth,
    like wine left on its dregs,
not poured from one jar to another—
    she has not gone into exile.
So she tastes as she did,
    and her aroma is unchanged.

The Lord
(voice only) But days are coming . . .
when I will send men who pour from jars,
    and they will pour her out;
they will empty her jars
    and smash her jugs.
Then Moab will be ashamed of Chemosh,
    as the house of Israel was ashamed
    when they trusted in Bethel.

Jeremiah How can you say,

Person We are warriors,
    men valiant in battle?

Jeremiah [The King, whose name is the LORD Almighty, declares:]

The Lord
(voice) Moab will be destroyed and her towns invaded;
    her finest young men will go down in the slaughter. . . .
The fall of Moab is at hand;
    her calamity will come quickly.

Jeremiah Mourn for her, all who live around her,
    all who know her fame . . .

Person How broken is the mighty scepter,
    how broken the glorious staff!

Jeremiah Come down from your glory
    and sit on the parched ground,
    O inhabitants of the Daughter of Dibon,
for he who destroys Moab
    will come up against you
    and ruin your fortified cities.
Stand by the road and watch,
    you who live in Aroer.
Ask the man fleeing and the woman escaping,
    ask them,

Person What has happened?

Refugee 1 Moab is disgraced, for she is shattered.

Refugee 2	Wail and cry out!
Refugee 1	Announce by the Arnon that Moab is destroyed. . . .
Jeremiah	[The LORD declares:]
The Lord (voice)	Moab's horn is cut off; her arm is broken. . . .

Cast: **Jeremiah, the Lord** (voice only), **Person, Refugee 1, Refugee 2**

A Message about Edom

Jeremiah 49:7–22

Jeremiah	Concerning Edom:
	This is what the LORD Almighty says:

The Lord
(voice only)
	Is there no longer wisdom in Teman?
	    Has counsel perished from the prudent?
	    Has their wisdom decayed?
	Turn and flee, hide in deep caves,
	    you who live in Dedan,
	for I will bring disaster on Esau
	    at the time I punish him.
	If grape pickers came to you,
	    would they not leave a few grapes?
	If thieves came during the night,
	    would they not steal only as much
	        as they wanted?
	But I will strip Esau bare;
	    I will uncover his hiding places,
	    so that he cannot conceal himself.
	His children, relatives and neighbors will perish,
	    and he will be no more.
	Leave your orphans; I will protect their lives.
	    Your widows too can trust in me.

Jeremiah	This is what the LORD says:
The Lord (voice)	If those who do not deserve to drink the cup must drink it, why should you go unpunished? You will not go unpunished, but must drink it. I swear by myself . . . that Bozrah will become a ruin and an object of horror, of reproach and of cursing; and all its towns will be in ruins forever.

Jeremiah	I have heard a message from the LORD:
The Lord (voice)	An envoy was sent to the nations to say,
Envoy	Assemble yourselves to attack it! Rise up for battle!
The Lord (voice)	Now I will make you small among the nations, despised among men.
Jeremiah	[Declares the LORD:]

The Lord (voice)	The terror you inspire
	    and the pride of your heart have deceived you,
	you who live in the clefts of the rocks,
	    who occupy the heights of the hill.
	Though you build your nest as high as the eagle's,
	    from there I will bring you down. . . . (PAUSE)
	Edom will become an object of horror;
	    all who pass by will be appalled and will scoff
	    because of all its wounds.
	As Sodom and Gomorrah were overthrown,
	    along with their neighboring towns . . .
	so no one will live there;
	    no man will dwell in it.
	
	Like a lion coming up from Jordan's thickets
	    to a rich pastureland,
	I will chase Edom from its land in an instant.
	    Who is the chosen one I will appoint for this?
	Who is like me and who can challenge me?
	    And what shepherd can stand against me?

Jeremiah	Therefore, hear what the LORD has planned against Edom, what he has purposed against those who live in Teman:
The Lord (voice)	The young of the flock will be dragged away.
Jeremiah	He will completely destroy their pasture because of them. At the sound of their fall the earth will tremble; their cry will resound to the Red Sea.
The Lord (voice)	Look! An eagle will soar and swoop down, spreading its wings over Bozrah.
Jeremiah	In that day the hearts of Edom's warriors will be like the heart of a woman in labor.

Cast: **Jeremiah**, **the Lord** (voice only), **Envoy**

God Speaks of Israel's Return

Jeremiah 50:4–10

Jeremiah   The people of Israel and the people of Judah together
                   will go in tears to seek the Lord their God.
              They will ask the way to Zion
                   and turn their faces toward it.
              They will come and bind themselves to the Lord
                   in an everlasting covenant
                   that will not be forgotten.

The Lord
  (voice only) My people have been lost sheep;
                   their shepherds have led them astray
                   and caused them to roam on the mountains.
              They wandered over mountain and hill
                   and forgot their own resting place.
              Whoever found them devoured them;
                   their enemies said:

Enemy 1   We are not guilty,
              for they sinned against the Lord, their true pasture—

Enemy 2   The Lord, the hope of their fathers.

The Lord
  (voice)   Flee out of Babylon;
                   leave the land of the Babylonians,
                   and be like the goats that lead the flock.
              For I will stir up and bring against Babylon
                   an alliance of great nations from the land of the north.
              They will take up their positions against her,
                   and from the north she will be captured.
              Their arrows will be like skilled warriors
                   who do not return empty-handed.

Jeremiah   [The Lord declares:]

The Lord
  (voice)   Babylonia will be plundered;
                   all who plunder her will have their fill. . . .

Cast: **Jeremiah, the Lord** (voice only), **Enemy 1, Enemy 2**

A Message about Babylon

Jeremiah 51:1, 8–14

Jeremiah   This is what the Lord says:

The Lord
  (voice only) Babylon will suddenly fall and be broken.

	Wail over her! Get balm for her pain; perhaps she can be healed.
Person 1	We would have healed Babylon, but she cannot be healed.
Person 2	Let us leave her and each go to his own land.
Person 1	For her judgment reaches to the skies.
Person 2	It rises as high as the clouds.
Person 1	The LORD has vindicated us.
Person 2	Come, let us tell in Zion what the LORD our God has done.

Jeremiah	Sharpen the arrows,
	   take up the shields!
	The LORD has stirred up the kings of the Medes,
	   because his purpose is to destroy Babylon.
	The LORD will take vengeance,
	   vengeance for his temple.

Officer 1	Lift up a banner against the walls of Babylon!
Officer 2	Reinforce the guard.
Officer 1	Station the watchmen.
Officer 2	Prepare an ambush!

Jeremiah	The LORD will carry out his purpose,
	   his decree against the people of Babylon.
	You who live by many waters
	   and are rich in treasures,
	your end has come,
	   the time for you to be cut off.
	The LORD Almighty has sworn by himself:

The Lord (voice)	I will surely fill you with men, as with a swarm of locusts, and they will shout in triumph over you.

Cast: **Jeremiah**, **the Lord** (voice only), **Person 1**, **Person 2** (can be the same as Person 1), **Officer 1**, **Officer 2** (can be the same as Officer 1)

A Hymn of Praise to God

Jeremiah 51:15–19

Singer 1	[God] made the earth by his power;
	   he founded the world by his wisdom
	   and stretched out the heavens by his understanding.

Singer 2   When he thunders, the waters in the heavens roar;
               he makes clouds rise from the ends of the earth.

Singer 3   He sends lightning with the rain
               and brings out the wind from his storehouses.

Singer 1   Every man is senseless and without knowledge;
               every goldsmith is shamed by his idols.
             His images are a fraud;
               they have no breath in them.

Singer 2   They are worthless, the objects of mockery;
               when their judgment comes, they will perish.

Singer 3   He who is the Portion of Jacob is not like these,
               for he is the Maker of all things,
             including the tribe of his inheritance—

Singers 1–3
(with
flourish)   The LORD Almighty is his name.

Cast: **Singer 1, Singer 2, Singer 3**

Babylonia

Jeremiah 51:1, 20–35

Jeremiah   This is what the LORD says:

The Lord
(voice only) You are my war club,
               my weapon for battle—
             with you I shatter nations,
               with you I destroy kingdoms,
             with you I shatter horse and rider,
               with you I shatter chariot and driver,
             with you I shatter man and woman,
               with you I shatter old man and youth,
               with you I shatter young man and maiden,
             with you I shatter shepherd and flock,
               with you I shatter farmer and oxen,
               with you I shatter governors and officials.

Jeremiah   [The LORD declares:]

The Lord
(voice)   Before your eyes I will repay Babylon and all who live in Babylonia for
             all the wrong they have done in Zion. . . .

Jeremiah   [The LORD declares:]

The Lord
(voice)   I am against you, O destroying mountain,

352

you who destroy the whole earth. . . .

Jeremiah   [The LORD declares:]

The Lord
(voice)

I will stretch out my hand against you,
    roll you off the cliffs,
    and make you a burned-out mountain.
No rock will be taken from you for a cornerstone,
    nor any stone for a foundation,
    for you will be desolate forever. . . . (PAUSE)

Voice 1   Lift up a banner in the land!

Voice 2   Blow the trumpet among the nations!

Voice 1   Prepare the nations for battle against her.

Voice 3   Summon against her these kingdoms:
    Ararat, Minni and Ashkenaz.

Voice 1   Appoint a commander against her.

Voice 2   Send up horses like a swarm of locusts.

Voice 1   Prepare the nations for battle against her—

Voice 3   The kings of the Medes,
    their governors and all their officials,
    and all the countries they rule.

Jeremiah   The land trembles and writhes,
    for the LORD's purposes against Babylon stand—
to lay waste the land of Babylon
    so that no one will live there.
Babylon's warriors have stopped fighting;
    they remain in their strongholds.
Their strength is exhausted;
    they have become like women.
Her dwellings are set on fire;
    the bars of her gates are broken.
One courier follows another
    and messenger follows messenger
to announce to the king of Babylon
    that his entire city is captured,
the river crossings seized,
    the marshes set on fire,
    and the soldiers terrified.

This is what the LORD Almighty, the God of Israel, says:

The Lord
(voice)

The Daughter of Babylon is like a threshing floor
    at the time it is trampled;
    the time to harvest her will soon come.

Jeremiah	[The inhabitants of Zion say:]
Person 1	Nebuchadnezzar king of Babylon has devoured us.
Person 2	He has thrown us into confusion.
Person 1	He has made us an empty jar.
Person 2	Like a serpent he has swallowed us and filled his stomach with our delicacies—
Person 1	And then has spewed us out.
Person 2	May the violence done to our flesh be upon Babylon. . . .
Jeremiah	[Jerusalem says:]
Person 1	May our blood be on those who live in Babylonia. . . .

Cast: **Jeremiah, the Lord** (voice only), **Voice 1, Voice 2, Voice 3, Person 1** (can be the same as Voice 1), **Person 2** (can be the same as Voice 2)

God's Message to the Israelites in Babylonia

Jeremiah 51:50–53

Jeremiah	[The Lord declares:]

The Lord
   (voice only)
	You who have escaped the sword,
	    leave and do not linger!

Jeremiah	Remember the Lord in a distant land, and think on Jerusalem.

Person 1	We are disgraced,
	    for we have been insulted
	    and shame covers our faces.

Person 2	Because foreigners have entered the holy places of the Lord's house.
Jeremiah	[The Lord declares:]

The Lord
   (voice)
	But days are coming . . .
	    when I will punish her idols,
	  and throughout her land
	    the wounded will groan.
	  Even if Babylon reaches the sky
	    and fortifies her lofty stronghold,
	    I will send destroyers against her. . . .

Cast: **Jeremiah, the Lord** (voice only), **Person 1, Person 2** (can be the same as Person 1)

Jeremiah's Message Is Sent to Babylonia

Jeremiah 51:59–64

Narrator　This is the message Jeremiah gave to the staff officer Seraiah son of Neriah, the son of Mahseiah, when he went to Babylon with Zedekiah king of Judah in the fourth year of his reign. Jeremiah had written on a scroll about all the disasters that would come upon Babylon—all that had been recorded concerning Babylon. He said to Seraiah:

Jeremiah　When you get to Babylon, see that you read all these words aloud. Then say—

Seraiah　O LORD, you have said you will destroy this place, so that neither man nor animal will live in it; it will be desolate forever.

Jeremiah　When you finish reading this scroll, tie a stone to it and throw it into the Euphrates. Then say:

Narrator　So will Babylon sink to rise no more because of the disaster I will bring upon her. And her people will fall.

(with
flourish)　The words of Jeremiah end here.

Cast: **Narrator, Jeremiah, Seraiah**

Lamentations

The Sorrows of Jerusalem

From Lamentations 1:1–20

Voice 1 How deserted lies the city,
   once so full of people!
How like a widow is she,
   who once was great among the nations!
She who was queen among the provinces
   has now become a slave.

Voice 2 Bitterly she weeps at night,
   tears are upon her cheeks.
Among all her lovers
   there is none to comfort her.
All her friends have betrayed her;
   they have become her enemies.

Voice 3 After affliction and harsh labor,
   Judah has gone into exile.
She dwells among the nations;
   she finds no resting place.
All who pursue her have overtaken her
   in the midst of her distress.

Voice 1 The roads to Zion mourn,
   for no one comes to her appointed feasts.
All her gateways are desolate,
   her priests groan,
her maidens grieve,
   and she is in bitter anguish.

Voice 2 Her foes have become her masters;
   her enemies are at ease.
The LORD has brought her grief
   because of her many sins.
Her children have gone into exile,
   captive before the foe.

Voice 3 All the splendor has departed
   from the Daughter of Zion.
Her princes are like deer
   that find no pasture;
in weakness they have fled
   before the pursuer.

Voice 1 In the days of her affliction and wandering
   Jerusalem remembers all the treasures

356

that were hers in days of old.
   When her people fell into enemy hands,
     there was no one to help her.
   Her enemies looked at her
     and laughed at her destruction.

Voice 2   Jerusalem has sinned greatly
     and so has become unclean.
   All who honored her despise her,
     for they have seen her nakedness;
   she herself groans
     and turns away.

Voice 3   Her filthiness clung to her skirts;
     she did not consider her future.
   Her fall was astounding;
     there was none to comfort her.

Person 1   Look, O Lord, on my affliction.
     For the enemy has triumphed. . . .

Person 2   Look, O Lord, and consider,
     for I am despised.

Person 1   Is it nothing to you, all you who pass by?
     Look around and see.
   Is any suffering like my suffering
     that was inflicted on me,
   that the Lord brought on me
     in the day of his fierce anger?

Person 2   From on high he sent fire,
     sent it down into my bones.
   He spread a net for my feet
     and turned me back.
   He made me desolate,
     faint all the day long.

Person 1   My sins have been bound into a yoke;
     by his hands they were woven together.
   They have come upon my neck
     and the Lord has sapped my strength.
   He has handed me over
     to those I cannot withstand. . . .

Person 2   This is why I weep
     and my eyes overflow with tears.
   No one is near to comfort me,
     no one to restore my spirit.
   My children are destitute
     because the enemy has prevailed. . . .

Person 1   The LORD is righteous,
        yet I rebelled against his command. . . .

(praying)   See, O LORD, how distressed I am!
        I am in torment within,
    and in my heart I am disturbed. . . .

Cast: **Voice 1, Voice 2, Voice 3, Person 1, Person 2**

The Lord's Punishment of Jerusalem

From Lamentations 2:1–19a

Voice 1   How the Lord has covered the Daughter of Zion
        with the cloud of his anger!
    He has hurled down the splendor of Israel
        from heaven to earth;
    he has not remembered his footstool
        in the day of his anger.

Voice 2   Without pity the Lord has swallowed up
        all the dwellings of Jacob;
    in his wrath he has torn down
        the strongholds of the Daughter of Judah.
    He has brought her kingdom and its princes
        down to the ground in dishonor. . . .

Voice 1   The Lord has rejected his altar
        and abandoned his sanctuary.
    He has handed over to the enemy
        the walls of her palaces;
    they have raised a shout in the house of the LORD
        as on the day of an appointed feast.

Voice 2   The LORD determined to tear down
        the wall around the Daughter of Zion.
    He stretched out a measuring line
        and did not withhold his hand from destroying.
    He made ramparts and walls lament;
        together they wasted away.

Voice 1   Her gates have sunk into the ground;
        their bars he has broken and destroyed.
    Her king and her princes are exiled among the nations,
        the law is no more,
    and her prophets no longer find
        visions from the LORD. . . .

Voice 2   My eyes fail from weeping,
        I am in torment within,

my heart is poured out on the ground
    because my people are destroyed,
because children and infants faint
    in the streets of the city. . . .

Voice 1   The visions of your prophets
    were false and worthless;
they did not expose your sin
    to ward off your captivity.
The oracles they gave you
    were false and misleading.

Voice 2   All who pass your way
    clap their hands at you;
they scoff and shake their heads
    at the Daughter of Jerusalem:

Person 1   Is this the city that was called
    the perfection of beauty?

Person 2   The joy of the whole earth?

Voice 2   All your enemies open their mouths
    wide against you;
they scoff and gnash their teeth
    and say:

Enemy 1   We have swallowed her up.

Enemy 2   This is the day we have waited for;
    we have lived to see it.

Voice 1   The Lord has done what he planned;
    he has fulfilled his word,
    which he decreed long ago.
He has overthrown you without pity,
    he has let the enemy gloat over you,
    he has exalted the horn of your foes.

Voice 2   The hearts of the people
    cry out to the Lord.
O wall of the Daughter of Zion,
    let your tears flow like a river
    day and night . . .

    Pour out your heart like water
    in the presence of the Lord.

Cast: **Voice 1, Voice 2, Person 1, Person 2, Enemy 1, Enemy 2**

Repentance and Hope (i)

From Lamentations 3:22–42

Voice 1   Because of the LORD's great love we are not consumed,
      for his compassions never fail.
They are new every morning.

Voice 2   Great is your faithfulness. . . .
The LORD is my portion;
      therefore I will wait for him.

Voice 1   The LORD is good to those whose hope is in him,
      to the one who seeks him.

Voice 2   It is good to wait quietly
      for the salvation of the LORD. . . .

Voice 1   For men are not cast off
      by the Lord forever.
Though he brings grief, he will show compassion,
      so great is his unfailing love.
He does not willingly bring affliction
      or grief to the children of men.

Voice 2   To crush underfoot
      all prisoners in the land,
to deny a man his rights
      before the Most High,
to deprive a man of justice—
      would not the Lord see such things?

Voice 1   Who can speak and have it happen
      if the Lord has not decreed it?
Is it not from the mouth of the Most High
      that both calamities and good things come?
Why should any living man complain
      when punished for his sins?

Voice 2   Let us examine our ways and test them,
      and let us return to the LORD.
Let us lift up our hearts and our hands
      to God in heaven, and say:

**Voices 1
and 2**   We have sinned and rebelled—

Voice 1   And you have not forgiven.

Cast: **Voice 1, Voice 2**

Repentance and Hope (ii)

From Lamentations 3:52–58

Voice 1   Those who were my enemies without cause
         hunted me like a bird.
They tried to end my life in a pit
         and threw stones at me;
the waters closed over my head,
         and I thought I was about to be cut off.

Voice 2   I called on your name, O Lord,
         from the depths of the pit.
You heard my plea . . . .

Voice 1   O Lord, you took up my case—

Voice 2   You redeemed my life.

Cast: **Voice 1, Voice 2**

Jerusalem after Its Fall

From Lamentations 4:1–18

Voice 1   How the gold has lost its luster,
         the fine gold become dull!
The sacred gems are scattered
         at the head of every street. . . .

Voice 2   The Lord has given full vent to his wrath;
         he has poured out his fierce anger.
He kindled a fire in Zion
         that consumed her foundations.

Voice 1   The kings of the earth did not believe,
         nor did any of the world's people,
that enemies and foes could enter
         the gates of Jerusalem.

Voice 2   But it happened because of the sins of her prophets
         and the iniquities of her priests,
who shed within her
         the blood of the righteous.

Now they grope through the streets
         like men who are blind.
They are so defiled with blood
         that no one dares to touch their garments.

Voice 1	[Men cry to them:]
Person 1	Go away!
Person 2	You are unclean!
Person 1	Away! Away!
Person 2	Don't touch us!
Voice 1	When they flee and wander about, people among the nations say:
Person 1	They can stay here no longer.
Person 2	The LORD himself has scattered them; he no longer watches over them.
Voice 2	The priests are shown no honor, the elders no favor.
Voice 1	Moreover, our eyes failed, looking in vain for help; from our towers we watched for a nation that could not save us. . . .
Voices 1 and 2	Our end was near, our days were numbered, for our end had come.

Cast: **Voice 1, Voice 2, Person 1, Person 2**

A Prayer for Mercy

From Lamentations 5:1–22

Voice 1	Remember, O LORD, what has happened to us.
Voice 2	Look, and see our disgrace. . . .
Voice 1	Joy is gone from our hearts.
Voice 2	Our dancing has turned to mourning.
Voice 1	The crown has fallen from our head.
Voices 1 and 2	Woe to us, for we have sinned!
Voice 2	Because of this our hearts are faint.
Voice 1	Because of these things our eyes grow dim. . . .

Voice 2	You, O LORD, reign forever.
Voice 1	Your throne endures from generation to generation. . . .
Voice 2	Restore us to yourself, O LORD, that we may return.
Voice 1	Renew our days as of old.
Voice 2	Unless you have utterly rejected us and are angry with us beyond measure.

Cast: **Voice 1, Voice 2**

Ezekiel

The Living Creatures and the Glory of the Lord

Ezekiel 1:1–28

Ezekiel   In the thirtieth year, in the fourth month on the fifth day, while I was among the exiles by the Kebar River, the heavens were opened and I saw visions of God.

Chronicler   On the fifth of the month—it was the fifth year of the exile of King Jehoiachin—

Ezekiel   The word of the LORD came to Ezekiel the priest, the son of Buzi, by the Kebar River in the land of the Babylonians. There the hand of the LORD was upon him.

I looked, and I saw a windstorm coming out of the north.

Voice 1   An immense cloud with flashing lightning and surrounded by brilliant light. The center of the fire looked like glowing metal.

Ezekiel   And in the fire was what looked like four living creatures. In appearance their form was that of a man.

Voice 2   Each of them had four faces and four wings. Their legs were straight; their feet were like those of a calf and gleamed like burnished bronze. Under their wings on their four sides they had the hands of a man. All four of them had faces and wings, and their wings touched one another. Each one went straight ahead; they did not turn as they moved.

Voice 3   Their faces looked like this: Each of the four had the face of a man, and on the right side each had the face of a lion, and on the left the face of an ox; each also had the face of an eagle. Such were their faces. Their wings were spread out upward; each had two wings, one touching the wing of another creature on either side, and two wings covering its body. Each one went straight ahead. Wherever the spirit would go, they would go, without turning as they went.

Voice 1   The appearance of the living creatures was like burning coals of fire or like torches. Fire moved back and forth among the creatures; it was bright, and lightning flashed out of it. The creatures sped back and forth like flashes of lightning.

Ezekiel   As I looked at the living creatures, I saw a wheel on the ground beside each creature with its four faces.

Voice 2   This was the appearance and structure of the wheels: They sparkled like chrysolite, and all four looked alike. Each appeared to be made like a wheel intersecting a wheel. As they moved, they would go in any one of the four directions the creatures faced; the wheels did not turn about as

	the creatures went. Their rims were high and awesome, and all four rims were full of eyes all around.
Voice 3	When the living creatures moved, the wheels beside them moved; and when the living creatures rose from the ground, the wheels also rose. Wherever the spirit would go, they would go, and the wheels would rise along with them, because the spirit of the living creatures was in the wheels. When the creatures moved, they also moved; when the creatures stood still, they also stood still; and when the creatures rose from the ground, the wheels rose along with them, because the spirit of the living creatures was in the wheels.
Voice 1	Spread out above the heads of the living creatures was what looked like an expanse, sparkling like ice, and awesome. Under the expanse their wings were stretched out one toward the other, and each had two wings covering its body.
Ezekiel	When the creatures moved, I heard the sound of their wings.
Voice 2	Like the roar of rushing waters, like the voice of the Almighty, like the tumult of an army.
Voice 3	When they stood still, they lowered their wings.
	Then there came a voice from above the expanse over their heads as they stood with lowered wings.
Voice 1	Above the expanse over their heads was what looked like a throne of sapphire, and high above on the throne was a figure like that of a man.
Ezekiel	I saw that from what appeared to be his waist up he looked like glowing metal, as if full of fire, and that from there down he looked like fire; and brilliant light surrounded him.
Voice 3	Like the appearance of a rainbow in the clouds on a rainy day, so was the radiance around him.
Voices 1–3	This was the appearance of the likeness of the glory of the LORD.
Ezekiel	When I saw it, I fell facedown, and I heard the voice of one speaking.

Cast: **Ezekiel, Chronicler, Voice 1, Voice 2, Voice 3**

God Calls Ezekiel to Be a Prophet

Ezekiel 1:1, 26–3:15

Ezekiel	In the thirtieth year, in the fourth month on the fifth day, while I was among the exiles by the Kebar River, the heavens were opened and I saw visions of God.
	[I saw] what looked like a throne of sapphire, and high above on the throne was a figure like that of a man. I saw that from what appeared to

365

be his waist up he looked like glowing metal, as if full of fire, and that from there down he looked like fire; and brilliant light surrounded him. Like the appearance of a rainbow in the clouds on a rainy day, so was the radiance around him.

This was the appearance of the likeness of the glory of the LORD. When I saw it, I fell facedown, and I heard the voice of one speaking. (PAUSE) He said to me:

The Lord
(voice only) Son of man, stand up on your feet and I will speak to you.

Ezekiel As he spoke, the Spirit came into me and raised me to my feet, and I heard him speaking to me.

The Lord
(voice) Son of man, I am sending you to the Israelites, to a rebellious nation that has rebelled against me; they and their fathers have been in revolt against me to this very day. The people to whom I am sending you are obstinate and stubborn. Say to them, "This is what the Sovereign LORD says." And whether they listen or fail to listen—for they are a rebellious house—they will know that a prophet has been among them. And you, son of man, do not be afraid of them or their words. Do not be afraid, though briers and thorns are all around you and you live among scorpions. Do not be afraid of what they say or terrified by them, though they are a rebellious house. You must speak my words to them, whether they listen or fail to listen, for they are rebellious.

Ezekiel [God said:]

The Lord
(voice) But you, son of man, listen to what I say to you. Do not rebel like that rebellious house; open your mouth and eat what I give you.

Ezekiel Then I looked, and I saw a hand stretched out to me. In it was a scroll, which he unrolled before me. On both sides of it were written words of lament and mourning and woe. (PAUSE) And he said to me:

The Lord
(voice) Son of man, eat what is before you, eat this scroll; then go and speak to the house of Israel.

Ezekiel So I opened my mouth, and he gave me the scroll to eat. (PAUSE) Then he said to me:

The Lord
(voice) Son of man, eat this scroll I am giving you and fill your stomach with it.

Ezekiel So I ate it, and it tasted as sweet as honey in my mouth. (PAUSE) He then said to me:

The Lord
(voice) Son of man, go now to the house of Israel and speak my words to them. You are not being sent to a people of obscure speech and difficult lan-

guage, but to the house of Israel—not to many peoples of obscure speech and difficult language, whose words you cannot understand. Surely if I had sent you to them, they would have listened to you. But the house of Israel is not willing to listen to you because they are not willing to listen to me, for the whole house of Israel is hardened and obstinate. But I will make you as unyielding and hardened as they are. I will make your forehead like the hardest stone, harder than flint. Do not be afraid of them or terrified by them, though they are a rebellious house. . . .

Son of man, listen carefully and take to heart all the words I speak to you. Go now to your countrymen in exile and speak to them. Say to them, "This is what the Sovereign LORD says," whether they listen or fail to listen.

Ezekiel Then the Spirit lifted me up, and I heard behind me a loud rumbling sound.

Creatures
(loudly) May the glory of the LORD be praised in his dwelling place!

Ezekiel The sound of the wings of the living creatures brushing against each other and the sound of the wheels beside them, a loud rumbling sound. The Spirit then lifted me up and took me away, and I went in bitterness and in the anger of my spirit, with the strong hand of the LORD upon me. I came to the exiles who lived at Tel Abib near the Kebar River. And there, where they were living, I sat among them for seven days—overwhelmed.

Cast: **Ezekiel, the Lord** (voice only), **Creatures**

Ezekiel Will Be Unable to Talk

Ezekiel 3:22–27

Ezekiel The hand of the LORD was upon me there, and he said to me:

The Lord
(voice only) Get up and go out to the plain, and there I will speak to you.

Ezekiel So I got up and went out to the plain. And the glory of the LORD was standing there, like the glory I had seen by the Kebar River, and I fell facedown.

Then the Spirit came into me and raised me to my feet. He spoke to me and said:

The Lord
(voice) Go, shut yourself inside your house. And you, son of man, they will tie with ropes; you will be bound so that you cannot go out among the people. I will make your tongue stick to the roof of your mouth so that you will be silent and unable to rebuke them, though they are a rebellious house. But when I speak to you, I will open your mouth and you shall say to them, "This is what the Sovereign LORD says." Whoever will

listen let him listen, and whoever will refuse let him refuse; for they are a rebellious house.

Cast: **Ezekiel, the Lord** (voice only)

Siege of Jerusalem Symbolized

From Ezekiel 4:1–17

The Lord
(voice only) Son of man, take a clay tablet, put it in front of you and draw the city of Jerusalem on it. Then lay siege to it: Erect siege works against it, build a ramp up to it, set up camps against it and put battering rams around it. Then take an iron pan, place it as an iron wall between you and the city and turn your face toward it. It will be under siege, and you shall besiege it. This will be a sign to the house of Israel.

Then lie on your left side and put the sin of the house of Israel upon yourself. You are to bear their sin for the number of days you lie on your side. I have assigned you the same number of days as the years of their sin. So for 390 days you will bear the sin of the house of Israel.

After you have finished this, lie down again, this time on your right side, and bear the sin of the house of Judah. I have assigned you 40 days, a day for each year. Turn your face toward the siege of Jerusalem and with bared arm prophesy against her. I will tie you up with ropes so that you cannot turn from one side to the other until you have finished the days of your siege.

Take wheat and barley, beans and lentils, millet and spelt; put them in a storage jar and use them to make bread for yourself. You are to eat it during the 390 days you lie on your side. Weigh out twenty shekels of food to eat each day and eat it at set times. . . .

In this way the people of Israel will eat defiled food among the nations where I will drive them.

Ezekiel Not so, Sovereign Lord! I have never defiled myself. From my youth until now I have never eaten anything found dead or torn by wild animals. No unclean meat has ever entered my mouth. . . .

The Lord
(voice) . . . I will cut off the supply of food in Jerusalem. The people will eat rationed food in anxiety and drink rationed water in despair, for food and water will be scarce. They will be appalled at the sight of each other and will waste away because of their sin.

Cast: **The Lord** (voice only), **Ezekiel**

The End Is Near for Israel

Ezekiel 7:1–14

Ezekiel	The word of the Lord came to me:
The Lord (voice only)	Son of man, this is what the Sovereign Lord says to the land of Israel: The end! The end has come upon the four corners of the land. The end is now upon you and I will unleash my anger against you. I will judge you according to your conduct and repay you for all your detestable practices. I will not look on you with pity or spare you; I will surely repay you for your conduct and the detestable practices among you. Then you will know that I am the Lord.
Ezekiel	This is what the Sovereign Lord says:
The Lord (voice)	Disaster! An unheard-of disaster is coming. The end has come! The end has come! It has roused itself against you. It has come! Doom has come upon you—you who dwell in the land. The time has come, the day is near; there is panic, not joy, upon the mountains. I am about to pour out my wrath on you and spend my anger against you; I will judge you according to your conduct and repay you for all your detestable practices. I will not look on you with pity or spare you; I will repay you in accordance with your conduct and the detestable practices among you. Then you will know that it is I the Lord who strikes the blow.
Ezekiel	The day is here! It has come! Doom has burst forth, the rod has budded, arrogance has blossomed! Violence has grown into a rod to punish wickedness; none of the people will be left, none of that crowd—no wealth, nothing of value. The time has come, the day has arrived. Let not the buyer rejoice nor the seller grieve, for wrath is upon the whole crowd. The seller will not recover the land he has sold as long as both of them live, for the vision concerning the whole crowd will not be reversed. Because of their sins, not one of them will preserve his life. Though they blow the trumpet and get everything ready, no one will go into battle, for [God's] wrath is upon the whole crowd.

Cast: **Ezekiel, the Lord** (voice only)

Punishment for Israel's Sins

Ezekiel 7:15–27

Ezekiel	Outside is the sword, inside are plague and famine; those in the country will die by the sword, and those in the city will be devoured by famine and plague. All who survive and escape will be in the mountains, moaning like doves of the valleys, each because of his sins. Every hand will go limp, and every knee will become as weak as water. They will put on sack-

cloth and be clothed with terror. Their faces will be covered with shame and their heads will be shaved. They will throw their silver into the streets, and their gold will be an unclean thing. Their silver and gold will not be able to save them in the day of the LORD's wrath. They will not satisfy their hunger or fill their stomachs with it, for it has made them stumble into sin.

The Lord

(voice only) They were proud of their beautiful jewelry and used it to make their detestable idols and vile images. Therefore I will turn these into an unclean thing for them. I will hand it all over as plunder to foreigners and as loot to the wicked of the earth, and they will defile it. I will turn my face away from them, and they will desecrate my treasured place; robbers will enter it and desecrate it.

Prepare chains, because the land is full of bloodshed and the city is full of violence. I will bring the most wicked of the nations to take possession of their houses; I will put an end to the pride of the mighty, and their sanctuaries will be desecrated.

Ezekiel When terror comes, they will seek peace, but there will be none. Calamity upon calamity will come, and rumor upon rumor. They will try to get a vision from the prophet; the teaching of the law by the priest will be lost, as will the counsel of the elders. The king will mourn, the prince will be clothed with despair, and the hands of the people of the land will tremble.

The Lord

(voice) I will deal with them according to their conduct, and by their own standards I will judge them. Then they will know that I am the LORD.

Cast: **Ezekiel, the Lord** (voice only)

Idolatry in the Temple

Ezekiel 8:1–18

Ezekiel In the sixth year, in the sixth month on the fifth day, while I was sitting in my house and the elders of Judah were sitting before me, the hand of the Sovereign LORD came upon me there. I looked, and I saw a figure like that of a man. From what appeared to be his waist down he was like fire, and from there up his appearance was as bright as glowing metal. He stretched out what looked like a hand and took me by the hair of my head. The Spirit lifted me up between earth and heaven and in visions of God he took me to Jerusalem, to the entrance to the north gate of the inner court, where the idol that provokes to jealousy stood. And there before me was the glory of the God of Israel, as in the vision I had seen in the plain. (PAUSE) Then he said to me:

The Lord
(voice only) Son of man, look toward the north.

Ezekiel So I looked, and in the entrance north of the gate of the altar I saw this idol of jealousy. (PAUSE) And he said to me:

The Lord
(voice) Son of man, do you see what they are doing—the utterly detestable things the house of Israel is doing here, things that will drive me far from my sanctuary? But you will see things that are even more detestable.

Ezekiel Then he brought me to the entrance to the court. I looked, and I saw a hole in the wall. He said to me:

The Lord
(voice) Son of man, now dig into the wall.

Ezekiel So I dug into the wall and saw a doorway there. (PAUSE) And he said to me:

The Lord
(voice) Go in and see the wicked and detestable things they are doing here.

Ezekiel So I went in and looked, and I saw portrayed all over the walls all kinds of crawling things and detestable animals and all the idols of the house of Israel. In front of them stood seventy elders of the house of Israel, and Jaazaniah son of Shaphan was standing among them. Each had a censer in his hand, and a fragrant cloud of incense was rising. (PAUSE) He said to me:

The Lord
(voice) Son of man, have you seen what the elders of the house of Israel are doing in the darkness, each at the shrine of his own idol? They say:

Jaazaniah The Lord does not see us.

Pelatiah The Lord has forsaken the land.

Ezekiel Again, he said:

The Lord
(voice) You will see them doing things that are even more detestable.

Ezekiel Then he brought me to the entrance to the north gate of the house of the Lord, and I saw women sitting there, mourning for Tammuz. (PAUSE) He said to me:

The Lord
(voice) Do you see this, son of man? You will see things that are even more detestable than this.

Ezekiel He then brought me into the inner court of the house of the Lord, and there at the entrance to the temple, between the portico and the altar, were about twenty-five men. With their backs toward the temple of the Lord and their faces toward the east, they were bowing down to the sun in the east. (PAUSE) He said to me:

The Lord
(voice) Have you seen this, son of man? Is it a trivial matter for the house of

Judah to do the detestable things they are doing here? Must they also fill the land with violence and continually provoke me to anger? Look at them putting the branch to their nose! Therefore I will deal with them in anger; I will not look on them with pity or spare them. Although they shout in my ears, I will not listen to them.

Cast: **Ezekiel**, **the Lord** (voice only), **Jaazaniah**, **Pelatiah** (can be the same as Jaazaniah)

Idolaters Killed

Ezekiel 9:1–11

Ezekiel	Then I heard [the LORD] call out in a loud voice:
The Lord (voice only, calling)	Bring the guards of the city here, each with a weapon in his hand.
Ezekiel	And I saw six men coming from the direction of the upper gate, which faces north, each with a deadly weapon in his hand. With them was a man clothed in linen who had a writing kit at his side. They came in and stood beside the bronze altar.
	Now the glory of the God of Israel went up from above the cherubim, where it had been, and moved to the threshold of the temple. Then the LORD called to the man clothed in linen who had the writing kit at his side and said to him:
The Lord (voice)	Go throughout the city of Jerusalem and put a mark on the foreheads of those who grieve and lament over all the detestable things that are done in it.
Ezekiel	As I listened, he said to the others:
The Lord (voice)	Follow him through the city and kill, without showing pity or compassion. Slaughter old men, young men and maidens, women and children, but do not touch anyone who has the mark. Begin at my sanctuary.
Ezekiel	So they began with the elders who were in front of the temple.
	Then he said to them:
The Lord (voice)	Defile the temple and fill the courts with the slain. Go!
Ezekiel	So they went out and began killing throughout the city. While they were killing and I was left alone, I fell facedown, crying out:
Young Ezekiel	Ah, Sovereign LORD! Are you going to destroy the entire remnant of Israel in this outpouring of your wrath on Jerusalem?

Ezekiel	He answered me:
The Lord (voice)	The sin of the house of Israel and Judah is exceedingly great; the land is full of bloodshed and the city is full of injustice. They say, "The LORD has forsaken the land; the LORD does not see." So I will not look on them with pity or spare them, but I will bring down on their own heads what they have done.
Ezekiel	Then the man in linen with the writing kit at his side brought back word, saying:
Man	I have done as you commanded.

Cast: **Ezekiel, the Lord** (voice only), **Young Ezekiel, Man**

Judgment on Israel's Leaders

Ezekiel 11:1–13

Ezekiel	Then the Spirit lifted me up and brought me to the gate of the house of the LORD that faces east. There at the entrance to the gate were twenty-five men, and I saw among them Jaazaniah son of Azzur and Pelatiah son of Benaiah, leaders of the people. The LORD said to me:
The Lord (voice only)	Son of man, these are the men who are plotting evil and giving wicked advice in this city. They say:
Man	Will it not soon be time to build houses? This city is a cooking pot, and we are the meat.
The Lord (voice)	Therefore prophesy against them; prophesy, son of man.
Ezekiel	Then the Spirit of the LORD came upon me, and he told me to say:
Young Ezekiel	This is what the LORD says: That is what you are saying, O house of Israel, but I know what is going through your mind. You have killed many people in this city and filled its streets with the dead.
	Therefore this is what the Sovereign LORD says: The bodies you have thrown there are the meat and this city is the pot, but I will drive you out of it. You fear the sword, and the sword is what I will bring against you, declares the Sovereign LORD. I will drive you out of the city and hand you over to foreigners and inflict punishment on you. You will fall by the sword, and I will execute judgment on you at the borders of Israel. Then you will know that I am the LORD. This city will not be a pot for you, nor will you be the meat in it; I will execute judgment on you at the borders of Israel. And you will know that I am the LORD, for you have not followed my decrees or kept my laws but have conformed to the

373

standards of the nations around you.

Ezekiel	Now as I was prophesying, Pelatiah son of Benaiah died. Then I fell face-down and cried out in a loud voice:
Young Ezekiel	Ah, Sovereign LORD! Will you completely destroy the remnant of Israel?

Cast: **Ezekiel, the Lord** (voice only), **Man, Young Ezekiel**

God's Promise to the Exiles

Ezekiel 11:14–25

Ezekiel	The word of the LORD came to me:
The Lord (voice only)	Son of man, your brothers—your brothers who are your blood relatives and the whole house of Israel—are those of whom the people of Jerusalem have said:
Person 1	They are far away from the LORD.
Person 2	This land was given to us as our possession.
The Lord (voice)	Therefore say: "This is what the Sovereign LORD says: Although I sent them far away among the nations and scattered them among the countries, yet for a little while I have been a sanctuary for them in the countries where they have gone."
	Therefore say: "This is what the Sovereign LORD says: I will gather you from the nations and bring you back from the countries where you have been scattered, and I will give you back the land of Israel again."
	They will return to it and remove all its vile images and detestable idols.
Ezekiel	[The Sovereign LORD declares:]
The Lord (voice)	I will give them an undivided heart and put a new spirit in them; I will remove from them their heart of stone and give them a heart of flesh. Then they will follow my decrees and be careful to keep my laws. They will be my people, and I will be their God. But as for those whose hearts are devoted to their vile images and detestable idols, I will bring down on their own heads what they have done. . . .
Ezekiel	Then the cherubim, with the wheels beside them, spread their wings, and the glory of the God of Israel was above them. The glory of the LORD went up from within the city and stopped above the mountain east of it. The Spirit lifted me up and brought me to the exiles in Babylonia in the vision given by the Spirit of God.

Then the vision I had seen went up from me, and I told the exiles everything the LORD had shown me.

Cast: **Ezekiel, the Lord** (voice only), **Person 1, Person 2**

God's Glory Leaves Jerusalem

Ezekiel 11:22–12:16

Ezekiel Then the cherubim, with the wheels beside them, spread their wings, and the glory of the God of Israel was above them. The glory of the LORD went up from within the city and stopped above the mountain east of it. The Spirit lifted me up and brought me to the exiles in Babylonia in the vision given by the Spirit of God.

Then the vision I had seen went up from me, and I told the exiles everything the LORD had shown me.

The word of the LORD came to me:

The Lord
(voice only) Son of man, you are living among a rebellious people. They have eyes to see but do not see and ears to hear but do not hear, for they are a rebellious people.

Therefore, son of man, pack your belongings for exile and in the daytime, as they watch, set out and go from where you are to another place. Perhaps they will understand, though they are a rebellious house. During the daytime, while they watch, bring out your belongings packed for exile. Then in the evening, while they are watching, go out like those who go into exile. While they watch, dig through the wall and take your belongings out through it. Put them on your shoulder as they are watching and carry them out at dusk. Cover your face so that you cannot see the land, for I have made you a sign to the house of Israel.

Ezekiel So I did as I was commanded. During the day I brought out my things packed for exile. Then in the evening I dug through the wall with my hands. I took my belongings out at dusk, carrying them on my shoulders while they watched.

In the morning the word of the LORD came to me:

The Lord
(voice) Son of man, did not that rebellious house of Israel ask you, "What are you doing?"

Say to them, "This is what the Sovereign LORD says: This oracle concerns the prince in Jerusalem and the whole house of Israel who are there." Say to them, "I am a sign to you."

As I have done, so it will be done to them. They will go into exile as captives.

375

The prince among them will put his things on his shoulder at dusk and leave, and a hole will be dug in the wall for him to go through. He will cover his face so that he cannot see the land. I will spread my net for him, and he will be caught in my snare; I will bring him to Babylonia, the land of the Chaldeans, but he will not see it, and there he will die. I will scatter to the winds all those around him—his staff and all his troops—and I will pursue them with drawn sword.

They will know that I am the LORD, when I disperse them among the nations and scatter them through the countries. But I will spare a few of them from the sword, famine and plague, so that in the nations where they go they may acknowledge all their detestable practices. Then they will know that I am the LORD.

Cast: **Ezekiel, the Lord** (voice only). (This reading overlaps with the previous one.)

A Popular Proverb and an Unpopular Message

Ezekiel 12:21–28

Ezekiel	The word of the LORD came to me:
The Lord (voice only)	Son of man, what is this proverb you have in the land of Israel:
Israelite	The days go by and every vision comes to nothing? . . .
Ezekiel	This is what the Sovereign LORD says:
The Lord (voice)	I am going to put an end to this proverb, and they will no longer quote it in Israel. Say to them, "The days are near when every vision will be fulfilled. For there will be no more false visions or flattering divinations among the people of Israel. But I the LORD will speak what I will, and it shall be fulfilled without delay. For in your days, you rebellious house, I will fulfill whatever I say. . . ."
[(with flourish)	[I have spoken!]]
Ezekiel	The word of the LORD came to me:
The Lord (voice)	Son of man, the house of Israel is saying, "The vision he sees is for many years from now, and he prophesies about the distant future."
	Therefore say to them, "This is what the Sovereign LORD says: None of my words will be delayed any longer. Whatever I say will be fulfilled, declares the Sovereign LORD."

Cast: **Ezekiel, the Lord** (voice only), **Israelite**

Jerusalem, a Useless Vine

Ezekiel 15:1–8

Ezekiel The word of the LORD came to me:

The Lord
(voice only) Son of man, how is the wood of a vine better than that of a branch on any of the trees in the forest? Is wood ever taken from it to make anything useful? Do they make pegs from it to hang things on? And after it is thrown on the fire as fuel and the fire burns both ends and chars the middle, is it then useful for anything? If it was not useful for anything when it was whole, how much less can it be made into something useful when the fire has burned it and it is charred?

Ezekiel Therefore this is what the Sovereign LORD says:

The Lord
(voice) As I have given the wood of the vine among the trees of the forest as fuel for the fire, so will I treat the people living in Jerusalem. I will set my face against them. Although they have come out of the fire, the fire will yet consume them. And when I set my face against them, you will know that I am the LORD. I will make the land desolate because they have been unfaithful.

Ezekiel
(with
flourish) Declares the Sovereign LORD.

Cast: **Ezekiel, the Lord** (voice only)

God Requires Repentance

Ezekiel 18:1–4, 20–32

Ezekiel The word of the LORD came to me:

The Lord
(voice only) What do you people mean by quoting this proverb about the land of Israel?

Israelite "The fathers eat sour grapes,
    and the children's teeth are set on edge."

Ezekiel [The Sovereign LORD says:]

The Lord
(voice) As surely as I live, declares the Sovereign LORD, you will no longer quote this proverb in Israel. For every living soul belongs to me, the father as well as the son—both alike belong to me. The soul who sins is the one who will die. . . .

The soul who sins is the one who will die. The son will not share the guilt of the father, nor will the father share the guilt of the son. The righteousness of the righteous man will be credited to him, and the wickedness of the wicked will be charged against him.

But if a wicked man turns away from all the sins he has committed and keeps all my decrees and does what is just and right, he will surely live; he will not die. None of the offenses he has committed will be remembered against him. Because of the righteous things he has done, he will live.

Ezekiel   [The Sovereign LORD asks:]

The Lord
(voice)

Do I take any pleasure in the death of the wicked? . . . Rather, am I not pleased when they turn from their ways and live?

But if a righteous man turns from his righteousness and commits sin and does the same detestable things the wicked man does, will he live? None of the righteous things he has done will be remembered. Because of the unfaithfulness he is guilty of and because of the sins he has committed, he will die. Yet you say:

Israelite   The way of the Lord is not just.

The Lord
(voice)

Hear, O house of Israel: Is my way unjust? Is it not your ways that are unjust? If a righteous man turns from his righteousness and commits sin, he will die for it; because of the sin he has committed he will die. But if a wicked man turns away from the wickedness he has committed and does what is just and right, he will save his life. Because he considers all the offenses he has committed and turns away from them, he will surely live; he will not die. Yet the house of Israel says:

Israelite   The way of the Lord is not just.

The Lord
(voice)

Are my ways unjust, O house of Israel? Is it not your ways that are unjust?

Therefore, O house of Israel, I will judge you, each one according to his ways.

Ezekiel   [The Sovereign LORD declares:] Repent! Turn away from all your offenses; then sin will not be your downfall. Rid yourselves of all the offenses you have committed, and get a new heart and a new spirit. Why will you die, O house of Israel? For I take no pleasure in the death of anyone. . . .

The Lord
(voice)   Repent and live!

Cast: **Ezekiel**, the **Lord** (voice only), **Israelite**

Ezekiel's Wife Dies

Ezekiel 24:15–27

Ezekiel The word of the LORD came to me:

The Lord
(voice only) Son of man, with one blow I am about to take away from you the delight of your eyes. Yet do not lament or weep or shed any tears. Groan quietly; do not mourn for the dead. Keep your turban fastened and your sandals on your feet; do not cover the lower part of your face or eat the customary food ˻of mourners˼.

Ezekiel So I spoke to the people in the morning, and in the evening my wife died. The next morning I did as I had been commanded.

Then the people asked me:

Person Won't you tell us what these things have to do with us?

Ezekiel So I said to them:

**Young
  Ezekiel** The word of the LORD came to me: Say to the house of Israel, "This is what the Sovereign LORD says":

The Lord
(voice) I am about to desecrate my sanctuary—the stronghold in which you take pride, the delight of your eyes, the object of your affection. The sons and daughters you left behind will fall by the sword. And you will do as I have done. You will not cover the lower part of your face or eat the customary food ˻of mourners˼. You will keep your turbans on your heads and your sandals on your feet. You will not mourn or weep but will waste away because of your sins and groan among yourselves. Ezekiel will be a sign to you; you will do just as he has done. When this happens, you will know that I am the Sovereign LORD.

[Ezekiel [The Lord said:]]

The Lord
(voice) And you, son of man, on the day I take away their stronghold, their joy and glory, the delight of their eyes, their heart's desire, and their sons and daughters as well—on that day a fugitive will come to tell you the news. At that time your mouth will be opened; you will speak with him and will no longer be silent. So you will be a sign to them, and they will know that I am the LORD.

Cast: **Ezekiel**, **the Lord** (voice only), **Person**, **Young Ezekiel**

A Prophecy against Tyre

From Ezekiel 26:1–21

Ezekiel	In the eleventh year, on the first day of the month, the word of the Lord came to me:
The Lord (voice only)	Son of man . . . Tyre has said of Jerusalem:
Person 1	Aha! The gate to the nations is broken.
Person 2	And its doors have swung open to me.
Person 1	Now that she lies in ruins I will prosper.
Ezekiel	Therefore this is what the Sovereign Lord says:
The Lord (voice)	I am against you, O Tyre, and I will bring many nations against you, like the sea casting up its waves. They will destroy the walls of Tyre and pull down her towers; I will scrape away her rubble and make her a bare rock. Out in the sea she will become a place to spread fishnets, for I have spoken, declares the Sovereign Lord. She will become plunder for the nations, and her settlements on the mainland will be ravaged by the sword. Then they will know that I am the Lord. . . .
Ezekiel	This is what the Sovereign Lord says to Tyre:
The Lord (voice)	Will not the coastlands tremble at the sound of your fall, when the wounded groan and the slaughter takes place in you? Then all the princes of the coast will step down from their thrones and lay aside their robes and take off their embroidered garments. Clothed with terror, they will sit on the ground, trembling every moment, appalled at you. Then they will take up a lament concerning you and say to you:
Kings 1 and 2	How you are destroyed, O city of renown, peopled by men of the sea!
King 1	You were a power on the seas, you and your citizens.
King 2	You put your terror on all who lived there.
King 1	Now the coastlands tremble on the day of your fall—
King 2	The islands in the sea are terrified at your collapse.
Ezekiel	This is what the Sovereign Lord says:

The Lord
(voice)   When I make you a desolate city, like cities no longer inhabited, and when I bring the ocean depths over you and its vast waters cover you, then I will bring you down with those who go down to the pit, to the people of long ago. I will make you dwell in the earth below, as in ancient ruins, with those who go down to the pit, and you will not return or take your place in the land of the living. I will bring you to a horrible end and you will be no more. You will be sought, but you will never again be found.

Ezekiel
(with
flourish)   Declares the Sovereign LORD.

Cast: **Ezekiel, the Lord** (voice only), **Person 1, Person 2, King 1, King 2**

A Cedar in Lebanon

From Ezekiel 31:1–18

Ezekiel   In the eleventh year, in the third month on the first day, the word of the LORD came to me:

The Lord
(voice only)   Son of man, say to Pharaoh king of Egypt and to his hordes:

Singer   Who can be compared with you in majesty?
Consider Assyria, once a cedar in Lebanon,
     with beautiful branches overshadowing the forest;
it towered on high,
     its top above the thick foliage.
The waters nourished it,
     deep springs made it grow tall;
their streams flowed
     all around its base
and sent their channels
     to all the trees of the field.
So it towered higher
     than all the trees of the field;
its boughs increased
     and its branches grew long,
     spreading because of abundant waters.
All the birds of the air
     nested in its boughs,
all the beasts of the field
     gave birth under its branches;
all the great nations
     lived in its shade.
It was majestic in beauty,

           with its spreading boughs,
        for its roots went down
           to abundant waters.
        The cedars in the garden of God
           could not rival it,
        nor could the pine trees
           equal its boughs,
        nor could the plane trees
           compare with its branches—
        no tree in the garden of God
           could match its beauty.
        I made it beautiful
           with abundant branches,
        the envy of all the trees of Eden
           in the garden of God.

The Lord
(voice)
    Therefore this is what the Sovereign Lord says: Because it towered on high, lifting its top above the thick foliage, and because it was proud of its height, I handed it over to the ruler of the nations, for him to deal with according to its wickedness. I cast it aside, and the most ruthless of foreign nations cut it down and left it. . . .

Ezekiel
    [The Sovereign Lord says:]

The Lord
(voice)
    [The tree is the king of Egypt and all his people.] Then all the trees of Eden, the choicest and best of Lebanon, all the trees that were well-watered, were consoled in the earth below. Those who lived in its shade, its allies among the nations, had also gone down to the grave with it, joining those killed by the sword.

    Which of the trees of Eden can be compared with you in splendor and majesty? Yet you, too, will be brought down with the trees of Eden to the earth below; you will lie among the uncircumcised, with those killed by the sword.

    This is Pharaoh and all his hordes, declares the Sovereign Lord.

Cast: **Ezekiel, the Lord** (voice only), **Singer** (who speaks the words of the Lord)

Individual Responsibility

From Ezekiel 33:10–19

Ezekiel
    [The Lord spoke to me:]

The Lord
(voice only)   Son of man, say to the house of Israel, This is what you are saying—

Israelite 1
    Our offenses and sins weigh us down.

Israelite 2	We are wasting away because of them.
Israelites 1 and 2	How then can we live?
The Lord (voice)	Say to them, "As surely as I live, declares the Sovereign LORD, I take no pleasure in the death of the wicked, but rather that they turn from their ways and live. Turn! Turn from your evil ways!" . . . And if I say to the wicked man, "You will surely die," but he then turns away from his sin and does what is just and right—if he gives back what he took in pledge for a loan, returns what he has stolen, follows the decrees that give life, and does no evil, he will surely live; he will not die. . . .
(deliberately)	And if a wicked man turns away from his wickedness and does what is just and right, he will live by doing so.

Cast: **Ezekiel**, **the Lord** (voice only), **Israelite 1**, **Israelite 2** (can be the same as Israelite 1)

Jerusalem's Fall Explained

Ezekiel 33:21–29

Ezekiel	In the twelfth year of our exile, in the tenth month on the fifth day, a man who had escaped from Jerusalem came to me and said:
Person 1	The city has fallen!
Ezekiel	Now the evening before the man arrived, the hand of the LORD was upon me, and he opened my mouth before the man came to me in the morning. So my mouth was opened and I was no longer silent. (PAUSE) Then the word of the LORD came to me:
The Lord (voice only)	Son of man, the people living in those ruins in the land of Israel are saying—
Person 2	Abraham was only one man, yet he possessed the land.
Person 1	But we are many; surely the land has been given to us as our possession.
The Lord (voice)	Therefore say to them, "This is what the Sovereign LORD says: Since you eat meat with the blood still in it and look to your idols and shed blood, should you then possess the land? You rely on your sword, you do detestable things, and each of you defiles his neighbor's wife. Should you then possess the land?"
	Say this to them: "This is what the Sovereign LORD says: As surely as I live, those who are left in the ruins will fall by the sword, those out in the country I will give to the wild animals to be devoured, and those in strongholds and caves will die of a plague. I will make the land a deso-

late waste, and her proud strength will come to an end, and the mountains of Israel will become desolate so that no one will cross them. Then they will know that I am the Lord, when I have made the land a desolate waste because of all the detestable things they have done."

Cast: **Ezekiel, the Lord** (voice only), **Person 1, Person 2**

The Results of the Prophet's Message

Ezekiel 33:30–33

Ezekiel [The Lord said:]

The Lord
(voice only) As for you, son of man, your countrymen are talking together about you by the walls and at the doors of the houses, saying to each other:

Person Come and hear the message that has come from the Lord.

The Lord
(voice) My people come to you, as they usually do, and sit before you to listen to your words, but they do not put them into practice. With their mouths they express devotion, but their hearts are greedy for unjust gain. Indeed, to them you are nothing more than one who sings love songs with a beautiful voice and plays an instrument well, for they hear your words but do not put them into practice.

When all this comes true—and it surely will—then they will know that a prophet has been among them.

Cast: **Ezekiel, the Lord** (voice only), **Person**

The Shepherds of Israel

Ezekiel 34:1–10

Ezekiel The word of the Lord came to me:

The Lord
(voice only) Son of man, prophesy against the shepherds of Israel. . . .

Ezekiel This is what the Sovereign Lord says:

The Lord
(voice) Woe to the shepherds of Israel who only take care of themselves! Should not shepherds take care of the flock? You eat the curds, clothe yourselves with the wool and slaughter the choice animals, but you do not take care of the flock. You have not strengthened the weak or healed the sick or bound up the injured. You have not brought back the strays or searched for the lost. You have ruled them harshly and brutally. So they

> were scattered because there was no shepherd, and when they were scattered they became food for all the wild animals. My sheep wandered over all the mountains and on every high hill. They were scattered over the whole earth, and no one searched or looked for them.

Ezekiel — Therefore, you shepherds, hear the word of the LORD: . . .

The Lord
(voice) — My flock lacks a shepherd and so has been plundered and has become food for all the wild animals. . . . My shepherds did not search for my flock but cared for themselves rather than for my flock.

Ezekiel — Therefore, O shepherds, hear the word of the LORD: This is what the Sovereign LORD says:

The Lord
(voice) — I am against the shepherds and will hold them accountable for my flock. I will remove them from tending the flock so that the shepherds can no longer feed themselves. I will rescue my flock from their mouths, and it will no longer be food for them.

Cast: **Ezekiel, the Lord** (voice only)

The Good Shepherd

Ezekiel 34:11–31

Voice 1 — For this is what the Sovereign LORD says: I myself will search for my sheep and look after them. As a shepherd looks after his scattered flock when he is with them, so will I look after my sheep. I will rescue them from all the places where they were scattered on a day of clouds and darkness.

Voice 2 — I will bring them out from the nations and gather them from the countries, and I will bring them into their own land.

Voice 3 — I will pasture them on the mountains of Israel, in the ravines and in all the settlements in the land.

Voice 1 — I will tend them in a good pasture, and the mountain heights of Israel will be their grazing land.

Voice 2 — There they will lie down in good grazing land, and there they will feed in a rich pasture on the mountains of Israel.

Voice 3 — I myself will tend my sheep and have them lie down, declares the Sovereign LORD.

Voices 1–3 — [I, the Sovereign LORD, have spoken.]

Voice 1 — I will search for the lost and bring back the strays. I will bind up the injured and strengthen the weak.

385

Voice 2	But the sleek and the strong I will destroy. I will shepherd the flock with justice.
Voice 3	As for you, my flock, this is what the Sovereign LORD says: I will judge between one sheep and another, and between rams and goats.
Voice 1	Is it not enough for you to feed on the good pasture? Must you also trample the rest of your pasture with your feet?
Voice 2	Is it not enough for you to drink clear water? Must you also muddy the rest with your feet?
Voice 3	Must my flock feed on what you have trampled and drink what you have muddied with your feet?
Voice 1	Therefore this is what the Sovereign LORD says to them: See, I myself will judge between the fat sheep and the lean sheep.
Voice 2	Because you shove with flank and shoulder, butting all the weak sheep with your horns until you have driven them away—
Voice 3	I will save my flock, and they will no longer be plundered.
Voice 1	I will judge between one sheep and another.
Voice 2	I will place over them one shepherd, my servant David, and he will tend them; he will tend them and be their shepherd.
Voice 3	I the LORD will be their God, and my servant David will be prince among them.
Voices 1–3	I the LORD have spoken.
Voice 1	I will make a covenant of peace with them and rid the land of wild beasts so that they may live in the desert and sleep in the forests in safety.
Voice 2	I will bless them and the places surrounding my hill.
Voice 3	I will send down showers in season; there will be showers of blessing.
Voice 1	The trees of the field will yield their fruit and the ground will yield its crops; the people will be secure in their land. They will know that I am the LORD, when I break the bars of their yoke and rescue them from the hands of those who enslaved them.
Voice 2	They will no longer be plundered by the nations, nor will wild animals devour them. They will live in safety, and no one will make them afraid.
Voice 3	I will provide for them a land renowned for its crops, and they will no longer be victims of famine in the land or bear the scorn of the nations. Then they will know that I, the LORD their God, am with them and that they, the house of Israel, are my people.
Voices 1–3	[I, the Sovereign LORD, have spoken.]
Voice 1	Declares the Sovereign LORD:

Voice 2	You my sheep, the sheep of my pasture, are people, and I am your God . . . .

Cast: **Voice 1, Voice 2, Voice 3**

The Valley of Dry Bones

Ezekiel 37:1–14

Ezekiel	The hand of the Lord was upon me, and he brought me out by the Spirit of the Lord and set me in the middle of a valley; it was full of bones. He led me back and forth among them, and I saw a great many bones on the floor of the valley, bones that were very dry. He asked me:
The Lord (voice only)	Son of man, can these bones live?
Ezekiel	I said, "O Sovereign Lord, you alone know." (PAUSE) [He said:]
The Lord (voice)	Prophesy to these bones and say to them, "Dry bones, hear the word of the Lord! This is what the Sovereign Lord says to these bones. I will make breath enter you, and you will come to life. I will attach tendons to you and make flesh come upon you and cover you with skin; I will put breath in you, and you will come to life. Then you will know that I am the Lord."
Ezekiel	So I prophesied as I was commanded. And as I was prophesying, there was a noise, a rattling sound, and the bones came together, bone to bone. I looked, and tendons and flesh appeared on them and skin covered them, but there was no breath in them. (PAUSE) Then he said to me:
The Lord (voice)	Prophesy to the breath; prophesy, son of man, and say to it, "This is what the Sovereign Lord says: Come from the four winds, O breath, and breathe into these slain, that they may live."
Ezekiel	So I prophesied as he commanded me, and breath entered them; they came to life and stood up on their feet—a vast army. (PAUSE) Then he said to me:
The Lord (voice)	Son of man, these bones are the whole house of Israel. They say, "Our bones are dried up and our hope is gone; we are cut off." Therefore prophesy and say to them: "This is what the Sovereign Lord says: O my people, I am going to open your graves and bring you up from them; I will bring you back to the land of Israel. Then you, my people, will know that I am the Lord, when I open your graves and bring you up from them. I will put my Spirit in you and you will live, and I will settle you in your own land. Then you will know that I the Lord have spoken, and I have done it, declares the Lord."

Cast: **Ezekiel, the Lord** (voice only)

Ezekiel Is Taken to the Temple

From Ezekiel 40:1–41:22 [41:23–42:14]

Ezekiel In the twenty-fifth year of our exile, at the beginning of the year, on the tenth of the month, in the fourteenth year after the fall of the city—on that very day the hand of the LORD was upon me and he took me there. In visions of God he took me to the land of Israel and set me on a very high mountain, on whose south side were some buildings that looked like a city. He took me there, and I saw a man whose appearance was like bronze; he was standing in the gateway with a linen cord and a measuring rod in his hand. The man said to me:

Man Son of man, look with your eyes and hear with your ears and pay attention to everything I am going to show you, for that is why you have been brought here. Tell the house of Israel everything you see.

Ezekiel I saw a wall completely surrounding the temple area. The length of the measuring rod in the man's hand was six long cubits, each of which was a cubit and a handbreadth. He measured the wall; it was one measuring rod thick and one rod high.

Then he went to the gate facing east. He climbed its steps and measured the threshold of the gate; it was one rod deep. The alcoves for the guards were one rod long and one rod wide, and the projecting walls between the alcoves were five cubits thick. And the threshold of the gate next to the portico facing the temple was one rod deep.

Then he measured the portico of the gateway; it was eight cubits deep and its jambs were two cubits thick. The portico of the gateway faced the temple. . . .

Then he brought me into the outer court. . . . Then he measured the distance from the inside of the lower gateway to the outside of the inner court; it was a hundred cubits on the east side as well as on the north.

Then he measured the length and width of the gate facing north, leading into the outer court. . . .

Then he led me to the south side and I saw a gate facing south. He measured its jambs and its portico, and they had the same measurements as the others. . . .

Then he brought me to the inner court on the east side, and he measured the gateway; it had the same measurements as the others. . . .

Then he brought me to the north gate and measured it. It had the same measurements as the others. . . . Its portico faced the outer court; palm trees decorated the jambs on either side, and eight steps led up to it.

Then the man brought me to the outer sanctuary and measured the jambs; the width of the jambs was six cubits on each side. . . .

Then he went into the inner sanctuary and measured the jambs of the entrance; each was two cubits wide. The entrance was six cubits wide, and the projecting walls on each side of it were seven cubits wide. And he measured the length of the inner sanctuary; it was twenty cubits, and its width was twenty cubits across the end of the outer sanctuary. He said to me:

Man   This is the Most Holy Place.

Ezekiel   Then he measured the wall of the temple; it was six cubits thick, and each side room around the temple was four cubits wide. The side rooms were on three levels, one above another, thirty on each level. There were ledges all around the wall of the temple to serve as supports for the side rooms, so that the supports were not inserted into the wall of the temple. . . .

In the space above the outside of the entrance to the inner sanctuary and on the walls at regular intervals all around the inner and outer sanctuary were carved cherubim and palm trees. Palm trees alternated with cherubim. Each cherub had two faces: the face of a man toward the palm tree on one side and the face of a lion toward the palm tree on the other. They were carved all around the whole temple. From the floor to the area above the entrance, cherubim and palm trees were carved on the wall of the outer sanctuary.

The outer sanctuary had a rectangular doorframe, and the one at the front of the Most Holy Place was similar. There was a wooden altar three cubits high and two cubits square; its corners, its base and its sides were of wood. The man said to me:

Man   This is the table that is before the LORD.

[Ezekiel   Both the outer sanctuary and the Most Holy Place had double doors. Each door had two leaves—two hinged leaves for each door. And on the doors of the outer sanctuary were carved cherubim and palm trees like those carved on the walls, and there was a wooden overhang on the front of the portico. On the sidewalls of the portico were narrow windows with palm trees carved on each side. The side rooms of the temple also had overhangs. . . .

Then he said to me:

Man   The north and south rooms facing the temple courtyard are the priests' rooms, where the priests who approach the LORD will eat the most holy offerings. There they will put the most holy offerings—the grain offerings, the sin offerings and the guilt offerings—for the place is holy. Once the priests enter the holy precincts, they are not to go into the outer court until they leave behind the garments in which they minister, for these are holy. They are to put on other clothes before they go near the places that are for the people.]

Cast: Ezekiel, Man

The Glory Returns to the Temple

Ezekiel 43:1–9

Ezekiel   Then the man brought me to the gate facing east, and I saw the glory of the God of Israel coming from the east. His voice was like the roar of rushing waters, and the land was radiant with his glory. The vision I saw was like the vision I had seen when he came to destroy the city and like the visions I had seen by the Kebar River, and I fell facedown. The glory of the Lord entered the temple through the gate facing east. Then the Spirit lifted me up and brought me into the inner court, and the glory of the Lord filled the temple.

While the man was standing beside me, I heard someone speaking to me from inside the temple. He said:

The Lord
(voice only)   Son of man, this is the place of my throne and the place for the soles of my feet. This is where I will live among the Israelites forever. The house of Israel will never again defile my holy name—neither they nor their kings—by their prostitution and the lifeless idols of their kings at their high places. When they placed their threshold next to my threshold and their doorposts beside my doorposts, with only a wall between me and them, they defiled my holy name by their detestable practices. So I destroyed them in my anger. Now let them put away from me their prostitution and the lifeless idols of their kings, and I will live among them forever.

Cast: **Ezekiel, the Lord** (voice only)

Rules for Admission to the Temple

Ezekiel 44:1–5

Ezekiel   Then the man brought me back to the outer gate of the sanctuary, the one facing east, and it was shut. The Lord said to me:

The Lord
(voice only)   This gate is to remain shut. It must not be opened; no one may enter through it. It is to remain shut because the Lord, the God of Israel, has entered through it. The prince himself is the only one who may sit inside the gateway to eat in the presence of the Lord. He is to enter by way of the portico of the gateway and go out the same way.

Ezekiel   Then the man brought me by way of the north gate to the front of the temple. I looked and saw the glory of the Lord filling the temple of the Lord, and I fell facedown. (PAUSE) The Lord said to me:

The Lord
(voice)   Son of man, look carefully, listen closely and give attention to every-

thing I tell you concerning all the regulations regarding the temple of the LORD. Give attention to the entrance of the temple and all the exits of the sanctuary.

Cast: **Ezekiel, the Lord** (voice only)

The River from the Temple

Ezekiel 47:1–12

Ezekiel The man brought me back to the entrance of the temple, and I saw water coming out from under the threshold of the temple toward the east (for the temple faced east). The water was coming down from under the south side of the temple, south of the altar. He then brought me out through the north gate and led me around the outside to the outer gate facing east, and the water was flowing from the south side.

As the man went eastward with a measuring line in his hand, he measured off a thousand cubits and then led me through water that was ankle-deep. He measured off another thousand cubits and led me through water that was knee-deep. He measured off another thousand and led me through water that was up to the waist. He measured off another thousand, but now it was a river that I could not cross, because the water had risen and was deep enough to swim in—a river that no one could cross. He asked me:

Man Son of man, do you see this?

Ezekiel Then he led me back to the bank of the river. When I arrived there, I saw a great number of trees on each side of the river. He said to me:

Man This water flows toward the eastern region and goes down into the Arabah, where it enters the Sea. When it empties into the Sea, the water there becomes fresh. Swarms of living creatures will live wherever the river flows. There will be large numbers of fish, because this water flows there and makes the salt water fresh; so where the river flows everything will live. Fishermen will stand along the shore; from En Gedi to En Eglaim there will be places for spreading nets. The fish will be of many kinds—like the fish of the Great Sea. But the swamps and marshes will not become fresh; they will be left for salt. Fruit trees of all kinds will grow on both banks of the river. Their leaves will not wither, nor will their fruit fail. Every month they will bear, because the water from the sanctuary flows to them. Their fruit will serve for food and their leaves for healing.

Cast: **Ezekiel, Man**

Daniel

Daniel's Training in Babylon

Daniel 1:1–21

Narrator 1   In the third year of the reign of Jehoiakim king of Judah, Nebuchadnez-zar king of Babylon came to Jerusalem and besieged it.

Narrator 2   And the Lord delivered Jehoiakim king of Judah into his hand, along with some of the articles from the temple of God. These he carried off to the temple of his god in Babylonia and put in the treasure house of his god.

Narrator 1   Then the king ordered Ashpenaz, chief of his court officials, to bring in some of the Israelites from the royal family and the nobility—young men without any physical defect, handsome, showing aptitude for every kind of learning, well informed, quick to understand, and qualified to serve in the king's palace. He was to teach them the language and literature of the Babylonians.

Narrator 2   The king assigned them a daily amount of food and wine from the king's table. They were to be trained for three years, and after that they were to enter the king's service.

Narrator 1   Among these were some from Judah: Daniel, Hananiah, Mishael and Azariah. The chief official gave them new names: to Daniel, the name Belteshazzar; to Hananiah, Shadrach; to Mishael, Meshach; and to Azariah, Abednego.

Narrator 2   But Daniel resolved not to defile himself with the royal food and wine, and he asked the chief official for permission not to defile himself this way. Now God had caused the official to show favor and sympathy to Daniel, but the official told Daniel:

Ashpenaz   I am afraid of my lord the king, who has assigned your food and drink. Why should he see you looking worse than the other young men your age? The king would then have my head because of you.

Narrator 2   Daniel then said to the guard whom the chief official had appointed over Daniel, Hananiah, Mishael and Azariah:

Daniel   Please test your servants for ten days: Give us nothing but vegetables to eat and water to drink. Then compare our appearance with that of the young men who eat the royal food, and treat your servants in accordance with what you see.

Narrator 2   So he agreed to this and tested them for ten days.

Narrator 1   At the end of the ten days they looked healthier and better nourished than any of the young men who ate the royal food. So the guard took

	away their choice food and the wine they were to drink and gave them vegetables instead.
Narrator 2	To these four young men God gave knowledge and understanding of all kinds of literature and learning. And Daniel could understand visions and dreams of all kinds.
Narrator 1	At the end of the time set by the king to bring them in, the chief official presented them to Nebuchadnezzar. The king talked with them, and he found none equal to Daniel, Hananiah, Mishael and Azariah; so they entered the king's service.
Narrator 2	In every matter of wisdom and understanding about which the king questioned them, he found them ten times better than all the magicians and enchanters in his whole kingdom.
Narrator 1	And Daniel remained there until the first year of King Cyrus.

Cast: **Narrator 1, Narrator 2, Ashpenaz, Daniel**

Nebuchadnezzar's Dream

Daniel 2:1–13

Narrator	In the second year of his reign, Nebuchadnezzar had dreams; his mind was troubled and he could not sleep. So the king summoned the magicians, enchanters, sorcerers and astrologers to tell him what he had dreamed. When they came in and stood before the king, he said to them:
King	I have had a dream that troubles me and I want to know what it means.
Narrator	Then the astrologers answered the king in Aramaic:
Adviser	O king, live forever! Tell your servants the dream, and we will interpret it.
Narrator	The king replied to the astrologers:
King	This is what I have firmly decided: If you do not tell me what my dream was and interpret it, I will have you cut into pieces and your houses turned into piles of rubble. But if you tell me the dream and explain it, you will receive from me gifts and rewards and great honor. So tell me the dream and interpret it for me.
Narrator	Once more they replied:
Adviser	Let the king tell his servants the dream, and we will interpret it.
Narrator	Then the king answered:
King	I am certain that you are trying to gain time, because you realize that this is what I have firmly decided: If you do not tell me the dream, there is just one penalty for you. You have conspired to tell me misleading and

wicked things, hoping the situation will change. So then, tell me the dream, and I will know that you can interpret it for me.

Narrator	The astrologers answered the king:
Adviser	There is not a man on earth who can do what the king asks! No king, however great and mighty, has ever asked such a thing of any magician or enchanter or astrologer. What the king asks is too difficult. No one can reveal it to the king except the gods, and they do not live among men.
Narrator	This made the king so angry and furious that he ordered the execution of all the wise men of Babylon. So the decree was issued to put the wise men to death, and men were sent to look for Daniel and his friends to put them to death.

Cast: **Narrator, King, Adviser**

God Shows Daniel What the Dream Means

Daniel 2:14–23

Narrator	When Arioch, the commander of the king's guard, had gone out to put to death the wise men of Babylon, Daniel spoke to him with wisdom and tact. He asked the king's officer:
Daniel	Why did the king issue such a harsh decree?
Narrator	Arioch then explained the matter to Daniel. At this, Daniel went in to the king and asked for time, so that he might interpret the dream for him.
	Then Daniel returned to his house and explained the matter to his friends Hananiah, Mishael and Azariah. He urged them to plead for mercy from the God of heaven concerning this mystery, so that he and his friends might not be executed with the rest of the wise men of Babylon. During the night the mystery was revealed to Daniel in a vision. Then Daniel praised the God of heaven and said:
Daniel	Praise be to the name of God for ever and ever;
	wisdom and power are his.
	He changes times and seasons;
	he sets up kings and deposes them.
	He gives wisdom to the wise
	and knowledge to the discerning.
	He reveals deep and hidden things;
	he knows what lies in darkness,
	and light dwells with him.
	I thank and praise you, O God of my fathers:
	You have given me wisdom and power,
	you have made known to me what we asked of you,
	you have made known to us the dream of the king.

Cast: **Narrator, Daniel**

Daniel Interprets the Dream

Daniel 2:24–49

Narrator	Then Daniel went to Arioch, whom the king had appointed to execute the wise men of Babylon, and said to him:
Daniel	Do not execute the wise men of Babylon. Take me to the king, and I will interpret his dream for him.
Narrator	Arioch took Daniel to the king at once and said:
Arioch	I have found a man among the exiles from Judah who can tell the king what his dream means.
Narrator	The king asked Daniel (also called Belteshazzar):
King	Are you able to tell me what I saw in my dream and interpret it?
Narrator	Daniel replied:
Daniel	No wise man, enchanter, magician or diviner can explain to the king the mystery he has asked about, but there is a God in heaven who reveals mysteries. He has shown King Nebuchadnezzar what will happen in days to come. Your dream and the visions that passed through your mind as you lay on your bed are these:

As you were lying there, O king, your mind turned to things to come, and the revealer of mysteries showed you what is going to happen. As for me, this mystery has been revealed to me, not because I have greater wisdom than other living men, but so that you, O king, may know the interpretation and that you may understand what went through your mind.

You looked, O king, and there before you stood a large statue—an enormous, dazzling statue, awesome in appearance. The head of the statue was made of pure gold, its chest and arms of silver, its belly and thighs of bronze, its legs of iron, its feet partly of iron and partly of baked clay. While you were watching, a rock was cut out, but not by human hands. It struck the statue on its feet of iron and clay and smashed them. Then the iron, the clay, the bronze, the silver and the gold were broken to pieces at the same time and became like chaff on a threshing floor in the summer. The wind swept them away without leaving a trace. But the rock that struck the statue became a huge mountain and filled the whole earth.

This was the dream, and now we will interpret it to the king. You, O king, are the king of kings. The God of heaven has given you dominion and power and might and glory; in your hands he has placed mankind and the beasts of the field and the birds of the air. Wherever they live, he has made you ruler over them all. You are that head of gold.

After you, another kingdom will rise, inferior to yours. Next, a third kingdom, one of bronze, will rule over the whole earth. Finally, there will be a fourth kingdom, strong as iron—for iron breaks and smashes everything—and as iron breaks things to pieces, so it will crush and break all the others. Just as you saw that the feet and toes were partly of baked clay and partly of iron, so this will be a divided kingdom; yet it will have some of the strength of iron in it, even as you saw iron mixed with clay. As the toes were partly iron and partly clay, so this kingdom will be partly strong and partly brittle. And just as you saw the iron mixed with baked clay, so the people will be a mixture and will not remain united, any more than iron mixes with clay.

In the time of those kings, the God of heaven will set up a kingdom that will never be destroyed, nor will it be left to another people. It will crush all those kingdoms and bring them to an end, but it will itself endure forever. This is the meaning of the vision of the rock cut out of a mountain, but not by human hands—a rock that broke the iron, the bronze, the clay, the silver and the gold to pieces.

The great God has shown the king what will take place in the future. The dream is true and the interpretation is trustworthy.

Narrator   Then King Nebuchadnezzar fell prostrate before Daniel and paid him honor and ordered that an offering and incense be presented to him. The king said to Daniel:

King   Surely your God is the God of gods and the Lord of kings and a revealer of mysteries, for you were able to reveal this mystery.

Narrator   Then the king placed Daniel in a high position and lavished many gifts on him. He made him ruler over the entire province of Babylon and placed him in charge of all its wise men. Moreover, at Daniel's request the king appointed Shadrach, Meshach and Abednego administrators over the province of Babylon, while Daniel himself remained at the royal court.

Cast: **Narrator, Daniel, Arioch, King**

Nebuchadnezzar Commands Everyone to Worship a Gold Statue

Daniel 3:1–7

Narrator   King Nebuchadnezzar made an image of gold, ninety feet high and nine feet wide, and set it up on the plain of Dura in the province of Babylon. He then summoned the satraps, prefects, governors, advisers, treasurers, judges, magistrates and all the other provincial officials to come to the dedication of the image he had set up. So the satraps, prefects, governors, advisers, treasurers, judges, magistrates and all the other provincial officials assembled for the dedication of the image that King Nebuchadnezzar had set up, and they stood before it. (PAUSE) Then the herald loudly proclaimed:

396

Herald
(calling)   This is what you are commanded to do, O peoples, nations and men of every language: As soon as you hear the sound of the horn, flute, zither, lyre, harp, pipes and all kinds of music, you must fall down and worship the image of gold that King Nebuchadnezzar has set up. Whoever does not fall down and worship will immediately be thrown into a blazing furnace.

Narrator   Therefore, as soon as they heard the sound of the horn, flute, zither, lyre, harp and all kinds of music, all the peoples, nations and men of every language fell down and worshiped the image of gold that King Nebuchadnezzar had set up.

Cast: **Narrator, Herald**

Daniel's Three Friends Are Accused of Disobedience

Daniel 3:7–18

Narrator   Therefore, as soon as they heard the sound of the horn, flute, zither, lyre, harp and all kinds of music, all the peoples, nations and men of every language fell down and worshiped the image of gold that King Nebuchadnezzar had set up.

At this time some astrologers came forward and denounced the Jews. They said to King Nebuchadnezzar:

Babylonian   O king, live forever! You have issued a decree, O king, that everyone who hears the sound of the horn, flute, zither, lyre, harp, pipes and all kinds of music must fall down and worship the image of gold, and that whoever does not fall down and worship will be thrown into a blazing furnace. But there are some Jews whom you have set over the affairs of the province of Babylon—Shadrach, Meshach and Abednego—who pay no attention to you, O king. They neither serve your gods nor worship the image of gold you have set up.

Narrator   Furious with rage, Nebuchadnezzar summoned Shadrach, Meshach and Abednego. So these men were brought before the king, and Nebuchadnezzar said to them:

King
(angrily)   Is it true, Shadrach, Meshach and Abednego, that you do not serve my gods or worship the image of gold I have set up? Now when you hear the sound of the horn, flute, zither, lyre, harp, pipes and all kinds of music, if you are ready to fall down and worship the image I made, very good. But if you do not worship it, you will be thrown immediately into a blazing furnace. Then what god will be able to rescue you from my hand?

Narrator   Shadrach, Meshach and Abednego replied to the king:

397

Shadrach	O Nebuchadnezzar, we do not need to defend ourselves before you in this matter. If we are thrown into the blazing furnace, the God we serve is able to save us from it, and he will rescue us from your hand, O king. But even if he does not, we want you to know, O king, that we will not serve your gods or worship the image of gold you have set up.

Cast: **Narrator, Babylonian, King, Shadrach.** (This reading overlaps with the previous one.)

Daniel's Three Friends in the Furnace

Daniel 3:19–30

Narrator	Nebuchadnezzar was furious with Shadrach, Meshach and Abednego, and his attitude toward them changed. He ordered the furnace heated seven times hotter than usual and commanded some of the strongest soldiers in his army to tie up Shadrach, Meshach and Abednego and throw them into the blazing furnace. So these men, wearing their robes, trousers, turbans and other clothes, were bound and thrown into the blazing furnace. The king's command was so urgent and the furnace so hot that the flames of the fire killed the soldiers who took up Shadrach, Meshach and Abednego, and these three men, firmly tied, fell into the blazing furnace.
	Then King Nebuchadnezzar leaped to his feet in amazement and asked his advisers:
King	Weren't there three men that we tied up and threw into the fire?
Officials 1 and 2	Certainly, O king.
King	Look! I see four men walking around in the fire, unbound and unharmed, and the fourth looks like a son of the gods.
Narrator	Nebuchadnezzar then approached the opening of the blazing furnace and shouted:
King	Shadrach, Meshach and Abednego, servants of the Most High God, come out! Come here!
Narrator	So Shadrach, Meshach and Abednego came out of the fire, and the satraps, prefects, governors and royal advisers crowded around them. They saw that the fire had not harmed their bodies, nor was a hair of their heads singed; their robes were not scorched, and there was no smell of fire on them.
Narrator	Then Nebuchadnezzar said:
King (amazed)	Praise be to the God of Shadrach, Meshach and Abednego, who has sent his angel and rescued his servants! They trusted in him and defied the king's command and were willing to give up their lives rather than serve or worship any god except their own God. (PAUSE) Therefore I decree that

the people of any nation or language who say anything against the God of Shadrach, Meshach and Abednego be cut into pieces and their houses be turned into piles of rubble, for no other god can save in this way.

Narrator Then the king promoted Shadrach, Meshach and Abednego in the province of Babylon.

Cast: **Narrator, King, Official 1, Official 2**

Nebuchadnezzar's Dream of a Tree

Daniel 4:1–18

Messenger King Nebuchadnezzar,

To the peoples, nations and men of every language, who live in all the world:

May you prosper greatly!

It is my pleasure to tell you about the miraculous signs and wonders that the Most High God has performed for me.

Singer How great are his signs,
  how mighty his wonders!
His kingdom is an eternal kingdom;
  his dominion endures from generation to generation.

Messenger I, Nebuchadnezzar, was at home in my palace, contented and prosperous. I had a dream that made me afraid. As I was lying in my bed, the images and visions that passed through my mind terrified me. So I commanded that all the wise men of Babylon be brought before me to interpret the dream for me. When the magicians, enchanters, astrologers and diviners came, I told them the dream, but they could not interpret it for me. Finally, Daniel came into my presence and I told him the dream. (He is called Belteshazzar, after the name of my god, and the spirit of the holy gods is in him.) I said:

King Belteshazzar, chief of the magicians, I know that the spirit of the holy gods is in you, and no mystery is too difficult for you. Here is my dream; interpret it for me. These are the visions I saw while lying in my bed: I looked, and there before me stood a tree in the middle of the land. Its height was enormous. The tree grew large and strong and its top touched the sky; it was visible to the ends of the earth. Its leaves were beautiful, its fruit abundant, and on it was food for all. Under it the beasts of the field found shelter, and the birds of the air lived in its branches; from it every creature was fed.

In the visions I saw while lying in my bed, I looked, and there before me was a messenger, a holy one, coming down from heaven. He called in a loud voice:

399

Angel	Cut down the tree and trim off its branches; strip off its leaves and scatter its fruit. Let the animals flee from under it and the birds from its branches. But let the stump and its roots, bound with iron and bronze, remain in the ground, in the grass of the field.
	Let him be drenched with the dew of heaven, and let him live with the animals among the plants of the earth. Let his mind be changed from that of a man and let him be given the mind of an animal, till seven times pass by for him.
	The decision is announced by messengers, the holy ones declare the verdict, so that the living may know that the Most High is sovereign over the kingdoms of men and gives them to anyone he wishes and sets over them the lowliest of men.
King	This is the dream that I, King Nebuchadnezzar, had. Now, Belteshazzar, tell me what it means, for none of the wise men in my kingdom can interpret it for me. But you can, because the spirit of the holy gods is in you.

Cast: **Messenger, Singer, King, Angel**

Daniel Interprets the Dream

Daniel 4:19–33

Narrator	Then Daniel (also called Belteshazzar) was greatly perplexed for a time, and his thoughts terrified him. So the king said:
King	Belteshazzar, do not let the dream or its meaning alarm you.
Narrator	Belteshazzar answered:
Daniel	My lord, if only the dream applied to your enemies and its meaning to your adversaries! The tree you saw, which grew large and strong, with its top touching the sky, visible to the whole earth, with beautiful leaves and abundant fruit, providing food for all, giving shelter to the beasts of the field, and having nesting places in its branches for the birds of the air—you, O king, are that tree! You have become great and strong; your greatness has grown until it reaches the sky, and your dominion extends to distant parts of the earth.
	You, O king, saw a messenger, a holy one, coming down from heaven and saying:
Angel	Cut down the tree and destroy it, but leave the stump, bound with iron and bronze, in the grass of the field, while its roots remain in the ground. Let him be drenched with the dew of heaven; let him live like the wild animals, until seven times pass by for him.
Daniel	This is the interpretation, O king, and this is the decree the Most High has issued against my lord the king: You will be driven away from people and will live with the wild animals; you will eat grass like cattle and be

400

drenched with the dew of heaven. Seven times will pass by for you until you acknowledge that the Most High is sovereign over the kingdoms of men and gives them to anyone he wishes. The command to leave the stump of the tree with its roots means that your kingdom will be restored to you when you acknowledge that Heaven rules. Therefore, O king, be pleased to accept my advice: Renounce your sins by doing what is right, and your wickedness by being kind to the oppressed. It may be that then your prosperity will continue.

Narrator	All this happened to King Nebuchadnezzar. Twelve months later, as the king was walking on the roof of the royal palace of Babylon, he said:
King	Is not this the great Babylon I have built as the royal residence, by my mighty power and for the glory of my majesty?
Narrator	The words were still on his lips when a voice came from heaven:
Voice	This is what is decreed for you, King Nebuchadnezzar: Your royal authority has been taken from you. You will be driven away from people and will live with the wild animals; you will eat grass like cattle. Seven times will pass by for you until you acknowledge that the Most High is sovereign over the kingdoms of men and gives them to anyone he wishes.
Narrator	Immediately what had been said about Nebuchadnezzar was fulfilled. He was driven away from people and ate grass like cattle. His body was drenched with the dew of heaven until his hair grew like the feathers of an eagle and his nails like the claws of a bird.

Cast: **Narrator, King, Daniel, Angel, Voice**

Nebuchadnezzar Praises God

Daniel 4:34–37

King	. . . I, Nebuchadnezzar, raised my eyes toward heaven, and my sanity was restored. Then I praised the Most High; I honored and glorified him who lives forever.

Singer	His dominion is an eternal dominion;
	    his kingdom endures from generation to generation.
	All the peoples of the earth
	    are regarded as nothing.
	He does as he pleases
	    with the powers of heaven
	    and the peoples of the earth.
	No one can hold back his hand
	    or say to him: "What have you done?"

King	At the same time that my sanity was restored, my honor and splendor were returned to me for the glory of my kingdom. My advisers and nobles sought me out, and I was restored to my throne and became even greater

than before. Now I, Nebuchadnezzar, praise and exalt and glorify the King of heaven, because everything he does is right and all his ways are just. And those who walk in pride he is able to humble.

Cast: **King, Singer**

Belshazzar's Banquet

Daniel 5:1–12

Narrator King Belshazzar gave a great banquet for a thousand of his nobles and drank wine with them. While Belshazzar was drinking his wine, he gave orders to bring in the gold and silver goblets that Nebuchadnezzar his father had taken from the temple in Jerusalem, so that the king and his nobles, his wives and his concubines might drink from them. So they brought in the gold goblets that had been taken from the temple of God in Jerusalem, and the king and his nobles, his wives and his concubines drank from them. As they drank the wine, they praised the gods of gold and silver, of bronze, iron, wood and stone.

Suddenly the fingers of a human hand appeared and wrote on the plaster of the wall, near the lampstand in the royal palace.

Voice
 (slowly) [MENE, MENE, TEKEL, PARSIN]

Narrator The king watched the hand as it wrote. His face turned pale and he was so frightened that his knees knocked together and his legs gave way.

The king called out for the enchanters, astrologers and diviners to be brought and said to these wise men of Babylon:

Belshazzar
 (anxiously) Whoever reads this writing and tells me what it means will be clothed in purple and have a gold chain placed around his neck, and he will be made the third highest ruler in the kingdom.

Narrator Then all the king's wise men came in, but they could not read the writing or tell the king what it meant. So King Belshazzar became even more terrified and his face grew more pale. His nobles were baffled.

The queen, hearing the voices of the king and his nobles, came into the banquet hall. [She said:]

Queen O king, live forever! Don't be alarmed! Don't look so pale! There is a man in your kingdom who has the spirit of the holy gods in him. In the time of your father he was found to have insight and intelligence and wisdom like that of the gods. King Nebuchadnezzar your father—your father the king, I say—appointed him chief of the magicians, enchanters, astrologers and diviners. This man Daniel, whom the king called Belteshazzar, was found to have a keen mind and knowledge and understanding, and also the ability to interpret dreams, explain riddles and solve difficult problems. Call for Daniel, and he will tell you what the writing means.

Cast: **Narrator, Voice, Belshazzar, Queen**

Daniel Explains the Writing

Daniel 5:13–31

Narrator   Daniel was brought before the king, and the king said to him:

Belshazzar   Are you Daniel, one of the exiles my father the king brought from Judah? I have heard that the spirit of the gods is in you and that you have insight, intelligence and outstanding wisdom. The wise men and enchanters were brought before me to read this writing and tell me what it means, but they could not explain it. Now I have heard that you are able to give interpretations and to solve difficult problems. If you can read this writing and tell me what it means, you will be clothed in purple and have a gold chain placed around your neck, and you will be made the third highest ruler in the kingdom.

Narrator   Then Daniel answered the king:

Daniel   You may keep your gifts for yourself and give your rewards to someone else. Nevertheless, I will read the writing for the king and tell him what it means. (PAUSE)

O king, the Most High God gave your father Nebuchadnezzar sovereignty and greatness and glory and splendor. Because of the high position he gave him, all the peoples and nations and men of every language dreaded and feared him. Those the king wanted to put to death, he put to death; those he wanted to spare, he spared; those he wanted to promote, he promoted; and those he wanted to humble, he humbled. But when his heart became arrogant and hardened with pride, he was deposed from his royal throne and stripped of his glory. He was driven away from people and given the mind of an animal; he lived with the wild donkeys and ate grass like cattle; and his body was drenched with the dew of heaven, until he acknowledged that the Most High God is sovereign over the kingdoms of men and sets over them anyone he wishes.

But you his son, O Belshazzar, have not humbled yourself, though you knew all this. Instead, you have set yourself up against the Lord of heaven. You had the goblets from his temple brought to you, and you and your nobles, your wives and your concubines drank wine from them. You praised the gods of silver and gold, of bronze, iron, wood and stone, which cannot see or hear or understand. But you did not honor the God who holds in his hand your life and all your ways. Therefore he sent the hand that wrote the inscription.

This is the inscription that was written:

Voice	MENE, MENE, TEKEL, PARSIN
Daniel	This is what these words mean:
Voice	*Mene:*
Daniel	God has numbered the days of your reign and brought it to an end.
Voice	*Tekel:*
Daniel	You have been weighed on the scales and found wanting.
Voice	*Peres:*
Daniel	Your kingdom is divided and given to the Medes and Persians.
Narrator	Then at Belshazzar's command, Daniel was clothed in purple, a gold chain was placed around his neck, and he was proclaimed the third highest ruler in the kingdom.
	That very night Belshazzar, king of the Babylonians, was slain, and Darius the Mede took over the kingdom, at the age of sixty-two.

Cast: **Narrator, Belshazzar, Daniel, Voice**

Daniel's Courage

Daniel 6:1–23

Narrator	It pleased Darius to appoint 120 satraps to rule throughout the kingdom, with three administrators over them, one of whom was Daniel. The satraps were made accountable to them so that the king might not suffer loss. Now Daniel so distinguished himself among the administrators and the satraps by his exceptional qualities that the king planned to set him over the whole kingdom. At this, the administrators and the satraps tried to find grounds for charges against Daniel in his conduct of government affairs, but they were unable to do so. They could find no corruption in him, because he was trustworthy and neither corrupt nor negligent. Finally these men said:
Enemy 1	We will never find any basis for charges against this man Daniel—
Enemy 2	Unless it has something to do with the law of his God.
Narrator	So the administrators and the satraps went as a group to the king and said:
Enemies 1 and 2	O King Darius, live forever!
Enemy 1	The royal administrators, prefects, satraps, advisers and governors have all agreed that the king should issue an edict—

Enemy 2	And enforce the decree that anyone who prays to any god or man during the next thirty days—
Enemy 1	Except to you, O king—
Enemy 2	shall be thrown into the lions' den. Now, O king, issue the decree and put it in writing so that it cannot be altered—in accordance with the laws of the Medes and Persians, which cannot be repealed.
Narrator	So King Darius put the decree in writing.
	Now when Daniel learned that the decree had been published, he went home to his upstairs room where the windows opened toward Jerusalem. Three times a day he got down on his knees and prayed, giving thanks to his God, just as he had done before. Then these men went as a group and found Daniel praying and asking God for help. So they went to the king and spoke to him about his royal decree:
Enemies 1 and 2	Did you not publish a decree that during the next thirty days anyone who prays to any god or man except to you, O king, would be thrown into the lions' den?
Narrator	The king answered:
Darius	The decree stands—in accordance with the laws of the Medes and Persians, which cannot be repealed.
Narrator	Then they said to the king:
Enemy 2	Daniel, who is one of the exiles from Judah, pays no attention to you, O king, or to the decree you put in writing.
Enemy 1	He still prays three times a day.
Narrator	When the king heard this, he was greatly distressed; he was determined to rescue Daniel and made every effort until sundown to save him.
	Then the men went as a group to the king and said to him:
Enemy 2	Remember, O king, that according to the law of the Medes and Persians no decree or edict that the king issues can be changed.
Narrator	So the king gave the order, and they brought Daniel and threw him into the lions' den. The king said to Daniel:
Darius (calling)	May your God, whom you serve continually, rescue you!
Narrator	A stone was brought and placed over the mouth of the den, and the king sealed it with his own signet ring and with the rings of his nobles, so that Daniel's situation might not be changed. Then the king returned to his palace and spent the night without eating and without any entertainment being brought to him. And he could not sleep. (PAUSE)
	At the first light of dawn, the king got up and hurried to the lions' den. When he came near the den, he called to Daniel in an anguished voice:

Darius (calling)	Daniel, servant of the living God, has your God, whom you serve continually, been able to rescue you from the lions?
Narrator	Daniel answered:
Daniel (unseen)	O king, live forever! My God sent his angel, and he shut the mouths of the lions. They have not hurt me, because I was found innocent in his sight. Nor have I ever done any wrong before you, O king.
Narrator	The king was overjoyed and gave orders to lift Daniel out of the den. (PAUSE) And when Daniel was lifted from the den, no wound was found on him, because he had trusted in his God.

Cast: **Narrator, Enemy 1, Enemy 2, Darius, Daniel** (preferably unseen)

King Darius Writes

Daniel 6:25–28

Narrator	Then King Darius wrote to all the peoples, nations and men of every language throughout the land:
Darius	May you prosper greatly!
	I issue a decree that in every part of my kingdom people must fear and reverence the God of Daniel.

Singer	For he is the living God
	    and he endures forever;
	his kingdom will not be destroyed,
	    his dominion will never end.
	He rescues and he saves;
	    he performs signs and wonders
	    in the heavens and on the earth.
	He has rescued Daniel
	    from the power of the lions.

Narrator	So Daniel prospered during the reign of Darius and the reign of Cyrus the Persian.

Cast: **Narrator, Darius, Singer**

Daniel's Dream of Four Beasts

Daniel 7:1–8

Voice 1	In the first year of Belshazzar king of Babylon, Daniel had a dream, and visions passed through his mind as he was lying on his bed. He wrote down the substance of his dream. Daniel said:

Voice 2	In my vision at night I looked, and there before me were the four winds of heaven churning up the great sea. Four great beasts, each different from the others, came up out of the sea.
	The first was like a lion, and it had the wings of an eagle. I watched until its wings were torn off and it was lifted from the ground so that it stood on two feet like a man, and the heart of a man was given to it.
Voice 3	And there before me was a second beast, which looked like a bear. It was raised up on one of its sides, and it had three ribs in its mouth between its teeth. It was told:
Voice 1	Get up and eat your fill of flesh!
Voice 2	After that, I looked, and there before me was another beast, one that looked like a leopard. And on its back it had four wings like those of a bird. This beast had four heads, and it was given authority to rule.
Voice 3	After that, in my vision at night I looked, and there before me was a fourth beast—terrifying and frightening and very powerful. It had large iron teeth; it crushed and devoured its victims and trampled underfoot whatever was left. It was different from all the former beasts, and it had ten horns.
Voice 1	While I was thinking about the horns, there before me was another horn, a little one, which came up among them; and three of the first horns were uprooted before it. This horn had eyes like the eyes of a man and a mouth that spoke boastfully.

Cast: **Voice 1, Voice 2, Voice 3**

The Vision of the One Who Has Been Living Forever

Daniel 7:1, 9–14

Voice 1	In the first year of Belshazzar king of Babylon, Daniel had a dream, and visions passed through his mind as he was lying on his bed. . . .
	As I looked, thrones were set in place.

Voice 2	And the Ancient of Days took his seat.
	His clothing was as white as snow;
	    the hair of his head was white like wool.
	His throne was flaming with fire,
	    and its wheels were all ablaze.

Voice 3	A river of fire was flowing,
	    coming out from before him.
	Thousands upon thousands attended him;
	    ten thousand times ten thousand stood before him.

The court was seated,
and the books were opened.

Voice 1 Then I continued to watch because of the boastful words the horn was speaking.

Voice 2 I kept looking until the beast was slain and its body destroyed and thrown into the blazing fire.

Voice 3 (The other beasts had been stripped of their authority, but were allowed to live for a period of time.)

Voice 1 In my vision at night I looked, and there before me was one like a son of man, coming with the clouds of heaven. He approached the Ancient of Days and was led into his presence. He was given authority, glory and sovereign power; all peoples, nations and men of every language worshiped him.

**Voices
1 and 2** His dominion is an everlasting dominion that will not pass away, and his kingdom is one that will never be destroyed.

Cast: **Voice 1, Voice 2, Voice 3.** (This reading overlaps with the previous one.)

The Visions Are Explained

Daniel 7:15–28

Daniel I, Daniel, was troubled in spirit, and the visions that passed through my mind disturbed me. I approached one of those standing there and asked him the true meaning of all this.

So he told me and gave me the interpretation of these things:

Witness The four great beasts are four kingdoms that will rise from the earth. But the saints of the Most High will receive the kingdom and will possess it forever—yes, for ever and ever.

Daniel Then I wanted to know the true meaning of the fourth beast, which was different from all the others and most terrifying, with its iron teeth and bronze claws—the beast that crushed and devoured its victims and trampled underfoot whatever was left. I also wanted to know about the ten horns on its head and about the other horn that came up, before which three of them fell—the horn that looked more imposing than the others and that had eyes and a mouth that spoke boastfully. As I watched, this horn was waging war against the saints and defeating them, until the Ancient of Days came and pronounced judgment in favor of the saints of the Most High, and the time came when they possessed the kingdom. He gave me this explanation:

Witness The fourth beast is a fourth kingdom that will appear on earth. It will be different from all the other kingdoms and will devour the whole earth, trampling it down and crushing it. The ten horns are ten kings who will come from this kingdom. After them another king will arise, different from the earlier ones; he will subdue three kings. He will speak against the Most High and oppress his saints and try to change the set times and the laws. The saints will be handed over to him for a time, times and half a time.

But the court will sit, and his power will be taken away and completely destroyed forever. Then the sovereignty, power and greatness of the kingdoms under the whole heaven will be handed over to the saints, the people of the Most High. His kingdom will be an everlasting kingdom, and all rulers will worship and obey him.

Daniel   This is the end of the matter. I, Daniel, was deeply troubled by my thoughts, and my face turned pale, but I kept the matter to myself.

Cast: **Daniel, Witness**

Daniel's Vision of a Ram and a Goat

From Daniel 8:1–11

Daniel   In the third year of King Belshazzar's reign, I, Daniel, had a vision, after the one that had already appeared to me. . . . I looked up, and there before me was a ram with two horns, standing beside the canal, and the horns were long. One of the horns was longer than the other but grew up later. I watched the ram as he charged toward the west and the north and the south. No animal could stand against him, and none could rescue from his power. He did as he pleased and became great.

As I was thinking about this, suddenly a goat with a prominent horn between his eyes came from the west, crossing the whole earth without touching the ground. He came toward the two-horned ram I had seen standing beside the canal and charged at him in great rage. I saw him attack the ram furiously, striking the ram and shattering his two horns. The ram was powerless to stand against him; the goat knocked him to the ground and trampled on him, and none could rescue the ram from his power. The goat became very great, but at the height of his power his large horn was broken off, and in its place four prominent horns grew up toward the four winds of heaven.

Out of one of them came another horn, which started small but grew in power to the south and to the east and toward the Beautiful Land. It grew until it reached the host of the heavens, and it threw some of the starry host down to the earth and trampled on them. It set itself up to be as great as the Prince of the host; it took away the daily sacrifice from him, and the place of his sanctuary was brought low. Because of rebellion, the host ˌof the saintsˌ and the daily sacrifice were given over to it. It prospered in everything it did, and truth was thrown to the ground.

Then I heard a holy one speaking, and another holy one said to him:

Angel 1   How long will it take for the vision to be fulfilled—the vision concerning the daily sacrifice, the rebellion that causes desolation, and the surrender of the sanctuary and of the host that will be trampled underfoot?

Daniel   He said to me:

Angel 2   It will take 2,300 evenings and mornings; then the sanctuary will be reconsecrated.

Cast: **Daniel, Angel 1, Angel 2**

The Interpretation of the Vision

Daniel 8:15–27

Daniel   While I, Daniel, was watching the vision and trying to understand it, there before me stood one who looked like a man. And I heard a man's voice from the Ulai calling:

Voice   Gabriel, tell this man the meaning of the vision.

Daniel   As he came near the place where I was standing, I was terrified and fell prostrate. [He said to me:]

Gabriel   Son of man . . . understand that the vision concerns the time of the end.

Daniel   While he was speaking to me, I was in a deep sleep, with my face to the ground. Then he touched me and raised me to my feet. He said:

Gabriel   I am going to tell you what will happen later in the time of wrath, because the vision concerns the appointed time of the end. The two-horned ram that you saw represents the kings of Media and Persia. The shaggy goat is the king of Greece, and the large horn between his eyes is the first king. The four horns that replaced the one that was broken off represent four kingdoms that will emerge from his nation but will not have the same power.

In the latter part of their reign, when rebels have become completely wicked, a stern-faced king, a master of intrigue, will arise. He will become very strong, but not by his own power. He will cause astounding devastation and will succeed in whatever he does. He will destroy the mighty men and the holy people. He will cause deceit to prosper, and he will consider himself superior. When they feel secure, he will destroy many and take his stand against the Prince of princes. Yet he will be destroyed, but not by human power.

The vision of the evenings and mornings that has been given you is true, but seal up the vision, for it concerns the distant future.

Daniel	I, Daniel, was exhausted and lay ill for several days. Then I got up and went about the king's business. I was appalled by the vision; it was beyond understanding.

Cast: **Daniel, Voice, Gabriel**

Daniel's Prayer

Daniel 9:1–19

Daniel	In the first year of Darius son of Xerxes (a Mede by descent), who was made ruler over the Babylonian kingdom—in the first year of his reign, I, Daniel, understood from the Scriptures, according to the word of the LORD given to Jeremiah the prophet, that the desolation of Jerusalem would last seventy years. So I turned to the Lord God and pleaded with him in prayer and petition, in fasting, and in sackcloth and ashes.

I prayed to the LORD my God and confessed: |
Voices 1 and 2	O Lord, the great and awesome God—
Voice 3	Who keeps his covenant of love with all who love him and obey his commands.
Voice 1	We have sinned—
Voice 2	And done wrong.
Voice 3	We have been wicked and have rebelled.
Voice 1	We have turned away from your commands and laws.
Voice 2	We have not listened to your servants the prophets, who spoke in your name to our kings, our princes and our fathers, and to all the people of the land.
Voice 3	Lord, you are righteous, but this day we are covered with shame—the men of Judah and people of Jerusalem and all Israel, both near and far, in all the countries where you have scattered us because of our unfaithfulness to you.
Voice 1	O LORD, we and our kings, our princes and our fathers are covered with shame because we have sinned against you.
Voice 2	The Lord our God is merciful and forgiving, even though we have rebelled against him.
Voice 3	We have not obeyed the LORD our God or kept the laws he gave us through his servants the prophets.
Voice 1	All Israel has transgressed your law and turned away, refusing to obey you.

411

Voice 2	Therefore the curses and sworn judgments written in the Law of Moses, the servant of God, have been poured out on us, because we have sinned against you.
Voice 3	You have fulfilled the words spoken against us and against our rulers by bringing upon us great disaster. Under the whole heaven nothing has ever been done like what has been done to Jerusalem.
Voice 1	Just as it is written in the Law of Moses, all this disaster has come upon us, yet we have not sought the favor of the LORD our God by turning from our sins and giving attention to your truth.
Voice 2	The LORD did not hesitate to bring the disaster upon us, for the LORD our God is righteous in everything he does; yet we have not obeyed him.
Voice 3	Now, O Lord our God, who brought your people out of Egypt with a mighty hand and who made for yourself a name that endures to this day.
Voices 2 and 3	We have sinned, we have done wrong.
Voice 1	O Lord, in keeping with all your righteous acts, turn away your anger and your wrath from Jerusalem, your city, your holy hill. Our sins and the iniquities of our fathers have made Jerusalem and your people an object of scorn to all those around us.
Daniel	Now, our God, hear the prayers and petitions of your servant. For your sake, O Lord, look with favor on your desolate sanctuary.
Voice 1	Give ear, O God, and hear!
Voice 2	Open your eyes and see the desolation of the city that bears your Name.
Voice 3	We do not make requests of you because we are righteous, but because of your great mercy.
Voice 1	O Lord, listen!
Voice 2	O Lord, forgive!
Voice 3	O Lord, hear and act!
Daniel	For your sake, O my God, do not delay, because your city and your people bear your Name.

Cast: **Daniel, Voice 1, Voice 2, Voice 3**

The Seventy "Sevens"

Daniel 9:20–27

Daniel	While I was speaking and praying, confessing my sin and the sin of my people Israel and making my request to the LORD my God for his holy hill—while I was still in prayer, Gabriel, the man I had seen in the ear-

lier vision, came to me in swift flight about the time of the evening sacrifice. He instructed me and said to me:

Gabriel   Daniel, I have now come to give you insight and understanding. As soon as you began to pray, an answer was given, which I have come to tell you, for you are highly esteemed. Therefore, consider the message and understand the vision:

Seventy "sevens" are decreed for your people and your holy city to finish transgression, to put an end to sin, to atone for wickedness, to bring in everlasting righteousness, to seal up vision and prophecy and to anoint the most holy.

Know and understand this: From the issuing of the decree to restore and rebuild Jerusalem until the Anointed One, the ruler, comes, there will be seven "sevens," and sixty-two "sevens." It will be rebuilt with streets and a trench, but in times of trouble. After the sixty-two "sevens," the Anointed One will be cut off and will have nothing. The people of the ruler who will come will destroy the city and the sanctuary. The end will come like a flood: War will continue until the end, and desolations have been decreed. He will confirm a covenant with many for one "seven." In the middle of the "seven" he will put an end to sacrifice and offering. And on a wing ⌞of the temple⌟ he will set up an abomination that causes desolation, until the end that is decreed is poured out on him.

Cast: **Daniel, Gabriel**

Daniel's Vision of a Man

Daniel 10:1–19

Narrator   In the third year of Cyrus king of Persia, a revelation was given to Daniel (who was called Belteshazzar). Its message was true and it concerned a great war. The understanding of the message came to him in a vision.

Daniel   At that time I, Daniel, mourned for three weeks. I ate no choice food; no meat or wine touched my lips; and I used no lotions at all until the three weeks were over.

On the twenty-fourth day of the first month, as I was standing on the bank of the great river, the Tigris, I looked up and there before me was a man dressed in linen, with a belt of the finest gold around his waist. His body was like chrysolite, his face like lightning, his eyes like flaming torches, his arms and legs like the gleam of burnished bronze, and his voice like the sound of a multitude.

I, Daniel, was the only one who saw the vision; the men with me did not see it, but such terror overwhelmed them that they fled and hid themselves. So I was left alone, gazing at this great vision; I had no strength left, my face turned deathly pale and I was helpless. Then I heard him speaking, and as I listened to him, I fell into a deep sleep, my face to the ground.

A hand touched me and set me trembling on my hands and knees. He said:

Angel Daniel, you who are highly esteemed, consider carefully the words I am about to speak to you, and stand up, for I have now been sent to you.

Daniel And when he said this to me, I stood up trembling. Then he continued:

Angel Do not be afraid, Daniel. Since the first day that you set your mind to gain understanding and to humble yourself before your God, your words were heard, and I have come in response to them. But the prince of the Persian kingdom resisted me twenty-one days. Then Michael, one of the chief princes, came to help me, because I was detained there with the king of Persia. Now I have come to explain to you what will happen to your people in the future, for the vision concerns a time yet to come.

Daniel While he was saying this to me, I bowed with my face toward the ground and was speechless. Then one who looked like a man touched my lips, and I opened my mouth and began to speak. I said to the one standing before me:

Young Daniel I am overcome with anguish because of the vision, my lord, and I am helpless. How can I, your servant, talk with you, my lord? My strength is gone and I can hardly breathe.

Daniel Again the one who looked like a man touched me and gave me strength.

Angel Do not be afraid, O man highly esteemed. Peace! Be strong now; be strong.

Daniel When he spoke to me, I was strengthened and said:

Young Daniel Speak, my lord, since you have given me strength.

Cast: **Narrator, Daniel, Angel, Young Daniel**

The End Times

From Daniel 12:1–13

Daniel At that time Michael, the great prince who protects your people, will arise. There will be a time of distress such as has not happened from the beginning of nations until then. But at that time your people—everyone whose name is found written in the book—will be delivered. Multitudes who sleep in the dust of the earth will awake: some to everlasting life, others to shame and everlasting contempt. Those who are wise will shine like the brightness of the heavens, and those who lead many to righteousness, like the stars for ever and ever. [He said to me:]

The Lord
(voice only) But you, Daniel, close up and seal the words of the scroll until the time of the end. Many will go here and there to increase knowledge.

Daniel	Then I, Daniel, looked, and there before me stood two others, one on this bank of the river and one on the opposite bank. One of them said to the man clothed in linen, who was above the waters of the river:
Angel	How long will it be before these astonishing things are fulfilled?
Daniel	The man clothed in linen, who was above the waters of the river, lifted his right hand and his left hand toward heaven, and I heard him swear by him who lives forever, saying:
Angel	It will be for a time, times and half a time. When the power of the holy people has been finally broken, all these things will be completed.
Daniel	I heard, but I did not understand. So I asked:
Young Daniel	My lord, what will the outcome of all this be?
Daniel	He replied:
Angel	Go your way, Daniel, because the words are closed up and sealed until the time of the end. Many will be purified, made spotless and refined, but the wicked will continue to be wicked. None of the wicked will understand, but those who are wise will understand. . . .
	As for you, go your way till the end. You will rest, and then at the end of the days you will rise to receive your allotted inheritance.

Cast: **Daniel, the Lord** (voice only), **Angel, Young Daniel** (can be the same as Daniel)

Hosea

Hosea's Wife and Children

Hosea 1:1–9 [10–2:1]

Narrator   The word of the LORD that came to Hosea son of Beeri during the reigns of Uzziah, Jotham, Ahaz and Hezekiah, kings of Judah, and during the reign of Jeroboam son of Jehoash king of Israel.

When the LORD began to speak through Hosea, the LORD said to him:

The Lord
(voice only)   Go, take to yourself an adulterous wife and children of unfaithfulness, because the land is guilty of the vilest adultery in departing from the LORD.

Narrator   So he married Gomer daughter of Diblaim, and she conceived and bore him a son. Then the LORD said to Hosea:

The Lord
(voice)   Call him Jezreel, because I will soon punish the house of Jehu for the massacre at Jezreel, and I will put an end to the kingdom of Israel. In that day I will break Israel's bow in the Valley of Jezreel.

Narrator   Gomer conceived again and gave birth to a daughter. Then the LORD said to Hosea:

The Lord
(voice)   Call her Lo-Ruhamah, for I will no longer show love to the house of Israel, that I should at all forgive them. Yet I will show love to the house of Judah; and I will save them—not by bow, sword or battle, or by horses and horsemen, but by the LORD their God.

Narrator   After she had weaned Lo-Ruhamah, Gomer had another son. Then the LORD said:

The Lord
(voice)   Call him Lo-Ammi, for you are not my people, and I am not your God. (PAUSE)

[Narrator   Yet the Israelites will be like the sand on the seashore, which cannot be measured or counted. In the place where it was said to them:

The Lord
(voice)   You are not my people.

Narrator   They will be called—

The Lord
(voice)   [You are] Sons of the living God.

Narrator	The people of Judah and the people of Israel will be reunited, and they will appoint one leader and will come up out of the land, for great will be the day of Jezreel.

Say of your brothers, "My people," and of your sisters, "My loved one."]

Cast: **Narrator** (speaks the words of the Lord), **the Lord** (voice only)

The Lord's Punishment for Unfaithful Israel

Hosea 2:2–13

Prophet	Rebuke your mother, rebuke her,
	    for she is not my wife,
	    and I am not her husband.
	Let her remove the adulterous look from her face
	    and the unfaithfulness from between her breasts.
	Otherwise I will strip her naked
	    and make her as bare as on the day she was born;
	I will make her like a desert,
	    turn her into a parched land,
	    and slay her with thirst.
	I will not show my love to her children,
	    because they are the children of adultery.
	Their mother has been unfaithful
	    and has conceived them in disgrace.
	She said:

Israel	I will go after my lovers,
	    who give me my food and my water,
	    my wool and my linen, my oil and my drink.

Prophet	Therefore I will block her path with thornbushes;
	    I will wall her in so that she cannot find her way.
	She will chase after her lovers but not catch them;
	    she will look for them but not find them.
	Then she will say:

Israel	I will go back to my husband as at first, for then I was better off than now.

Prophet	She has not acknowledged that I was the one
	    who gave her the grain, the new wine and oil,
	who lavished on her the silver and gold—
	    which they used for Baal.
	
	Therefore I will take away my grain when it ripens,
	    and my new wine when it is ready.
	I will take back my wool and my linen,
	    intended to cover her nakedness.

So now I will expose her lewdness
  before the eyes of her lovers;
    no one will take her out of my hands.
I will stop all her celebrations:
  her yearly festivals, her New Moons,
    her Sabbath days—all her appointed feasts.
I will ruin her vines and her fig trees,
  which she said were her pay from her lovers;
I will make them a thicket,
  and wild animals will devour them.
I will punish her for the days
  she burned incense to the Baals;
she decked herself with rings and jewelry,
  and went after her lovers,
    but me she forgot, (PAUSE)

declares the LORD.

Cast: **Prophet, Israel**

The Lord's Love for His People

Hosea 2:14–23

Prophet "Therefore I am now going to allure her;
  I will lead her into the desert
    and speak tenderly to her.
There I will give her back her vineyards,
  and will make the Valley of Achor a door of hope.
There she will sing as in the days of her youth,
  as in the day she came up out of Egypt.

"In that day," declares the LORD,
  "you will call me 'my husband';
    you will no longer call me 'my master.'
I will remove the names of the Baals from her lips;
  no longer will their names be invoked.
In that day I will make a covenant for them
  with the beasts of the field and the birds of the air
    and the creatures that move along the ground.
Bow and sword and battle
  I will abolish from the land,
    so that all may lie down in safety.

Poet "I will betroth you to me forever;
  I will betroth you in righteousness and justice,
    in love and compassion.
I will betroth you in faithfulness,
  and you will acknowledge the LORD.

418

"In that day I will respond,"
  declares the LORD—
"I will respond to the skies,
  and they will respond to the earth;
and the earth will respond to the grain,
  the new wine and oil,
  and they will respond to Jezreel.
I will plant her for myself in the land;
  I will show my love to the one I called 'Not my loved one.'
I will say to those called 'Not my people,' 'You are my people';
  and they will say, 'You are my God.'"

Cast: **Prophet, Poet**

Hosea's Reconciliation with His Wife

Hosea 3:1–5

Hosea   The LORD said to me:

The Lord
 (voice only)   Go, show your love to your wife again, though she is loved by another and is an adulteress. Love her as the LORD loves the Israelites, though they turn to other gods and love the sacred raisin cakes.

Hosea   So I bought her for fifteen shekels of silver and about a homer and a lethek of barley. Then I told her:

Young Hosea   You are to live with me many days; you must not be a prostitute or be intimate with any man, and I will live with you.

Hosea   For the Israelites will live many days without king or prince, without sacrifice or sacred stones, without ephod or idol. Afterward the Israelites will return and seek the LORD their God and David their king. They will come trembling to the LORD and to his blessings in the last days.

Cast: **Hosea, the Lord** (voice only), **Young Hosea**

Judgment against Israel

From Hosea 5:1–15

Hosea   [The Lord says:]

The Lord
 (voice only)   Hear this, you priests!
  Pay attention, you Israelites!
Listen, O royal house!
  This judgment is against you:
You have been a snare at Mizpah,
  a net spread out on Tabor.

419

The rebels are deep in slaughter.
   I will discipline all of them.
I know all about Ephraim;
   Israel is not hidden from me.
Ephraim, you have now turned to prostitution;
   Israel is corrupt.

Hosea   Their deeds do not permit them
        to return to their God.
A spirit of prostitution is in their heart;
   they do not acknowledge the LORD.
Israel's arrogance testifies against them;
   the Israelites, even Ephraim, stumble in their sin;
   Judah also stumbles with them.
When they go with their flocks and herds
   to seek the LORD,
they will not find him;
   he has withdrawn himself from them.
They are unfaithful to the LORD;
   they give birth to illegitimate children.
Now their New Moon festivals
   will devour them and their fields.

Commander 1 Sound the trumpet in Gibeah.

Commander 2 The horn in Ramah.

Commander 1 Raise the battle cry in Beth Aven.

Commander 2 Lead on, O Benjamin.

Hosea   Ephraim will be laid waste
        on the day of reckoning.
Among the tribes of Israel
   I proclaim what is certain. . . .

The Lord
  (voice)   Then I will go back to my place
        until they admit their guilt.
And they will seek my face;
   in their misery they will earnestly seek me.

Cast: **Hosea, the Lord** (voice only), **Commander 1, Commander 2**

Israel Unrepentant

Hosea 6:1–7:2

Prophet   [The people say:]

**Persons 1
and 2**   Come, let us return to the LORD.

Person 1   He has torn us to pieces
but he will heal us.

Person 2   He has injured us
but he will bind up our wounds.

Person 1   After two days he will revive us;
on the third day he will restore us,
that we may live in his presence.

Person 2   Let us acknowledge the LORD;
let us press on to acknowledge him.
As surely as the sun rises,
he will appear;
he will come to us like the winter rains,
like the spring rains that water the earth.

[Prophet   [But the Lord says:]]

The Lord
(voice only) What can I do with you, Ephraim?
What can I do with you, Judah?
Your love is like the morning mist,
like the early dew that disappears.
Therefore I cut you in pieces with my prophets,
I killed you with the words of my mouth;
my judgments flashed like lightning upon you.
For I desire mercy, not sacrifice,
and acknowledgment of God rather than burnt offerings.
Like Adam, they have broken the covenant—
they were unfaithful to me there.
Gilead is a city of wicked men,
stained with footprints of blood.
As marauders lie in ambush for a man,
so do bands of priests;
they murder on the road to Shechem,
committing shameful crimes.
I have seen a horrible thing
in the house of Israel.
There Ephraim is given to prostitution
and Israel is defiled.

Also for you, Judah,
a harvest is appointed.

Whenever I would restore the fortunes of my people,
whenever I would heal Israel,
the sins of Ephraim are exposed
and the crimes of Samaria revealed.
They practice deceit,
thieves break into houses,
bandits rob in the streets;

but they do not realize
    that I remember all their evil deeds.
Their sins engulf them;
    they are always before me.

Cast: **Prophet, Person 1, Person 2** (can be the same as Person 1), **the Lord** (voice only)

The Prophet Speaks about Israel

Hosea 10:1–8

Prophet   Israel was a spreading vine;
    he brought forth fruit for himself.
As his fruit increased,
    he built more altars;
as his land prospered,
    he adorned his sacred stones.
Their heart is deceitful,
    and now they must bear their guilt.
The LORD will demolish their altars
    and destroy their sacred stones.

Then they will say:

Person 1   We have no king
    because we did not revere the LORD.

Person 2   But even if we had a king,
    what could he do for us?

Prophet   They make many promises,
    take false oaths
    and make agreements;
therefore lawsuits spring up
    like poisonous weeds in a plowed field.
The people who live in Samaria fear
    for the calf-idol of Beth Aven.
Its people will mourn over it,
    and so will its idolatrous priests,
those who had rejoiced over its splendor,
    because it is taken from them into exile.
It will be carried to Assyria
    as tribute for the great king.
Ephraim will be disgraced;
    Israel will be ashamed of its wooden idols.
Samaria and its king will float away
    like a twig on the surface of the waters.
The high places of wickedness will be destroyed—
    it is the sin of Israel.
Thorns and thistles will grow up

and cover their altars.
Then they will say to the mountains:

**Persons 1
and 2**   Cover us!

Prophet   And to the hills:

**Persons 1
and 2**   Fall on us!

Cast: **Prophet, Person 1, Person 2**

God's Love for Israel

Hosea 11:1–9

Voice 1   When Israel was a child, I loved him,
and out of Egypt I called my son.

Voice 2   But the more I called Israel,
the further they went from me.
They sacrificed to the Baals
and they burned incense to images.

Voice 1   It was I who taught Ephraim to walk,
taking them by the arms.

Voice 2   But they did not realize
it was I who healed them.

Voice 1   I led them with cords of human kindness,
with ties of love;
I lifted the yoke from their neck
and bent down to feed them.

Voice 2   Will they not return to Egypt
and will not Assyria rule over them
because they refuse to repent?
Swords will flash in their cities,
will destroy the bars of their gates
and put an end to their plans.
My people are determined to turn from me.
Even if they call to the Most High,
he will by no means exalt them.

Voice 1   How can I give you up, Ephraim?
How can I hand you over, Israel?
How can I treat you like Admah?
How can I make you like Zeboiim?
My heart is changed within me;
all my compassion is aroused.

> I will not carry out my fierce anger,
>> nor will I turn and devastate Ephraim.
> For I am God, and not man—
>> the Holy One among you.
> I will not come in wrath.

Cast: **Voice 1** (caring), **Voice 2** (warning)

Further Words of Judgment

Hosea 12:7–14

Prophet   [The Lord says:]

The Lord
(voice only) The merchant uses dishonest scales;
>> he loves to defraud.
> Ephraim boasts:

Israelites 1
and 2   [We are] very rich.

Israelite 1   [We] have become wealthy.

Israelite 2   With all [our] wealth they will not find in [us]
>> any iniquity or sin.

The Lord
(voice)   I am the LORD your God,
>> ⌞who brought you⌟ out of Egypt;
> I will make you live in tents again,
>> as in the days of your appointed feasts.
> I spoke to the prophets,
>> gave them many visions
>> and told parables through them.

> Is Gilead wicked?
>> Its people are worthless!
> Do they sacrifice bulls in Gilgal?
>> Their altars will be like piles of stones
>> on a plowed field.

Prophet   Jacob fled to the country of Aram;
>> Israel served to get a wife,
>> and to pay for her he tended sheep.
> The LORD used a prophet to bring Israel up from Egypt,
>> by a prophet he cared for him.
> But Ephraim has bitterly provoked him to anger;

424

> his Lord will leave upon him the guilt of his bloodshed
> and will repay him for his contempt.

Cast: **Prophet**, the **Lord** (voice only), **Israelite 1**, **Israelite 2** (can be the same as Israelite 1)

The Lord's Anger against Israel

Hosea 13:1–9

Prophet When Ephraim spoke, men trembled;
> he was exalted in Israel.
> But he became guilty of Baal worship and died.
> Now they sin more and more;
> they make idols for themselves from their silver,
> cleverly fashioned images,
> all of them the work of craftsmen.
> It is said of these people:

Person They offer human sacrifice
> and kiss the calf-idols

Prophet Therefore they will be like the morning mist,
> like the early dew that disappears,
> like chaff swirling from a threshing floor,
> like smoke escaping through a window. (PAUSE)

The Lord
(voice only) But I am the LORD your God,
> ⌐who brought you⌐ out of Egypt.
> You shall acknowledge no God but me,
> no Savior except me.
> I cared for you in the desert,
> in the land of burning heat.
> When I fed them, they were satisfied;
> when they were satisfied, they became proud;
> then they forgot me.
> So I will come upon them like a lion,
> like a leopard I will lurk by the path.
> Like a bear robbed of her cubs,
> I will attack them and rip them open.
> Like a lion I will devour them;
> a wild animal will tear them apart.

> You are destroyed, O Israel,
> because you are against me, against your helper.

Cast: **Prophet, Person, the Lord** (voice only)

Repentance to Bring Blessing

Hosea 14:1–9

Prophet   Return, O Israel, to the LORD your God.
    Your sins have been your downfall!
Take words with you
    and return to the LORD.
Say to him:

Israelite 1   Forgive all our sins
and receive us graciously,
    that we may offer the fruit of our lips.

Israelite 2   Assyria cannot save us;
    we will not mount war-horses.

Israelite 1   We will never again say "Our gods"
    to what our own hands have made.

Israelite 2   For in you the fatherless find compassion.

Prophet   [The Lord says:]

The Lord
  (voice only) I will heal their waywardness
    and love them freely,
    for my anger has turned away from them.
I will be like the dew to Israel;
    he will blossom like a lily.
Like a cedar of Lebanon
    he will send down his roots;
    his young shoots will grow.
His splendor will be like an olive tree,
    his fragrance like a cedar of Lebanon.
Men will dwell again in his shade.
    He will flourish like the grain.
He will blossom like a vine,
    and his fame will be like the wine from Lebanon.
O Ephraim, what more have I to do with idols?
    I will answer him and care for him.
I am like a green pine tree;
    your fruitfulness comes from me.

Prophet   Who is wise? He will realize these things.
    Who is discerning? He will understand them.
The ways of the LORD are right;
    the righteous walk in them,
    but the rebellious stumble in them.

Cast: **Prophet, Israelite 1, Israelite 2** (can be the same as Israelite 1), **the Lord** (voice only)

Joel

The People Mourn the Destruction of the Crops

Joel 1:1–20

Voice 1	The word of the LORD that came to Joel son of Pethuel.
Voice 2	Hear this, you elders;

Voice 2
Hear this, you elders;
   listen, all who live in the land.
Has anything like this ever happened in your days
   or in the days of your forefathers?
Tell it to your children,
   and let your children tell it to their children,
   and their children to the next generation.
What the locust swarm has left
   the great locusts have eaten;
what the great locusts have left
   the young locusts have eaten;
what the young locusts have left
   other locusts have eaten.

Voice 3
Wake up, you drunkards, and weep!
   Wail, all you drinkers of wine;
wail because of the new wine,
   for it has been snatched from your lips.
A nation has invaded my land,
   powerful and without number;
it has the teeth of a lion,
   the fangs of a lioness.
It has laid waste my vines
   and ruined my fig trees.
It has stripped off their bark
   and thrown it away,
   leaving their branches white.

Voice 1
Mourn like a virgin in sackcloth
   grieving for the husband of her youth.
Grain offerings and drink offerings
   are cut off from the house of the LORD.
The priests are in mourning,
   those who minister before the LORD.

Voice 2
The fields are ruined,
   the ground is dried up;
the grain is destroyed,
   the new wine is dried up,
   the oil fails.
Despair, you farmers,

wail, you vine growers;
    grieve for the wheat and the barley,
        because the harvest of the field is destroyed.
    The vine is dried up
        and the fig tree is withered;
    the pomegranate, the palm and the apple tree—
        all the trees of the field—are dried up.
    Surely the joy of mankind
        is withered away.

Voice 3   Put on sackcloth, O priests, and mourn;
                 wail, you who minister before the altar.
             Come, spend the night in sackcloth,
                 you who minister before my God;
             for the grain offerings and drink offerings
                 are withheld from the house of your God.
             Declare a holy fast;
                 call a sacred assembly.
             Summon the elders
                 and all who live in the land
             to the house of the LORD your God,
                 and cry out to the LORD.

             Alas for that day!
                 For the day of the LORD is near;
                 it will come like destruction from the Almighty.

Voice 1   Has not the food been cut off
                 before our very eyes—
             joy and gladness
                 from the house of our God?
             The seeds are shriveled
                 beneath the clods.
             The storehouses are in ruins,
                 the granaries have been broken down,
                 for the grain has dried up.
             How the cattle moan!
                 The herds mill about
             because they have no pasture;
                 even the flocks of sheep are suffering.

Voice 2   To you, O LORD, I call,
                 for fire has devoured the open pastures
                 and flames have burned up all the trees of the field.
             Even the wild animals pant for you;
                 the streams of water have dried up
                 and fire has devoured the open pastures.

Cast: **Voice 1, Voice 2, Voice 3**

An Army of Locusts

Joel 2:1–11

Voices 1 and 2	Blow the trumpet in Zion.
Voice 3	Sound the alarm on my holy hill.
Voice 1	Let all who live in the land tremble.
Voice 2	For the day of the LORD is coming.
Voice 3	It is close at hand— a day of darkness and gloom.
Voices 1 and 2	A day of clouds and blackness.
Voice 1	Like dawn spreading across the mountains a large and mighty army comes.
Voice 2	Such as never was of old nor ever will be in ages to come.
Voice 3	Before them fire devours, behind them a flame blazes.
Voice 1	Before them the land is like the garden of Eden.
Voice 2	Behind them, a desert waste— nothing escapes them.
Voice 3	They have the appearance of horses.
Voice 1	They gallop along like cavalry.
Voice 2	With a noise like that of chariots.
Voice 3	They leap over the mountaintops, like a crackling fire consuming stubble.
Voice 1	Like a mighty army drawn up for battle.
Voice 2	At the sight of them, nations are in anguish—
Voices 1 and 3	Every face turns pale.
Voice 3	They charge like warriors.
Voice 1	They scale walls like soldiers.
Voice 3	They all march in line, not swerving from their course.
Voice 1	They do not jostle each other; each marches straight ahead.

429

Voice 2	They plunge through defenses without breaking ranks.
Voice 1	They rush upon the city.
Voice 2	They run along the wall.
Voice 1	They climb into the houses.
Voice 2	Like thieves they enter through the windows.
Voices 1 and 2	Before them the earth shakes.
Voices 2 and 3	The sky trembles.
Voice 2	The sun and moon are darkened.
Voice 3	And the stars no longer shine.
Voice 1	The LORD thunders at the head of his army.
Voice 2	His forces are beyond number, and mighty are those who obey his command.
Voices 1–3	The day of the LORD is great; it is dreadful.
Voice 3	Who can endure it?

Cast: **Voice 1, Voice 2, Voice 3**

Rend Your Heart

Joel 2:12–17

Joel	[The Lord says:]
The Lord (voice only)	Even now . . . return to me with all your heart, with fasting and weeping and mourning.
	Rend your heart and not your garments.
Joel	Return to the LORD your God, for he is gracious and compassionate, slow to anger and abounding in love, and he relents from sending calamity. Who knows? He may turn and have pity and leave behind a blessing—

	grain offerings and drink offerings for the LORD your God.
(calling)	Blow the trumpet in Zion, declare a holy fast, call a sacred assembly. Gather the people, consecrate the assembly; bring together the elders, gather the children, those nursing at the breast. Let the bridegroom leave his room and the bride her chamber. Let the priests, who minister before the LORD, weep between the temple porch and the altar. Let them say:
Priest 1	Spare your people, O LORD.
Priest 2	Do not make your inheritance an object of scorn, a byword among the nations. Why should they say among the peoples—
Priests 1 and 2	Where is their God?

Cast: **Joel**, **the Lord** (voice only), **Priest 1**, **Priest 2** (can be the same as Priest 1)

The Lord's Answer

Joel 2:18–27

Joel	Then the LORD will be jealous for his land and take pity on his people.
	The LORD will reply to them:
The Lord (voice only)	I am sending you grain, new wine and oil, enough to satisfy you fully; never again will I make you an object of scorn to the nations.
	I will drive the northern army far from you, pushing it into a parched and barren land, with its front columns going into the eastern sea and those in the rear into the western sea. And its stench will go up; its smell will rise.
	Surely he has done great things.

Joel	Be not afraid, O land;
	    be glad and rejoice.
	Surely the LORD has done great things.
	    Be not afraid, O wild animals,
	        for the open pastures are becoming green.
	The trees are bearing their fruit;
	    the fig tree and the vine yield their riches.
	Be glad, O people of Zion,
	    rejoice in the LORD your God,
	for he has given you
	    the autumn rains in righteousness.
	He sends you abundant showers,
	    both autumn and spring rains, as before.

The Lord
(voice)   The threshing floors will be filled with grain;
        the vats will overflow with new wine and oil.

        I will repay you for the years the locusts have eaten—
        the great locust and the young locust,
        the other locusts and the locust swarm—
    my great army that I sent among you.

Joel   You will have plenty to eat, until you are full,
        and you will praise the name of the LORD your God,
        who has worked wonders for you;
    never again will my people be shamed.

The Lord
(voice)   Then you will know that I am in Israel,
        that I am the LORD your God,
        and that there is no other;
    never again will my people be shamed.

Cast: **Joel, the Lord** (voice only)

The Day of the Lord

Joel 2:28–32

The Lord
(voice only) And afterward,
        I will pour out my Spirit on all people.
    Your sons and daughters will prophesy,
        your old men will dream dreams,
        your young men will see visions.
    Even on my servants, both men and women,
        I will pour out my Spirit in those days. (PAUSE)
    I will show wonders in the heavens

and on the earth,
blood and fire and billows of smoke.

Joel	The sun will be turned to darkness
	and the moon to blood
	before the coming of the great and dreadful day of the LORD.
	And everyone who calls
	on the name of the LORD will be saved.

[For, as the LORD has said:]

The Lord (voice)	On Mount Zion and in Jerusalem
	there will be deliverance. . . .
Joel	Among the survivors
	whom the LORD calls.

Cast: **The Lord** (voice only), **Joel**

The Nations Judged

Joel 3:9–15

The Lord (voice only)	Proclaim this among the nations:
Heralds 1 and 2	Prepare for war!
Herald 2	Rouse the warriors!
	Let all the fighting men draw near and attack.
Herald 1	Beat your plowshares into swords
	and your pruning hooks into spears.
Herald 2	Let the weakling say,
	"I am strong!"
Herald 1	Come quickly, all you nations from every side,
	and assemble there.
Joel	Bring down your warriors, O LORD!
The Lord (voice)	Let the nations be roused;
	let them advance into the Valley of Jehoshaphat,
	for there I will sit
	to judge all the nations on every side.
	Swing the sickle,
	for the harvest is ripe.
	Come, trample the grapes,

for the winepress is full
and the vats overflow—
so great is their wickedness!

Joel   Multitudes, multitudes
in the valley of decision!
For the day of the Lord is near
in the valley of decision.
The sun and moon will be darkened,
and the stars no longer shine.

Cast: **The Lord** (voice only), **Herald 1**, **Herald 2** (Heralds 1 and 2 can be the same as the Lord; they speak the Lord's words), **Joel**

Amos

God's Judgment

Amos 1:1–2:8

Narrator　　The words of Amos, one of the shepherds of Tekoa—what he saw concerning Israel two years before the earthquake, when Uzziah was king of Judah and Jeroboam son of Jehoash was king of Israel. He said:

Amos　　The LORD roars from Zion
　　　and thunders from Jerusalem;
　　the pastures of the shepherds dry up,
　　　and the top of Carmel withers.

(with
flourish)　　This is what the LORD says:

The Lord
(voice only) For three sins of Damascus,
　　　　even for four, I will not turn back ⌐my wrath⌐.
　　Because she threshed Gilead
　　　with sledges having iron teeth,
　　I will send fire upon the house of Hazael
　　　that will consume the fortresses of Ben-Hadad.
　　I will break down the gate of Damascus;
　　　I will destroy the king who is in the Valley of Aven
　　and the one who holds the scepter in Beth Eden.
　　　The people of Aram will go into exile to Kir. . . .

Amos
(with
flourish)　　This is what the LORD says:

The Lord
(voice)　　For three sins of Gaza,
　　　　even for four, I will not turn back ⌐my wrath⌐.
　　Because she took captive whole communities
　　　and sold them to Edom,
　　I will send fire upon the walls of Gaza
　　　that will consume her fortresses.
　　I will destroy the king of Ashdod
　　　and the one who holds the scepter in Ashkelon.
　　I will turn my hand against Ekron,
　　　till the last of the Philistines is dead. . . .

Amos
(with
flourish)　　This is what the LORD says:

The Lord
  (voice)

For three sins of Tyre,
  even for four, I will not turn back ˻my wrath˼.
Because she sold whole communities of captives to Edom,
  disregarding a treaty of brotherhood,
I will send fire upon the walls of Tyre
  that will consume her fortresses.

Amos
  (with
  flourish)

This is what the Lord says:

The Lord
  (voice)

For three sins of Edom,
  even for four, I will not turn back ˻my wrath˼.
Because he pursued his brother with a sword,
  stifling all compassion,
because his anger raged continually
  and his fury flamed unchecked,
I will send fire upon Teman
  that will consume the fortresses of Bozrah.

Amos
  (with
  flourish)

This is what the Lord says:

The Lord
  (voice)

For three sins of Ammon,
  even for four, I will not turn back ˻my wrath˼.
Because he ripped open the pregnant women of Gilead
  in order to extend his borders,
I will set fire to the walls of Rabbah
  that will consume her fortresses
amid war cries on the day of battle,
  amid violent winds on a stormy day.
Her king will go into exile,
  he and his officials together. . . .

Amos
  (with
  flourish)

This is what the Lord says:

The Lord
  (voice)

For three sins of Moab,
  even for four, I will not turn back ˻my wrath˼.
Because he burned, as if to lime,
  the bones of Edom's king,
I will send fire upon Moab
  that will consume the fortresses of Kerioth.
Moab will go down in great tumult
  amid war cries and the blast of the trumpet.

436

I will destroy her ruler
  and kill all her officials with him. . . .

Amos

(with
flourish)   This is what the LORD says:

The Lord

(voice)   For three sins of Judah,
  even for four, I will not turn back ⌐my wrath⌐.
Because they have rejected the law of the LORD
  and have not kept his decrees,
because they have been led astray by false gods,
  the gods their ancestors followed,
I will send fire upon Judah
  that will consume the fortresses of Jerusalem.

Amos

(with
flourish)   This is what the LORD says:

The Lord

(voice)   For three sins of Israel,
  even for four, I will not turn back ⌐my wrath⌐.
They sell the righteous for silver,
  and the needy for a pair of sandals.
They trample on the heads of the poor
  as upon the dust of the ground
  and deny justice to the oppressed.
Father and son use the same girl
  and so profane my holy name.
They lie down beside every altar
  on garments taken in pledge.
In the house of their god
  they drink wine taken as fines.

Cast: **Narrator, Amos, the Lord** (voice only)

Judgment on Israel

Amos 2:9–3:2

Amos

(with
flourish)   [The LORD says:]

The Lord

(voice only) I destroyed the Amorite before them,
  though he was tall as the cedars
  and strong as the oaks.

I destroyed his fruit above
  and his roots below.

I brought you up out of Egypt,
  and I led you forty years in the desert
  to give you the land of the Amorites.
I also raised up prophets from among your sons
  and Nazirites from among your young men.
Is this not true, people of Israel? . . .
But you made the Nazirites drink wine
  and commanded the prophets not to prophesy.

Now then, I will crush you
  as a cart crushes when loaded with grain.
The swift will not escape,
  the strong will not muster their strength,
  and the warrior will not save his life.
The archer will not stand his ground,
  the fleet-footed soldier will not get away,
  and the horseman will not save his life.
Even the bravest warriors
  will flee naked on that day. . . .

Amos   Hear this word the LORD has spoken against you, O people of Israel—
against the whole family I brought up out of Egypt:

You only have I chosen
  of all the families of the earth;
therefore I will punish you
  for all your sins.

Cast: **Amos, the Lord** (voice only)

The Prophet's Task

Amos 3:3–8

Voice 1   Do two walk together
  unless they have agreed to do so?

Voice 2   Does a lion roar in the thicket
  when he has no prey?

Voice 1   Does he growl in his den
  when he has caught nothing?

Voice 2   Does a bird fall into a trap on the ground
  where no snare has been set?

Voice 1   Does a trap spring up from the earth
  when there is nothing to catch?

Voice 2   When a trumpet sounds in a city,
    do not the people tremble?

Voice 1   When disaster comes to a city,
    has not the LORD caused it?

Voice 2   Surely the Sovereign LORD does nothing
    without revealing his plan
    to his servants the prophets.

Voice 1   The lion has roared—
    who will not fear?
    The Sovereign LORD has spoken—
    who can but prophesy?

Cast: **Voice 1, Voice 2**

The Doom of Samaria

Amos 3:9–4:3

Amos   Proclaim to the fortresses of Ashdod
    and to the fortresses of Egypt:

Herald   Assemble yourselves on the mountains of Samaria;
    see the great unrest within her
    and the oppression among her people.

Amos
(with
flourish)   They do not know how to do right . . .
    who hoard plunder and loot in their fortresses.

    Therefore this is what the Sovereign LORD says:

The Lord
(voice only)   An enemy will overrun the land;
    he will pull down your strongholds
    and plunder your fortresses.

Amos
(with
flourish)   This is what the LORD says:

The Lord
(voice)   As a shepherd saves from the lion's mouth
    only two leg bones or a piece of an ear,
    so will the Israelites be saved,
  those who sit in Samaria
    on the edge of their beds
    and in Damascus on their couches.

    Hear this and testify against the house of Jacob. . . .

Amos
(with
flourish)   [This is what the LORD says:]

The Lord
(voice)   On the day I punish Israel for her sins,
     I will destroy the altars of Bethel;
the horns of the altar will be cut off
     and fall to the ground.
I will tear down the winter house
     along with the summer house;
the houses adorned with ivory will be destroyed
     and the mansions will be demolished. . . .

Amos   Hear this word, you cows of Bashan on Mount Samaria,
     you women who oppress the poor and crush the needy
     and say to your husbands, "Bring us some drinks!"
The Sovereign LORD has sworn by his holiness:

The Lord
(voice)   The time will surely come
when you will be taken away with hooks,
     the last of you with fishhooks.
You will each go straight out
     through breaks in the wall,
     and you will be cast out toward Harmon. . . .

Cast: **Amos, Herald** (can be the same as Amos), **the Lord** (voice only)

Israel's Failure to Learn

Amos 4:4–13

Amos   [The Sovereign Lord says:]

Voice 1   Go to Bethel and sin;
     go to Gilgal and sin yet more.

Voice 2   Bring your sacrifices every morning,
     your tithes every three years.

Voice 3   Burn leavened bread as a thank offering
     and brag about your freewill offerings—
boast about them, you Israelites,
     for this is what you love to do. . . .

Voice 1   I gave you empty stomachs in every city
     and lack of bread in every town,
     yet you have not returned to me. . . .

Voice 2	I also withheld rain from you when the harvest was still three months away.
Voice 3	I sent rain on one town, but withheld it from another. One field had rain; another had none and dried up. People staggered from town to town for water but did not get enough to drink—
Voice 1	Yet you have not returned to me. . . .
Voice 2	Many times I struck your gardens and vineyards, I struck them with blight and mildew. Locusts devoured your fig and olive trees, yet you have not returned to me. . . .
Voice 3	I sent plagues among you as I did to Egypt. I killed your young men with the sword, along with your captured horses. I filled your nostrils with the stench of your camps, yet you have not returned to me. . . .
Voice 1	I overthrew some of you as I overthrew Sodom and Gomorrah. You were like a burning stick snatched from the fire, yet you have not returned to me. . . .
Amos	[The Lord says:]
Voices 1–3	Therefore this is what I will do to you, Israel, and because I will do this to you, prepare to meet your God, O Israel.
Amos (slowly)	He who forms the mountains, creates the wind, and reveals his thoughts to man, he who turns dawn to darkness, and treads the high places of the earth— the Lord God Almighty is his name.

Cast: **Amos, Voice 1, Voice 2, Voice 3** (Voices speak words of the Lord)

A Lament and Call to Repentance

Amos 5:1–9

Amos	Hear this word, O house of Israel, this lament I take up concerning you:

Singer	Fallen is Virgin Israel,
	    never to rise again,
	deserted in her own land,
	    with no one to lift her up.

Amos (with flourish)	This is what the Sovereign LORD says:

The Lord
(voice only)
	The city that marches out a thousand strong for Israel
	    will have only a hundred left;
	the town that marches out a hundred strong
	    will have only ten left.

Amos	This is what the LORD says to the house of Israel:

The Lord
(voice)
	Seek me and live;
	    do not seek Bethel,
	do not go to Gilgal,
	    do not journey to Beersheba.
	For Gilgal will surely go into exile,
	    and Bethel will be reduced to nothing.

Amos	Seek the LORD and live,
	    or he will sweep through the house of Joseph like a fire;
	it will devour,
	    and Bethel will have no one to quench it.
	
	You who turn justice into bitterness
	    and cast righteousness to the ground.

Singer	(He who made the Pleiades and Orion,
	    who turns blackness into dawn
	    and darkens day into night,
	who calls for the waters of the sea
	    and pours them out over the face of the land—
	    the LORD is his name—
	he flashes destruction on the stronghold
	    and brings the fortified city to ruin.)

Cast: **Amos, Singer, the Lord** (voice only)

The Day of the Lord

Amos 5:10–27

Amos	You hate the one who reproves in court and despise him who tells the truth.

You trample on the poor
   and force him to give you grain.
Therefore, though you have built stone mansions,
   you will not live in them;
though you have planted lush vineyards,
   you will not drink their wine.
For I know how many are your offenses
   and how great your sins.

You oppress the righteous and take bribes
   and you deprive the poor of justice in the courts.
Therefore the prudent man keeps quiet in such times,
   for the times are evil.

Seek good, not evil,
   that you may live.
Then the Lord God Almighty will be with you,
   just as you say he is.
Hate evil, love good;
   maintain justice in the courts.
Perhaps the Lord God Almighty will have mercy
   on the remnant of Joseph.

Therefore this is what the Lord, the Lord God Almighty, says:

The Lord
(voice only) There will be wailing in all the streets
   and cries of anguish in every public square.
The farmers will be summoned to weep
   and the mourners to wail.
There will be wailing in all the vineyards,
   for I will pass through your midst. . . .

Amos Woe to you who long
   for the day of the Lord!
Why do you long for the day of the Lord?
   That day will be darkness, not light.
It will be as though a man fled from a lion
   only to meet a bear,
as though he entered his house
   and rested his hand on the wall
   only to have a snake bite him.
Will not the day of the Lord be darkness, not light—
   pitch-dark, without a ray of brightness?

(with
flourish) [The Lord says:]

The Lord
(voice) I hate, I despise your religious feasts;
   I cannot stand your assemblies.
Even though you bring me burnt offerings and grain offerings,

443

I will not accept them.
Though you bring choice fellowship offerings,
   I will have no regard for them.
Away with the noise of your songs!
   I will not listen to the music of your harps.
But let justice roll on like a river,
   righteousness like a never-failing stream!

Did you bring me sacrifices and offerings
   forty years in the desert, O house of Israel?
You have lifted up the shrine of your king,
   the pedestal of your idols,
   the star of your god—
which you made for yourselves.
Therefore I will send you into exile beyond Damascus.

Amos
(with flourish) Says the LORD, whose name is God Almighty.

Cast: **Amos, the Lord** (voice only)

Woe to the Complacent

Amos 6:1–14

Amos   Woe to you who are complacent in Zion,
   and to you who feel secure on Mount Samaria,
you notable men of the foremost nation,
   to whom the people of Israel come!
Go to Calneh and look at it;
   go from there to great Hamath,
   and then go down to Gath in Philistia.
Are they better off than your two kingdoms?
   Is their land larger than yours?
You put off the evil day
   and bring near a reign of terror.
You lie on beds inlaid with ivory
   and lounge on your couches.
You dine on choice lambs
   and fattened calves.
You strum away on your harps like David
   and improvise on musical instruments.
You drink wine by the bowlful
   and use the finest lotions,
   but you do not grieve over the ruin of Joseph.
Therefore you will be among the first to go into exile;
   your feasting and lounging will end.

444

(deliberately)	The Sovereign LORD has sworn by himself—the LORD God Almighty declares:

The Lord (voice only)	I abhor the pride of Jacob
	    and detest his fortresses;
	I will deliver up the city
	    and everything in it.

Amos	If ten men are left in one house, they too will die. And if a relative who is to burn the bodies comes to carry them out of the house and asks anyone still hiding there:
Voice 1	Is anyone with you?
[Amos	[A voice will answer:]]
Voice 2	No.
[Amos	[Then a voice will answer:]]
Voice 1	Hush! We must not mention the name of the LORD.

Amos	For the LORD has given the command,
	    and he will smash the great house into pieces
	and the small house into bits.
	
	Do horses run on the rocky crags?
	    Does one plow there with oxen?
	But you have turned justice into poison
	    and the fruit of righteousness into bitterness—
	you who rejoice in the conquest of Lo Debar
	    and say, "Did we not take Karnaim by our own strength?"

Amos (with flourish)	For the LORD God Almighty declares:
The Lord (voice)	I will stir up a nation against you, O house of Israel, that will oppress you all the way from Lebo Hamath to the valley of the Arabah.

Cast: **Amos**, **the Lord** (voice only), **Voice 1**, **Voice 2**

Locusts, Fire, and a Plumb Line

Amos 7:1–9

Amos	This is what the Sovereign LORD showed me: He was preparing swarms of locusts after the king's share had been harvested and just as the sec-

ond crop was coming up. When they had stripped the land clean, I cried out:

Young Amos	Sovereign Lord, forgive! How can Jacob survive? He is so small!
Amos	So the Lord relented.
The Lord (voice only)	This will not happen. . . .
Amos	This is what the Sovereign Lord showed me: The Sovereign Lord was calling for judgment by fire; it dried up the great deep and devoured the land. Then I cried out:
Young Amos	Sovereign Lord, I beg you, stop! How can Jacob survive? He is so small!
Amos	So the Lord relented.
The Lord (voice)	This will not happen either. . . .
Amos	This is what he showed me: The Lord was standing by a wall that had been built true to plumb, with a plumb line in his hand. And the Lord asked me:
The Lord (voice)	What do you see, Amos?
Young Amos	A plumb line.
Amos	Then the Lord said:
The Lord (voice)	Look, I am setting a plumb line among my people Israel; I will spare them no longer.

	The high places of Isaac will be destroyed
	   and the sanctuaries of Israel will be ruined;
	   with my sword I will rise against the house of Jeroboam.

Cast: **Amos, Young Amos, the Lord** (voice only)

Amos and Amaziah

Amos 7:10–17

Narrator	Then Amaziah the priest of Bethel sent a message to Jeroboam king of Israel:
Amaziah (as if writing a letter)	Amos is raising a conspiracy against you in the very heart of Israel. The land cannot bear all his words.

For this is what Amos is saying:

"Jeroboam will die by the sword,
    and Israel will surely go into exile,
    away from their native land."

Narrator Then Amaziah said to Amos:

Amaziah
(to Amos) Get out, you seer! Go back to the land of Judah. Earn your bread there and do your prophesying there. Don't prophesy anymore at Bethel, because this is the king's sanctuary and the temple of the kingdom.

Narrator Amos answered Amaziah:

Amos I was neither a prophet nor a prophet's son, but I was a shepherd, and I also took care of sycamore-fig trees. But the Lord took me from tending the flock and said to me, "Go, prophesy to my people Israel." Now then, hear the word of the Lord. You say,

"Do not prophesy against Israel,
    and stop preaching against the house of Isaac."

Therefore this is what the Lord says:

"Your wife will become a prostitute in the city,
    and your sons and daughters will fall by the sword.
Your land will be measured and divided up,
    and you yourself will die in a pagan country.
And Israel will certainly go into exile,
    away from their native land."

Cast: **Narrator, Amaziah, Amos**

A Vision of a Basket of Fruit

Amos 8:1–3

Amos This is what the Sovereign Lord showed me: a basket of ripe fruit.

The Lord
(voice only) What do you see, Amos?

Young Amos A basket of ripe fruit.

Amos Then the Lord said to me:

The Lord
(voice) The time is ripe for my people Israel; I will spare them no longer.

In that day . . . the songs in the temple will turn to wailing. Many, many bodies—flung everywhere! Silence!

Cast: **Amos, the Lord** (voice only), **Young Amos**

Israel's Doom

Amos 8:4–14

Amos   Hear this, you who trample the needy
      and do away with the poor of the land,

       saying:

Israelite 1 When will the New Moon be over
      that we may sell grain?

Israelite 2 And the Sabbath be ended
      that we may market wheat?

Israelite 1 Skimping the measure,
      boosting the price
      and cheating with dishonest scales.

Israelite 2 Buying the poor with silver
      and the needy for a pair of sandals.

Israelite 1 Selling even the sweepings with the wheat.

Amos
(with
flourish) The LORD has sworn by the Pride of Jacob:

The Lord
(voice only) I will never forget anything they have done.

      Will not the land tremble for this,
       and all who live in it mourn?
      The whole land will rise like the Nile;
       it will be stirred up and then sink
       like the river of Egypt.

      In that day . . .

      I will make the sun go down at noon
       and darken the earth in broad daylight.
      I will turn your religious feasts into mourning
       and all your singing into weeping.
      I will make all of you wear sackcloth
       and shave your heads.
      I will make that time like mourning for an only son
       and the end of it like a bitter day.

      The days are coming . . .
       when I will send a famine through the land—
      not a famine of food or a thirst for water,
       but a famine of hearing the words of the LORD.
      Men will stagger from sea to sea
       and wander from north to east,

searching for the word of the Lord,
  but they will not find it.

In that day

the lovely young women and strong young men
  will faint because of thirst.
They who swear by the shame of Samaria,
  or say:

Israelite 1   As surely as your god lives, O Dan,
  or

Israelite 2   As surely as the god of Beersheba lives—

The Lord
  (voice)   they will fall,
  never to rise again.

Cast: **Amos**, **Israelite 1**, **Israelite 2** (can be the same as Israelite 1), **the Lord** (voice only)

Israel to Be Destroyed

Amos 9:1–10

Amos
  (with
  flourish)   I saw the Lord standing by the altar—and he said:

The Lord
  (voice only)   Strike the tops of the pillars
  so that the thresholds shake.
Bring them down on the heads of all the people;
  those who are left I will kill with the sword.
Not one will get away,
  none will escape.
Though they dig down to the depths of the grave,
  from there my hand will take them.
Though they climb up to the heavens,
  from there I will bring them down.
Though they hide themselves on the top of Carmel,
  there I will hunt them down and seize them.
Though they hide from me at the bottom of the sea,
  there I will command the serpent to bite them.
Though they are driven into exile by their enemies,
  there I will command the sword to slay them.
I will fix my eyes upon them
  for evil and not for good.

Singer 1   The Lord, the Lord Almighty,
  he who touches the earth and it melts,
  and all who live in it mourn—

the whole land rises like the Nile,
then sinks like the river of Egypt.

Singer 2   [The Lord] builds his lofty palace in the heavens
and sets its foundation on the earth,
who calls for the waters of the sea
and pours them out over the face of the land—

**Singers
1** and **2**   The LORD is his name.

**[Amos
(with
flourish)**   [The Lord says:]]

**The Lord
(voice)**   Are not you Israelites
the same to me as the Cushites? . . .
Did I not bring Israel up from Egypt,
the Philistines from Caphtor
and the Arameans from Kir?

Surely the eyes of the Sovereign LORD
are on the sinful kingdom.
I will destroy it
from the face of the earth—
yet I will not totally destroy
the house of Jacob. . . .
For I will give the command,
and I will shake the house of Israel
among all the nations
as grain is shaken in a sieve,
and not a pebble will reach the ground.
All the sinners among my people
will die by the sword,
all those who say,
"Disaster will not overtake or meet us."

Cast: **Amos, the Lord** (voice only), **Singer 1, Singer 2** (Singers can be the same as Amos)

Israel's Restoration

Amos 9:11–15

**Amos
(with
flourish)**   In that day I will restore
David's fallen tent.
I will repair its broken places,
restore its ruins,

and build it as it used to be,
so that they may possess the remnant of Edom
and all the nations that bear my name,
declares the LORD, who will do these things.

[Amos
(with
flourish)   [So says the Lord, who will cause this to happen!
The Lord says:]]

The Lord
(voice only) The days are coming . . .

when the reaper will be overtaken by the plowman
and the planter by the one treading grapes.
New wine will drip from the mountains
and flow from all the hills.
I will bring back my exiled people Israel;
they will rebuild the ruined cities and live in them.
They will plant vineyards and drink their wine;
they will make gardens and eat their fruit.
I will plant Israel in their own land,
never again to be uprooted
from the land I have given them. . . .

[Amos
(with
flourish)   [The Lord your God has spoken!]]

Cast: **Amos, the Lord** (voice only)

Obadiah

The Lord Will Punish Edom

Obadiah 1:1–14

Announcer   The vision of Obadiah.

This is what the Sovereign LORD says about Edom:

Obadiah   We have heard a message from the LORD:
    An envoy was sent to the nations to say:

The Lord
(voice only) Rise, and let us go against her for battle.

[Obadiah   [The Lord says to Edom:]]

The Lord
(voice)   See, I will make you small among the nations;
    you will be utterly despised.
  The pride of your heart has deceived you,
    you who live in the clefts of the rocks
    and make your home on the heights,
  you who say to yourself:

Edomite   Who can bring me down to the ground?

The Lord
(voice)   Though you soar like the eagle
    and make your nest among the stars,
    from there I will bring you down. . . .
  If thieves came to you,
    if robbers in the night—
  Oh, what a disaster awaits you—
    would they not steal only as much as they wanted?
  If grape pickers came to you,
    would they not leave a few grapes?
  But how Esau will be ransacked,
    his hidden treasures pillaged!
  All your allies will force you to the border;
    your friends will deceive and overpower you;
  those who eat your bread will set a trap for you,
    but you will not detect it.

  In that day . . .
    will I not destroy the wise men of Edom,
    men of understanding in the mountains of Esau?
  Your warriors, O Teman, will be terrified,
    and everyone in Esau's mountains
    will be cut down in the slaughter.

Because of the violence against your brother Jacob,
  you will be covered with shame;
  you will be destroyed forever.
On the day you stood aloof
  while strangers carried off his wealth
and foreigners entered his gates
  and cast lots for Jerusalem,
  you were like one of them.
You should not look down on your brother
  in the day of his misfortune,
nor rejoice over the people of Judah
  in the day of their destruction,
nor boast so much
  in the day of their trouble.
You should not march through the gates of my people
  in the day of their disaster,
nor look down on them in their calamity
  in the day of their disaster,
nor seize their wealth
  in the day of their disaster.
You should not wait at the crossroads
  to cut down their fugitives,
nor hand over their survivors
  in the day of their trouble.

Cast: **Announcer, Obadiah, the Lord** (voice only), **Edomite**

Jonah

Jonah Flees from the Lord

Jonah 1:1–17

Narrator	The word of the LORD came to Jonah son of Amittai:
The Lord (voice only)	Go to the great city of Nineveh and preach against it, because its wickedness has come up before me.
Narrator	But Jonah ran away from the LORD and headed for Tarshish. He went down to Joppa, where he found a ship bound for that port. After paying the fare, he went aboard and sailed for Tarshish to flee from the LORD.
	Then the LORD sent a great wind on the sea, and such a violent storm arose that the ship threatened to break up. All the sailors were afraid and each cried out to his own god. And they threw the cargo into the sea to lighten the ship.
	But Jonah had gone below deck, where he lay down and fell into a deep sleep. The captain went to him and said:
Captain	How can you sleep? Get up and call on your god! Maybe he will take notice of us, and we will not perish.
Narrator	Then the sailors said to each other:
Sailors 1 and 2	Come, let us cast lots—
Sailor 2	To find out who is responsible for this calamity.
Narrator	They cast lots and the lot fell on Jonah. So they asked him:
Sailor 2	Tell us, who is responsible for making all this trouble for us?
Sailor 1	What do you do?
Sailor 2	Where do you come from?
Sailor 1	What is your country?
Sailor 2	From what people are you?
Narrator	He answered:
Jonah	I am a Hebrew and I worship the LORD, the God of heaven, who made the sea and the land.
Narrator	This terrified them and they asked:
Sailor 2	What have you done?

454

Commen- tator	(They knew he was running away from the LORD, because he had already told them so.)
Narrator	The sea was getting rougher and rougher. So they asked him:
Sailor 1	What should we do to you to make the sea calm down for us?
Jonah	Pick me up and throw me into the sea, and it will become calm. I know that it is my fault that this great storm has come upon you.
Narrator	Instead, the men did their best to row back to land. But they could not, for the sea grew even wilder than before. Then they cried to the LORD:
Sailor 2	O LORD, please do not let us die for taking this man's life.
Sailor 1	Do not hold us accountable for killing an innocent man.
Sailor 2	For you, O LORD, have done as you pleased.
Narrator	Then they took Jonah and threw him overboard, and the raging sea grew calm. At this the men greatly feared the LORD, and they offered a sacrifice to the LORD and made vows to him.
	But the LORD provided a great fish to swallow Jonah, and Jonah was inside the fish three days and three nights.

Cast: **Narrator, the Lord** (voice only), **Captain, Sailor 1, Sailor 2** (can be the same as Captain), **Jonah**

Jonah's Prayer

Jonah 2:1–10

Narrator	From inside the fish Jonah prayed to the LORD his God. He said:

Jonah	In my distress I called to the LORD,
	    and he answered me.
	From the depths of the grave I called for help,
	    and you listened to my cry.
	You hurled me into the deep,
	      into the very heart of the seas,
	      and the currents swirled about me;
	all your waves and breakers
	    swept over me.
	I said, "I have been banished
	    from your sight;
	yet I will look again
	    toward your holy temple."
	The engulfing waters threatened me,

the deep surrounded me;
    seaweed was wrapped around my head.
To the roots of the mountains I sank down;
    the earth beneath barred me in forever.
But you brought my life up from the pit,
    O LORD my God.

When my life was ebbing away,
    I remembered you, LORD,
and my prayer rose to you,
    to your holy temple.

Those who cling to worthless idols
    forfeit the grace that could be theirs.
But I, with a song of thanksgiving,
    will sacrifice to you.
What I have vowed I will make good.
    Salvation comes from the LORD.

Narrator   And the LORD commanded the fish, and it vomited Jonah onto dry land.

Cast: **Narrator, Jonah**

Jonah Goes to Nineveh

Jonah 3:1–10

Narrator   Then the word of the LORD came to Jonah a second time:

The Lord
  (voice only) Go to the great city of Nineveh and proclaim to it the message I give you.

Narrator   Jonah obeyed the word of the LORD and went to Nineveh. Now Nineveh was a very important city—a visit required three days. On the first day, Jonah started into the city. He proclaimed:

Jonah
  (calling) Forty more days and Nineveh will be overturned.

Narrator   The Ninevites believed God. They declared a fast, and all of them, from the greatest to the least, put on sackcloth.

When the news reached the king of Nineveh, he rose from his throne, took off his royal robes, covered himself with sackcloth and sat down in the dust. Then he issued a proclamation in Nineveh:

King   By the decree of the king and his nobles:

Do not let any man or beast, herd or flock, taste anything; do not let them eat or drink. But let man and beast be covered with sackcloth. Let everyone call urgently on God. Let them give up their evil ways and their violence. Who knows? God may yet relent and with compassion turn from his fierce anger so that we will not perish.

Narrator   When God saw what they did and how they turned from their evil ways, he had compassion and did not bring upon them the destruction he had threatened.

Cast: **Narrator, the Lord** (voice only), **Jonah, King**

Jonah's Anger at the Lord's Compassion

Jonah 4:1–11

Narrator   But Jonah was greatly displeased and became angry. He prayed to the LORD:

Jonah (angry)   O LORD, is this not what I said when I was still at home? That is why I was so quick to flee to Tarshish. I knew that you are a gracious and compassionate God, slow to anger and abounding in love, a God who relents from sending calamity. Now, O LORD, take away my life, for it is better for me to die than to live.

[Narrator   But the LORD replied:]

The Lord
(voice only)   Have you any right to be angry?

Narrator   Jonah went out and sat down at a place east of the city. There he made himself a shelter, sat in its shade and waited to see what would happen to the city. Then the LORD God provided a vine and made it grow up over Jonah to give shade for his head to ease his discomfort, and Jonah was very happy about the vine. But at dawn the next day God provided a worm, which chewed the vine so that it withered. When the sun rose, God provided a scorching east wind, and the sun blazed on Jonah's head so that he grew faint. He wanted to die, and said:

Jonah
(petulant)   It would be better for me to die than to live.

[Narrator   But God said to Jonah:]

The Lord
(voice,
concil-
iatory)   Do you have a right to be angry about the vine?

Jonah (bitter)   I do. I am angry enough to die.

[Narrator   But the LORD said:]

The Lord
(voice)   You have been concerned about this vine, though you did not tend it

457

or make it grow. It sprang up overnight and died overnight. But Nineveh has more than a hundred and twenty thousand people who cannot tell their right hand from their left, and many cattle as well. Should I not be concerned about that great city?

Cast: **Narrator, Jonah, the Lord** (voice only)

Micah

An Introduction to Micah

Micah 1:1–9

Narrator	The word of the LORD that came to Micah of Moresheth during the reigns of Jotham, Ahaz and Hezekiah, kings of Judah—the vision he saw concerning Samaria and Jerusalem.

Micah	Hear, O peoples, all of you,
	    listen, O earth and all who are in it,
	that the Sovereign LORD may witness against you,
	    the Lord from his holy temple.
	
	Look! The LORD is coming from his dwelling place;
	    he comes down and treads the high places of the earth.
	The mountains melt beneath him
	    and the valleys split apart,
	like wax before the fire,
	    like water rushing down a slope.
	All this is because of Jacob's transgression,
	    because of the sins of the house of Israel.

Questioner	What is Jacob's transgression?
Micah	Is it not Samaria?
Questioner	What is Judah's high place?
Micah	Is it not Jerusalem?

The Lord
(voice only)
	I will make Samaria a heap of rubble,
	    a place for planting vineyards.
	I will pour her stones into the valley
	    and lay bare her foundations.
	All her idols will be broken to pieces;
	    all her temple gifts will be burned with fire;
	    I will destroy all her images.
	Since she gathered her gifts from the wages of prostitutes,
	    as the wages of prostitutes they will again be used.

[Narrator	[Then Micah said:]]

Micah	Because of this I will weep and wail;
	    I will go about barefoot and naked.
	I will howl like a jackal
	    and moan like an owl.
	For her wound is incurable;
	    it has come to Judah.

It has reached the very gate of my people,
even to Jerusalem itself.

Cast: **Narrator, Micah, Questioner** (can be the same as Narrator), **the Lord** (voice only)

The Fate of Those Who Oppress the Poor

Micah 2:1–13

Micah Woe to those who plan iniquity,
to those who plot evil on their beds!
At morning's light they carry it out
because it is in their power to do it.
They covet fields and seize them,
and houses, and take them.
They defraud a man of his home,
a fellowman of his inheritance.

[Therefore, the LORD says:]

The Lord
(voice only) I am planning disaster against this people,
from which you cannot save yourselves.
You will no longer walk proudly,
for it will be a time of calamity.
In that day men will ridicule you;
they will taunt you with this mournful song:

**Singers 1
and 2** We are utterly ruined—

Singer 1 My people's possession is divided up.

Singer 2 He takes it from me!
He assigns our fields to traitors.

Micah Therefore you will have no one in the assembly of the LORD
to divide the land by lot.

[The people preach at me and say:]

**Persons 1
and 2** Do not prophesy. . . .

Person 1 Do not prophesy about these things;
disgrace will not overtake us.

The Lord
(voice) Should it be said, O house of Jacob:

Person 2 Is the Spirit of the LORD angry?

Person 1 Does he do such things?

460

Person 2	Do not my words do good to him whose ways are upright?
[Micah	[The Lord replies:]]

The Lord
  (voice)
	Lately my people have risen up
	    like an enemy.
	You strip off the rich robe
	    from those who pass by without a care,
	    like men returning from battle.
	You drive the women of my people
	    from their pleasant homes.
	You take away my blessing
	    from their children forever.
	Get up, go away!
	    For this is not your resting place,
	because it is defiled,
	    it is ruined, beyond all remedy.
	If a liar and deceiver comes and says,
	    "I will prophesy for you plenty of wine and beer,"
	    he would be just the prophet for this people!
	
	I will surely gather all of you, O Jacob;
	    I will surely bring together the remnant of Israel
	I will bring them together like sheep in a pen,
	    like a flock in its pasture;
	    the place will throng with people.

Micah	One who breaks open the way will go up before them;
	    they will break through the gate and go out.
	Their king will pass through before them,
	    the LORD at their head.

Cast: **Micah, the Lord** (voice only), **Singer 1, Singer 2** (can be the same as Singer 1), **Person 1, Person 2** (can be the same as Person 1)

Leaders and Prophets Rebuked

Micah 3:1–12

Micah	Listen, you leaders of Jacob,
	    you rulers of the house of Israel.
	Should you not know justice,
	    you who hate good and love evil;
	who tear the skin from my people
	    and the flesh from their bones;
	who eat my people's flesh,
	    strip off their skin
	    and break their bones in pieces;

461

who chop them up like meat for the pan,
   like flesh for the pot?

Then they will cry out to the Lord,
   but he will not answer them.
At that time he will hide his face from them
   because of the evil they have done. . . .

As for the prophets
   who lead my people astray,
if one feeds them,
   they proclaim "peace";
if he does not,
   they prepare to wage war against him.

The Lord
(voice only) Therefore night will come over you, without visions,
   and darkness, without divination.
The sun will set for the prophets,
   and the day will go dark for them.

Micah The seers will be ashamed
   and the diviners disgraced.
They will all cover their faces
   because there is no answer from God.

But as for me, I am filled with power,
   with the Spirit of the Lord,
   and with justice and might,
to declare to Jacob his transgression,
   to Israel his sin.
Hear this, you leaders of the house of Jacob,
   you rulers of the house of Israel,
who despise justice
   and distort all that is right;
who build Zion with bloodshed,
   and Jerusalem with wickedness.
Her leaders judge for a bribe,
   her priests teach for a price,
   and her prophets tell fortunes for money.
Yet they lean upon the Lord and say:

Person 1 Is not the Lord among us?

Person 2 No disaster will come upon us.

Micah Therefore because of you,
   Zion will be plowed like a field,
Jerusalem will become a heap of rubble,
   the temple hill a mound overgrown with thickets.

Cast: **Micah, the Lord** (voice only), **Person 1, Person 2**

The Mountain of the Lord

Micah 4:1–4 [5]

Micah	In the last days

the mountain of the LORD's temple will be established
    as chief among the mountains;
it will be raised above the hills,
    and peoples will stream to it.

Many nations will come and say:

Person 1   Come, let us go up to the mountain of the LORD,
    to the house of the God of Jacob.

Person 2   He will teach us his ways,
    so that we may walk in his paths.

Micah   The law will go out from Zion,
    the word of the LORD from Jerusalem.
He will judge between many peoples
    and will settle disputes for strong nations far and wide.
They will beat their swords into plowshares
    and their spears into pruning hooks.
Nation will not take up sword against nation,
    nor will they train for war anymore.
Every man will sit under his own vine
    and under his own fig tree,
and no one will make them afraid—

Cast   For the LORD Almighty has spoken.

[Micah   All the nations may walk
    in the name of their gods—

Cast   We will walk in the name of the LORD
    our God for ever and ever.]

Cast: **Micah, Person 1, Person 2**

Israel Will Return from Exile

Micah 4:6–5:1

The Lord
(voice only) In that day—

Micah
(with
flourish)   Declares the LORD,

The Lord
   (voice)   I will gather the lame;
               I will assemble the exiles
               and those I have brought to grief.
        I will make the lame a remnant,
               those driven away a strong nation.
        The Lord will rule over them in Mount Zion
               from that day and forever.

Micah   As for you, O watchtower of the flock,
               O stronghold of the Daughter of Zion,
        the former dominion will be restored to you;
               kingship will come to the Daughter of Jerusalem.

        Why do you now cry aloud—
               have you no king?
        Has your counselor perished,
               that pain seizes you like that of a woman in labor?
        Writhe in agony, O Daughter of Zion,
               like a woman in labor,
        for now you must leave the city
               to camp in the open field.
        You will go to Babylon;
               there you will be rescued.
        There the Lord will redeem you
               out of the hand of your enemies.

        But now many nations
               are gathered against you.
        They say:

Attacker 1   Let her be defiled.

Attacker 2   Let our eyes gloat over Zion!

Micah   But they do not know
               the thoughts of the Lord;
        they do not understand his plan,
               he who gathers them like sheaves to the threshing floor.

        [The Lord says:]

The Lord
   (voice)   Rise and thresh, O Daughter of Zion,
               for I will give you horns of iron;
        I will give you hoofs of bronze
               and you will break to pieces many nations.

        You will devote their ill-gotten gains to the Lord,
               their wealth to the Lord of all the earth.

Micah   Marshal your troops, O city of troops,
               for a siege is laid against us.

> They will strike Israel's ruler
> on the cheek with a rod.

Cast: **The Lord** (voice only), **Micah, Attacker 1, Attacker 2**

A Promised Ruler from Bethlehem

Micah 5:2–5

Micah
(with
flourish)   [The Lord says:]

The Lord
(voice only) But you, Bethlehem Ephrathah,
> though you are small among the clans of Judah,
> out of you will come for me
> > one who will be ruler over Israel,
>
> whose origins are from of old,
> > from ancient times.

Micah   Therefore Israel will be abandoned
> until the time when she who is in labor gives birth
> and the rest of his brothers return
> > to join the Israelites.

> He will stand and shepherd his flock
> > in the strength of the Lord,
> > in the majesty of the name of the Lord his God.
>
> And they will live securely, for then his greatness
> > will reach to the ends of the earth.
> > And he will be their peace.

> When the Assyrian invades our land
> > and marches through our fortresses,
>
> we will raise against him seven shepherds,
> > even eight leaders of men.

Cast: **Micah, the Lord** (voice only). (See also Appendix: Christmas Readings, New Testament, page 415.)

Deliverance and Punishment

Micah 5:5–6:5

Micah   He will be their peace.

> When the Assyrian invades our land
> > and marches through our fortresses,

465

we will raise against him seven shepherds,
  even eight leaders of men.
They will rule the land of Assyria with the sword,
  the land of Nimrod with drawn sword.
He will deliver us from the Assyrian
  when he invades our land
  and marches into our borders.

The remnant of Jacob will be
  in the midst of many peoples
like dew from the LORD,
  like showers on the grass,
which do not wait for man
  or linger for mankind.
The remnant of Jacob will be among the nations,
  in the midst of many peoples,
like a lion among the beasts of the forest,
  like a young lion among flocks of sheep,
which mauls and mangles as it goes,
  and no one can rescue.
Your hand will be lifted up in triumph over your enemies,
  and all your foes will be destroyed.

[(with
flourish)   [The Lord says:]]

The Lord
(voice only) In that day . . .

I will destroy your horses from among you
  and demolish your chariots.
I will destroy the cities of your land
  and tear down all your strongholds.
I will destroy your witchcraft
  and you will no longer cast spells.
I will destroy your carved images
  and your sacred stones from among you;
you will no longer bow down
  to the work of your hands.
I will uproot from among you your Asherah poles
  and demolish your cities.
I will take vengeance in anger and wrath
  upon the nations that have not obeyed me.

Micah
(to
audience)   Listen to what the LORD says:

(to
the Lord)   Stand up, plead your case before the mountains;
  let the hills hear what you have to say.

(calling)	Hear, O mountains, the LORD's accusation;
	listen, you everlasting foundations of the earth.
	For the LORD has a case against his people;
	he is lodging a charge against Israel.
(with	
flourish)	[The Lord says:]
The Lord	
(voice)	My people, what have I done to you?
	How have I burdened you?
	Answer me.
	I brought you up out of Egypt
	and redeemed you from the land of slavery.
	I sent Moses to lead you,
	also Aaron and Miriam.
	My people, remember
	what Balak king of Moab counseled
	and what Balaam son of Beor answered.
	Remember ⌐your journey⌐ from Shittim to Gilgal,
	that you may know the righteous acts of the LORD.

Cast· Micah, the Lord (voice only)

What the Lord Requires

Micah 6:6–16

Micah	With what shall I come before the LORD
	and bow down before the exalted God?
	Shall I come before him with burnt offerings,
	with calves a year old?
	Will the LORD be pleased with thousands of rams,
	with ten thousand rivers of oil?
	Shall I offer my firstborn for my transgression,
	the fruit of my body for the sin of my soul?
	He has showed you, O man, what is good.
	And what does the LORD require of you?
	To act justly and to love mercy
	and to walk humbly with your God.
(with	
flourish)	Listen! The LORD is calling to the city—
(to	
the Lord)	[LORD,] to fear your name is wisdom—
The Lord	
(voice only)	Heed the rod and the One who appointed it.
	Am I still to forget, O wicked house,

your ill-gotten treasures
and the short ephah, which is accursed?
Shall I acquit a man with dishonest scales,
    with a bag of false weights?
Her rich men are violent;
    her people are liars
and their tongues speak deceitfully.
Therefore, I have begun to destroy you,
    to ruin you because of your sins.
You will eat but not be satisfied;
    your stomach will still be empty.
You will store up but save nothing,
    because what you save I will give to the sword.
You will plant but not harvest;
    you will press olives but not use the oil on yourselves,
    you will crush grapes but not drink the wine.
You have observed the statutes of Omri
    and all the practices of Ahab's house,
    and you have followed their traditions.
Therefore I will give you over to ruin
    and your people to derision;
    you will bear the scorn of the nations.

Cast: **Micah, the Lord** (voice only)

Nahum

The Lord's Judgment

Nahum 1:2–10

Voice 1   The Lord is a jealous and avenging God;
      the Lord takes vengeance and is filled with wrath.
    The Lord takes vengeance on his foes
      and maintains his wrath against his enemies.

Voice 2   The Lord is slow to anger and great in power;
      the Lord will not leave the guilty unpunished.

Voice 3   His way is in the whirlwind and the storm,
      and clouds are the dust of his feet.

Voice 1   He rebukes the sea and dries it up;
      he makes all the rivers run dry.
    Bashan and Carmel wither
      and the blossoms of Lebanon fade.

Voice 2   The mountains quake before him
      and the hills melt away.

Voice 3   The earth trembles at his presence,
      the world and all who live in it.

Voice 1   Who can withstand his indignation?

Voice 2   Who can endure his fierce anger?

Voice 3   His wrath is poured out like fire;
      the rocks are shattered before him.

Voice 1   The Lord is good,
      a refuge in times of trouble.
    He cares for those who trust in him.

Voice 2   But with an overwhelming flood
    he will make an end of ⌊Nineveh⌋;
      he will pursue his foes into darkness.

Voice 3   Whatever they plot against the Lord—

Voice 1   He will bring to an end.

Voice 2   Trouble will not come a second time.

Voice 3   They will be entangled among thorns
      and drunk from their wine;
      they will be consumed like dry stubble.

Cast: **Voice 1, Voice 2, Voice 3**

Habakkuk

Habakkuk Complains of Injustice

Habakkuk 1:1–17

Announcer   The oracle that Habakkuk the prophet received.

Habakkuk   How long, O LORD, must I call for help,
    but you do not listen?
Or cry out to you, "Violence!"
    but you do not save?
Why do you make me look at injustice?
    Why do you tolerate wrong?
Destruction and violence are before me;
    there is strife, and conflict abounds.
Therefore the law is paralyzed,
    and justice never prevails.
The wicked hem in the righteous,
    so that justice is perverted.

The Lord
  (voice only) Look at the nations and watch—
    and be utterly amazed.
For I am going to do something in your days
    that you would not believe,
    even if you were told.
I am raising up the Babylonians,
    that ruthless and impetuous people,
who sweep across the whole earth
    to seize dwelling places not their own.
They are a feared and dreaded people;
    they are a law to themselves
    and promote their own honor.
Their horses are swifter than leopards,
    fiercer than wolves at dusk.
Their cavalry gallops headlong;
    their horsemen come from afar.
They fly like a vulture swooping to devour;
    they all come bent on violence.
Their hordes advance like a desert wind
    and gather prisoners like sand.
They deride kings
    and scoff at rulers.
They laugh at all fortified cities;
    they build earthen ramps and capture them.

Then they sweep past like the wind and go on—
  guilty men, whose own strength is their god.

Habakkuk   O Lord, are you not from everlasting?
  My God, my Holy One, we will not die.
O Lord, you have appointed them to execute judgment;
  O Rock, you have ordained them to punish.
Your eyes are too pure to look on evil;
  you cannot tolerate wrong.
Why then do you tolerate the treacherous?
  Why are you silent while the wicked
  swallow up those more righteous than themselves?
You have made men like fish in the sea,
  like sea creatures that have no ruler.
The wicked foe pulls all of them up with hooks,
  he catches them in his net,
he gathers them up in his dragnet;
  and so he rejoices and is glad.
Therefore he sacrifices to his net
  and burns incense to his dragnet,
for by his net he lives in luxury
  and enjoys the choicest food.
Is he to keep on emptying his net,
  destroying nations without mercy?

Cast: **Announcer, Habakkuk, the Lord** (voice only)

Habakkuk Receives the Lord's Answer

Habakkuk 2:1–4

Habakkuk   I will stand at my watch
  and station myself on the ramparts;
I will look to see what he will say to me,
  and what answer I am to give to this complaint. (PAUSE)

[Then the Lord replied:]

The Lord
(voice only) Write down the revelation
  and make it plain on tablets
  so that a herald may run with it.
For the revelation awaits an appointed time;
  it speaks of the end
  and will not prove false.
Though it linger, wait for it;
  it will certainly come and will not delay.

>See, he is puffed up;
>>his desires are not upright—
>>but the righteous will live by his faith.

Cast: **Habakkuk, the Lord** (voice only)

Doom on the Unrighteous

Habakkuk 2:5–14

Habakkuk   Wine betrays [the wicked foe];
>>he is arrogant and never at rest.
>Because he is as greedy as the grave
>>and like death is never satisfied,
>he gathers to himself all the nations
>>and takes captive all the peoples.

Will not all of them taunt him with ridicule and scorn, saying:

Person 1   Woe to him who piles up stolen goods
>>and makes himself wealthy by extortion!

Person 2   How long must this go on?

Habakkuk   Will not your debtors suddenly arise?
>>Will they not wake up and make you tremble?
>>Then you will become their victim.
>Because you have plundered many nations,
>>the peoples who are left will plunder you.
>For you have shed man's blood;
>>you have destroyed lands and cities and everyone in them.

Person 1   Woe to him who builds his realm by unjust gain
>>to set his nest on high,
>>to escape the clutches of ruin!

Habakkuk   You have plotted the ruin of many peoples,
>>shaming your own house and forfeiting your life.
>The stones of the wall will cry out,
>>and the beams of the woodwork will echo it.

Person 2   Woe to him who builds a city with bloodshed
>>and establishes a town by crime!

Habakkuk   Has not the Lord Almighty determined
>>that the people's labor is only fuel for the fire,
>>that the nations exhaust themselves for nothing?
>For the earth will be filled with the knowledge
>>>of the glory of the Lord,
>>as the waters cover the sea.

Cast: **Habakkuk, Person 1, Person 2**

Idols

Habakkuk 2:18–20

Habakkuk   Of what value is an idol, since a man has carved it?
   Or an image that teaches lies?
For he who makes it trusts in his own creation;
   he makes idols that cannot speak.
Woe to him who says to wood:

Person   Come to life!

Habakkuk   Or to lifeless stone:

Person   Wake up!

Habakkuk   Can it give guidance?
   It is covered with gold and silver;
   there is no breath in it.
But the LORD is in his holy temple;
   let all the earth be silent before him.

Cast: **Habakkuk, Person**

Habakkuk's Prayer

From Habakkuk 3:1–19

Announcer   A prayer of Habakkuk the prophet.

Voice 1   LORD, I have heard of your fame;
   I stand in awe of your deeds, O LORD.
Renew them in our day,
   in our time make them known;
   in wrath remember mercy.

Voice 2   God came from Teman,
   the Holy One from Mount Paran.
His glory covered the heavens
   and his praise filled the earth.
His splendor was like the sunrise;
   rays flashed from his hand,
   where his power was hidden.
Plague went before him;
   pestilence followed his steps.
He stood, and shook the earth;
   he looked, and made the nations tremble.
The ancient mountains crumbled
   and the age-old hills collapsed.
   His ways are eternal. . . .

473

Voice 1   Were you angry with the rivers, O Lᴏʀᴅ?
          Was your wrath against the streams?
       Did you rage against the sea
          when you rode with your horses
          and your victorious chariots?
       You uncovered your bow,
          you called for many arrows.
       You split the earth with rivers;
          the mountains saw you and writhed.
       Torrents of water swept by;
          the deep roared
          and lifted its waves on high.

Voice 2   Sun and moon stood still in the heavens
          at the glint of your flying arrows,
          at the lightning of your flashing spear.
       In wrath you strode through the earth
          and in anger you threshed the nations.
       You came out to deliver your people,
          to save your anointed one.
       You crushed the leader of the land of wickedness,
          you stripped him from head to foot.
       With his own spear you pierced his head
          when his warriors stormed out to scatter us,
       gloating as though about to devour
          the wretched who were in hiding.
       You trampled the sea with your horses,
          churning the great waters.

Voice 1   I heard and my heart pounded,
          my lips quivered at the sound;
       decay crept into my bones,
          and my legs trembled. (ᴘᴀᴜꜱᴇ)
       Yet I will wait patiently for the day of calamity
          to come on the nation invading us.

Voice 2   Though the fig tree does not bud
          and there are no grapes on the vines,
       though the olive crop fails
          and the fields produce no food,
       though there are no sheep in the pen
          and no cattle in the stalls,
       yet I will rejoice in the Lᴏʀᴅ,
          I will be joyful in God my Savior.

       The Sovereign Lᴏʀᴅ is my strength;
          he makes my feet like the feet of a deer,
          he enables me to go on the heights.

Cast: **Announcer, Voice 1, Voice 2**

Zephaniah

The Day of the Lord's Judgment

Zephaniah 1:1–18

Announcer　The word of the LORD that came to Zephaniah son of Cushi, the son of Gedaliah, the son of Amariah, the son of Hezekiah, during the reign of Josiah son of Amon king of Judah:

The Lord
(voice only)　I will sweep away everything
　　　　from the face of the earth. . . .
　　　I will sweep away both men and animals;
　　　　I will sweep away the birds of the air
　　　　and the fish of the sea.
　　　The wicked will have only heaps of rubble
　　　　when I cut off man from the face of the earth. . . .

　　　I will stretch out my hand against Judah
　　　　and against all who live in Jerusalem.
　　　I will cut off from this place every remnant of Baal,
　　　　the names of the pagan and the idolatrous priests—
　　　those who bow down on the roofs
　　　　to worship the starry host,
　　　those who bow down and swear by the LORD
　　　　and who also swear by Molech,
　　　those who turn back from following the LORD
　　　　and neither seek the LORD nor inquire of him.

Zephaniah　Be silent before the Sovereign LORD,
　　　　for the day of the LORD is near.
　　　The LORD has prepared a sacrifice;
　　　　he has consecrated those he has invited.
　　　On the day of the LORD's sacrifice
　　　　I will punish the princes
　　　　and the king's sons
　　　and all those clad
　　　　in foreign clothes.

The Lord
(voice)　On that day I will punish
　　　　all who avoid stepping on the threshold,
　　　who fill the temple of their gods
　　　　with violence and deceit.

Zephaniah　On that day . . .
　　　　a cry will go up from the Fish Gate,
　　　　wailing from the New Quarter,

and a loud crash from the hills.
Wail, you who live in the market district;
  all your merchants will be wiped out,
  all who trade with silver will be ruined.

The Lord
  (voice)

At that time I will search Jerusalem with lamps
  and punish those who are complacent,
  who are like wine left on its dregs,
who think;

Person

The LORD will do nothing,
  either good or bad.

The Lord
  (voice)

Their wealth will be plundered,
  their houses demolished.
They will build houses
  but not live in them;
they will plant vineyards
  but not drink the wine.

Zephaniah

The great day of the LORD is near—
  near and coming quickly.
Listen! The cry on the day of the LORD will be bitter,
  the shouting of the warrior there.
That day will be a day of wrath,
  a day of distress and anguish,
a day of trouble and ruin,
  a day of darkness and gloom,
  a day of clouds and blackness,
a day of trumpet and battle cry
  against the fortified cities
  and against the corner towers.

The Lord
  (voice)

I will bring distress on the people
  and they will walk like blind men,
  because they have sinned against the LORD.
Their blood will be poured out like dust
  and their entrails like filth.

Zephaniah

Neither their silver nor their gold
  will be able to save them
  on the day of the LORD's wrath.
In the fire of his jealousy
  the whole world will be consumed,
for he will make a sudden end
  of all who live in the earth.

Cast: **Announcer, the Lord** (voice only), **Zephaniah, Person**

The Doom of the Nations around Israel

Zephaniah 2:1–11

Zephaniah

(sternly)   Gather together, gather together,
    O shameful nation,
before the appointed time arrives
    and that day sweeps on like chaff,
before the fierce anger of the Lord comes upon you,
    before the day of the Lord's wrath comes upon you.

(kindly)   Seek the Lord, all you humble of the land,
    you who do what he commands.
Seek righteousness, seek humility;
    perhaps you will be sheltered
    on the day of the Lord's anger.

(sternly)   Gaza will be abandoned
    and Ashkelon left in ruins.
At midday Ashdod will be emptied
    and Ekron uprooted.
Woe to you who live by the sea,
    O Kerethite people;
the word of the Lord is against you,
    O Canaan, land of the Philistines.

The Lord

(voice only) I will destroy you,
    and none will be left.

Zephaniah   The land by the sea, where the Kerethites dwell,
    will be a place for shepherds and sheep pens.

(kindly)   It will belong to the remnant of the house of Judah;
    there they will find pasture.
In the evening they will lie down
    in the houses of Ashkelon.
The Lord their God will care for them;
    he will restore their fortunes.

The Lord

(voice)   I have heard the insults of Moab
    and the taunts of the Ammonites,
who insulted my people
    and made threats against their land.
Therefore, as surely as I live . . .
surely Moab will become like Sodom,
    the Ammonites like Gomorrah—
a place of weeds and salt pits,
    a wasteland forever.
The remnant of my people will plunder them;
    the survivors of my nation will inherit their land.

Zephaniah	This is what they will get in return for their pride,
	    for insulting and mocking the people of the Lord Almighty.
	The Lord will be awesome to them
	    when he destroys all the gods of the land.
	The nations on every shore will worship him,
	    every one in its own land.

Cast: **Zephaniah, the Lord** (voice only)

The Future of Jerusalem

Zephaniah 3:1–13

Zephaniah

(sternly)   Woe to the city of oppressors,
        rebellious and defiled!
She obeys no one,
    she accepts no correction.
She does not trust in the Lord,
    she does not draw near to her God.
Her officials are roaring lions,
    her rulers are evening wolves,
    who leave nothing for the morning.
Her prophets are arrogant;
    they are treacherous men.
Her priests profane the sanctuary
    and do violence to the law.

(gently)   The Lord within her is righteous;
    he does no wrong.
Morning by morning he dispenses his justice,
    and every new day he does not fail,
    yet the unrighteous know no shame.

The Lord

(voice only) I have cut off nations;
    their strongholds are demolished.
I have left their streets deserted,
    with no one passing through.
Their cities are destroyed;
    no one will be left—no one at all.
I said to the city,
    "Surely you will fear me
    and accept correction!"
Then her dwelling would not be cut off,
    nor all my punishments come upon her.
But they were still eager
    to act corruptly in all they did.

Zephaniah	[The Lord declares:]
The Lord (voice)	Therefore wait for me . . . for the day I will stand up to testify. I have decided to assemble the nations, to gather the kingdoms and to pour out my wrath on them— all my fierce anger. The whole world will be consumed by the fire of my jealous anger.

Then will I purify the lips of the peoples,
that all of them may call on the name of the Lord
and serve him shoulder to shoulder.
From beyond the rivers of Cush
my worshipers, my scattered people,
will bring me offerings.
On that day you will not be put to shame
for all the wrongs you have done to me,
because I will remove from this city
those who rejoice in their pride.
Never again will you be haughty
on my holy hill.
But I will leave within you
the meek and humble,
who trust in the name of the Lord.
The remnant of Israel will do no wrong;
they will speak no lies,
nor will deceit be found in their mouths.
They will eat and lie down
and no one will make them afraid.

Cast: **Zephaniah, the Lord** (voice only)

A Song of Joy

Zephaniah 3:14–20

Zephaniah	Sing, O Daughter of Zion; shout aloud, O Israel! Be glad and rejoice with all your heart, O Daughter of Jerusalem! The Lord has taken away your punishment, he has turned back your enemy. The Lord, the King of Israel, is with you; never again will you fear any harm. On that day they will say to Jerusalem:
Person 1	Do not fear, O Zion!

Person 2	Do not let your hands hang limp.
Person 1	The Lord your God is with you, he is mighty to save.
Person 2	He will take great delight in you, he will quiet you with his love.
Person 1	He will rejoice over you with singing.
[Zephaniah	[The Lord says:]]

The Lord
(voice only) The sorrows for the appointed feasts
    I will remove from you;
        they are a burden and a reproach to you.
    At that time I will deal
        with all who oppressed you;
    I will rescue the lame
        and gather those who have been scattered.
    I will give them praise and honor
        in every land where they were put to shame.
    At that time I will gather you;
        at that time I will bring you home.
    I will give you honor and praise
        among all the peoples of the earth
    when I restore your fortunes
        before your very eyes. . . .

Cast: **Zephaniah, Person 1, Person 2** (can be the same as Person 1), **the Lord** (voice only)

Haggai

A Call to Build the House of the Lord

Haggai 1:1–15

Narrator
In the second year of King Darius, on the first day of the sixth month, the word of the LORD came through the prophet Haggai to Zerubbabel son of Shealtiel, governor of Judah, and to Joshua son of Jehozadak, the high priest:

This is what the LORD Almighty says:

The Lord
(voice only) These people say, "The time has not yet come for the LORD's house to be built."

Narrator
Then the word of the LORD came through the prophet Haggai:

Haggai
Is it a time for you yourselves to be living in your paneled houses, while this house remains a ruin?

Now this is what the LORD Almighty says:

The Lord
(voice) Give careful thought to your ways. You have planted much, but have harvested little. You eat, but never have enough. You drink, but never have your fill. You put on clothes, but are not warm. You earn wages, only to put them in a purse with holes in it.

Haggai
This is what the LORD Almighty says:

The Lord
(voice) Give careful thought to your ways. Go up into the mountains and bring down timber and build the house, so that I may take pleasure in it and be honored. . . . You expected much, but see, it turned out to be little. What you brought home, I blew away. Why? . . . Because of my house, which remains a ruin, while each of you is busy with his own house. Therefore, because of you the heavens have withheld their dew and the earth its crops. I called for a drought on the fields and the mountains, on the grain, the new wine, the oil and whatever the ground produces, on men and cattle, and on the labor of your hands.

Narrator
Then Zerubbabel son of Shealtiel, Joshua son of Jehozadak, the high priest, and the whole remnant of the people obeyed the voice of the LORD their God and the message of the prophet Haggai, because the LORD their God had sent him. And the people feared the LORD.

Then Haggai, the LORD's messenger, gave this message of the LORD to the people—

Haggai
[The LORD declares:]

The Lord
(voice)   I am with you. . . .

Narrator   So the LORD stirred up the spirit of Zerubbabel son of Shealtiel, governor of Judah, and the spirit of Joshua son of Jehozadak, the high priest, and the spirit of the whole remnant of the people. They came and began to work on the house of the LORD Almighty, their God, on the twenty-fourth day of the sixth month in the second year of King Darius.

Cast: **Narrator, the Lord** (voice only), **Haggai** (can be the same as the Lord)

The Promised Glory of the New House

Haggai 2:1–9

Narrator   On the twenty-first day of the seventh month, the word of the LORD came through the prophet Haggai: "Speak to Zerubbabel son of Shealtiel, governor of Judah, to Joshua son of Jehozadak, the high priest, and to the remnant of the people. Ask them":

The Lord
(voice only) Who of you is left who saw this house in its former glory? How does it look to you now? Does it not seem to you like nothing? But now be strong, O Zerubbabel. . . . Be strong, O Joshua son of Jehozadak, the high priest. Be strong, all you people of the land . . . and work. For I am with you. . . . This is what I covenanted with you when you came out of Egypt. And my Spirit remains among you. Do not fear. . . .

      . . . In a little while I will once more shake the heavens and the earth, the sea and the dry land. I will shake all nations, and the desired of all nations will come, and I will fill this house with glory. . . . The silver is mine and the gold is mine. . . . The glory of this present house will be greater than the glory of the former house. . . . And in this place I will grant peace. . . .

Haggai
(with
flourish)   [The LORD Almighty has spoken!]

Cast: **Narrator, the Lord** (voice only), **Haggai**

The Prophet Consults the Priests

Haggai 2:10–14

Narrator   On the twenty-fourth day of the ninth month, in the second year of Darius, the word of the LORD came to the prophet Haggai:

Haggai	"This is what the Lord Almighty says":
The Lord (voice only)	Ask the priests what the law says: If a person carries consecrated meat in the fold of his garment, and that fold touches some bread or stew, some wine, oil or other food, does it become consecrated?
Narrator	The priests answered:
Priest(s)	No.
Narrator	Then Haggai said:
Haggai	If a person defiled by contact with a dead body touches one of these things, does it become defiled?
Narrator	[The priests answered:]
Priest(s)	Yes . . . it becomes defiled.
The Lord (voice)	So it is with this people and this nation in my sight. . . .
Haggai	Whatever they do and whatever they offer there is defiled.

Cast: **Narrator, Haggai, the Lord** (voice only), **Priest(s)**

The Lord Promises His Blessing

Haggai 2:15–23

Haggai	Now give careful thought to this from this day on—consider how things were before one stone was laid on another in the Lord's temple. When anyone came to a heap of twenty measures, there were only ten. When anyone went to a wine vat to draw fifty measures, there were only twenty.
The Lord (voice only)	I struck all the work of your hands with blight, mildew and hail, yet you did not turn to me. . . .
Haggai	From this day on, from this twenty-fourth day of the ninth month, give careful thought to the day when the foundation of the Lord's temple was laid. Give careful thought: Is there yet any seed left in the barn?
The Lord (voice)	Until now, the vine and the fig tree, the pomegranate and the olive tree have not borne fruit.
	From this day on I will bless you.
Narrator	The word of the Lord came to Haggai a second time on the twenty-fourth day of the month:
The Lord (voice)	Tell Zerubbabel governor of Judah that I will shake the heavens and the

earth. I will overturn royal thrones and shatter the power of the foreign kingdoms. I will overthrow chariots and their drivers; horses and their riders will fall, each by the sword of his brother.

On that day . . . I will take you, my servant Zerubbabel son of Shealtiel . . . and I will make you like my signet ring, for I have chosen you. . . .

Haggai
(with
flourish)   [The LORD Almighty has spoken!]

Cast: **Haggai, the Lord** (voice only), **Narrator**

Zechariah

The Man among the Myrtle Trees

Zechariah 1:7–17

Zechariah	On the twenty-fourth day of the eleventh month, the month of Shebat, in the second year of Darius, the word of the Lord came to the prophet Zechariah son of Berekiah, the son of Iddo.
	During the night I had a vision—and there before me was a man riding a red horse! He was standing among the myrtle trees in a ravine. Behind him were red, brown and white horses. I asked:
Young Zechariah	What are these, my lord?
Narrator	The angel who was talking with me answered:
Angel	I will show you what they are.
Zechariah	Then the man standing among the myrtle trees explained:
Rider 1	They are the ones the Lord has sent to go throughout the earth.
Zechariah	And they reported to the angel of the Lord, who was standing among the myrtle trees:
Rider 2	We have gone throughout the earth and found the whole world at rest and in peace.
Zechariah	Then the angel of the Lord said:
Angel	Lord Almighty, how long will you withhold mercy from Jerusalem and from the towns of Judah, which you have been angry with these seventy years?
Zechariah	So the Lord spoke kind and comforting words to the angel who talked with me.
	Then the angel who was speaking to me said:
Angel	Proclaim this word: This is what the Lord Almighty says:
The Lord (voice only)	I am very jealous for Jerusalem and Zion, but I am very angry with the nations that feel secure. I was only a little angry, but they added to the calamity.
Angel	Therefore, this is what the Lord says:
The Lord (voice)	I will return to Jerusalem with mercy, and there my house will be rebuilt.
Angel	[The Lord Almighty declares:]

The Lord (voice)	The measuring line will be stretched out over Jerusalem. . . .
Angel	Proclaim further:
Young Zechariah	This is what the LORD Almighty says:
The Lord (voice)	My towns will again overflow with prosperity.
Zechariah	And the LORD will again comfort Zion and choose Jerusalem.

Cast: **Zechariah, Young Zechariah, Narrator, Angel, Rider 1, Rider 2, the Lord** (voice only)

Four Horns and Four Craftsmen

Zechariah 1:18–21

Zechariah	Then I looked up—and there before me were four horns! I asked the angel who was speaking to me:
Young Zechariah	What are these?
Zechariah	He answered me:
Angel	These are the horns that scattered Judah, Israel and Jerusalem.
Zechariah	Then the LORD showed me four craftsmen. (PAUSE) I asked:
Young Zechariah	What are these coming to do?
Zechariah	He answered:
Angel	These are the horns that scattered Judah so that no one could raise his head, but the craftsmen have come to terrify them and throw down these horns of the nations who lifted up their horns against the land of Judah to scatter its people.

Cast: **Zechariah, Young Zechariah, Angel**

A Man with a Measuring Line

Zechariah 2:1–5

Zechariah	Then I looked up—and there before me was a man with a measuring line in his hand! (PAUSE) I asked:
Young Zechariah	Where are you going?
Zechariah	He answered me:

Man	To measure Jerusalem, to find out how wide and how long it is.
Zechariah	Then the angel who was speaking to me left, and another angel came to meet him [and said to him:]
Angel	Run, tell that young man, "Jerusalem will be a city without walls because of the great number of men and livestock in it."
Zechariah	[The Lord declares:]
The Lord (voice only)	And I myself will be a wall of fire around it . . . and I will be its glory within.

Cast: **Zechariah, Young Zechariah, Man, Angel, the Lord** (voice only)

The Exiles Are Called to Come Home

Zechariah 2:6–13

Zechariah	[The Lord said to his people:]
The Lord (voice only)	Come! Come! Flee from the land of the north . . . for I have scattered you to the four winds of heaven. . . .
	Come, O Zion! Escape, you who live in the Daughter of Babylon!
Zechariah	This is what the Lord Almighty says:
The Lord (voice)	After he has honored me and has sent me against the nations that have plundered you—
Zechariah	For whoever touches you touches the apple of his eye—
The Lord (voice)	I will surely raise my hand against them so that their slaves will plunder them.
Zechariah	Then you will know that the Lord Almighty has sent me. (PAUSE)
	[The Lord says:]
The Lord (voice)	Shout and be glad, O Daughter of Zion. For I am coming, and I will live among you. . . .
Zechariah	Many nations will be joined with the Lord in that day and will become my people. I will live among you and you will know that the Lord Almighty has sent me to you. The Lord will inherit Judah as his portion in the holy land and will again choose Jerusalem. (PAUSE) Be still before the Lord, all mankind, because he has roused himself from his holy dwelling.

Cast: **Zechariah, the Lord** (voice only)

Clean Garments for the High Priest

Zechariah 3:1–10

Zechariah	Then he showed me Joshua the high priest standing before the angel of the Lord, and Satan standing at his right side to accuse him. The Lord said to Satan:
Angel	The Lord rebuke you, Satan! The Lord, who has chosen Jerusalem, rebuke you! Is not this man a burning stick snatched from the fire?
Zechariah	Now Joshua was dressed in filthy clothes as he stood before the angel. The angel said to those who were standing before him:
Angel	Take off his filthy clothes.
Zechariah	Then he said to Joshua:
Angel	See, I have taken away your sin, and I will put rich garments on you.
Zechariah	Then I said, "Put a clean turban on his head." So they put a clean turban on his head and clothed him, while the angel of the Lord stood by.
	The angel of the Lord gave this charge to Joshua:
Angel	This is what the Lord Almighty says:
The Lord (voice only)	If you will walk in my ways and keep my requirements, then you will govern my house and have charge of my courts, and I will give you a place among these standing here.
	Listen, O high priest Joshua and your associates seated before you, who are men symbolic of things to come: I am going to bring my servant, the Branch. See, the stone I have set in front of Joshua! There are seven eyes on that one stone, and I will engrave an inscription on it . . . and I will remove the sin of this land in a single day.
	In that day each of you will invite his neighbor to sit under his vine and fig tree. . . .

Cast: **Zechariah, Angel, the Lord** (voice only)

The Gold Lampstand and the Two Olive Trees

From Zechariah 4:1–14

Zechariah	Then the angel who talked with me returned and wakened me, as a man is wakened from his sleep. He asked me:
Angel	What do you see?
Zechariah	I answered:

Young Zechariah	I see a solid gold lampstand with a bowl at the top and seven lights on it, with seven channels to the lights. Also there are two olive trees by it, one on the right of the bowl and the other on its left.
Zechariah	I asked the angel who talked with me:
Young Zechariah	What are these, my lord? . . .
Angel	(These seven are the eyes of the Lord, which range throughout the earth.)
Young Zechariah	. . . What are these two olive trees on the right and the left of the lampstand? . . . What are these two olive branches beside the two gold pipes that pour out golden oil?
Angel	Do you not know what these are?
Young Zechariah	No, my lord.
Angel	These are the two who are anointed to serve the Lord of all the earth.

Cast: **Zechariah, Angel, Young Zechariah**

God's Promise to Zerubbabel

Zechariah 4:6–10

Zechariah	This is the word of the Lord to Zerubbabel:
The Lord (voice only)	Not by might nor by power, but by my Spirit. . . .
Zechariah	[The Lord Almighty says:]
The Lord (voice)	What are you, O mighty mountain? Before Zerubbabel you will become level ground. Then he will bring out the capstone to shouts of:
Person 1	God bless it!
Persons 1 and 2	God bless it!
Zechariah	Then the word of the Lord came to me:
The Lord (voice)	The hands of Zerubbabel have laid the foundation of this temple; his hands will also complete it.
Zechariah	Then you will know that the Lord Almighty has sent me to you.

489

The Lord
(voice)   Who despises the day of small things? Men will rejoice when they see the plumb line in the hand of Zerubbabel.

Zechariah   (These seven are the eyes of the LORD, which range throughout the earth.)

Cast: **Zechariah, the Lord** (voice only), **Person 1**, **Person 2** (can be the same as Person 1). (As in the Good News Bible, verses 6–10 are moved after verses 10b–14 in order to retain the natural order of the narrative.)

Zechariah's Visions

Zechariah 5:1–6:8

Zechariah   I looked again—and there before me was a flying scroll! (PAUSE) [The angel] asked me:

Angel   What do you see?

**Young
Zechariah**   I see a flying scroll, thirty feet long and fifteen feet wide.

Zechariah   And he said to me:

Angel   This is the curse that is going out over the whole land; for according to what it says on one side, every thief will be banished, and according to what it says on the other, everyone who swears falsely will be banished. The LORD Almighty declares:

The Lord
(voice only)   I will send it out, and it will enter the house of the thief and the house of him who swears falsely by my name. It will remain in his house and destroy it, both its timbers and its stones.

Zechariah   Then the angel who was speaking to me came forward and said to me:

Angel   Look up and see what this is that is appearing.

**Young
Zechariah**   What is it?

Angel   It is a measuring basket. . . . This is the iniquity of the people throughout the land.

Zechariah   Then the cover of lead was raised, and there in the basket sat a woman! [The angel said:]

Angel   This is wickedness.

Zechariah   And he pushed her back into the basket and pushed the lead cover down over its mouth.

Then I looked up—and there before me were two women, with the wind in their wings! They had wings like those of a stork, and they lifted up the basket between heaven and earth.

Young **Zechariah**	[I asked the angel who was speaking to me:] Where are they taking the basket?
Angel	To the country of Babylonia to build a house for it. When it is ready, the basket will be set there in its place.
Zechariah	I looked up again—and there before me were four chariots coming out from between two mountains—mountains of bronze! The first chariot had red horses, the second black, the third white, and the fourth dappled—all of them powerful. I asked the angel who was speaking to me:
Young **Zechariah**	What are these, my lord?
Angel	These are the four spirits of heaven, going out from standing in the presence of the Lord of the whole world. The one with the black horses is going toward the north country, the one with the white horses toward the west, and the one with the dappled horses toward the south.
Zechariah	When the powerful horses went out, they were straining to go throughout the earth. And he said,
Angel (moving away)	Go throughout the earth!
Zechariah	So they went throughout the earth. (PAUSE) Then he called to me:
Angel (calling)	Look, those going toward the north country have given my Spirit rest in the land of the north.

Cast: **Zechariah, Angel, Young Zechariah, the Lord** (voice only)

A Crown for Joshua

Zechariah 6:9–15

Zechariah	The word of the LORD came to me:
Young **Zechariah**	Take ⌞silver and gold⌟ from the exiles Heldai, Tobijah and Jedaiah, who have arrived from Babylon. Go the same day to the house of Josiah son of Zephaniah. Take the silver and gold and make a crown, and set it on the head of the high priest, Joshua son of Jehozadak. Tell him this is what the LORD Almighty says:
The Lord (voice only)	Here is the man whose name is the Branch, and he will branch out from his place and build the temple of the LORD. It is he who will build the temple of the LORD, and he will be clothed with majesty and will sit and rule on his throne. And he will be a priest on his throne. And there will

be harmony between the two.

Young
  Zechariah The crown will be given to Heldai, Tobijah, Jedaiah and Hen son of Zephaniah as a memorial in the temple of the LORD.

Zechariah Those who are far away will come and help to build the temple of the LORD, and you will know that the LORD Almighty has sent me to you. This will happen if you diligently obey the LORD your God.

Cast: **Zechariah, Young Zechariah, the Lord** (voice only)

Justice and Mercy, Not Fasting

Zechariah 7:1–7

Zechariah In the fourth year of King Darius, the word of the LORD came to [me] on the fourth day of the ninth month, the month of Kislev. (PAUSE) The people of Bethel had sent Sharezer and Regem-Melech, together with their men, to entreat the LORD by asking the priests of the house of the LORD Almighty and the prophets:

Questioner Should I mourn and fast in the fifth month, as I have done for so many years?

Zechariah Then the word of the LORD Almighty came to me:

The Lord
  (voice only) Ask all the people of the land and the priests, "When you fasted and mourned in the fifth and seventh months for the past seventy years, was it really for me that you fasted? And when you were eating and drinking, were you not just feasting for yourselves?"

Zechariah Are these not the words the LORD proclaimed through the earlier prophets when Jerusalem and its surrounding towns were at rest and prosperous, and the Negev and the western foothills were settled?

Cast: **Zechariah, Questioner, the Lord** (voice only)

Disobedience, the Cause of Exile

Zechariah 7:8–14

Zechariah The word of the LORD came again to [me]:

The Lord
  (voice only) This is what the LORD Almighty says:

Voice	Administer true justice; show mercy and compassion to one another. Do not oppress the widow or the fatherless, the alien or the poor. In your hearts do not think evil of each other.
Zechariah	But they refused to pay attention; stubbornly they turned their backs and stopped up their ears. They made their hearts as hard as flint and would not listen to the law or to the words that the LORD Almighty had sent by his Spirit through the earlier prophets. So the LORD Almighty was very angry.
	When I called, they did not listen; so when they called, I would not listen. . . . I scattered them with a whirlwind among all the nations, where they were strangers. The land was left so desolate behind them that no one could come or go. This is how they made the pleasant land desolate.

Cast: **Zechariah, the Lord** (voice only), **Voice** (speaks words of the Lord)

The Lord Promises to Bless Jerusalem (i)

From Zechariah 8:1–13

Narrator	Again the word of the LORD Almighty came to me. This is what the LORD Almighty says:
The Lord (voice only)	I am very jealous for Zion; I am burning with jealousy for her.
Zechariah	This is what the LORD says:
The Lord (voice)	I will return to Zion and dwell in Jerusalem.
Zechariah	Then Jerusalem will be called the City of Truth, and the mountain of the LORD Almighty will be called the Holy Mountain.
	This is what the LORD Almighty says:
The Lord (voice)	Once again men and women of ripe old age will sit in the streets of Jerusalem, each with cane in hand because of his age. The city streets will be filled with boys and girls playing there. . . .
	The seed will grow well, the vine will yield its fruit, the ground will produce its crops, and the heavens will drop their dew. I will give all these things as an inheritance to the remnant of this people. As you have been an object of cursing among the nations, O Judah and Israel, so will I save you, and you will be a blessing. Do not be afraid, but let your hands be strong.

Cast: **Narrator, the Lord** (voice only), **Zechariah**

The Lord Promises to Bless Jerusalem (ii)

Zechariah 8:14–23

Zechariah   This is what the LORD Almighty says:

The Lord
(voice only) Just as I had determined to bring disaster upon you and showed no pity when your fathers angered me . . . so now I have determined to do good again to Jerusalem and Judah. Do not be afraid. (PAUSE) These are the things you are to do: Speak the truth to each other, and render true and sound judgment in your courts; do not plot evil against your neighbor, and do not love to swear falsely. I hate all this. . . .

Zechariah   Again the word of the LORD Almighty came to me . . . :

The Lord
(voice)   The fasts of the fourth, fifth, seventh and tenth months will become joyful and glad occasions and happy festivals for Judah. Therefore love truth and peace.

Zechariah   This is what the LORD Almighty says:

The Lord
(voice)   Many peoples and the inhabitants of many cities will yet come, and the inhabitants of one city will go to another and say:

Citizen 1   Let us go at once to entreat the LORD and seek the LORD Almighty.

Citizen 2   I myself am going.

Zechariah   Many peoples and powerful nations will come to Jerusalem to seek the LORD Almighty and to entreat him.

This is what the LORD Almighty says:

The Lord
(voice)   In those days ten men from all languages and nations will take firm hold of one Jew by the hem of his robe and say:

Foreigner   Let us go with you, because we have heard that God is with you.

Cast: **Zechariah, the Lord** (voice only), **Citizen 1, Citizen 2, Foreigner**

Judgment on Israel's Enemies

Zechariah 9:1–8

Zechariah   The word of the LORD is against the land of Hadrach
      and will rest upon Damascus—
   for the eyes of men and all the tribes of Israel
      are on the LORD—

and upon Hamath too, which borders on it,
  and upon Tyre and Sidon, though they are very skillful.
Tyre has built herself a stronghold;
  she has heaped up silver like dust,
  and gold like the dirt of the streets.
But the Lord will take away her possessions
  and destroy her power on the sea,
  and she will be consumed by fire.

The Lord
  (voice only) Ashkelon will see it and fear;
  Gaza will writhe in agony,
  and Ekron too, for her hope will wither.
Gaza will lose her king
  and Ashkelon will be deserted.
Foreigners will occupy Ashdod,
  and I will cut off the pride of the Philistines.
I will take the blood from their mouths,
  the forbidden food from between their teeth.
Those who are left will belong to our God
  and become leaders in Judah,
  and Ekron will be like the Jebusites.
But I will defend my house
  against marauding forces.
Never again will an oppressor overrun my people,
  for now I am keeping watch.

Cast: **Zechariah, the Lord** (voice only)

The Coming of Zion's King

Zechariah 9:9–10

Voice 1   Rejoice greatly, O Daughter of Zion!

Voice 2   Shout, Daughter of Jerusalem!

Voices
  1 and 2   See, your king comes to you,
  righteous and having salvation,
  gentle and riding on a donkey,
  on a colt, the foal of a donkey.

The Lord
  (voice only) I will take away the chariots from Ephraim
  and the war-horses from Jerusalem,
  and the battle bow will be broken.
He will proclaim peace to the nations.

His rule will extend from sea to sea
and from the River to the ends of the earth.

Cast: **Voice 1, Voice 2, the Lord** (voice only)

The Restoration of God's People

From Zechariah 9:11–17

Zechariah
(with
flourish)   [The Lord says:]

The Lord
(voice only) As for you, because of the blood of my covenant with you,
I will free your prisoners from the waterless pit.
Return to your fortress, O prisoners of hope;
even now I announce that I will restore twice as much to you.
I will bend Judah as I bend my bow
and fill it with Ephraim.
I will rouse your sons, O Zion,
against your sons, O Greece,
and make you like a warrior's sword. . . .

Zechariah   The LORD their God will save them on that day
as the flock of his people.
They will sparkle in his land
like jewels in a crown.
How attractive and beautiful they will be!
Grain will make the young men thrive,
and new wine the young women.

Cast: **Zechariah, the Lord** (voice only)

The Lord Will Care for Judah

From Zechariah 10:1–12

Zechariah   Ask the LORD for rain in the springtime;
it is the LORD who makes the storm clouds.
He gives showers of rain to men,
and plants of the field to everyone.
The idols speak deceit,
diviners see visions that lie;
they tell dreams that are false,
they give comfort in vain.

Therefore the people wander like sheep
   oppressed for lack of a shepherd.

(with
flourish)   [The Lord says:]

The Lord
(voice only) My anger burns against the shepherds,
   and I will punish the leaders.

Zechariah   For the LORD Almighty will care
   for his flock, the house of Judah,
   and make them like a proud horse in battle.
From Judah will come the cornerstone,
   from him the tent peg,
   from him the battle bow,
   from him every ruler.
Together they will be like mighty men
   trampling the muddy streets in battle.
Because the LORD is with them,
   they will fight and overthrow the horsemen.

The Lord
(voice)   I will strengthen the house of Judah
   and save the house of Joseph.
I will restore them
   because I have compassion on them.
They will be as though
   I had not rejected them,
for I am the LORD their God
   and I will answer them. . . .
I will signal for them
   and gather them in.
Surely I will redeem them;
   they will be as numerous as before.
Though I scatter them among the peoples,
   yet in distant lands they will remember me.
They and their children will survive,
   and they will return.
I will bring them back from Egypt
   and gather them from Assyria.
I will bring them to Gilead and Lebanon,
   and there will not be room enough for them.
They will pass through the sea of trouble;
   the surging sea will be subdued
   and all the depths of the Nile will dry up.
Assyria's pride will be brought down
   and Egypt's scepter will pass away.
I will strengthen them in the LORD
   and in his name they will walk. . . .

Zechariah
(with
flourish)   [The LORD has spoken!]

Cast: **Zechariah, the Lord** (voice only)

Two Shepherds

From Zechariah 11:4–17

Zechariah   This is what the LORD my God says:

The Lord
(voice only) Pasture the flock marked for slaughter. Their buyers slaughter them and
go unpunished. Those who sell them say—

Owners
1 and 2   Praise the LORD!

Owner 2   I am rich!

The Lord
(voice)   Their own shepherds do not spare them. . . .

Zechariah   So I pastured the flock marked for slaughter, particularly the oppressed
of the flock. Then I took two staffs and called one Favor and the other
Union, and I pastured the flock. In one month I got rid of the three shepherds.

The flock detested me, and I grew weary of them and said:

Young
Zechariah   I will not be your shepherd. Let the dying die, and the perishing perish.
Let those who are left eat one another's flesh.

Zechariah   Then I took my staff called Favor and broke it, revoking the covenant I
had made with all the nations. It was revoked on that day, and so the
afflicted of the flock who were watching me knew it was the word of the
LORD. (PAUSE) I told them:

Young
Zechariah   If you think it best, give me my pay; but if not, keep it.

Zechariah   So they paid me thirty pieces of silver. (PAUSE) And the LORD said to me:

The Lord
(voice)   Throw it to the potter—the handsome price at which they priced me!

Zechariah   So I took the thirty pieces of silver and threw them into the house of the
LORD to the potter.

Then I broke my second staff called Union, breaking the brotherhood
between Judah and Israel.

Then the LORD said to me:

The Lord
(voice)   Take again the equipment of a foolish shepherd. For I am going to raise up a shepherd over the land who will not care for the lost, or seek the young, or heal the injured, or feed the healthy, but will eat the meat of the choice sheep, tearing off their hoofs.

Zechariah   Woe to the worthless shepherd,
            who deserts the flock!
        May the sword strike his arm and his right eye!
            May his arm be completely withered,
            his right eye totally blinded!

Cast: **Zechariah**, **the Lord** (voice only), **Owner 1**, **Owner 2** (can be the same as Owner 1), **Young Zechariah**

Malachi

Jacob Loved, Esau Hated

Malachi 1:1–5

Narrator	An oracle: The word of the LORD to Israel through Malachi.
Malachi	[The LORD says:]
The Lord (voice only)	I have loved you. . . . But you ask:
Person 1	How have you loved us?
Person 2	Was not Esau Jacob's brother? . . .
Malachi	[The LORD answers:]
The Lord (voice)	Yet I have loved Jacob, but Esau I have hated, and I have turned his mountains into a wasteland and left his inheritance to the desert jackals.
Malachi	Edom may say:
Edomite	Though we have been crushed, we will rebuild the ruins.
Malachi	But this is what the LORD Almighty says:
The Lord (voice)	They may build, but I will demolish.
Malachi	They will be called the Wicked Land, a people always under the wrath of the LORD. You will see it with your own eyes and say:
Persons **1 and 2**	Great is the LORD—
Person 2	Even beyond the borders of Israel!

Cast: **Narrator, Malachi, the Lord** (voice only), **Person 1, Person 2** (can be the same as Person 1), **Edomite** (can be the same as Person 1)

Blemished Sacrifices

Malachi 1:6–14

Malachi	[The LORD Almighty says:]
The Lord (voice only)	A son honors his father, and a servant his master. If I am a father, where is the honor due me? If I am a master, where is the respect due

	me? . . . It is you, O priests, who show contempt for my name. (PAUSE) But you ask:
Priest 1	How have we shown contempt for your name?
The Lord (voice)	You place defiled food on my altar. (PAUSE) But you ask:
Priest 2	How have we defiled you?
The Lord (voice)	By saying that the LORD's table is contemptible. When you bring blind animals for sacrifice, is that not wrong? When you sacrifice crippled or diseased animals, is that not wrong? Try offering them to your governor! Would he be pleased with you? Would he accept you? . . .
Malachi	Now implore God to be gracious to us. With such offerings from your hands, will he accept you? . . .
The Lord (voice)	Oh, that one of you would shut the temple doors, so that you would not light useless fires on my altar! I am not pleased with you . . . and I will accept no offering from your hands. My name will be great among the nations, from the rising to the setting of the sun. In every place incense and pure offerings will be brought to my name, because my name will be great among the nations. . . .
	But you profane it by saying of the Lord's table. . . . and of its food:
Priest 1	It is defiled! . . .
Priest 2	It is contemptible.
Priest 1	What a burden!
The Lord (voice)	And you sniff at it contemptuously.
	When you bring injured, crippled or diseased animals and offer them as sacrifices, should I accept them from your hands? . . .
Malachi	Cursed is the cheat who has an acceptable male in his flock and vows to give it, but then sacrifices a blemished animal to the Lord.
The Lord (voice)	For I am a great king . . . and my name is to be feared among the nations.

Cast: **Malachi, the Lord** (voice only), **Priest 1, Priest 2**

Judah Unfaithful

From Malachi 2:10–16

Speaker 1	Have we not all one Father?
Speaker 2	Did not one God create us?

Speaker 1	Why do we profane the covenant of our fathers by breaking faith with one another? . . .
Malachi	Another thing you do: You flood the LORD's altar with tears. You weep and wail because he no longer pays attention to your offerings or accepts them with pleasure from your hands.
Speaker 1	[Judah has broken faith. A detestable thing has been committed in Israel and in Jerusalem—
Speaker 2	Judah has desecrated the sanctuary the LORD loves, by marrying the daughter of a foreign god.]
Malachi	[You ask:
Speaker 1	Why?
Malachi	It is because the LORD is acting as the witness between you and the wife of your youth, because you have broken faith with her, though she is your partner, the wife of your marriage covenant.]
Speaker 1	Has not ⸢the LORD⸤ made them one? In flesh and spirit they are his. And why one?
Speaker 2	Because he was seeking godly offspring.
Malachi	So guard yourself in your spirit, and do not break faith with the wife of your youth. [The LORD Almighty says:]
The Lord (voice only)	I hate divorce . . . and I hate a man's covering himself with violence as well as with his garment. . . .
Malachi	So guard yourself in your spirit, and do not break faith.

Cast: **Speaker 1, Speaker 2, Malachi, the Lord** (voice only)

The Day of Judgment

Malachi 2:17–3:6

Malachi	You have wearied the LORD with your words.
Persons 1 and 2	How have we wearied him?
Malachi	By saying:
Person 1	All who do evil are good in the eyes of the LORD, and he is pleased with them.
Malachi	Or [by asking:]
Person 2	Where is the God of justice?
Malachi	[The LORD Almighty answers:]

502

The Lord

(voice only) See, I will send my messenger, who will prepare the way before me. Then suddenly the Lord you are seeking will come to his temple; the messenger of the covenant, whom you desire, will come. . . .

But who can endure the day of his coming? Who can stand when he appears? For he will be like a refiner's fire or a launderer's soap. He will sit as a refiner and purifier of silver; he will purify the Levites and refine them like gold and silver.

Malachi Then the LORD will have men who will bring offerings in righteousness, and the offerings of Judah and Jerusalem will be acceptable to the LORD, as in days gone by, as in former years.

(with
flourish) [The LORD Almighty says:]

The Lord

(voice) So I will come near to you for judgment. I will be quick to testify against sorcerers, adulterers and perjurers, against those who defraud laborers of their wages, who oppress the widows and the fatherless, and deprive aliens of justice, but do not fear me. . . .

I the LORD do not change. So you, O descendants of Jacob, are not destroyed.

Cast: **Malachi, Person 1, Person 2** (can be the same as Person 1), **the Lord** (voice only)

The Lord Calls for Tithes

Malachi 3:6–12

The Lord

(voice only) I the LORD do not change. So you, O descendants of Jacob, are not destroyed. Ever since the time of your forefathers you have turned away from my decrees and have not kept them. Return to me, and I will return to you. . . . (PAUSE) But you ask:

Person(s) How are we to return?

The Lord

(voice) Will a man rob God? Yet you rob me. (PAUSE) But you ask:

Person(s) How do we rob you?

The Lord

(voice) In tithes and offerings. You are under a curse—the whole nation of you—because you are robbing me. Bring the whole tithe into the storehouse, that there may be food in my house. Test me in this . . . and see if I will not throw open the floodgates of heaven and pour out so much blessing that you will not have room enough for it. I will prevent pests from devouring your crops, and the vines in your fields will not cast their

503

fruit. . . . Then all the nations will call you blessed, for yours will be a delightful land. . . .

Cast: **The Lord** (voice only), **Person(s)**

God's Promise of Mercy

Malachi 3:13–18

Malachi	[The LORD says:]
The Lord (voice only)	You have said harsh things against me. . . . (PAUSE) Yet you ask:
Person 1 and 2	What have we said against you?
The Lord (voice)	You have said:
Person 1	It is futile to serve God.
Person 2	What did we gain by carrying out his requirements and going about like mourners before the LORD Almighty?
Person 1	But now we call the arrogant blessed.
Person 2	Certainly the evildoers prosper, and even those who challenge God escape.
Malachi	Then those who feared the LORD talked with each other, and the LORD listened and heard. A scroll of remembrance was written in his presence concerning those who feared the LORD and honored his name. [The LORD Almighty says:]
The Lord (voice)	They will be mine . . . in the day when I make up my treasured possession. I will spare them, just as in compassion a man spares his son who serves him. And you will again see the distinction between the righteous and the wicked, between those who serve God and those who do not.

Cast: **Malachi, the Lord** (voice only), **Person 1, Person 2**

The Day of the Lord

Malachi 4:1–6

Malachi	[The LORD Almighty says:]
The Lord (voice only)	Surely the day is coming; it will burn like a furnace. All the arrogant and

every evildoer will be stubble, and that day that is coming will set them on fire. . . . Not a root or a branch will be left to them. But for you who revere my name, the sun of righteousness will rise with healing in its wings. And you will go out and leap like calves released from the stall. Then you will trample down the wicked; they will be ashes under the soles of your feet on the day when I do these things. . . .

Remember the law of my servant Moses, the decrees and laws I gave him at Horeb for all Israel.

See, I will send you the prophet Elijah before that great and dreadful day of the Lord comes. He will turn the hearts of the fathers to their children, and the hearts of the children to their fathers; or else I will come and strike the land with a curse.

Cast: **Malachi, the Lord** (voice only)

Subject Index

507

Scripture Index

Character Index

515

Thematic Index

Boldface type indicates the volume number within the three-volume set of *The Dramatized Bible.*